40 Model Essays

A Portable Anthology

40
Model Essays
A Portable Anthology

JANE E. AARON

Bedford/St. Martin's   BOSTON   ◆   NEW YORK

Production Supervisor: Christopher Gross
Senior Marketing Manager: Rachel Falk
Art Director: Lucy Krikorian
Text Design: Sandra Rigney
Copy Editor: Sally Scott
Cover Design: Donna Lee Dennison
Cover Photo: © Steve Terrill / CORBIS
Composition: Macmillan India Ltd
Printing and Binding: Haddon Craftsmen, Inc., an R. R. Donnelley &
Sons Company

President: Joan E. Feinberg
Editorial Director: Denise B. Wydra
Editor in Chief: Karen Henry
Director of Marketing: Karen Melton Soeltz
Director of Editing, Design, and Production: Marcia Cohen
Managing Editor: Erica T. Appel

Library of Congress Control Number: 2004114579

Manufactured in the United States of America.

0 9 8 7 6 5
f e d c b a

For information, write: Bedford/St. Martin's, 75 Arlington Street,
Boston, MA 02116   (617-399-4000)

ISBN: 0-312-43829-X

EAN: 978-0-312-43829-6

Acknowledgments

Acknowledgments and copyrights can be found at the back of the book on
pages 380–81, which constitute an extension of the copyright page. It is a violation
of the law to reproduce these selections by any means whatsoever without the
written permission of the copyright holder.

Preface for Instructors

40 Model Essays: A Portable Anthology is a brief and affordable rhetorically arranged reader. With about half the usual number of selections and for about half the price of similar books, *40 Model Essays* provides a manageable collection of carefully chosen readings and clear, concrete guidance on reading and writing.

40 Model Essays offers a selection of classic and contemporary readings proven to be successful in the classroom. Joining favorites by such writers as E. B. White, Joan Didion, Martin Luther King, Jr., and Virginia Woolf are newer voices including David Sedaris, Anne Lamott, and Malcolm Gladwell. The selections vary in length to accommodate different teaching needs, but all are clear, well-crafted models of the rhetorical methods.

40 Model Essays adapts the concise, effective writing instruction of my text *The Compact Reader: Short Essays by Method and Theme,* Seventh Edition:

- The general introduction helps students become better critical readers and writers. To demonstrate the reading process, it includes a sample passage annotated by a student and a detailed analysis of a professional essay, Barbara Lazear Ascher's "The Box Man." The discussion of the writing process guides students through each stage, from prewriting and considering subject, purpose, audience, and thesis through revising and editing.

- The chapter introductions offer detailed, practical instruction in the ten methods of development: description, narration, example, division or analysis, classification, process analysis, comparison and contrast, definition, cause-and-effect analysis, and argument and persuasion. Each introduction discusses basic concepts and then suggests strategies for starting, organizing, drafting, revising, and editing an essay using the method.

- Apparatus helps students make good use of the selections. Each reading includes a separate headnote for the writer and for the essay. Following each selection are four sets of detailed questions on meaning, purpose and audience, method and structure, and language. A question labeled "Other Methods" highlights the writer's use of combined rhetorical methods. Finally, several writing topics after each selection guide students in creating their own essays.

- Additional writing topics at the end of each chapter list further ideas for applying the chapter's method of development.

40 Model Essays comes with helpful supplements as well. *Resources for Teaching 40 MODEL ESSAYS*, the manual that accompanies the text, includes tips for teaching with each essay and detailed possible answers for the discussion questions. And the companion Web site (bedfordstmartins.com/40modelessays) provides students with annotated links to the best Web sites for further exploring the authors and topics of the text's readings. It also provides quick access to grammar practice through Exercise Central—an online bank of editing exercises—as well as to Bedford/St. Martin's collection of Web resources that help students improve their online research skills.

I am grateful to the many teachers and students who contributed to *The Compact Reader* over five editions and thus substantially to this book as well. And yet again I happily thank my colleagues at Bedford/St. Martin's, who this time saw the need for *40 Model Essays* and helped to shape it: Joan Feinberg, Denise Wydra, Karen Henry, Steve Scipione, Erica Appel, Ryan Sullivan, and especially Karin Halbert.

Contents

vii

Introduction

READING AND WRITING

This collection of essays has one purpose: to help you become a more proficient reader and writer. It combines examples of good writing with explanations of the writers' methods, questions to guide your reading, and ideas for your own writing. In doing so, it shows how you can adapt the processes and techniques of others as you learn to communicate clearly and effectively on paper.

Writing well is not an inborn skill but an acquired one: you will become proficient only by writing and rewriting, experimenting with different strategies, listening to the responses of readers. How, then, can it help to read the work of other writers?

- Reading others' ideas can introduce you to new information and give you new perspectives on your own experience. Many of the essays collected here demonstrate that personal experience is a rich and powerful source of material for writing. But the knowledge gained from reading can help pinpoint just what is remarkable in your experience. And by introducing varieties of behavior and ways of thinking that would otherwise remain unknown to you, reading can also help you understand where you fit in the scheme of things. Such insight not only reveals subjects for writing but also improves your ability to communicate with others whose experiences naturally differ from your own.

- Reading exposes you to a broad range of strategies and styles. Just seeing that these vary as much as the writers themselves should assure you that there is no fixed standard of writing, while it should also encourage you to find your own strategies and style.

At the same time, you will see that writers do make choices to suit their subjects, their purposes, and especially their readers. Writing is rarely easy, even for the pros; but the more options you have to choose from, the more likely you are to succeed at it.

- Reading makes you sensitive to the role of audience in writing. As you become adept at reading the work of other writers critically, discovering intentions and analyzing choices, you will see how a writer's decisions affect you as audience. Training yourself to read consciously and critically is a first step to becoming a more objective reader of your own writing.

The rest of this chapter offers strategies for making the most of your reading and writing for this course and elsewhere. But first you should understand the book's organization. The essays are arranged to introduce ten methods of developing a piece of writing:

description	process analysis
narration	comparison and contrast
example	definition
division or analysis	cause-and-effect analysis
classification	argument and persuasion

These methods correspond to basic and familiar patterns of thought and expression, common in our daily musings and conversations as well as in writing for all sorts of purposes and audiences: college term papers, lab reports, and examinations; business memos and reports; letters to the editors of newspapers; articles in popular magazines. The methods provide a context for critical reading and also stimulate writing by helping you generate and shape ideas. Detailed chapter introductions explain each method and give advice for using it to develop your own essays. Then the essays in each chapter provide clear examples that you can analyze and learn from (with the help of specific questions) and can refer to while writing (with the help of specific writing suggestions).

READING

When we look for something to watch on television or listen to on the radio, we often tune in one station after another, pausing just long enough each time to catch the program or music being broadcast before settling on one choice. Much of the reading we do is similar: we skim a newspaper, magazine, or Web page, noting headings and scanning text to get the gist of the content. But such skimming is not really reading, for it neither involves us deeply in the subject nor engages us in interaction with the writer.

Reading Critically

To get the most out of reading, we must invest something of ourselves in the process, applying our own ideas and emotions and attending not just to the substance but also to the writer's interpretation of it. This kind of reading is **critical** because it looks beneath the surface of a piece of writing. (The common meaning of *critical* as "negative" doesn't apply here: critical reading may result in positive, negative, or even neutral reactions.)

Critical reading can be enormously rewarding, but of course it takes care and time. A good method for developing your own skill in critical reading is to prepare yourself beforehand and then read the work at least twice to uncover what it has to offer. Preparation can involve just a few minutes as you form some ideas about the author, the work, and your likely response to the work:

- What is the author's background, what qualifications does he or she bring to the subject, and what approach is he or she likely to take? The biographical information provided before each essay in this book should help answer these questions; many periodicals and books include similar information on their authors.
- What does the title convey about the subject and the author's attitude toward it? Note, for instance, the quite different attitudes conveyed by these three titles on the same subject: "Safe Hunting," "In Touch with Ancient Spirits," and "Killing Animals for Fun and Profit."
- What can you predict about your own response to the work? What might you already know about the subject? Based on the title and other clues, are you likely to agree or disagree with the author's views?

After developing some expectations about the piece of writing, read it through carefully to acquaint yourself with the subject, the author's reason for writing about it, and the way the author presents it. (Each essay in this book is short enough to be read at one sitting.) Try not to read passively, letting the words wash over you, but instead interact directly with the work to discover its meaning, the author's intentions, and your own responses.

One of the best aids to active reading is to make notes on separate sheets of paper or, preferably (if you own the book), on the pages themselves. As you practice making notes, you will probably develop a personal code meaningful only to you. As a start, however, try this system:

- Underline or bracket passages that you find particularly effective or that seem especially important to the author's purpose.
- Circle words you don't understand so that you can look them up when you finish.
- Put question marks in the margins next to unclear passages.
- Jot down associations that occur to you, such as examples from your own experience or disagreements with the author's assumptions or arguments.

When you have finished such an active reading, your annotations might look like those below. (The paragraph is from the end of the essay reprinted on pp. 5–9.)

The first half of our lives is spent stubbornly denying it. As children we acquire language to make ourselves understood and soon learn from the blank stares in response to our babblings that even these, our saviors, our parents, are strangers. In adolescence when we replay earlier dramas with peers in the place of parents, we begin the quest for the best friend, that person who will receive all thoughts as if they were her own. Later we assert that true love will find the way. True love finds many ways, but no escape from exile. The shores are littered with us, Annas and Ophelias, Emmas and Juliets, all outcasts from the dream of perfect understanding. We might as well draw the night around us and find solace there and a friend in our own voice.

true?

What about his own? Audience = women?

Ophelia+ Juliet from Shakespeare. Others also?

In other words, just give up?

Before leaving the essay after such an initial reading, try to answer your own questions by looking up unfamiliar words and figuring out the meaning of unclear passages. Then let the essay rest in your mind for at least an hour or two before approaching it again.

When rereading the essay, write a one- or two-sentence summary of each paragraph—in your own words—to increase your mastery of the material. Aim to answer the following questions:

- Why did the author write about this subject?
- What impression did the author wish to make on readers?

- How do the many parts of the work—for instance, the sequencing of information, the tone, the evidence—contribute to the author's purpose?
- How effective is the essay, and why?

A procedure for such an analysis—and the insights to be gained from it—can best be illustrated by examining an actual essay. The paragraph on page 4 comes from "The Box Man" by Barbara Lazear Ascher. The entire essay is reprinted here in the same format as other selections in the book, with a note on the author and a note on the essay.

BARBARA LAZEAR ASCHER

Born in 1946, American writer Barbara Lazear Ascher is known for her insightful, inspiring essays. She obtained a BA from Bennington College in 1968 and a JD from Cardozo School of Law in 1979. After practicing law for two years, Ascher turned to writing full-time. Her essays have appeared in a diverse assortment of periodicals, including the New York Times, Vogue, *the* Yale Review, Redbook, *and* National Geographic Traveler. *Ascher has also published a memoir of her brother, who died of AIDS,* Landscape Without Gravity: A Memoir of Grief *(1993), and several collections of essays:* Playing After Dark *(1986),* The Habit of Loving *(1989), and* Dancing in the Dark: Romance, Yearning, and the Search for the Sublime *(1999).*

The Box Man

In this essay from Playing After Dark, *the evening ritual of a homeless man prompts Ascher's reflection on the nature of solitude. By describing the Box Man alongside two other solitary people, Ascher distinguishes between chosen and unchosen loneliness.*

The Box Man was at it again. It was his lucky night. 1

The first stroke of good fortune occurred as darkness fell and the 2 night watchman at 220 East Forty-fifth Street neglected to close the door as he slipped out for a cup of coffee. I saw them before the Box Man did. Just inside the entrance, cardboard cartons, clean and with their top flaps intact. With the silent fervor of a mute at a horse race, I willed him toward them.

It was slow going. His collar was pulled so high that he appeared   3
headless as he shuffled across the street like a man who must feel Earth with his toes to know that he walks there.

Standing unselfconsciously in the white glare of an overhead   4
light, he began to sort through the boxes, picking them up, one by one, inspecting tops, insides, flaps. Three were tossed aside. They looked perfectly good to me, but then, who knows what the Box Man knows? When he found the one that suited his purpose, he dragged it up the block and dropped it in a doorway.

Then, as if dogged by luck, he set out again and discovered,   5
behind the sign at the parking garage, a plastic Dellwood box, strong and clean, once used to deliver milk. Back in the doorway the grand design was revealed as he pushed the Dellwood box against the door and set its cardboard cousin two feet in front — the usual distance between coffee table and couch. Six full shopping bags were distributed even on either side.

He eased himself with slow care onto the stronger box, reached   6
into one of the bags, pulled out a *Daily News*, and snapped it open against his cardboard table. All done with the ease of IRT Express passengers whose white-tipped, fair-haired fingers reach into attaché cases as if radar-directed to the *Wall Street Journal*. They know how to fold it. They know how to stare at the print, not at the girl who stares at them.

That's just what the Box Man did, except that he touched his   7
tongue to his fingers before turning each page, something grand-mothers do.

One could live like this. Gathering boxes to organize a life.   8
Wandering through the night collecting comforts to fill a doorway.

When I was a child, my favorite book was *The Boxcar Children*.   9
If I remember correctly, the young protagonists were orphaned, and rather than live with cruel relatives, they ran away to the woods to live life on their own terms. An abandoned boxcar was turned into a home, a bubbling brook became an icebox. Wild berries provided abundant desserts and days were spent in the happy, adultless pursuit of joy. The children never worried where the next meal would come from or what February's chill might bring. They had unquestioning faith that berries would ripen and

streams run cold and clear. And unlike Thoreau,[1] whose deliberate living was self-conscious and purposeful, theirs had the ease of children at play.

Even now, when life seems complicated and reason slips, I long to 10 live like a Boxcar Child, to have enough open space and freedom of movement to arrange my surroundings according to what I find. To turn streams into iceboxes. To be ingenious with simple things. To let the imagination hold sway.

Who is to say that the Box Man does not feel as Thoreau did in his 11 doorway, not ". . . crowded or confined in the least," with "pasture enough for . . . imagination." Who is to say that his dawns don't bring back heroic ages? That he doesn't imagine a goddess trailing her garments across his blistered legs?

His is a life of the mind, such as it is, and voices only he can hear. 12 Although it would appear to be a life of misery, judging from the bandages and chill of night, it is of his choosing. He will ignore you if you offer an alternative. Last winter, Mayor Koch[2] tried, coaxing him with promises and the persuasive tones reserved for rabid dogs. The Box Man backed away, keeping a car and paranoia between them.

He is not to be confused with the lonely ones. You'll find them 13 everywhere. The lady who comes into our local coffee shop each evening at five-thirty, orders a bowl of soup and extra Saltines. She drags it out as long as possible, breaking the crackers into smaller and smaller pieces, first in halves and then halves of halves and so on until the last pieces burst into salty splinters and fall from dry fingers onto the soup's shimmering surface. By 6 PM, it's all over. What will she do with the rest of the night?

You can tell by the vacancy of expression that no memories linger 14 there. She does not wear a gold charm bracelet with silhouettes of boys and girls bearing grandchildren's birthdates and a chip of the appropriate birthstone. When she opens her black purse to pay, there is only a crumpled Kleenex and a wallet inside, no photographs spill onto her lap. Her children, if there are any, live far away and prefer not to visit. If she worked as a secretary for forty years in a downtown office, she was given a retirement party, a cake, a reproduction of an

---

[1]Henry David Thoreau (1817–62) was an American essayist and poet who for two years lived a solitary and simple life in the woods. He wrote of his experiences in *Walden* (1854). [Editor's note.]

[2]Edward Koch was the mayor of New York City from 1978 through 1989. [Editor's note.]

antique perfume atomizer and sent on her way. Old colleagues—those who traded knitting patterns and brownie recipes over the water cooler, who discussed the weather, health, and office scandal while applying lipstick and blush before the ladies' room mirror—they are lost to time and the new young employees who take their places in the typing pool.

Each year she gets a Christmas card from her ex-boss. The envelope is canceled in the office mailroom and addressed by memory typewriter. Within is a family in black and white against a wooded Connecticut landscape. The boss, his wife, who wears her hair in a gray page boy, the three blond daughters, two with tall husbands and an occasional additional grandchild. All assembled before a worn stone wall.

Does she watch game shows? Talk to a parakeet, feed him cuttlebone, and call him Pete? When she rides the buses on her Senior Citizen pass, does she go anywhere or wait for something to happen? Does she have a niece like the one in Cynthia Ozick's story "Rosa," who sends enough money to keep her aunt at a distance?

There's a lady across the way whose lights and television stay on all night. A crystal chandelier in the dining room and matching Chinese lamps on Regency end tables in the living room. She has six cats, some Siamese, others Angora and Abyssinian. She pets them and waters her plethora of plants—African violets, a ficus tree, a palm, and geraniums in season. Not necessarily a lonely life except that 3 AM lights and television seem to proclaim it so.

The Box Man welcomes the night, opens to it like a lover. He moves in darkness and prefers it that way. He's not waiting for the phone to ring or an engraved invitation to arrive in the mail. Not for him a P.O. number. Not for him the overcrowded jollity of office parties, the hot anticipation of a singles' bar. Not even for him a holiday handout. People have tried and he shuffled away.

The Box Man knows that loneliness chosen loses its sting and claims no victims. He declares what we all know in the secret passages of our own nights, that although we long for perfect harmony, communion, and blending with another soul, that this is a solo voyage.

The first half of our lives is spent stubbornly denying it. As children we acquire language to make ourselves understood and soon learn from the blank stares in response to our babblings that even these, our saviors, our parents, are strangers. In adolescence when we replay earlier dramas with peers in the place of parents, we begin the quest for the best friend, that person who will receive all thoughts as if they were her own. Later we assert that true love will find the way.

True love finds many ways, but no escape from exile. The shores are littered with us, Annas and Ophelias, Emmas and Juliets,[3] all outcasts from the dream of perfect understanding. We might as well draw the night around us and find solace there and a friend in our own voice.

One could do worse than be a collector of boxes.   21

Even read quickly, Ascher's essay would not be difficult to comprehend: the author draws on examples of three people to make a point at the end about solitude. In fact, a quick reading might give the impression that Ascher produced the essay effortlessly, artlessly. But close, critical reading reveals a carefully conceived work whose parts work independently and together to achieve the author's purpose.

Asking Questions

One way to uncover the underlying intentions and relations in a piece of writing is to work through questions like the ones following. These questions proceed from the general to the specific—from overall meaning to particular word choices. They are accompanied by possible answers for Ascher's essay. (The paragraph numbers can help you locate the appropriate passages in Ascher's essay as you follow the analysis.)

Meaning

What is the main idea of the essay—the chief point the writer makes about the subject, to which all other ideas and details relate? What are the subordinate ideas that contribute to the main idea?

Ascher states her main idea near the end of her essay: in choosing solitude, the Box Man confirms the essential aloneness of human beings (paragraph 19) but also demonstrates that we can "find solace" within ourselves (20). (Writers sometimes postpone stating their main idea, as Ascher does here. Perhaps more often, they state it near the beginning of the essay. See p. 15.) Ascher leads up to and supports her idea with three examples—the Box Man (paragraphs 1–7, 11–12)

---

[3]These are all doomed heroines of literature. Anna is the title character of Leo Tolstoy's novel *Anna Karenina* (1876). Emma is the title character of Gustave Flaubert's novel *Madame Bovary* (1856). Ophelia and Juliet are in Shakespeare's plays—the lovers, respectively, of Hamlet and Romeo. [Editor's note.]

and, in contrast, two women whose loneliness seems unchosen (13–16, 17). These examples are developed with specific details from Ascher's observations (such as the nearly empty purse, 14) and from the imagined lives these observations suggest (such as the remote, perhaps nonexistent children, 14).

Purpose and Audience

Why did the author write the essay? What did the author hope readers would gain from it? What did the author assume about the knowledge and interests of readers, and how are these assumptions reflected in the essay?

Ascher seems to have written her essay for two interlocking reasons: to show and thus explain that solitude need not always be lonely and to argue gently for defeating loneliness by becoming one's own friend. In choosing the Box Man as her main example, she reveals perhaps a third purpose as well—to convince readers that a homeless person can have dignity and may achieve a measure of self-satisfaction lacking in some people who do have homes.

Ascher seems to assume that her readers, like her, are people with homes, people to whom the Box Man and his life might seem completely foreign: she comments on the Box Man's slow shuffle (paragraph 3), his mysterious discrimination among boxes (4), his "blistered legs" (11), how miserable his life looks (12), his bandages (12), the cold night he inhabits (12), the fearful or condescending approaches of strangers (12, 18). Building from this assumption that her readers will find the Box Man strange, Ascher takes pains to show the dignity of the Box Man—his "grand design" for furniture (5), his resemblance to commuters (6), his grandmotherly finger licking (7), his refusal of handouts (18).

Several other apparent assumptions about her audience also influence Ascher's selection of details, if less significantly. First, she assumes some familiarity with literature—at least with the writings of Thoreau (9, 11) and the characters named in paragraph 20. Second, Ascher seems to address women: in paragraph 20 she speaks of each person confiding in "her" friend, and she chooses only female figures from literature to illustrate "us, . . . all outcasts from the dream of perfect understanding." Finally, Ascher seems to address people who are familiar with, if not actually residents of, New York City: she refers to a New York street address (2); alludes to a New York newspaper, the *Daily News*, and a New York subway line, the IRT Express

(6); and mentions the city's mayor (12). However, readers who do not know the literature Ascher cites, who are not women, and who do not know New York City are still likely to understand and appreciate Ascher's main point.

Method and Structure

What method or methods does the author use to develop the main idea, and how do the methods serve the author's purpose? How does the organization serve the author's purpose?

As nonfiction writers often do, Ascher develops her main idea with a combination of the methods discussed in this book. Her primary support for her idea consists of three examples (Chapter 3)— specific instances of solitary people. These examples are developed with description (Chapter 1), especially of the Box Man and the two women (as in paragraphs 6–7), and with narration (Chapter 2) of the Box Man's activities (1–7). Narration figures as well in the summary of the lifelong search for understanding (20). In addition, Ascher uses division or analysis (Chapter 4) to tease apart the elements of her three characters' lives. And she relies on comparison and contrast (Chapter 7) to show the differences between the Box Man and the other two characters (13, 17–18).

While using many methods to develop her idea, Ascher keeps her organization fairly simple. She does not begin with a formal introduction or a statement of her idea but instead starts right off with her main example, the inspiration for her idea. In the first seven paragraphs she narrates and describes the Box Man's activities. Then, in paragraphs 8–12, she explains what appeals to her about circumstances like the Box Man's and she applies those thoughts to what she imagines are his thoughts. Still delaying a statement of her main idea, Ascher contrasts the Box Man and two other solitary people, whose lives she sees as different from his (13–17). Finally, she returns to the Box Man (18–19) and zeroes in on her main idea (19–20). Although she has withheld this idea until the end, we see that everything in the essay has been controlled by it and directed toward it.

Language

How are the author's main idea and purpose revealed at the level of sentences and words? How does the author use language to convey his or her attitudes toward the subject and to make meaning clear and vivid?

Perhaps Ascher's most striking use of language to express and support her idea is in paragraph 20, where she paints a picture of isolation with such words as "blank stares," "strangers," "exile," "littered," and "outcasts." But earlier she also depicts the Box Man's existence and her feeling for it in much warmer terms; she watches him with "silent fervor" (paragraph 2); he seems "dogged by luck" (5); he sits with "slow care" and opens the newspaper with "ease" (6); his page turning reminds Ascher of "grandmothers" (7); it is conceivable that, in Thoreau's word, the Box Man's imagination has "pasture" to roam, that he dreams of "heroic ages" and a "goddess trailing her garments" (11). The contrast between these passages and the later one is so marked that it emphasizes Ascher's point about the individual's ability to find comfort in solitude.

In describing the two other solitary people—those who evidently have not found comfort in aloneness—Ascher uses words that emphasize the heaviness of time and the sterility of existence. The first woman "drags" her meal out and crumbles crackers between "dry fingers" (13), a "vacancy of expression" on her face (14). She lacks even the trinkets of attachment—a "gold charm bracelet" with pictures of grandchildren (14). A vividly imagined photograph of her ex-boss and his family (15)—the wife with "her hair in a gray page boy," "the three blond daughters"—emphasizes the probable absence of such scenes in the woman's own life.

Ascher occasionally uses incomplete sentences (or sentence fragments) to stress the accumulation of details or the quickness of her impressions. For example, in paragraph 10 the incomplete sentences beginning "To . . ." sketch Ascher's dream. And in paragraph 18 the incomplete sentences beginning "Not . . ." emphasize the Box Man's withdrawal. Both of these sets of incomplete sentences gain emphasis from **parallelism,** the use of similar grammatical form for ideas of equal importance. (See the Glossary.) The parallelism begins in the complete sentences preceding each set of incomplete sentences— for example, ". . . I long to live like a Boxcar Child. . . . To turn streams into iceboxes. To be ingenious with simple things. To let the imagination hold sway." Although incomplete sentences can be unclear, these and the others in Ascher's essay are clear: she uses them deliberately and carefully, for a purpose. (Inexperienced writers usually find it safer to avoid any incomplete sentences until they have mastered the complete sentence.)

These notes on Ascher's essay show how one can arrive at a deeper, more personal understanding of a piece of writing by attentive, thoughtful analysis. Every other essay in this book will also repay such close analysis. Guided by the questions at the end of each essay and by your own sense of what works and why, you'll find similar lessons and pleasures in all of this book's readings.

WRITING

An analysis like the preceding one is valuable in itself, helping you better understand and appreciate whatever you read. But it can make you a better writer, too, by showing you how to read your own work critically, broadening the range of strategies available to you, and suggesting subjects for you to write about.

Accompanying the questions on the essays in this book are writing topics — ideas for you to adapt and develop into essays of your own. Some of these call for your analysis of the essay; others lead you to examine your own experiences or outside sources in light of the essay's ideas. At the end of each chapter is an additional set of writing topics that provides a range of subjects for using the chapter's method of development.

To help you develop essays using the various methods, each chapter's introduction gives specific advice arranged by stages of the writing process described below: getting started, organizing, drafting, and revising. Actually, these stages are quite arbitrary, for writers do not move in straight lines through fixed steps, like locomotives over tracks. Instead, just as they do when thinking, writers continually circle back over covered territory, each time picking up more information or seeing new relationships, until their meaning is clear to themselves and can be made clear to readers. No two writers proceed in exactly the same way, either, so your writing process may differ considerably from your classmates'. A successful writing process is the one that works for you.

Getting Started

Every writing situation involves several elements: you communicate an *idea* about a subject to an *audience* of readers for a particular *purpose*. At first you may not be sure of your idea or your purpose. You may not know how you want to approach your readers, even when you know who they are. Your job in getting started, then, is to explore options and make choices.

Subject, Purpose, and Thesis

A subject for writing may arise from any source, including your own experience or reading, a suggestion in this book, or an assignment specified by your instructor. Barbara Ascher's essay demonstrates how an excellent subject can be found from observing one's surroundings. Whatever its source, the subject should be something you care enough about to probe deeply and to stamp with your own perspective.

This personal stamp comprises both your main idea or **thesis,** the central point you want to make about the subject, and your **purpose,** your reason for writing. The purpose may be one of the following:

- To explain the subject so that readers understand it or see it in a new light.
- To persuade readers to accept or reject an opinion or to take a certain action.
- To entertain readers with a humorous or exciting story.
- To express the thoughts and emotions triggered by a revealing or instructive experience.

A single essay may sometimes have more than one purpose: for instance, a writer might both explain what it's like to be disabled and try to persuade readers to respect special parking zones for the disabled. Your purpose and your thesis may occur to you early on, arising out of the subject and its significance for you. But you may need to explore your subject for a while—even to the point of writing a draft—before they become clear to you.

When your purpose and thesis are clear, you should try to state them in a **thesis sentence** or sentences, an assertion about the subject. In the following two sentences from the end of "The Box Man" (p. 9), Barbara Ascher asserts the point of her essay:

> [We are] all outcasts from the dream of perfect understanding. We might as well draw the night around us and find solace there and a friend in our own voice.

Because your thesis itself may change over the course of the writing process, your thesis sentence may also change, sometimes considerably. The following thesis sentences show how one writer shifted his opinion and moved from an explanatory to a persuasive purpose between the early stages of the writing process and the final draft.

Tentative: With persistence, adopted children can often locate information about their birth parents.

Final: Adopted children are unfairly hampered in seeking information about their birth parents.

Even though your thesis sentence may change, it's a good idea to draft it early on because it can help keep you focused as you generate more ideas, seek information, organize your thoughts, and so on. If you state it near the beginning of your essay, the thesis sentence can also serve as a promise to readers — a commitment to examine a specific subject from a particular perspective — that can help control your writing and revising. However, as Ascher's essay demonstrates, the thesis sentence may come elsewhere as long as it still controls the whole essay. It may even go unstated, as some of the essays in this book illustrate, but it still must govern every element of the work as if it were announced.

Audience

Either very early, when you first begin exploring your subject, or later, as a check on what you have generated, you may want to make a few notes on your anticipated audience. The notes are optional, but thinking about audience definitely is not. Your purpose and main idea as well as supporting ideas, details and examples, organization, style, tone, and language — all should reflect your answers to the following questions:

- What impression do you want to make on readers?
- What do readers already know about your subject? What do they need to know?
- What are readers' likely expectations and assumptions about your subject?
- How can you build on readers' previous knowledge, expectations, and assumptions to bring them around to your view?

These considerations are obviously crucial to achieve the fundamental purpose of all public writing: communication. Accordingly, they come up again and again in the chapter introductions and the questions after each essay.

Invention

Ideas for your writing—whether your subject or your thesis or the many smaller ideas and details that build your thesis—may come to you in a rush, or you may need to search for them. Writers use a variety of searching techniques, from jotting down thoughts while they pursue other activities to writing concentratedly for a set period. Here are a few techniques you might try.

Journal writing.   Many writers keep a **journal,** a record of thoughts and observations. Whether in a notebook or in a computer file, journal entries give you an opportunity to explore ideas just for yourself, free of concerns about readers who will judge what you say or how you say it. Regular journal entries can also make you more comfortable with the act of writing and build your confidence. Indeed, writing teachers often require their students to keep journals for these reasons.

In a journal you can write about whatever interests, puzzles, or disturbs you. For example, you might analyze a relationship that's causing you problems, explore your reactions to a movie or a music album, or confide your dreams and fears. Any of this material could provide a seed for a writing assignment, but you can also use a journal deliberately to develop ideas for assignments. For instance, after reading Barbara Ascher's "The Box Man" (p. 5), you might explore your feelings about homeless people, recount a particular encounter with a homeless person, or respond to Ascher's ideas about homelessness. Writing for yourself, you will feel free to explore what is on your mind, without worrying about correctness.

Freewriting.   Another effective invention technique is **freewriting,** exploratory writing in which you write without stopping for ten or fifteen minutes, following ideas wherever they lead, paying no attention to completeness or correctness. Like journal writing, freewriting is rough: the tone is usually informal; thoughts might be left dangling; some sentences might be shapeless or incomplete; words can be misspelled. But none of this matters because the freewriting is just exploratory. (If you have difficulty writing without correcting and you compose on a word processor, you might try **invisible writing:** turn the computer's monitor off while you freewrite, so that you can't see what you're producing. When your time is up, turn the monitor back on to work with the material.)

Using the methods of development.   The methods of development discussed in this book can also be useful tools for probing a subject. They suggest questions that can spark ideas by opening up different approaches.

- *Description:* How does the subject look, sound, smell, taste, and feel?
- *Narration:* What is the story in the subject? How did it happen?
- *Example:* How can the subject be illustrated? What are instances of it?
- *Division or analysis:* What are the subject's parts, and what is their relationship or significance?
- *Classification:* What groups can the subject be sorted into?
- *Process analysis:* How does the subject work, or how does one do it?
- *Comparison and contrast:* How is the subject similar to or different from something else?
- *Definition:* What are the subject's characteristics and boundaries?
- *Cause-and-effect analysis:* Why did the subject happen? What were or may be its consequences?
- *Argument and persuasion:* Why do I believe as I do about the subject? Why do others have different opinions? How can I convince others to accept my opinion or believe as I do?

Organizing

Writers vary in the extent to which they arrange their material before they begin writing, but most do establish some plan. For you, the plan may consist of a list of key points, a fuller list including specifics as well, or even a detailed formal outline—whatever provides direction for your essay and thus promises to relieve some of the pressure of writing. You will find that some subjects and methods of development demand fuller plans than others: a chronological narrative of a personal experience, for instance, would not require as much prearrangement as a comparison of two complex social policies. Most of the methods of development also suggest specific structures, as you will find in reading the chapter introductions and essays.

Most essays consist of three parts: an introduction and a conclusion (discussed on p. 18) and the **body,** the most substantial and longest part that develops the main idea or thesis. As you explore your subject, you will discover both ideas that directly support your thesis and more specific examples, details, and other evidence that support these ideas. Each supporting idea, or subpoint, may take a paragraph or more to develop with specifics.

When you seek a plan in your ideas, look first for your subpoints, the main supports for your thesis. Use these as your starting points to work out your essay one chunk (or paragraph) at a time. You can fill in the supporting evidence in your organizational plan, or you can wait until you begin drafting to get into the specifics.

As you plan the body of your essay, you can also be thinking of how you want to begin and end it. An effective opening or closing may not become apparent until after you have drafted the body of the essay. But considering how you want to approach readers and what you want to leave them with can help channel your thoughts while you draft.

- The basic **introduction** draws readers into the essay and focuses their attention on the main idea and purpose—often stated in a thesis sentence.
- The basic **conclusion** ties together the elements of the essay and provides a final impression for readers to take away with them.

These basic forms allow considerable room for variation. Especially as you are developing your writing skills, you will find it helpful to state your thesis sentence near the beginning of the essay; but sometimes you can place it effectively at the end, or you can let it direct what you say in the essay but never state it at all. One essay may need two paragraphs of introduction but only a one-sentence conclusion, whereas another essay may require no formal introduction but a lengthy conclusion. How you begin and end depends on your subject and purpose, the kind of essay you are writing, and the likely responses of your readers. Specific ideas for opening and closing essays are included in each chapter introduction.

Drafting

However detailed your organizational plan is, you should not view it as a rigid taskmaster while you are drafting your essay. If you are like most writers, you will discover much of what you have to say while drafting. In fact, if your subject is complex or difficult for you to write about, you may need several drafts just to work out your ideas and their relationships.

While drafting, remember: write first; then revise. Concentrate on *what* you are saying, not on *how* you are saying it. Awkwardness, repetition, wrong words, grammatical errors, spelling mistakes—these and other more superficial concerns can be attended to in a later draft. The same goes for considering your readers' needs. Like many writers, you may find that attention to readers during the first draft inhibits the flow of ideas. If so, then postpone that attention until the second or third draft.

You may find it helpful to start your draft with your thesis sentence—or to keep it in front of you as you write—as a reminder of your purpose and main idea. But if you find yourself pulled away from the thesis by a new idea, you may want to let go and follow, at least for a while. After all, drafting is your opportunity to find what you have to say. If your purpose and main idea change as a result of such exploration, you can always revise your thesis accordingly.

Revising

In a rough draft you have the chance to work out your meaning without regard for what others may think. Eventually, though, you must look critically at a draft. In this stage, called **revision** (literally, "re-seeing"), you see the draft as a reader sees it, mere words on a page that are only as clear, interesting, and significant as you have made them. To gain something like a reader's distance from your work, try one or more of the following techniques:

- Put your first draft aside for at least a few hours before attempting to revise it. You may have further thoughts in the interval, and you will be able to see your work more objectively when you return to it.

- Ask another person to read and comment on your draft. Your writing teacher may ask you and your classmates to exchange your drafts so that you can help each other revise. But even without such a procedure, you can benefit from others' responses. Keep an open mind to your readers' comments, and ask questions when you need more information.

- Make an outline of your draft by listing what you cover in each paragraph. Such an outline can show gaps, overlaps, and problems in organization.

- Read the draft aloud or into a tape recorder. Speaking the words and hearing them can help to create distance from them.

- Imagine you are someone else—a friend, perhaps, or a particular person in your intended audience—and read the draft through that person's eyes, as if for the first time.

- If you write on a word processor, print out a copy of your draft with double spacing. It's much more difficult to see errors on the computer screen than on paper, and you can spread out the pages of a printout to see the whole paper at once.

For most writers, revision actually divides in two: a phase for fundamental changes in content and structure; and a phase for more superficial changes in style, grammar, and the like. In the first phase, you might ask yourself the following questions:

- Is the purpose clear and consistent?
- Do subordinate points relate to the thesis sentence and support it fully?
- Have you provided enough facts, examples, and other evidence for readers to understand your meaning and find your ideas convincing?
- Does your organization channel readers' attention as you intended?
- Does each sentence and each paragraph relate clearly and logically to the ones before and after?

In editing you turn from what the text says to how it sounds and looks.

- Are transitions smooth between paragraphs and sentences?
- Are sentences clear and concise, and do their lengths and structures vary to suit your meaning and purpose?
- Do concrete, specific words sharpen your meaning?
- Are details vivid enough to help your readers see your subject as you want them to?
- Are grammar, punctuation, and spelling correct?

Once you are satisfied that your essay achieves your purpose and is as clear as possible, prepare the final draft, the one you will submit. Proofread the draft carefully to correct spelling errors, typographical mistakes, and other minor problems.

By finishing with revising and editing, we have circled back to the beginning of this chapter. Good writers are good readers. Reading the essays in this book will give you pleasure and set you thinking. But analyzing and writing about them will also increase your flexibility as a writer and train you to read your own work critically.

Chapter One

DESCRIPTION

USING THE METHOD

Whenever you use words to depict or re-create a scene, an object, a person, or a feeling, you use **description.** You draw on the perceptions of your five senses—sight, hearing, smell, taste, and touch—to understand and communicate your experience of the world. Description is a mainstay of conversation between people, and it is likely to figure in almost any writing situation: an e-mail home may describe a new roommate's spiky yellow hair; a laboratory report may describe the colors and odors of chemicals; a business memo may distinguish between the tastes of two competitors' chicken potpies.

Your purpose in writing and your involvement with the subject will largely determine how objective or subjective your description is.

- In **objective description** you strive for precision and objectivity, trying to convey the subject impersonally, without emotion. This is the kind of description required in scientific writing—for instance, a medical diagnosis or a report on an experiment in psychology— where cold facts and absence of feeling are essential for readers to judge the accuracy of procedures and results. It is also the method of news reports and of reference works such as encyclopedias.

- In **subjective description,** in contrast, you draw explicitly on your emotions, giving an impression of the subject filtered through your experience of it. Instead of withdrawing to the background, you invest feelings in the subject and let those feelings

21

determine which details to describe and how to describe them. Your state of mind—perhaps loneliness, anger, or joy—can be re-created by reference to sensory details such as numbness, heat, or sweetness.

In general, you should favor objective description when your purpose is explanation and subjective description when your purpose is self-expression or entertainment. But the categories are not exclusive, and most descriptive writing mixes the two. A news report on a trop-ical storm, for instance, might objectively describe bent and broken trees, fallen wires, and lashing rains, but your selection of details would give a subjective impression of the storm's fearsomeness.

Whether objective or subjective or a mixture of the two, effective description requires a **dominant impression**—a central theme or idea about the subject to which readers can relate all the details. The dom-inant impression may be something you see in the subject, such as the apparent purposefulness of city pedestrians or the expressiveness of an actor. Or it may derive from your emotional response to the subject, perhaps pleasure (or depression) at all the purposefulness, perhaps admiration (or disdain) for the actor's technique. Whatever its source, the dominant impression serves as a unifying principle that guides your selection of details and the reader's understanding of the subject.

One aid to creating a dominant impression is a consistent **point of view,** a position from which you approach the subject. Point of view in description has two main elements:

- You take a real or imagined *physical* relation to the subject: you could view a mountain, for instance, from the bottom looking up, from fifteen miles away across a valley, or from an airplane pass-ing overhead. The first two points of view are fixed because you remain in one position and scan the scene from there; the third is moving because you change position.
- You take a *psychological* relation to the subject, a relation partly conveyed by pronouns. In subjective description, where your feel-ings are part of the message, you might use *I* and *you* freely to narrow the distance between yourself and the subject and between yourself and the reader. But in the most objective, imper-sonal description, you will use *one* ("One can see the summit") or avoid self-reference altogether in order to appear distant from and unbiased toward the subject.

Once you establish a physical and psychological point of view, readers come to depend on it. Thus a sudden and inexplicable shift from one view to another—zooming in from fifteen miles away to the foot of a mountain, abandoning *I* for the more removed *one*—can disorient readers and distract them from the dominant impression you are trying to create.

DEVELOPING A DESCRIPTIVE ESSAY

Getting Started

The subject for a descriptive essay may be any object, place, person, or state of mind that you have observed closely enough or experienced sharply enough to invest with special significance. A chair, a tree, a room, a shopping mall, a movie actor, a passerby on the street, a feeling of fear, a sense of achievement—anything you have a strong impression of can prompt effective description.

When you have your subject, specify in a sentence the impression that you want to create for readers. The sentence will help keep you on track while you search for details, and later it may serve as the thesis of your essay. It should evoke a quality or an atmosphere or an effect, as these examples do:

> His fierce anger at the world shows in every word and gesture.
>
> The mall is a thoroughly unnatural place, like a space station in a science-fiction movie.

A sentence like one of these should give you a good start in choosing the sensory details that will make your description concrete and vivid. Observe your subject directly, if possible, or recall it as completely as you can. Jot down the details that seem to contribute most to the impression you're trying to convey. You needn't write the description of them yet—that can wait for drafting—but you do want to capture the possibilities in your subject. While exploring, try to remain alert to any variations in your dominant impression so that it can continue to guide your search.

At this stage you should start to consider the needs and expectations of your readers. If the subject is something readers have never seen or felt before, you will need enough objective details to create a complete picture in their minds. A description of a friend, for example, might focus on his distinctive voice and laugh, but readers will also want to know something about his appearance. If the subject is essentially abstract, like an emotion, you will need details to make it concrete for readers. And if the subject is familiar to readers, as a shopping mall or an old spruce tree on campus probably would be, you will want to skip obvious objective information in favor of fresh observations that will make readers see the subject anew.

Organizing

Though the details of a subject may not occur to you in any particular order, you should arrange them so that readers are not confused by your shifts among features. You can give readers a sense of the whole subject in the introduction to the essay: objective details of location or size or shape, the incident leading to a state of mind, or the reasons for describing a familiar object. In the introduction, also, you may want to state your thesis—the dominant impression you will create. An explicit thesis is not essential in description; sometimes you may prefer to let the details build to a conclusion. But the thesis should hover over the essay nonetheless, governing the selection of every detail and making itself as clear to readers as if it were stated outright.

The organization of the body of the essay depends partly on point of view and partly on dominant impression. If you take a moving point of view—say, strolling down a city street—the details will probably arrange themselves naturally. But a fixed point of view, scanning a subject from one position, requires your intervention. When the subject is a landscape, a person, or an object, you'll probably want to use a spatial organization: near to far, top to bottom, left to right, or vice versa. Other subjects, such as a shopping mall, might be better treated in groups of features: shoppers, main concourses, insides of stores. Or a description of an emotional state might follow the chronological sequence of the event that aroused it (thus overlapping description and narration, the subject of the next chapter). The order itself is not important, as long as there is an order that channels readers' attention.

Drafting

The challenge of drafting your description will be bringing the subject to life. Whether it is in front of you or in your mind, you may find it helpful to consider the subject one sense at a time—what you can see, hear, smell, touch, taste. Of course, not all senses will be applicable to all subjects; a chair, for instance, may not have a noticeable odor, and you're unlikely to know its taste. But proceeding sense by sense can help you uncover details, such as the smell of a tree or the sound of a person's voice, that you may have overlooked.

Examining one sense at a time is also one of the best ways to conceive of concrete words and figures of speech to represent sensations and feelings. For instance, does *acid* describe the taste of fear? Does an actor's appearance suggest the smell of soap? Does a shopping mall smell like new dollar bills? In creating distinct physical sensations for readers, such representations make meaning inescapably clear.

Revising and Editing

When you are ready to revise and edit, use the following questions as a guide.

- *Have you in fact created the dominant impression you intended to create?* Check that you have plenty of specific details and that each one helps to pin down one crucial feature of your subject. Delete irrelevant details that may have crept in. What counts is not the number of details but their quality and the strength of the impression they make.

- *Are your point of view and organization clear and consistent?* Watch for confusing shifts from one vantage point or organizational scheme to another. Watch also for confusing and unnecessary shifts in pronouns, such as from *I* to *one* or vice versa. Any shifts in point of view or organization should be clearly essential for your purpose and for the impression you want to create.

- *Have you used the most specific, concrete language you can muster?* Keep a sharp eye out for vague words like *delicious, handsome, loud,* and *short* that force readers to create their own impressions or, worse, leave them with no impression at all. Using details that call on readers' sensory experiences, say why delicious or why handsome, how loud or how short. At the same time, cut or change fancy language that simply calls attention to itself without adding to your meaning.

E. B. WHITE

With an infallible ear for language and a keen eye for detail, Elwyn Brooks White earned a place among America's finest writers. White was born in 1899 in Mount Vernon, New York, where he also grew up. After graduating from Cornell University in 1921, he traveled for a time in the West before heading back to settle in Manhattan. In 1927 he joined the staff of the New Yorker, *which was a little over a year old, and for decades his contributions of essays, poems, editorials, and cartoon captions helped shape the magazine. With his wife, Katharine Sergeant White (herself an influential* New Yorker *editor), and their son, Joel, White moved in 1938 to Maine, where he took up farming and animal husbandry while continuing to write. Among his nineteen books are many essay collections; three works for children, including the classic* Charlotte's Web *(1952); and* The Elements of Style *(4th ed., 2000), his revision of the composition textbook he used at Cornell, by his teacher William Strunk, Jr. In his last decade, White published his* Letters *(1976),* Essays *(1977), and* Poems and Sketches *(1981), and he edited a collection of Katharine White's essays on gardening, published two years after her death in 1977. White died in 1985 on the Maine farm they had shared.*

Once More to the Lake

Probably White's best-known essay, "Once More to the Lake" was written in 1941 and collected in One Man's Meat *(1944) along with White's other contributions to* Harper's Magazine. *Mingling past and present, reflection and observation, poetic images and spoken rhythms, the essay describes White's visit to a scene of his boyhood, a place "linking the generations in a strong indestructible chain."*

One summer, along about 1904, my father rented a camp on a lake   1
in Maine and took us all there for the month of August. We all got
ringworm from some kittens and had to rub Pond's Extract on our
arms and legs night and morning, and my father rolled over in a
canoe with all his clothes on; but outside of that the vacation was a
success and from then on none of us ever thought there was any

place in the world like that lake in Maine. We returned summer after summer—always on August 1 for one month. I have since become a salt-water man, but sometimes in summer there are days when the restlessness of the tides and the fearful cold of the sea water and the incessant wind that blows across the afternoon and into the evening make me wish for the placidity of a lake in the woods. A few weeks ago this feeling got so strong I bought myself a couple of bass hooks and a spinner and returned to the lake where we used to go, for a week's fishing and to revisit old haunts.

I took along my son, who had never had any fresh water up his   2
nose and who had seen lily pads only from train windows. On the journey over to the lake I began to wonder what it would be like. I wondered how time would have marred this unique, this holy spot— the coves and streams, the hills that the sun set behind, the camps and the paths behind the camps. I was sure that the tarred road would have found it out, and I wondered in what other ways it would be desolated. It is strange how much you can remember about places like that once you allow your mind to return into the grooves that lead back. You remember one thing, and that suddenly reminds you of another thing. I guess I remembered clearest of all the early mornings, when the lake was cool and motionless, remembered how the bedroom smelled of the lumber it was made of and of the wet woods whose scent entered through the screen. The partitions in the camp were thin and did not extend clear to the top of the rooms, and as I was always the first up I would dress softly so as not to wake the others, and sneak out into the sweet outdoors and start out in the canoe, keeping close along the shore in the long shadows of the pines. I remembered being very careful never to rub my paddle against the gunwale for fear of disturbing the stillness of the cathedral.

The lake had never been what you would call a wild lake. There   3
were cottages sprinkled around the shores, and it was in farming country although the shores of the lake were quite heavily wooded. Some of the cottages were owned by nearby farmers, and you would live at the shore and eat your meals at the farmhouse. That's what our family did. But although it wasn't wild, it was a fairly large and undisturbed lake and there were places in it that, to a child at least, seemed infinitely remote and primeval.

I was right about the tar: it led to within half a mile of the shore.   4
But when I got back there, with my boy, and we settled into a camp near a farmhouse and into the kind of summertime I had known, I could tell it was going to be pretty much the same as it had been

before—I knew it, lying in bed the first morning, smelling the bedroom and hearing the boy sneak quietly out and go off along the shore in a boat. I began to sustain the illusion that he was I, and therefore, by simple transposition, that I was my father. This sensation persisted, kept cropping up all the time we were there. It was not an entirely new feeling, but in this setting it grew much stronger. I seemed to be living a dual existence. I would be in the middle of some simple act, I would be picking up a bait box or laying down a table fork, or I would be saying something, and suddenly it would be not I but my father who was saying the words or making the gesture. It gave me a creepy sensation.

We went fishing the first morning. I felt the same damp moss covering the worms in the bait can, and saw the dragonfly alight on the tip of my rod as it hovered a few inches from the surface of the water. It was the arrival of this fly that convinced me beyond any doubt that everything was as it always had been, that the years were a mirage and that there had been no years. The small waves were the same, chucking the rowboat under the chin as we fished at anchor, and the boat was the same boat, the same color green and the ribs broken in the same places, and under the floorboards the same freshwater leavings and débris—the dead helgramite, the wisps of moss, the rusty discarded fishhook, the dried blood from yesterday's catch. We stared silently at the tips of our rods, at the dragonflies that came and went. I lowered the tip of mine into the water, tentatively, pensively dislodging the fly, which darted two feet away, posed, darted two feet back, and came to rest again a little farther up the rod. There had been no years between the ducking of this dragonfly and the other one—the one that was part of memory. I looked at the boy, who was silently watching his fly, and it was my hands that held his rod, my eyes watching. I felt dizzy and didn't know which rod I was at the end of. 5

We caught two bass, hauling them in briskly as though they were mackerel, pulling them over the side of the boat in a businesslike manner without any landing net, and stunning them with a blow on the back of the head. When we got back for a swim before lunch, the lake was exactly were we had left it, the same number of inches from the dock, and there was only the merest suggestion of a breeze. This seemed an utterly enchanted sea, this lake you could leave to its own devices for a few hours and come back to, and find that it had not stirred, this constant and trustworthy body of water. In the shallows, the dark, water-soaked sticks and twigs, smooth and old, were undulating in clusters on the bottom against the clean 6 ribbed sand, and the track of the mussel was plain. A school of minnows swam by, each minnow with its small individual shadow, doubling the attendance, so clear and sharp in the sunlight. Some of the other campers were in swimming, along the shore, one of them with a cake of soap, and the water felt thin and clear and unsubstantial. Over the years there had been this person with the cake of soap, this cultist, and here he was. There had been no years.

Up to the farmhouse to dinner through the teeming, dusty field, the road under our sneakers was only a two-track road. The middle track was missing, the one with the marks of the hooves and the splotches of dried, flaky manure. There had always been three tracks to choose from in choosing which track to walk in; now the choice was narrowed down to two. For a moment I missed terribly the middle alternative. But the way led past the tennis court, and something about the way it lay there in the sun reassured me; the tape had loosened along the backline, the alleys were green with plantains and other weeds, and the net (installed in June and removed in September) sagged in the dry noon, and the whole place steamed with midday heat and hunger and emptiness. There was a choice of pie for dessert, and one was blueberry and one was apple, and the waitresses were the same country girls, there having been no passage of time, only the illusion of it as in a dropped curtain—the waitresses were still fifteen; their hair had been washed, that was the only difference—they had been to the movies and seen the pretty girls with the clean hair.

Summertime, oh, summertime, pattern of life indelible, the fade-proof lake, the woods unshatterable, the pasture with the sweetfern and the juniper forever and ever, summer without end; this was the background, and the life along the shore was the design, the cottagers with their innocent and tranquil design, their tiny docks with the flagpole and the American flag floating against the white clouds in the blue sky, the little paths over the roots of the trees leading from camp to camp and the paths leading back to the outhouses and the can of lime for sprinkling, and at the souvenir counters at the store the miniature birch-bark canoes and the postcards that showed things looking a little better than they looked. This was the American family at play, escaping the city heat, wondering whether the newcomers in the camp at the head of the cove were "common" or "nice," wondering whether it was true that the people who drove up for Sunday dinner at the farmhouse were turned away because there wasn't enough chicken.

It seemed to me, as I kept remembering all this, that those times   9
and those summers had been infinitely precious and worth saving.
There had been jollity and peace and goodness. The arriving (at the
beginning of August) had been so big a business in itself, at the rail-
way station the farm wagon drawn up, the first smell of the pine-
laden air, the first glimpse of the smiling farmer, and the great
importance of the trunks and your father's enormous authority in
such matters, and the feel of the wagon under you for the long ten-
mile haul, and at the top of the last long hill catching the first view
of the lake after eleven months of not seeing this cherished body of
water. The shouts and cries of the other campers when they saw you,
and the trunks to be unpacked, to give up their rich burden. (Arriving
was less exciting nowadays, when you sneaked up in your car and
parked it under a tree near the camp and took out the bags and in
five minutes it was all over, no fuss, no loud wonderful fuss about
trunks.)

Peace and goodness and jollity. The only thing that was wrong   10
now, really, was the sound of the place, an unfamiliar nervous sound
of the outboard motors. This was the note that jarred, the one thing
that would sometimes break the illusion and set the years moving. In
those other summertimes all motors were inboard; and when they
were at a little distance, the noise they made was a sedative, an ingre-
dient of summer sleep. They made one-cylinder and two-cylinder
engines, and some were make-and-break and some were jump-spark,
but they all made a sleepy sound across the lake. The one-lungers
throbbed and fluttered, and the twin-cylinder ones purred and purred,
and that was a quiet sound, too. But now the campers all had out-
boards. In the daytime, in the hot mornings, these motors made a
petulant, irritable sound; at night, in the still evening when the after-
glow lit the water, they whined about one's ears like mosquitoes. My
boy loved our rented outboard, and his great desire was to achieve
single-handed mastery over it, and authority, and he soon learned
the trick of choking it a little (but not too much), and the adjust-
ment of the needle valve. Watching him I would remember the
things you could do with the old one-cylinder engine with the heavy
flywheel, how you could have it eating out of your hand if you got
really close to it spiritually. Motorboats in those days didn't have
clutches, and you would make a landing by shutting off the motor
at the proper time and coasting in with a dead rudder. But there was
a way of reversing them, if you learned the trick, by cutting the
switch and putting it on again exactly on the final dying revolution
of the flywheel, so that it would kick back against compression and

begin reversing. Approaching a dock in a strong following breeze, it was difficult to slow up sufficiently by the ordinary coasting method, and if a boy felt he had complete mastery over his motor, he was tempted to keep it running beyond its time and then reverse it a few feet from the dock. It took a cool nerve, because if you threw the switch a twentieth of a second too soon you would catch the flywheel when it still had speed enough to go up past center, and the boat would leap ahead, charging bull-fashion at the dock.

We had a good week at the camp. The bass were biting well and the 11 sun shone endlessly, day after day. We would be tired at night and lie down in the accumulated heat of the little bedrooms after the long hot day and the breeze would stir almost imperceptibly outside and the smell of the swamp drift in through the rusty screens. Sleep would come easily and in the morning the red squirrel would be on the roof, tapping out his gay routine. I kept remembering everything, lying in bed in the mornings—the small steamboat that had a long rounded stern like the lip of a Ubangi, and how quietly she ran on the moonlight sails, when the older boys played their mandolins and the girls sang and we ate doughnuts dipped in sugar, and how sweet the music was on the water in the shining night, and what it had felt like to think about girls then. After breakfast we would go up to the store and the things were in the same place—the minnows in a bottle, the plugs and spinners disarranged and pawed over by the youngsters from the boys' camp, the Fig Newtons and the Beeman's gum. Outside, the road was tarred and cars stood in front of the store. Inside, all was just as it had always been, except there was more Coca-Cola and not so much Moxie and root beer and birch beer and sarsaparilla. We would walk out with the bottle of pop apiece and sometimes the pop would backfire up our noses and hurt. We explored the streams, quietly, where the turtles slid off the sunny logs and dug their way into the soft bottom; and we lay on the town wharf and fed worms to the tame bass. Everywhere we went I had trouble making out which was I, the one walking at my side, the one walking in my pants.

One afternoon while we were there at the lake a thunderstorm 12 came up. It was like the revival of an old melodrama that I had seen long ago with childish awe. The second-act climax of the drama of the electrical disturbance over a lake in America had not changed in any important respect. This was the big scene, still the big scene. The whole thing was so familiar, the first feeling of oppression and heat and a general air around camp of not wanting to go very far away. In midafternoon (it was all the same) a curious darkening of the sky, and a lull in everything that had made life tick; and then the way the boats suddenly swung the other way at their moorings with the coming of a breeze out of the new quarter, and the premonitory rumble. Then the kettle drum, then the snare, then the bass drum and cymbals, then crackling light against the dark, and the gods grinning and licking their chops in the hills. Afterward the calm, the rain steadily rustling in the calm lake, the return of light and hope and spirits, and the campers running out in joy and relief to go swimming in the rain, their bright cries perpetuating the deathless joke about how they were getting simply drenched, and the children screaming with delight at the new sensation of bathing in the rain, and the joke about getting drenched linking the generations in a strong indestructible chain. And the comedian who waded in carrying an umbrella.

When the others went swimming, my son said he was going in, 13 too. He pulled his dripping trunks from the line where they had hung all through the shower and wrung them out. Languidly, and with no thought of going in, I watched him, his hard little body, skinny and bare, saw him wince slightly as he pulled up around his vitals the small, soggy, icy garment. As he buckled the swollen belt, suddenly my groin felt the chill of death.

Meaning

1. The main idea of White's essay is fully revealed only in the last paragraph. What is this idea? Why, after White had identified so closely with his son, reliving his own boyhood, does he suddenly feel the "chill of death"?

2. In the opening paragraph White mentions that he sought escape from "the restlessness of the tides and the fearful cold of the sea water and the incessant wind" to the "placidity of a lake in the woods." His escape seems complete but for the "creepy sensation" (paragraph 4) and the "dizzy" feeling (5) accompanying the illusion that time has stood still since his boyhood. What causes these uneasy feelings, and how do they relate to the main idea of the essay?

3. Why do you think it disturbs White momentarily that the road offers only two tracks to choose from, not the three of his boyhood (paragraph 7)? How does this observation relate to the main idea of the essay?

Purpose and Audience

1. Do you think White's purpose is solely to express his feelings, or does he want to explain something as well? If so, what does he want to explain?

2. To what extent does White seem to consider readers unlike himself— say, young adults with no children and no experience of lakeside

vacations? Does he succeed in making you identify with the perceptions and feelings prompted by his experience? What details or passages do you find particularly effective or ineffective, and why?

3. Why do you think White devotes such detail to boat handling (paragraph 10)? In answering, consider especially the significance of the idea of getting "really close to [the boat] spiritually," the many undefined boating terms, and the context of comparison between inboard and outboard motors and between his son's experiences and his own.

Method and Structure

1. Why do you think White chose mainly subjective description to explore the themes of this essay? Would objective description have the same effect? Why, or why not?

2. Locate the many flashbacks in which White remembers being a boy at the lake. (See p. 61 for an explanation of *flashback*.) What events in the present trigger these flashbacks? Note that in some passages (paragraph 8, for instance) the time is neither clearly present nor clearly past. Why?

3. **Other Methods**   Though primarily a descriptive essay, "Once More to the Lake" is also developed by narration and by comparison and contrast. Locate examples of both methods just in paragraph 12, and analyze what they contribute to the essay as whole.

Language

1. How would you characterize White's tone? What, for example, is the effect of "holy," "sweet," and "cathedral" (paragraph 2), "sleepy" (10), and similar words throughout the essay? (If necessary, see *tone* in the Glossary.)

2. White's sense that time has stood still is repeated or restated many times throughout the essay—not only explicitly, as in "There had been no years" (paragraph 5), but also in single words, such as "indelible" (8). Locate both the restatements and the single words in paragraphs 4–11. How does White intensify this theme in his description of the oncoming storm (12)? How do the figures of speech in the description of the storm and the lingering over the "deathless joke" forecast the essay's last sentence? (If necessary, consult the Glossary for *figures of speech*.)

Writing Topics

1. Think of a situation in which you observed a child undergoing an experience or making a decision that recalls your own childhood. (The child may be a brother, sister, son, daughter, cousin, neighbor, or

even a stranger.) Write a narrative essay linking your observations with your memories, making sure that you lead the reader to see the insights you gained.

2. Recall a time when you accompanied a parent or other adult (aunt, uncle, grandparent, and so on) to a place he or she knew well but you were seeing for the first time. It could be a place where the person grew up, went to school, lived for a time, or vacationed. Write an essay in which you compare your reactions to the place with what you remember of the adult's reactions or what, with hindsight, you think the adult's reactions might have been.

JOAN DIDION

One of America's leading nonfiction writers, Joan Didion consistently applies a journalist's eye for detail and a terse, understated style to the cultural dislocation pervading modern American society. She was born in 1934 in Sacramento, a fifth-generation Californian, and she has attended closely to the distinctive people and places of the American West. After graduating from the University of California at Berkeley in 1956, Didion lived for nearly a decade in New York City before returning permanently to California, a place that she scrutinizes in her most recent book, Where I Was From *(2003). She has contributed to many periodicals, and her essays have been published in* Slouching Towards Bethlehem *(1968),* The White Album *(1979),* Salvador *(1983),* Essays and Conversations *(1984),* Miami *(1987),* After Henry *(1992), and* Political Fictions *(2001). Didion has also published five novels:* Run River *(1963),* Play It as It Lays *(1970),* A Book of Common Prayer *(1977),* Democracy *(1984), and* The Last Thing He Wanted *(1996). With her late husband, the writer John Gregory Dunne, she wrote screenplays for movies, among them* Panic in Needle Park *(1971),* A Star Is Born *(1976),* True Confessions *(1981), and* Up Close and Personal *(1996).*

The Santa Ana

In describing the violent effects of a hot, dry wind on Los Angeles, Didion ranges typically outward from herself to the people figuring in local news reports. "The Santa Ana" first appeared in the Saturday Evening Post *in 1967 and later appeared as part of "Los Angeles Notebook," an essay collected in* Slouching Towards Bethlehem.

There is something uneasy in the Los Angeles air this afternoon, 1 some unnatural stillness, some tension. What it means is that to-night a Santa Ana will begin to blow, a hot wind from the northeast whining down through the Cajon and San Gorgonio Passes, blowing up sandstorms out along Route 66, drying the hills and the nerves to the flash point. For a few days now we will see smoke back in the canyons, and hear sirens in the night. I have neither heard nor read that a Santa Ana is due, but I know it, and almost everyone

I have seen today knows it too. We know it because we feel it. The baby frets. The maid sulks. I rekindle a waning argument with the telephone company, then cut my losses and lie down, given over to whatever it is in the air. To live with the Santa Ana is to accept, consciously or unconsciously, a deeply mechanistic view of human behavior.

I recall being told, when I first moved to Los Angeles and was living on an isolated beach, that the Indians would throw themselves into the sea when the bad wind blew. I could see why. The Pacific turned ominously glossy during a Santa Ana period, and one woke in the night troubled not only by the peacocks screaming in the olive trees but by the eerie absence of surf. The heat was surreal. The sky had a yellow cast, the kind of light sometimes called "earthquake weather." My only neighbor would not come out of her house for days, and there were no lights at night, and her husband roamed the place with a machete. One day he would tell me that he had heard a trespasser, the next a rattlesnake.

"On nights like that," Raymond Chandler[1] once wrote about the Santa Ana, "every booze party ends in a fight. Meek little wives feel the edge of the carving knife and study their husbands' necks. Anything can happen." That was the kind of wind it was. I did not know then that there was any basis for the effect it had on all of us, but it turns out to be another of those cases in which science bears out folk wisdom. The Santa Ana, which is named for one of the canyons it rushes through, is a *foehn* wind, like the *foehn* of Austria and Switzerland and the *hamsin* of Israel. There are a number of persistent malevolent winds, perhaps the best known of which are the mistral of France and the Mediterranean sirocco, but a *foehn* wind has distinct characteristics: it occurs on the leeward slope of a mountain range and, although the air begins as a cold mass, it is warmed as it comes down the mountain and appears finally as a hot dry wind. Whenever and wherever a *foehn* blows, doctors hear about headaches and nausea and allergies, about "nervousness," about "depression." In Los Angeles some teachers do not attempt to conduct formal classes during a Santa Ana, because the children become unmanageable. In Switzerland the suicide rate goes up during the *foehn*, and in the courts of some Swiss cantons the wind is considered a mitigating circumstance for crime. Surgeons are said to watch the wind, because blood does not clot normally during a *foehn*.

[1]Chandler (1888–1959) is best known for his detective novels featuring Philip Marlowe. [Editor's note.]

A few years ago an Israeli physicist discovered that not only during such winds, but for the ten or twelve hours which precede them, the air carries an unusually high ratio of positive to negative ions. No one seems to know exactly why that should be; some talk about friction and others suggest solar disturbances. In any case the positive ions are there, and what an excess of positive ions does, in the simplest terms, is make people unhappy. One cannot get much more mechanistic than that.

Easterners commonly complain that there is no "weather" at   4
all in Southern California, that the days and the seasons slip by relentlessly, numbingly bland. That is quite misleading. In fact the climate is characterized by infrequent but violent extremes: two periods of torrential subtropical rains which continue for weeks and wash out the hills and send subdivisions sliding toward the sea; about twenty scattered days a year of the Santa Ana, which, with its incendiary dryness, invariably means fire. At the first prediction of a Santa Ana, the Forest Service flies men and equipment from northern California into the southern forests, and the Los Angeles Fire Department cancels its ordinary nonfirefighting routines. The Santa Ana caused Malibu to burn the way it did in 1956, and Bel Air in 1961, and Santa Barbara in 1964. In the winter of 1966–67 eleven men were killed fighting a Santa Ana fire that spread through the San Gabriel Mountains.

Just to watch the front-page news out of Los Angeles during a   5
Santa Ana is to get very close to what it is about the place. The longest single Santa Ana period in recent years was in 1957, and it lasted not the usual three or four days but fourteen days, from November 21 until December 4. On the first day 25,000 acres of the San Gabriel Mountains were burning, with gusts reaching 100 miles an hour. In town, the wind reached Force 12, or hurricane force, on the Beaufort Scale; oil derricks were toppled and people ordered off the downtown streets to avoid injury from flying objects. On November 22 the fire in the San Gabriels was out of control. On November 24 six people were killed in automobile accidents, and by the end of the week the Los Angeles *Times* was keeping a box score of traffic deaths. On November 26 a prominent Pasadena attorney, depressed about money, shot and killed his wife, their two sons, and himself. On November 27 a South Gate divorcée, twenty-two, was murdered and thrown from a moving car. On November 30 the San Gabriel fire was still out of control, and the wind in town was blowing eighty miles an hour. On the first day of December four people died violently, and on the third the wind began to break.

It is hard for people who have not lived in Los Angeles to realize   6
how radically the Santa Ana figures in the local imagination. The
city burning is Los Angeles's deepest image of itself: Nathanael West
perceived that, in *The Day of the Locust*; and at the time of the 1965
Watts riots what struck the imagination most indelibly were the
fires.[2] For days one could drive the Harbor Freeway and see the city
on fire, just as we had always known it would be in the end. Los
Angeles weather is the weather of catastrophe, of apocalypse, and,
just as the reliably long and bitter winters of New England determine
the way life is lived there, so the violence and the unpredictability
of the Santa Ana affect the entire quality of life in Los Angeles,
accentuate its impermanence, its unreliability. The wind shows us
how close to the edge we are.

Meaning

1. Does Didion describe purely for the sake of describing, or does she
   have a thesis she wants to convey? If so, where does she most explicitly state this thesis?
2. What is the dominant impression Didion creates of the Santa Ana
   wind? What effect does it have on residents of Los Angeles?
3. Explain what Didion means by a "mechanistic view of human behavior" (paragraph 1). What would the opposite of such a view of human
   behavior be?
4. How might Didion's last sentence have two meanings?

Purpose and Audience

1. Why do you think Didion felt compelled to write about the Santa
   Ana? Consider whether she might have had a dual purpose.
2. What kind of audience is Didion writing for? Primarily people from
   Los Angeles? How do you know? Does Didion identify herself as an
   Angelina?

Method and Structure

1. Didion doesn't describe the Santa Ana wind itself as much as its effects.
   Why does she approach her subject this way? What effects does she
   focus on?

[2]*The Day of the Locust* (1939), a novel about Hollywood, ends in riot and fire.
The August 1965 disturbances in the Watts neighborhood of Los Angeles resulted
in millions of dollars in damage from fires. [Editor's note.]

2. Didion alternates between passages of mostly objective and mostly subjective description. Trace this movement throughout the essay.

3. What is the function of the quotation from Raymond Chandler at the beginning of paragraph 3? How does it serve as a transition?

4. **Other Methods**   The essay is full of examples of the wind's effects on human beings. How do these examples help Didion achieve her purpose?

Language

1. Note Didion's frequent use of the first person (*I* and *we*) and of the present tense. What does she achieve with this point of view?

2. What is the effect of the vivid imagery in paragraph 2? In what way is this imagery "surreal" (fantastic or dreamlike)?

Writing Topics

1. Using Didion's essay as a model, write a descriptive essay about something that annoys, frightens, or even crazes you and others. Your subject could be a natural phenomenon, such as the one Didion describes, or something else: bumper-to-bumper traffic at rush hour, long lines at the department of motor vehicles or another government agency, lengthy and complicated voice-mail menus that end up in busy signals. You may use examples from your own experience and observation, from experiences you have read or heard about, or, like Didion, from both sources.

2. Didion tries to explain the Santa Ana phenomenon scientifically in paragraph 3 as having something to do with an excess of positive ions in the air. But she admits that nobody knows why there are more positive than negative ions or why that fact should translate into human unhappiness. To what extent do you think our moods can be explained by science? Are our emotions simply the by-products of brain chemistry, as some scientists would suggest? Write an essay, using description and narration, about someone you know (or know of) whose moods are affected by forces beyond his or her control. Be sure to include enough detail to create a vivid portrait for your readers.

3. Didion perceives the Santa Ana as a cultural phenomenon in Los Angeles that affects the attitudes, relationships, and activities of residents "just as the reliably long and bitter winters of New England determine the way life is lived there" (paragraph 6). Consider a place you know well and describe how some aspect of the climate or weather affects the culture, "the way life is lived," not only during a particular event or season but throughout the year.

JUDITH ORTIZ COFER

Judith Ortiz Cofer, who was born in Puerto Rico, is a writer and a teacher of literature and writing at the University of Georgia in Athens. Her works include The Latin Deli *(1993) and many other books of poems and stories. She has been anthologized in* The Best American Essays, The Norton Book of Women's Lives, The Pushcart Prize, *and the* O. Henry Prize Stories. *She received a PEN/Martha Albrand Special Citation in nonfiction for* Silent Dancing *(1990) as well as the Anisfield Wolf Book Award for* The Latin Deli. *She recently coedited an anthology of essays,* Sleeping with One Eye Open: Women Writers and the Art of Survival *(1999). Cofer has received fellowships from the National Endowment for the Arts and the Witter Bynner Foundation for poetry. Her most recent books include the novel* The Meaning of Consuelo *(2003) and several works for young adults.*

Silent Dancing

Describing old home movies and fragments of dreams, Cofer re-creates her childhood in an immigrant family that moved from Puerto Rico to New Jersey when she was three years old. The essay was first published in the Georgia Review *and later appeared as the title essay in Cofer's collection* Silent Dancing.

We have a home movie of this party. Several times my mother and I have watched it together, and I have asked questions about the silent revelers coming in and out of focus. It is grainy and of short duration, but it's a great visual aid to my memory of life at that time. And it is in color—the only complete scene in color I can recall from those years. 1

We lived in Puerto Rico until my brother was born in 1954. Soon after, because of economic pressures on our growing family, my father joined the United States Navy. He was assigned to duty on a ship in Brooklyn Yard—a place of cement and steel that was to be his home base in the States until his retirement more than twenty years later. He left the Island first, alone, going to New York City and tracking down his uncle who lived with his family across the Hudson 2

40

River in Paterson, New Jersey. There my father found a tiny apartment in a huge tenement that had once housed Jewish families but was just being taken over and transformed by Puerto Ricans, overflowing from New York City. In 1955 he sent for us. My mother was only twenty years old, I was not quite three, and my brother was a toddler when we arrived at El Building, as the place had been christened by its newest residents.

My memories of life in Paterson during those first few years are   3
all in shades of gray. Maybe I was too young to absorb vivid colors and details, or to discriminate between the slate blue of the winter sky and the darker hues of the snow-bearing clouds, but that single color washes over the whole period. The building we lived in was gray, as were the streets, filled with slush the first few months of my life there. The coat my father had bought for me was similar in color and too big; it sat heavily on my thin frame.

I do remember the way the heater pipes banged and rattled, star-   4
tling all of us out of sleep until we got so used to the sound that we automatically shut it out or raised our voices above the racket. The hiss from the valve punctuated my sleep (which has always been fitful) like a nonhuman presence in the room — a dragon sleeping at the entrance of my childhood. But the pipes were also a connection to all the other lives being lived around us. Having come from a house designed for a single family back in Puerto Rico — my mother's extended-family home — it was curious to know that strangers lived under our floor and above our heads, and that the heater pipe went through everyone's apartment. (My first spanking in Paterson came as a result of playing tunes on the pipes in my room to see if there would be an answer.) My mother was as new to this concept of beehive life as I was, but she had been given strict orders by my father to keep the doors locked, the noise down, ourselves to ourselves.

It seems that Father had learned some painful lessons about prej-   5
udice while searching for an apartment in Paterson. Not until years later did I hear how much resistance he had encountered with landlords who were panicking at the influx of Latinos into a neighborhood that had been Jewish for a couple of generations. It made no difference that it was the American phenomenon of ethnic turnover which was changing the urban core of Paterson, and that the human flood could not be held back with an accusing finger.

"You Cuban?" one man had asked my father, pointing at his name   6
tag on the navy uniform — even though my father had the fair skin and light brown hair of his northern Spanish background, and the

name Ortiz is as common in Puerto Rico as Johnson is in the United States.

"No," my father had answered, looking past the finger into his   7
adversary's angry eyes. "I'm Puerto Rican."

"Same shit." And the door closed.   8

My father could have passed as European, but we couldn't. My   9
brother and I both have our mother's black hair and olive skin, and so
we lived in El Building and visited our great-uncle and his fair children
on the next block. It was their private joke that they were the German
branch of the family. Not many years later that area too would be
mainly Puerto Rican. It was as if the heart of the city map were being
gradually colored brown—*café con leche*¹ brown. Our color.

The movie opens with a sweep of the living room. It is "typical"   10
immigrant Puerto Rican decor for the time: The sofa and chairs are
square and hard-looking, upholstered in bright colors (blue and yellow
in this instance) and covered with the transparent plastic that furni-
ture salesmen then were so adept at convincing women to buy. The
linoleum on the floor is light blue; where it had been subjected to spike
heels, as it was in most places, there were dime-size indentations all
over it that cannot be seen in this movie. The room is full of people
dressed up: dark suits for the men, red dresses for the women. When I
have asked my mother why most of the women are in red that night,
she has shrugged and said, "I don't remember. Just a coincidence." She
doesn't have my obsession for assigning symbolism to everything.

The three women in red sitting on the couch are my mother, my   11
eighteen-year-old cousin, and her brother's girlfriend. The novia² *is just*
up from the Island, which is apparent in her body language. She sits
up formally, her dress pulled over her knees. She is a pretty girl, but her
posture makes her look insecure, lost in her full-skirted dress, which
she has carefully tucked around her to make room for my gorgeous
cousin, her future sister-in-law. My cousin has grown up in Paterson
and is in her last year of high school. She doesn't have a trace of what
Puerto Ricans call la mancha *(literally, the stain: the mark of the new*
immigrant—something about the posture, the voice, or the humble
demeanor that makes it obvious to everyone the person has just
arrived on the mainland). My cousin is wearing a tight, sequined,
cocktail dress. Her brown hair has been lightened with peroxide
around the bangs, and she is holding a cigarette expertly between her

¹Spanish for "coffee with milk." [Editor's note.]

²Fiancée, or a girl just arrived from Puerto Rico. [Editor's note.]

fingers, bringing it up to her mouth in a sensuous arc of her arm as she
talks animatedly. My mother, who has come up to sit between the two
women, both only a few years younger than herself, is somewhere
between the poles they represent in our culture.

It became my father's obsession to get out of the barrio, and thus   12
we were never permitted to form bonds with the place or with the
people who lived there. Yet El Building was a comfort to my mother,
who never got over yearning for *la isla*.[3] She felt surrounded by her
language: The walls were thin, and voices speaking and arguing in
Spanish could be heard all day. *Salsas* blasted out of radios, turned
on early in the morning and left on for company. Women seemed to
cook rice and beans perpetually—the strong aroma of boiling red
kidney beans permeated the hallways.

Though Father preferred that we do our grocery shopping at the   13
supermarket when he came home on weekend leaves, my mother
insisted that she could cook only with products whose labels she
could read. Consequently, during the week I accompanied her and
my little brother to La Bodega—a hole-in-the-wall grocery store
across the street from El Building. There we squeezed down three
narrow aisles jammed with various products. Goya and Libby's—
those were the trademarks that were trusted by her *mamá*, so my
mother bought many cans of Goya beans, soups, and condiments,
as well as little cans of Libby's fruit juices for us. And she also
bought Colgate toothpaste and Palmolive soap. (The final *e* is pronounced in both these products in Spanish, so for many years I
believed that they were manufactured on the Island. I remember
my surprise at first hearing a commercial on television in which
"Colgate" rhymed with "ate.") We always lingered at La Bodega, for
it was there that Mother breathed best, taking in the familiar aro-
mas of the foods she knew from Mamá's kitchen. It was also there
that she got to speak to the other women of El Building without
violating outright Father's dictates against fraternizing with our
neighbors.

Yet Father did his best to make our "assimilation" painless. I can still   14
see him carrying a real Christmas tree up several flights of stairs to our
apartment, leaving a trail of aromatic pine. He carried it formally, as if
it were a flag in a parade. We were the only ones in El Building that I
knew of who got presents on both Christmas and *día de Reyes*, the day
when the Three Kings brought gifts to Christ and to Hispanic children.

[3]The island. [Editor's note.]

Our supreme luxury in El Building was having our own television 15
set. It must have been a result of Father's guilt feelings over the isolation he had imposed on us, but we were among the first in the barrio to have one. My brother quickly became an avid watcher of Captain Kangaroo and Jungle Jim, while I loved all the series showing families. By the time I started first grade, I could have drawn a map of Middle America as exemplified by the lives of characters in *Father Knows Best, The Donna Reed Show, Leave It to Beaver, My Three Sons*, and (my favorite) *Bachelor Father*, where John Forsythe treated his adopted teenage daughter like a princess because he was rich and had a Chinese houseboy to do everything for him. In truth, compared to our neighbors in El Building, *we* were rich. My father's navy check provided us with financial security and a standard of living that the factory workers envied. The only thing his money could not buy us was a place to live away from the barrio—his greatest wish, Mother's greatest fear.

In the home movie the men are shown next, sitting around a card 16
table set up in one corner of the living room, playing dominoes. The clack of the ivory pieces was a familiar sound. I heard it in many houses on the Island and in many apartments in Paterson. In Leave It to Beaver, *the Cleavers played bridge in every other episode; in my childhood, the men started every social occasion with a hotly debated round of dominoes. The women would sit around and watch, but they never participated in the games.*

Here and there you can see a small child. Children were always 17
brought to parties and, whenever they got sleepy, were put to bed in the host's bedroom. Babysitting was a concept unrecognized by the Puerto Rican women I knew: A responsible mother did not leave her children with any stranger. And in a culture where children are not considered intrusive, there was no need to leave the children at home. We went where our mother went.

Of my preschool years I have only impressions: the sharp bite of 18
the wind in December as we walked with our parents toward the brightly lit stores downtown; how I felt like a stuffed doll in my heavy coat, boots, and mittens; how good it was to walk into the five-and-dime and sit at the counter drinking hot chocolate. On Saturdays our whole family would walk downtown to shop at the big department stores on Broadway. Mother bought all our clothes at Penney's and Sears, and she liked to buy her dresses at the women's specialty shops like Lerner's and Diana's. At some point we'd go into Woolworth's and sit at the soda fountain to eat.

We never ran into other Latinos at these stores or when eating   19
out, and it became clear to me only years later that the women from
El Building shopped mainly in other places—stores owned by other
Puerto Ricans or by Jewish merchants who had philosophically
accepted our presence in the city and decided to make us their good
customers, if not real neighbors and friends. These establishments
were located not downtown but in the blocks around our street, and
they were referred to generically as La Tienda, El Bazar, La Bodega,
La Botánica. Everyone knew what was meant. These were the stores
where your face did not turn a clerk to stone, where your money was
as green as anyone else's.

One New Year's Eve we were dressed up like child models in the   20
Sears catalogue: my brother in a miniature man's suit and bow tie,
and I in black patent-leather shoes and a frilly dress with several lay-
ers of crinoline underneath. My mother wore a bright red dress that
night, I remember, and spike heels; her long black hair hung to her
waist. Father, who usually wore his navy uniform during his short
visits home, had put on a dark civilian suit for the occasion: We
had been invited to his uncle's house for a big celebration. Everyone
was excited because my mother's brother—Hernan—a bachelor who
could indulge himself with luxuries—had bought a home movie
camera, which he would be trying out that night.

Even the home movie cannot fill in the sensory details such a   21
gathering left imprinted in a child's brain. The thick sweetness of
women's perfumes mixing with the ever-present smells of food cooking in the kitchen: meat and plantain *pasteles*, as well as the ubiqui-
tous rice dish made special with pigeon peas—*gandules*—and
seasoned with precious *sofrito* sent up from the Island by somebody's mother or smuggled in by a recent traveler. *Sofrito* was one of
the items that women hoarded, since it was hardly ever in stock at
La Bodega. It was the flavor of Puerto Rico.

The men drank Palo Viejo rum, and some of the younger ones got   22
weepy. The first time I saw a grown man cry was at a New Year's Eve
party: He had been reminded of his mother by the smells in the kitchen.
But what I remember most were the boiled *pasteles*, plantain or yucca
rectangles stuffed with corned beef or other meats, olives, and many
other savory ingredients, all wrapped in banana leaves. Everybody had
to fish one out with a fork. There was always a "trick" *pastel*—one without stuffing—and whoever got that one was the "New Year's Fool."

There was also the music. Long-playing albums were treated like   23
precious china in these homes. Mexican recordings were popular,

but the songs that brought tears to my mother's eyes were sung by the melancholy Daniel Santos, whose life as a drug addict was the stuff of legend. Felipe Rodríguez was a particular favorite of couples, since he sang about faithless women and broken-hearted men. There is a snatch of one lyric that has stuck in my mind like a needle on a worn groove: *De piedra ha de ser mi cama, de piedra la cabezera . . . la mujer que a mi me quiera . . . ha de quererme de veras. Ay, Ay, Ay, corazón, porque no amas . . .* I must have heard it a thousand times since the idea of a bed made of stone, and its connection to love, first troubled me with its disturbing images.

The five-minute home movie ends with people dancing in a circle—   24
the creative filmmaker must have set it up, so that all of them could file past him. It is both comical and sad to watch silent dancing. Since there is no justification for the absurd movements that music provides for some of us, people appear frantic, their faces embarrassingly intense. It's as if you were watching sex. Yet for years, I've had dreams in the form of this home movie. In a recurring scene, familiar faces push themselves forward into my mind's eye, plastering their features into distorted close-ups. And I'm asking them: "Who is *she*? Who is the old woman I don't recognize? Is she an aunt? Somebody's wife? Tell me who she is."

"See the beauty mark on her cheek as big as a hill on the lunar land-   25
scape of her face—well, that runs in the family. The women on your father's side of the family wrinkle early; it's the price they pay for that fair skin. The young girl with the green stain on her wedding dress is *la novia*—just up from the Island. See, she lowers her eyes when she approaches the camera, as she's supposed to. Decent girls never look at you directly in the face. *Humilde*, humble, a girl should express humility in all her actions. She will make a good wife for your cousin. He should consider himself lucky to have met her only weeks after she arrived here. If he marries her quickly, she will make him a good Puerto Rican–style wife; but if he waits too long, she will be corrupted by the city, just like your cousin there."

"She means me. I do what I want. This is not some primitive island I   26
live on. Do they expect me to wear a black mantilla on my head and go to mass every day? Not me. I'm an American woman, and I will do as I please. I can type faster than anyone in my senior class at Central High, and I'm going to be a secretary to a lawyer when I graduate. I can pass for an American girl anywhere—I've tried it. At least for Italian, anyway— I never speak Spanish in public. I hate these parties, but I wanted the dress. I look better than any of these *humildes* here. My life is going to

be different. I have an American boyfriend. He is older and has a car. My parents don't know it, but I sneak out of the house late at night sometimes to be with him. If I marry him, even my name will be American. I hate rice and beans — that's what makes these women fat."

"Your *prima*[4] is pregnant by that man she's been sneaking around 27 with. Would I lie to you? I'm your *tía política*,[5] your great-uncle's common-law wife — the one he abandoned on the Island to go marry your cousin's mother. *I* was not invited to this party, of course, but I came anyway. I came to tell you that story about your cousin that you've always wanted to hear. Do you remember the comment your mother made to a neighbor that has always haunted you? The only thing you heard was your cousin's name, and then you saw your mother pick up your doll from the couch and say: 'It was as big as this doll when they flushed it down the toilet.' This image has bothered you for years, hasn't it? You had nightmares about babies being flushed down the toilet, and you wondered why anyone would do such a horrible thing. You didn't dare ask your mother about it. She would only tell you that you had not heard her right, and yell at you for listening to adult conversations. But later, when you were old enough to know about abortions, you suspected.

"I am here to tell you that you were right. Your cousin was growing 28 an *americanito* in her belly when this movie was made. Soon after, she put something long and pointy into her pretty self, thinking maybe she could get rid of the problem before breakfast and still make it to her first class at the high school. Well, *niña*,[6] her screams could be heard downtown. Your aunt, her *mamá*, who had been a midwife on the Island, managed to pull the little thing out. Yes, they probably flushed it down the toilet. What else could they do with it — give it a Christian burial in a little white casket with blue bows and ribbons? Nobody wanted that baby — least of all the father, a teacher at her school with a house in West Paterson that he was filling with real children, and a wife who was a natural blonde.

"Girl, the scandal sent your uncle back to the bottle. And guess 29 where your cousin ended up? Irony of ironies. She was sent to a village in Puerto Rico to live with a relative on her mother's side: a place so far away from civilization that you have to ride a mule to reach it. A real change in scenery. She found a man there — women like that cannot live without male company — but believe me, the men in Puerto Rico know how to put a saddle on a woman like her. *La gringa*,[7] they call her. Ha, ha, ha. *La gringa* is what she always wanted to be . . ."

[4]Cousin. [Editor's note.]
[5]Aunt-in-law. [Editor's note.]
[6]Child. [Editor's note.]
[7]Foreigner or outsider, especially a North American or Briton. [Editor's note.]

The old woman's mouth becomes a cavernous black hole I fall 30
into. And as I fall, I can feel the reverberations of her laughter. I hear
the echoes of her last mocking words: *la gringa, la gringa!* And the
conga line keeps moving silently past me. There is no music in my
dream for the dancers.

When Odysseus visits Hades to see the spirit of his mother,[8] he 31
makes an offering of sacrificial blood, but since all the souls crave an
audience with the living, he has to listen to many of them before he
can ask questions. I, too, have to hear the dead and the forgotten
speak in my dream. Those who are still part of my life remain silent,
going around and around in their dance. The others keep pressing
their faces forward to say things about the past.

My father's uncle is last in line. He is dying of alcoholism, shrunken 32
and shriveled like a monkey, his face a mass of wrinkles and broken
arteries. As he comes closer I realize that in his features I can see my
whole family. If you were to stretch that rubbery flesh, you could find
my father's face, and deep within *that* face—my own. I don't want to
look into those eyes ringed in purple. In a few years he will retreat into
silence, and take a long, long time to die. *Move back, Tío,* I tell him. *I
don't want to hear what you have to say. Give the dancers room to move.
Soon it will be midnight. Who is the New Year's Fool this time?*

Meaning

1. Of her father, Cofer writes, "The only thing his money could not buy
   us was a place to live away from the barrio—his greatest wish,
   Mother's greatest fear" (paragraph 15). Why was moving her father's
   greatest wish? Why did her mother fear it? What passages from the
   essay support your answer?
2. Are the quoted speeches in paragraphs 25–29 real or imagined? Use
   evidence from the essay to support your answer.

Purpose and Audience

1. What do you think is Cofer's purpose in this essay? Does she have
   something specific she wants the reader to understand?
2. What assumptions does Cofer make about her audience? How familiar do readers have to be with Puerto Rican culture in order to understand Cofer's dominant impression?

---

[8]An episode in the *Odyssey*, usually attributed to Homer, who flourished in
the ninth or eighth century BC. In Greek mythology, Hades rules the underworld.
[Editor's note.]

Method and Structure

1. What does Cofer's description of Paterson and her childhood apartment (paragraphs 3–4) tell us about Cofer herself as a child?
2. What are the contents of the passages in italics (paragraphs 1, 10–11, 16–17) and the ones in smaller type (25–29)? How do these passages work with those in regular type? What is their effect?
3. How well does the observation in paragraph 24, "It is both comical and sad to watch silent dancing," convey the dominant impression of Cofer's essay? What, if anything, would you add to "comical and sad"?
4. **Other Methods**   Paragraph 11 offers three examples of Puerto Rican women: Cofer's mother, her assimilated cousin, and the cousin's brother's girlfriend. How do these three examples illustrate a cultural shift Puerto Rican immigrants were experiencing at the time the home movie was made?

Language

1. How might "silent dancing" serve as a metaphor for memory? (If necessary, see the Glossary for a definition of *metaphor*.)
2. What larger meaning can we infer from this sentence in paragraph 23: "Long-playing albums were treated like precious china in these homes"?

Writing Topics

1. In an essay, describe a dream you've had that stays with you for some reason. Try to interpret the dream in the context of your life when you had it. What do you think it meant? Why did you have it when you did? What did it tell you?
2. Have you had the experience of being isolated from your surroundings, whether because of language or culture or because of some other barrier—being new in town, feeling friendless, or even just having to study when everyone else was having fun? Describe the experience in an essay, using plenty of details to help your readers understand your feelings.
3. Analyze the different tones of Cofer herself, her cousin (paragraph 26), and her *tía política* (25, 27–29). How do their tones convey the different experiences and expectations of these three women?

N. SCOTT MOMADAY

One of the country's most respected writers about Native Americans'
traditions, myths, and landscapes, Navarre Scott Momaday was born
in 1934 on the Kiowa Indian Reservation in Oklahoma. He attended
the University of New Mexico (BA, 1958) and Stanford University
(PhD, 1963), and since then has earned his living as a teacher
and writer. The son of a Kiowa father and a mother descended from
white pioneers, Momaday often writes about characters who navi-
gate similar multicultural backgrounds. His novel House Made of
Dawn *won the Pulitzer Prize in 1969, and his other works include*
the memoir The Names *(1976) and numerous collections of stories,*
essays, poetry, and artwork. Most recently, Momaday published the
collection In the Bear's House *(1999) and the children's book* Circle
of Wonder *(2001).*

The Way to Rainy Mountain

The introduction to Momaday's book of the same title, published in
1961, "The Way to Rainy Mountain" describes the writer's trek to his
grandmother's grave. Along the way, he visits sites of great signifi-
cance to his Kiowa heritage.

A single knoll rises out of the plain in Oklahoma, north and west of   1
the Wichita Range.[1] For my people, the Kiowas, it is an old landmark, and they gave it the name Rainy Mountain. The hardest
weather in the world is there. Winter brings blizzards, hot tornadic
winds arise in the spring, and in summer the prairie is an anvil's
edge. The grass turns brittle and brown, and it cracks beneath your
feet. There are green belts along the rivers and creeks, linear groves
of hickory and pecan, willow and witch hazel. At a distance in July
or August the steaming foliage seems almost to writhe in fire. Great
green and yellow grasshoppers are everywhere in the tall grass, popping up like corn to sting the flesh, and tortoises crawl about on the
red earth, going nowhere in the plenty of time. Loneliness is an aspect
of the land. All things in the plain are isolate; there is no confusion of

[1]The Wichita Mountains are southwest of Oklahoma City. [Editor's note.]

objects in the eye, but *one* hill or *one* tree or *one* man. To look upon
that landscape in the early morning, with the sun at your back, is to
lose the sense of proportion. Your imagination comes to life, and
this, you think, is where Creation was begun.

I returned to Rainy Mountain in July. My grandmother had died   2
in the spring, and I wanted to be at her grave. She had lived to be
very old and at last infirm. Her only living daughter was with her
when she died, and I was told that in death her face was that of a
child.

I like to think of her as a child. When she was born, the Kiowas   3
were living that last great moment of their history. For more than a
hundred years they had controlled the open range from the Smoky
Hill River to the Red, from the headwaters of the Canadian to the
fork of the Arkansas and Cimarron.[2] In alliance with the Comanches,
they had ruled the whole of the southern plains. War was their sacred
business, and they were among the finest horsemen the world has
ever known. But warfare for the Kiowas was preeminently a matter
of disposition rather than of survival, and they never understood the
grim, unrelenting advance of the US Cavalry. When at last, divided
and ill-provisioned, they were driven onto the Staked Plains in the
cold rains of autumn, they fell into panic. In Palo Duro Canyon they
abandoned their crucial stores to pillage and had nothing then but
their lives. In order to save themselves, they surrendered to the soldiers at Fort Sill and were imprisoned in the old stone corral that
now stands as a military museum. My grandmother was spared
the humiliation of those high gray walls by eight or ten years, but she
must have known from birth the affliction of defeat, the dark brood-
ing of old warriors.

Her name was Aho, and she belonged to the last culture to evolve   4
in North America. Her forebears came down from the high country
in western Montana nearly three centuries ago. They were a mountain people, a mysterious tribe of hunters whose language has never
been positively classified in any major group. In the late seventeenth
century they began a long migration to the south and east. It was a
journey toward the dawn, and it led to a golden age. Along the way
the Kiowas were befriended by the Crows, who gave them the culture and religion of the Plains. They acquired horses, and their

[2]Momaday describes an area covering much of present-day Kansas and
Oklahoma as well as the Texas Panhandle and parts of Colorado and New Mexico.
Later in this paragraph, Palo Duro Canyon is south of Amarillo, Texas, and Fort
Sill is southwest of Oklahoma City, near the Wichita Mountains. [Editor's note.]

ancient nomadic spirit was suddenly free of the ground. They acquired Tai-me, the sacred Sun Dance doll, from that moment the object and symbol of their worship, and so shared in the divinity of the sun. Not least, they acquired the sense of destiny, therefore courage and pride. When they entered upon the southern Plains they had been transformed. No longer were they slaves to the simple necessity of survival; they were a lordly and dangerous society of fighters and thieves, hunters and priests of the sun. According to their origin myth, they entered the world through a hollow log. From one point of view, their migration was the fruit of an old prophecy, for indeed they emerged from a sunless world.

Although my grandmother lived out her long life in the shadow of   5
Rainy Mountain, the immense landscape of the continental interior lay like memory in her blood. She could tell of the Crows, whom she had never seen, and of the Black Hills,[3] where she had never been. I wanted to see in reality what she had seen more perfectly in the mind's eye, and traveled fifteen hundred miles to begin my pilgrimage.

Yellowstone, it seemed to me, was the top of the world, a region   6
of deep lakes and dark timber, canyons and waterfalls. But, beautiful as it is, one might have the sense of confinement there. The skyline in all directions is close at hand, the high wall of the woods and deep cleavages of shade. There is a perfect freedom in the mountains, but it belongs to the eagle and the elk, the badger and the bear. The Kiowas reckoned their stature by the distance they could see, and they were bent and blind in the wilderness.

Descending eastward, the highland meadows are a stairway to the   7
plain. In July the inland slope of the Rockies is luxuriant with flax and buckwheat, stonecrop and larkspur. The earth unfolds and the limit of the land recedes. Clusters of trees, and animals grazing far in the distance, cause the vision to reach away and wonder to build upon the mind. The sun follows a longer course in the day, and the sky is immense beyond all comparison. The great billowing clouds that sail upon it are shadows that move upon the grain like water, dividing light. Farther down, in the land of the Crows and Blackfeet, the plain is yellow. Sweet clover takes hold of the hills and bends upon itself to cover and seal the soil. There the Kiowas paused on their way; they had come to the place where they must change their lives. The sun is at home on the plains. Precisely there does it have

[3]The Black Hills are in western South Dakota. Yellowstone (next paragraph) is in northwestern Wyoming. In paragraphs 7–8, Momaday describes movement eastward across the top of Wyoming. [Editor's note.]

the certain character of a god. When the Kiowas came to the land of the Crows, they could see the dark lees of the hills at dawn across the Bighorn River, the profusion of light on the grain shelves, the oldest deity ranging after the solstices. Not yet would they veer southward to the caldron of the land that lay below; they must wean their blood from the northern winter and hold the mountains a while longer in their view. They bore Tai-me in procession to the east.

A dark mist lay over the Black Hills, and the land was like iron. At the top of a ridge I caught sight of Devil's Tower[4] upthrust against the gray sky as if in the birth of time the core of the earth had broken through its crust and the motion of the world was begun. There are things in nature that engender an awful quiet in the heart of man; Devil's Tower is one of them. Two centuries ago, because they could not do otherwise, the Kiowas made a legend at the base of the rock. My grandmother said: $\qquad$ 8

> Eight children were there at play, seven sisters and their brother. Suddenly the boy was struck dumb; he trembled and began to run upon his hands and feet. His fingers became claws, and his body was covered with fur. Directly there was a bear where the boy had been. The sisters were terrified; they ran, and the bear after them. They came to the stump of a great tree, and the tree spoke to them. It bade them climb upon it, and as they did so it began to rise into the air. The bear came to kill them, but they were just beyond its reach. It reared against the tree and scored the bark all around with its claws. The seven sisters were borne into the sky, and they became the stars of the Big Dipper.

From that moment, and so long as the legend lives, the Kiowas have kinsmen in the night sky. Whatever they were in the mountains, they could be no more. However tenuous their well-being, however much they had suffered and would suffer again, they had found a way out of the wilderness.

My grandmother had a reverence for the sun, a holy regard that now is all but gone out of mankind. There was a wariness in her, and an ancient awe. She was a Christian in her later years, but she had come a long way about, and she never forgot her birthright. As a child she had been to the Sun Dances; she had taken part in those annual rites, and by them she had learned the restoration of her people in the presence of Tai-me. She was about seven when the last   9

[4]An 865-foot stone outcropping in northeastern Wyoming, now a national monument. [Editor's note.]

Kiowa Sun Dance was held in 1887 on the Washita River above Rainy Mountain Creek.[5] The buffalo were gone. In order to consummate the ancient sacrifice—to impale the head of a buffalo bull upon the medicine tree—a delegation of old men journeyed into Texas, there to beg and barter for an animal from the Goodnight herd. She was ten when the Kiowas came together for the last time as a living Sun Dance culture. They could find no buffalo; they had to hang an old hide from the sacred tree. Before the dance could begin, a company of soldiers rode out from Fort Sill under orders to disperse the tribe. Forbidden without cause the essential act of their faith, having seen the wild herds slaughtered and left to rot upon the ground, the Kiowas backed away forever from the medicine tree. That was July 20, 1890, at the great bend of the Washita. My grandmother was there. Without bitterness, and for as long as she lived, she bore a vision of deicide.[6]

Now that I can have her only in memory, I see my grandmother 10 in the several postures that were peculiar to her: standing at the wood stove on a winter morning and turning meat in a great iron skillet; sitting at the south window, bent above her beadwork, and afterwards, when her vision failed, looking down for a long time into the fold of her hands; going out upon a cane, very slowly as she did when the weight of age came upon her; praying. I remember her most often at prayer. She made long, rambling prayers out of suffering and hope, having seen many things. I was never sure that I had the right to hear, so exclusive were they of all mere custom and company. The last time I saw her she prayed standing by the side of her bed at night, naked to the waist, the light of a kerosene lamp moving upon her dark skin. Her long, black hair, always drawn and braided in the day, lay upon her shoulders and against her breasts like a shawl. I do not speak Kiowa, and I never understood her prayers, but there was something inherently sad in the sound, some merest hesitation upon the syllables of sorrow. She began in a high and descending pitch, exhausting her breath to silence; then again and again—and always the same intensity of effort, of something that is, and is not, like urgency in the human voice. Transported so in the dancing light among the shadows of her room, she seemed beyond the reach of time. But that was illusion; I think I knew then that I should not see her again.

[5]The Washita runs halfway between Oklahoma City and the Wichita Mountains. [Editor's note.]

[6]The killing of a divine being or beings (from Latin words meaning "god" and "kill"). [Editor's note.]

Houses are like sentinels in the plain, old keepers of the weather 11
watch. There, in a very little while, wood takes on the appearance of
great age. All colors wear soon away in the wind and rain, and then
the wood is burned gray and the grain appears and the nails turn red
with rust. The windowpanes are black and opaque; you imagine
there is nothing within, and indeed there are many ghosts, bones
given up to the land. They stand here and there against the sky, and
you approach them for a longer time than you expect. They belong
in the distance; it is their domain.

Once there was a lot of sound in my grandmother's house, a lot of 12
coming and going, feasting and talk. The summers there were full of
excitement and reunion. The Kiowas are a summer people; they
abide the cold and keep to themselves, but when the season turns
and the land becomes warm and vital they cannot hold still; an old love
of going returns upon them. The aged visitors who came to my grandmother's house when I was a child were made of lean and leather, and
they bore themselves upright. They wore great black hats and bright
ample shirts that shook in the wind. They rubbed fat upon their hair
and wound their braids with strips of colored cloth. Some of them
painted their faces and carried the scars of old and cherished enmi-
ties. They were an old council of warlords, come to remind and be
reminded of who they were. Their wives and daughters served them
well. The women might indulge themselves; gossip was at once the
mark and compensation of their servitude. They made loud and
elaborate talk among themselves, full of jest and gesture, fright and
false alarm. They went abroad in fringed and flowered shawls, bright
beadwork and German silver. They were at home in the kitchen, and
they prepared meals that were banquets.

There were frequent prayer meetings, and great nocturnal feasts. 13
When I was a child I played with my cousins outside, where the lamp-
light fell upon the ground and the singing of the old people rose up
around us and carried away into the darkness. There were a lot of
good things to eat, a lot of laughter and surprise. And afterwards,
when the quiet returned, I lay down with my grandmother and could
hear the frogs away by the river and feel the motion of the air.

Now there is a funeral silence in the rooms, the endless wake of 14
some final word. The walls have closed in upon my grandmother's
house. When I returned to it in mourning, I saw for the first time
in my life how small it was. It was late at night, and there was a
white moon, nearly full. I sat for a long time on the stone steps by
the kitchen door. From there I could see out across the land; I could
see the long row of trees by the creek, the low light upon the rolling

plains, and the stars of the Big Dipper. Once I looked at the moon and caught sight of a strange thing. A cricket had perched upon the handrail, only a few inches away from me. My line of vision was such that the creature filled the moon like a fossil. It had gone there, I thought, to live and die, for there, of all places, was its small definition made whole and eternal. A warm wind rose up and purled like the longing within me.

The next morning I awoke at dawn and went out on the dirt road   15 to Rainy Mountain. It was already hot, and the grasshoppers began to fill the air. Still, it was early in the morning, and the birds sang out of the shadows. The long yellow grass on the mountain shone in the bright light, and a scissortail hied above the land. There, where it ought to be, at the end of a long and legendary way, was my grandmother's grave. Here and there on the dark stones were ancestral names. Looking back once, I saw the mountain and came away.

Meaning

1. What is the significance of Momaday's statement that the Kiowas "reckoned their stature by the distance they could see" (paragraph 6)? How does this statement relate to the ultimate fate of the Kiowas?
2. Remembering his grandmother, Momaday writes, "She made long, rambling prayers out of suffering and hope, having seen many things" (paragraph 10). What is the key point here, and how does the concept of prayer connect with the essay as a whole?
3. What do you think Momaday's main idea is? What thread links all the essay's parts?

Purpose and Audience

1. What seems to be Momaday's purpose in writing this essay? Can we read this as more than a personal story about a visit to his grandmother's grave?
2. Who is Momaday's audience? Do you think he is writing for other Kiowa descendants? for non-Indians? for others who have lost an older relative?

Method and Structure

1. "Loneliness is an aspect of the land," Momaday writes (paragraph 1). To what extent do you think this sentence captures the dominant impression of the essay? If you perceive a different impression, what is it?

2. How does Momaday organize his essay? (It may help to plot the structure by preparing a rough outline.) How effective do you find this organization, and why?

3. **Other Methods** Besides description, Momaday relies on other methods as well, such as narration, example, comparison and contrast, and cause and effect. What is the purpose of the comparison in paragraphs 12–14?

Language

1. Momaday uses many vivid figures of speech. Locate at least one use each of metaphor, simile, and hyperbole (review these terms under *figures of speech* in the Glossary). What does each of these figures convey?

2. Momaday's first and last paragraphs present contrasting images of Rainy Mountain and the surrounding plain: At first, "the prairie is an anvil's edge" and the "grass turns brittle and brown"; in the end, "the birds sang out of the shadows" and the "long yellow grass on the mountain shone in the bright light." How does this contrast serve Momaday's purpose?

3. Notice Momaday's use of parallelism in describing the visitors to his grandmother's house (paragraph 12)— for instance, "They wore.... They rubbed.... They made...." What does the parallelism convey about the people being described? (If necessary, consult the Glossary for the definition of *parallelism.*)

Writing Topics

1. Think of somebody special to you and a specific place that you associate with this person. Develop an essay that describes both the person and the place, using concrete and specific details to make the connection between them clear to your readers.

2. Momaday writes about his ancestors and a way of life very different from that of the present. For this assignment you may need to investigate your family's history. Write an essay that describes your ancestors' way of life. (Your ancestors may be as recent as your grandparents or as distant as your research allows.) Who were these people? How did they live? How does that way of life differ from the way you and your family live now? Be specific in your description and comparison, providing concrete details and examples for clarity.

3. In an essay, analyze Momaday's attitudes toward the Kiowas as revealed in the language he uses to describe them. Support your thesis (your idea about Momaday's attitudes) with specific quotations from the essay.

Writing with the Method
Description

Choose one of the following topics, or any topic they suggest, for an essay developed by description. The topic you decide on should be something you care about so that description is a means of communicating an idea, not an end in itself.

PEOPLE
1. An exceptionally neat or messy person
2. A person whose appearance and mannerisms are at odds with his or her real self
3. A person you admire or respect
4. An irritating child

PLACES
5. A frightening place
6. A place near water (ocean, lake, pond, river, swimming pool)
7. A place you daydream about
8. A prison cell, police station, or courtroom
9. A cellar, attic, or garage
10. Your room

ANIMALS AND THINGS
11. A work of art
12. A pet or an animal in a zoo
13. A prized possession or favorite childhood toy
14. The look and taste of a favorite or detested food

SCENES
15. The devastation caused by a natural disaster
16. A scene of environmental destruction
17. Late night or early morning
18. The scene at a concert (rock, country, rap, classical, jazz)

SENSATIONS

19. Waiting for important news
20. Being freed of some restraint
21. Writing
22. Skating, running, body surfing, skydiving, or some other activity
23. Extreme hunger, thirst, cold, heat, or fatigue

Chapter Two

NARRATION

USING THE METHOD

To **narrate** is to tell a story, to relate a sequence of events that are linked in time. We narrate when we tell of a funny experience, report a baseball game, or trace a historical event. By arranging events in an orderly progression, we illuminate the stages leading to a result.

Sometimes the emphasis in narration is on the story itself, as in fiction, biography, autobiography, some history, and much journalism. But often a narrative serves some larger point, as when a paragraph or a brief story about an innocent person's death helps to strengthen an argument for stricter handling of drunk drivers. When used as a primary means of developing an essay, such pointed narration usually relates a sequence of events that led to new knowledge or had a notable outcome. The point of the narrative—the idea the reader is to take away—then determines the selection of events, the amount of detail devoted to them, and their arrangement.

Though narration arranges events in time, narrative time is not real time. An important event may fill whole pages, even though it took only minutes to unfold; and a less important event may be dispensed with in a sentence, even though it lasted hours. Suppose, for instance, that a writer wants to narrate the experience of being mugged in order to show how courage came unexpectedly to his aid. He might provide a slow-motion account of the few minutes' encounter with the muggers, including vivid details of the setting and of the attackers' appearance, a moment-by-moment replay of his emotions, and exact dialogue. At the same time, he will compress events that merely fill in background or link main events, such as how he got to the scene of the mugging or the follow-up questioning by a police detective. And he will entirely omit many events, such as a conversation overheard at the police station, that have no significance for his point.

The point of a narrative influences not only which events are covered and how fully but also how the events are arranged. There are several possibilities:

- A straight chronological sequence is usually the easiest to manage because it relates events in the order of their actual occurrence. It is particularly useful for short narratives, for those in which the last event is the most dramatic, or for those in which the events preceding and following the climax contribute to the point being made.
- The final event, such as a self-revelation, may come first, followed by an explanation of the events leading up to it.
- The entire story may be summarized first and then examined in detail.
- **Flashbacks**—shifts backward rather than forward in time—may recall events whose significance would not have been apparent earlier. Flashbacks are common in movies and fiction: a character in the midst of one scene mentally replays a different scene.

In addition to providing a clear organization, you can also help readers by adopting a consistent **point of view,** a position relative to the events, conveyed in two main ways:

- Pronouns indicate your place in the story: the first-person *I* if you are a direct participant; the third-person *he, she, it,* and *they* if you are an observer or reporter.
- Verb tense indicates your relation in time to the sequence of events: present (*is, run*) or past (*was, ran*).

Combining the first-person pronoun with the present tense can create great immediacy ("I feel the point of the knife in my back"). At the other extreme, combining third-person pronouns with the past tense creates more distance and objectivity ("He felt the point of the knife in his back"). In between extremes, you can combine first person with past tense ("I felt . . .") or third person with present tense ("He feels . . ."). The choice depends on your actual involvement in the narrative and on your purpose.

DEVELOPING A NARRATIVE ESSAY

Getting Started

You'll find narration useful whenever relating a sequence of events can help you make a point, sometimes to support the thesis of a larger paper, sometimes *as* the thesis of a paper. If you're assigned a narrative essay, probe your own experiences for a situation such as an argument involving strong emotion, a humorous or embarrassing incident, a dramatic scene you witnessed, or a learning experience like a job. If you have the opportunity to do research, you might choose a topic dealing with the natural world (such as the Big Bang scenario for the origin of the universe) or an event in history or politics (such as how a local activist worked to close down an animal-research lab).

Whatever your subject, you should have some point to make about it: Why was the incident or experience significant? What does it teach or illustrate? Phrase this point in a sentence if you can at this stage (later it can serve as your thesis sentence). For instance:

> I used to think small-town life was boring, but one taste of the city made me appreciate the leisurely pace of home.

> A recent small earthquake demonstrated the hazards of inadequate civil-defense measures.

Sometimes you may need to draft your story before the point of it becomes clear to you, especially if the experience was personal and too recent to have sunk in.

Explore your subject by listing all the events in sequence as they happened. At this stage you may find the traditional journalist's questions helpful: *Who was involved? What happened? When did it happen? Where did it happen? Why did it happen? How did it happen?* These questions will lead you to examine your subject from all angles. Then you need to decide which events should be developed in great detail because they are central to your point; which merit compression because they merely contribute background or tie the main events together; and which should be omitted altogether because they add nothing to your point and might clutter your narrative.

While you are weighing the relative importance of events, consider also what your readers need to know in order to understand and appreciate your narrative.

- What information will help locate readers in the narrative's time and place?
- How will you expand and compress events to keep readers' attention?
- What details about people, places, and feelings will make the events vivid for readers?
- What is your attitude toward the subject—lighthearted, sarcastic, bitter, serious?—and how will you convey it to readers in your choice of events and details?
- What should your point of view be? Do you want to involve readers intimately by using the first person and the present tense? Or does that seem overdramatic, less appropriate than the more detached, objective view that would be conveyed by the past tense or the third person or both?

Organizing

Narrative essays often begin without formal introductions, instead drawing the reader in with one of the more dramatic events in the sequence. But you may find an introduction useful to set the scene for your narrative, summarize the events leading up to it, or otherwise establish the context for it. Such an opening may lead to a statement of your thesis so that readers know why you are bothering to tell them your story. Then again, to intensify the drama of your story you may decide to withhold your thesis sentence for the conclusion or omit it altogether. (Remember, though, that the thesis must be evident to readers even if it isn't stated: the narrative needs a point.)

The arrangement of events in the body of your essay depends on the actual order in which they occurred and the point you want to make. To narrate a trip during which one thing after another went wrong, you might find a strict chronological order most effective. To narrate an earthquake that began and ended in an instant, you might sort simultaneous events into groups—say, what happened to buildings and what happened to people—or you might arrange a few people's experiences in order of increasing drama. To narrate your experience of city life, you might interweave events in the city with contrasting flashbacks to your life in a small town, or you might start by relating one especially bad experience in the city, drop back to explain how you ended up in that situation, and then go on to tell what happened afterward. Narrative time can be manipulated in any number of ways, but your scheme should have a purpose that your readers can see, and you should stick to it.

Let the ending of your essay be determined by the effect you want to leave with readers. You can end with the last event in your sequence, or the one you have saved for last, if it conveys your point and provides a strong finish. Or you can summarize the aftermath of the story if it contributes to the point. You can also end with a formal conclusion that states your point—your thesis—explicitly. Such a conclusion is especially useful if your point unfolds gradually throughout the narrative and you want to emphasize it at the finish.

Drafting

Drafting a narrative can be less of a struggle than drafting other kinds of papers, especially if you're close to the events and you use a straight chronological order. But the relative ease of storytelling can be misleading if it causes you to describe events too quickly or write without making a point. While drafting, be as specific as possible. Tell what the people in your narrative were wearing, what expressions their faces held, how they gestured, what they said. Specify the time of day, and describe the weather and the surroundings (buildings, vegetation, and the like). All these details may be familiar to you, but they won't be to your readers.

At the same time, try to remain open to what the story means to you, so that you can convey that meaning in your selection and description of events. If you know before you begin what your thesis is, let it guide you. But the first draft may turn out to be a search for your thesis, so that you'll need another draft to make it evident in the way you relate events.

In your draft you may want to experiment with dialogue—quotations of what participants said, in their words. Dialogue can add immediacy and realism as long as it advances the narrative and doesn't ramble beyond its usefulness. In reconstructing dialogue from memory, try to recall not only the actual words but also the sounds of speakers' voices and the expressions on their faces—information that will help you represent each speaker distinctly. And keep the dialogue natural sounding by using constructions typical of speech. For instance, most speakers prefer contractions like *don't* and *shouldn't* to the longer forms *do not* and *should not*; and few speakers begin sentences with *although*, as in the formal-sounding "Although we could hear our mother's voice, we refused to answer her."

Whether you are relating events in strict chronological order or manipulating them for some effect, try to make their sequence in real time and the distance between them clear to readers. Instead of signaling sequence with the monotonous *and then . . . and then . . . and then* or *next . . . next . . . next,* use informative transitions that signal the order of events (*afterward, earlier*), the duration of events (*for an hour, in that time*), or the amount of time between events (*the next morning, a week later*).

Revising and Editing

When your draft is complete, revise and edit it by answering the following questions.

- *Is the point of your narrative clear, and does every event you relate contribute to it?* Whether or not you state your thesis, it should be obvious to readers. They should be able to see why you have lingered over some events and compressed others, and they should not be distracted by insignificant events and details.
- *Is your organization clear?* Be sure that your readers will understand any shifts backward or forward in time.
- *Have you used transitions to help readers follow the sequence of events?* Transitions such as *meanwhile* or *soon afterward* serve a dual purpose: they keep the reader on track, and they link sentences and paragraphs so that they flow smoothly.
- *If you have used dialogue, is it purposeful and natural?* Be sure all quoted speeches move the action ahead. And read all dialogue aloud to check that it sounds like something someone would actually say.

LANGSTON HUGHES

A poet, fiction writer, playwright, critic, and humorist, Langston Hughes described his writing as "largely concerned with depicting Negro life in America." He was born in 1902 in Joplin, Missouri, and grew up in Illinois, Kansas, and Ohio. After dropping out of Columbia University in the early 1920s, Hughes worked at odd jobs while struggling to gain recognition as a writer. His first book of poems, The Weary Blues *(1925), helped seed the Harlem Renaissance, a flowering of African American music and literature centered in the Harlem district of New York City during the 1920s. The book also generated a scholarship that enabled Hughes to finish college at Lincoln University. In all of his work—including* The Negro Mother *(1931),* The Ways of White Folks *(1934),* Shakespeare in Harlem *(1942),* Montage of a Dream Deferred *(1951),* Ask Your Mama *(1961), and* The Best of Simple *(1961)—Hughes captured and projected the rhythms of jazz and the distinctive speech, subtle humor, and deep traditions of African American people. He died in New York City in 1967.*

Salvation

A chapter in Hughes's autobiography, The Big Sea *(1940), "Salvation" is a simple yet compelling narrative about a moment of deceit and disillusionment for a boy of twelve. As you read Hughes's account, notice how the opening two sentences set up every twist of the story.*

I was saved from sin when I was going on thirteen. But not really 1 saved. It happened like this. There was a big revival at my Auntie Reed's church. Every night for weeks there had been much preaching, singing, praying, and shouting, and some very hardened sinners had been brought to Christ, and the membership of the church had grown by leaps and bounds. Then just before the revival ended, they held a special meeting for children, "to bring the young lambs to the fold." My aunt spoke of it for days ahead. That night, I was escorted to the front row and placed on the mourner's bench with all the other young sinners, who had not yet been brought to Jesus.

My aunt told me that when you were saved you saw a light, and 2 something happened to you inside! And Jesus came into your life!

And God was with you from then on! She said you could see and hear and feel Jesus in your soul. I believed her. I have heard a great many old people say the same thing and it seemed to me they ought to know. So I sat there calmly in the hot, crowded church, waiting for Jesus to come to me.

The preacher preached a wonderful rhythmical sermon, all 3 moans and shouts and lonely cries and dire pictures of hell, and then he sang a song about the ninety and nine safe in the fold, but one little lamb was left out in the cold. Then he said: "Won't you come? Won't you come to Jesus? Young lambs, won't you come?" And he held out his arms to all us young sinners there on the mourner's bench. And the little girls cried. And some of them jumped up and went to Jesus right away. But most of us just sat there.

A great many old people came and knelt around us and prayed, 4 old women with jet-black faces and braided hair, old men with work-gnarled hands. And the church sang a song about the lower lights are burning, some poor sinners to be saved. And the whole building rocked with prayer and song.

Still I kept waiting to *see* Jesus. 5

Finally all the young people had gone to the altar and were saved, 6 but one boy and me. He was a rounder's son named Westley. Westley and I were surrounded by sisters and deacons praying. It was very hot in the church, and getting late now. Finally Westley said to me in a whisper: "God damn! I'm tired o' sitting here. Let's get up and be saved." So he got up and was saved.

Then I was left all alone on the mourner's bench. My aunt came 7 and knelt at my knees and cried, while prayers and songs swirled all around me in the little church. The whole congregation prayed for me alone, in a mighty wail of moans and voices. And I kept waiting serenely for Jesus, waiting, waiting—but he didn't come. I wanted to see him, but nothing happened to me. Nothing! I wanted something to happen to me, but nothing happened.

I heard the songs and the minister saying: "Why don't you come? 8 My dear child, why don't you come to Jesus? Jesus is waiting for you. He wants you. Why don't you come? Sister Reed, what is this child's name?"

"Langston," my aunt sobbed. 9

"Langston, why don't you come? Why don't you come and be 10 saved? Oh, Lamb of God! Why don't you come?"

Now it was really getting late. I began to be ashamed of myself, 11 holding everything up so long. I began to wonder what God thought about Westley, who certainly hadn't seen Jesus either, but who was now sitting proudly on the platform, swinging his knickerbockered legs and grinning down at me, surrounded by deacons and old women on their knees praying. God had not struck Westley dead for taking his name in vain or for lying in the temple. So I decided that maybe to save further trouble, I'd better lie, too, and say that Jesus had come, and get up and be saved.

So I got up.   12

Suddenly the whole room broke into a sea of shouting, as they   13
saw me rise. Waves of rejoicing swept the place. Women leaped in the air. My aunt threw her arms around me. The minister took me by the hand and led me to the platform.

When things quieted down, in a hushed silence, punctuated by a   14
few ecstatic "Amens," all the new young lambs were blessed in the name of God. Then joyous singing filled the room.

That night, for the last time in my life but one—for I was a big   15
boy twelve years old—I cried. I cried, in bed alone, and couldn't stop. I buried my head under the quilts, but my aunt heard me. She woke up and told my uncle I was crying because the Holy Ghost had come into my life, and because I had seen Jesus. But I was really crying because I couldn't bear to tell her that I had lied, that I had deceived everybody in the church, that I hadn't seen Jesus, and that now I didn't believe there was a Jesus anymore, since he didn't come to help me.

Meaning

1. What is the main point of Hughes's narrative? What change occurs in him as a result of his experience?
2. What finally makes Hughes decide to get up and be saved? How does this decision affect him afterward?
3. What do you make of the title and the first two sentences? What is Hughes saying here about "salvation"?

Purpose and Audience

1. Why do you think Hughes wrote "Salvation" as part of his autobiography more than two decades after the experience? Was his purpose simply to express feelings prompted by a significant event in his life? Did he want to criticize his aunt and the other adults in the congregation? Did he want to explain something about childhood or about the distance between generations? What passages support your answer?

2. What does Hughes seem to assume about his readers' familiarity with the kind of service he describes? What details help make the procedure clear?

3. How do dialogue, lines from hymns, and details of other sounds (paragraphs 3–10) help re-create the increasing pressure Hughes feels? What other details contribute to this sense of pressure?

Method and Structure

1. Why do you think Hughes chose narration to explore the themes of this essay? Can you imagine an argumentative essay (Chapter 10) that would deal with the same themes? What might its title be?

2. Where in his narrative does Hughes insert explanations, compress time by summarizing events, or jump ahead in time by omitting events? Where does he expand time by drawing moments out? How does each of these insertions and manipulations of time relate to Hughes's main point?

3. In paragraph 1 Hughes uses several transitions to signal the sequence of events and the passage of time: "for weeks," "Then just before," "for days ahead," "That night." Where does he use similar signals in the rest of the essay?

4. **Other Methods**   Hughes's narrative also explains a process: we learn how a revival meeting works. Why is this process analysis essential to the essay?

Language

1. What does Hughes's language reveal about his adult attitudes toward his experience? Does he feel anger? bitterness? sorrow? guilt? shame? amusement? What words and passages support your answer?

2. Hughes relates his experience in an almost childlike style, using many short sentences and beginning many sentences with *And*. What effect do you think he is trying to achieve with this style?

3. Hughes expects to "see" Jesus when he is saved (paragraphs 2, 5, 7), and afterward his aunt thinks that he has "seen" Jesus (15). What does each of them mean by *see*? What is the significance of the difference in Hughes's story?

Writing Topics

1. Write a narrative essay about a time when others significantly influenced the way you thought, looked, or acted—perhaps against your own true beliefs or values. What was the appeal of the others' attitudes,

appearance, or behavior? What did you gain by conforming? What did you lose? Use specific details to explain how and why the experience affected you.

2. Hughes says, "I have heard a great many old people say the same thing and it seemed to me they ought to know" (paragraph 2). Think of a piece of information or advice that you heard over and over again from adults when you were a child. Write a narrative essay about an experience in which you were helped or misled by that information or advice.

3. It seems that Hughes wants to be saved largely because of the influence of his family and his community. Westley (paragraphs 6 and 11) represents another kind of influence, peer pressure, that often works against family and community. Think of an incident in your own life when you felt pressured by peers to go against your parents, religion, school, or another authority. Write a narrative essay telling what happened and making it clear why the situation was important to you. What were the results?

ANNIE DILLARD

A poet and essayist, Annie Dillard is part naturalist, part mystic. She was born in 1945 in Pittsburgh. Growing up in that city, she was an independent child given to exploration and reading. (As an adult, she reads nearly a hundred books a year.) After graduating from Hollins College in the Blue Ridge Mountains of Virginia, Dillard settled in the area to investigate her natural surroundings and to write. Her early books were Tickets for a Prayer Wheel *(1974), a collection of poems, and* Pilgrim at Tinker Creek *(1974), a series of related essays that demonstrate Dillard's intense, passionate involvement with the world of nature and the world of the mind.* Pilgrim *earned her national recognition and a Pulitzer Prize. It was followed by* Holy the Firm *(1977), a prose poem;* Teaching a Stone to Talk *(1982), a collection of essays;* Living by Fiction *(1982), a collection of critical essays;* Encounters with Chinese Writers *(1984); the autobiography* An American Childhood *(1987);* The Writing Life *(1989); and* The Living *(1992). More recently, Dillard published a collection of essays,* For the Time Being *(1999). In 1999 she was inducted into the American Academy of Arts and Letters.*

The Chase

In her autobiography, An American Childhood, *Dillard's enthusiasm for life in its many forms colors her recollections of her own youth. "The Chase" (editor's title) is a self-contained chapter from the book that narrates a few minutes of glorious excitement.*

Some boys taught me to play football. This was fine sport. You thought 1 up a new strategy for every play and whispered it to the others. You went out for a pass, fooling everyone. Best, you got to throw yourself mightily at someone's running legs. Either you brought him down or you hit the ground flat out on your chin, with your arms empty before you. It was all or nothing. If you hesitated in fear, you would miss and get hurt: you would take a hard fall while the kid got away, or you would get kicked in the face while the kid got away. But if you flung yourself wholeheartedly at the back of his knees—if you gathered and joined body and soul and pointed them diving fearlessly—then you likely wouldn't get hurt, and you'd stop the ball. Your fate, and your team's score, depended on your concentration and courage. Nothing girls did could compare with it.

Boys welcomed me at baseball, too, for I had, through enthusiastic practice, what was weirdly known as a boy's arm. In winter, in the snow, there was neither baseball nor football, so the boys and I threw snowballs at passing cars. I got in trouble throwing snowballs, and have seldom been happier since.

On one weekday morning after Christmas, six inches of new snow had just fallen. We were standing up to our boot tops in snow on a front yard on trafficked Reynolds Street, waiting for cars. The cars traveled Reynolds Street slowly and evenly; they were targets all but wrapped in red ribbons, cream puffs. We couldn't miss.

I was seven; the boys were eight, nine, and ten. The oldest two Fahey boys were there—Mikey and Peter—polite blond boys who lived near me on Lloyd Street, and who already had four brothers and sisters. My parents approved of Mikey and Peter Fahey. Chickie McBride was there, a tough kid, and Billy Paul and Mackie Kean too, from across Reynolds, where the boys grew up dark and furious, grew up skinny, knowing, and skilled. We had all drifted from our houses that morning looking for action, and had found it here on Reynolds Street.

It was cloudy but cold. The cars' tires laid behind them on the snowy street a complex trail of beige chunks like crenellated castle walls. I had stepped on some earlier; they squeaked. We could have wished for more traffic. When a car came, we all popped it one. In the intervals between cars we reverted to the natural solitude of children.

I started making an iceball—a perfect iceball, from perfectly white snow, perfectly spherical, and squeezed perfectly translucent so no snow remained all the way through. (The Fahey boys and I considered it unfair actually to throw an iceball at somebody, but it had been known to happen.)

I had just embarked on the iceball project when we heard tire chains come clanking from afar. A black Buick was moving toward us down the street. We all spread out, banged together some regular snowballs, took aim, and, when the Buick drew nigh, fired.

A soft snowball hit the driver's windshield right before the driver's face. It made a smashed star with a hump in the middle.

Often, of course, we hit our target, but this time, the only time in all of life, the car pulled over and stopped. Its wide black door

opened; a man got out of it, running. He didn't even close the car
door.

He ran after us, and we ran away from him, up the snowy   10
Reynolds sidewalk. At the corner, I looked back; incredibly, he was
still after us. He was in city clothes: a suit and tie, street shoes. Any
normal adult would have quit, having sprung us into flight and made
his point. This man was gaining on us. He was a thin man, all action.
All of a sudden, we were running for our lives.

Wordless, we split up. We were on our turf; we could lose our-   11
selves in the neighborhood backyards, everyone for himself. I paused
and considered. Everyone had vanished except Mike Fahey, who was
just rounding the corner of a yellow brick house. Poor Mikey, I
trailed him. The driver of the Buick sensibly picked the two of us to
follow. The man apparently had all day.

He chased Mikey and me around the yellow house and up a back-   12
yard path we knew by heart: under a low tree, up a bank, through a
hedge, down some snowy steps, and across the grocery store's delivery driveway. We smashed through a gap in another hedge, entered
a scruffy backyard and ran around its back porch and tight between
houses to Edgerton Avenue; we ran across Edgerton to an alley and
up our own sliding woodpile to the Halls' front yard; he kept coming. We ran up Lloyd Street and wound through mazy backyards
toward the steep hilltop at Willard and Lang.

He chased us silently, block after block. He chased us silently over   13
picket fences, through thorny hedges, between houses, around
garbage cans, and across streets. Every time I glanced back, choking
for breath, I expected he would have quit. He must have been as
breathless as we were. His jacket strained over his body. It was an
immense discovery, pounding into my hot head with every sliding,
joyous step, that this ordinary adult evidently knew what I thought
only children who trained at football knew: that you have to fling
yourself at what you're doing, you have to point yourself, forget
yourself, aim, dive.

Mikey and I had nowhere to go, in our own neighborhood or out   14
of it, but away from this man who was chasing us. He impelled us
forward; we compelled him to follow our route. The air was cold;
every breath tore my throat. We kept running, block after block; we
kept improvising, backyard after backyard, running a frantic course
and choosing it simultaneously, failing always to find small places or
hard places to slow him down, and discovering always, exhilarated,
dismayed, that only bare speed could save us—for he would never
give up, this man—and we were losing speed.

He chased us through the backyard labyrinths of ten blocks 15
before he caught us by our jackets. He caught us and we all stopped.

We three stood staggering, half blinded, coughing, in an obscure 16
hilltop backyard: a man in his twenties, a boy, a girl. He had released
our jackets, our pursuer, our captor, our hero: he knew we weren't
going anywhere. We all played by the rules. Mikey and I unzipped
our jackets. I pulled off my sopping mittens. Our tracks multiplied in
the backyard's new snow. We had been breaking new snow all morning. We didn't look at each other. I was cherishing my excitement.
The man's lower pants legs were wet; his cuffs were full of snow, and
there was a prow of snow beneath them on his shoes and socks.
Some trees bordered the little flat backyard, some messy winter
trees. There was no one around: a clearing in a grove, and we the
only players.

It was a long time before he could speak. I had some difficulty at 17
first recalling why we were there. My lips felt swollen; I couldn't see
out of the sides of my eyes; I kept coughing.

"You stupid kids," he began perfunctorily.   18

We listened perfunctorily indeed, if we listened at all, for the 19
chewing out was redundant, a mere formality, and beside the point.
The point was that he had chased us passionately without giving up,
and so he had caught us. Now he came down to earth. I wanted the
glory to last forever.

But how could the glory have lasted forever? We could have run 20
through every backyard in North America until we got to Panama.
But when he trapped us at the lip of the Panama Canal, what precisely could he have done to prolong the drama of the chase and cap
its glory? I brooded about this for the next few years. He could only
have fried Mikey Fahey and me in boiling oil, say, or dismembered
us piecemeal, or staked us to anthills. None of which I really wanted,
and none of which any adult was likely to do, even in the spirit of
fun. He could only chew us out there in the Panamanian jungle, after
months or years of exalting pursuit. He could only begin, "You stupid kids," and continue in his ordinary Pittsburgh accent with his
normal righteous anger and the usual common sense.

If in that snowy backyard the driver of the black Buick had cut off 21
our heads, Mikey's and mine, I would have died happy, for nothing has
required so much of me since as being chased all over Pittsburgh in
the middle of winter—running terrified, exhausted—by this sainted,
skinny, furious red-headed man who wished to have a word with us.
I don't know how he found his way back to his car.

Meaning

1. What lesson did Dillard learn from the experience of the chase? Where is her point explicitly revealed?
2. In paragraph 2 Dillard writes, "I got in trouble throwing snowballs, and have seldom been happier since." What exactly is Dillard saying about the relationship between trouble and happiness? Do you think she is recommending "getting in trouble" as a means to happiness? Why, or why not?

Purpose and Audience

1. What seems to be Dillard's purpose in "The Chase": to encourage children to get into trouble? to encourage adults to be more tolerant of children who get into trouble? something else?
2. In her first paragraph, Dillard deliberately shifts from the first-person point of view (using *me*) to the second (using *you*). What is the effect of this shift, and how does it contribute to Dillard's purpose?

Method and Structure

1. Why do you think Dillard chose narration to illustrate her point about the difference between children and adults? What does she gain from this method? What other methods might she have used?
2. In this straightforward narrative, Dillard expands some events and summarizes others: for instance, she provides much more detail about the chase in paragraph 12 than in paragraphs 13 and 14. Why might she first provide and then pull back from the detail in paragraph 12?
3. How does the last sentence of paragraph 2 — "I got in trouble throwing snowballs, and have seldom been happier since" — serve to set up the story Dillard is about to tell?
4. **Other Methods** Dillard makes extensive use of description. Locate examples of this method and analyze what they contribute to the essay as a whole.

Language

1. How would you characterize Dillard's style? How does the style reflect the fact that the adult Dillard is writing from a child's point of view?
2. What does Dillard mean by calling the man who chases her "sainted" (paragraph 21)? What is her attitude toward this man? What words and passages support your answer?

3. Consider Dillard's description of cars: traveling down the street, they looked like "targets all but wrapped in red ribbons, cream puffs" (paragraph 3), and their tires in the snow left "a complex trail of beige chunks like crenellated castle walls" (5). What is the dominant impression created here?

Writing Topics

1. Write a narrative essay about a time you misbehaved as a child. Use the first-person *I*, strong verbs, and plenty of descriptive details to render vividly the event and its effects on you and others.

2. Write a narrative essay about a time you discovered that "an ordinary adult" knew some truth you thought only children knew. What was that truth, and why did you believe until that moment that only children knew it? What did this adult do to change your mind?

3. Though Dillard focuses on a time when no harm was done, the consequences of throwing snowballs at moving cars could be quite serious. Rewrite the essay from the point of view of someone who would *not* glorify the children's behavior—the man driving the Buick, for instance, or one of the children's parents. How might one of these people narrate these events? On what might he or she focus?

4. Childhood pranks like throwing snowballs at cars are tolerated more in some cultural groups than in others. In a narrative essay, retell an event in your childhood when you felt you were testing the rules of behavior in your culture. Make your motivations as clear as possible, and reflect on the results of your action.

MAYA ANGELOU

Maya Angelou was born Marguerite Johnson in Saint Louis in 1928. Angelou's childhood was troubled—she was shuttled between the homes of her divorced parents and her grandmother, was raped as a young girl, and became an unwed mother as a teenager. She went on, however, to become a prolific writer whose work is filled with joy and hope. Though she is best known for her poetry, novels, and six auto-biographies, beginning with I Know Why the Caged Bird Sings *(1970) through* A Song Flung Up to Heaven *(2002), Angelou has also worked in theater, film, and television. She appeared in off-Broadway plays, wrote and produced several television-special series, costarred in the movie* How to Make an American Quilt *(1995), and directed the film* Down in the Delta *(1998). She has taught at the University of Kansas, Wichita State University, California State University at Sacramento, and Wake Forest University, where she is Reynolds Professor of American Studies.*

Champion of the World

Rich in detail, this chapter from I Know Why the Caged Bird Sings *captures the suspense of a memorable moment in Angelou's childhood—the night when African American boxer Joe Louis, the "Brown Bomber," defended his heavyweight title against a white con-tender. The narrative is set in her grandmother and Uncle Willie's store, where the community of Angelou's Arkansas hometown gath-ered to listen to the fight.*

The last inch of space was filled, yet people continued to wedge them- 1
selves along the walls of the Store. Uncle Willie had turned the radio
up to its last notch so that youngsters on the porch wouldn't miss a
word. Women sat on kitchen chairs, dining-room chairs, stools, and
upturned wooden boxes. Small children and babies perched on every
lap available and men leaned on the shelves or on each other.

The apprehensive mood was shot through with shafts of gaiety, as 2
a black sky is streaked with lightning.

"I ain't worried 'bout this fight. Joe's gonna whip that cracker like 3
it's open season."

"He gone whip him till that white boy call him Momma."   4

At last the talking finished and the string-along songs about razor   5
blades were over and the fight began.

"A quick jab to the head." In the Store the crowd grunted. "A   6
left to the head and a right and another left." One of the listeners
cackled like a hen and was quieted.

"They're in a clinch, Louis is trying to fight his way out."   7

Some bitter comedian on the porch said, "That white man don't   8
mind hugging that niggah now, I betcha."

"The referee is moving in to break them up, but Louis finally   9
pushed the contender away and it's an uppercut to the chin. The contender is hanging on, now he's backing away. Louis catches him with
a short left to the jaw."

A tide of murmuring assent poured out the door and into the yard.   10

"Another left and another left. Louis is saving that mighty   11
right . . ." The mutter in the Store had grown into a baby roar and it
was pierced by the clang of a bell and the announcer's "That's the bell
for round three, ladies and gentlemen."

As I pushed my way into the Store I wondered if the announcer   12
gave any thought to the fact that he was addressing as "ladies and
gentlemen" all the Negroes around the world who sat sweating and
praying, glued to their "Master's voice."[1]

There were only a few calls for RC Colas, Dr Peppers, and Hires   13
root beer. The real festivities would begin after the fight. Then even
the old Christian ladies who taught their children and tried themselves to practice turning the other cheek would buy soft drinks, and
if the Brown Bomber's victory was a particularly bloody one they
would order peanut patties and Baby Ruths also.

Bailey and I laid the coins on top of the cash register. Uncle Willie   14
didn't allow us to ring up sales during a fight. It was too noisy and
might shake up the atmosphere. When the gong rang for the next
round we pushed through the near-sacred quiet to the herd of children outside.

"He's got Louis against the ropes and now it's a left to the body   15
and a right to the ribs. Another right to the body, it looks like it was
low . . . Yes, ladies and gentlemen, the referee is signaling but the
contender keeps raining the blows on Louis. It's another to the body,
and it looks like Louis is going down."

---

[1]"His master's voice," accompanied by a picture of a little dog listening to a
phonograph, was a familiar advertising slogan. (The picture still appears on some
RCA recordings.) [Editor's note.]

My race groaned. It was our people falling. It was another lynch- 16
ing, yet another Black man hanging on a tree. One more woman
ambushed and raped. A Black boy whipped and maimed. It was
hounds on the trail of a man running through slimy swamps. It was
a white woman slapping her maid for being forgetful.

The men in the Store stood away from the walls and at attention. 17
Women greedily clutched the babes on their laps while on the porch
the shufflings and smiles, flirtings and pinching of a few minutes
before were gone. This might be the end of the world. If Joe lost we
were back in slavery and beyond help. It would all be true, the accusations that we were lower types of human beings. Only a little higher
than apes. True that we were stupid and ugly and lazy and dirty and,
unlucky and worst of all, that God Himself hated us and ordained us
to be hewers of wood and drawers of water, forever and ever, world
without end.

We didn't breathe. We didn't hope. We waited. 18

"He's off the ropes, ladies and gentlemen. He's moving towards 19
the center of the ring." There was no time to be relieved. The worst
might still happen.

"And now it looks like Joe is mad. He's caught Carnera with a left 20
hook to the head and a right to the head. It's a left jab to the body and
another left to the head. There's a left cross and a right to the head.
The contender's right eye is bleeding and he can't seem to keep his
block up. Louis is penetrating every block. The referee is moving in,
but Louis sends a left to the body and it's an uppercut to the chin and
the contender is dropping. He's on the canvas, ladies and gentlemen."

Babies slid to the floor as women stood up and men leaned 21
toward the radio.

"Here's the referee. He's counting. One, two, three, four, five, six, 22
seven . . . Is the contender trying to get up again?"

All the men in the store shouted, "NO." 23

"—eight, nine, ten." There were a few sounds from the audience, 24
but they seemed to be holding themselves in against tremendous
pressure.

"The fight is all over, ladies and gentlemen. Let's get the micro- 25
phone over to the referee . . . Here he is. He's got the Brown Bomber's
hand, he's holding it up . . . Here he is . . ."

Then the voice, husky and familiar, came to wash over us—"The 26
winnah, and still heavyweight champeen of the world . . . Joe Louis."

Champion of the world. A Black boy. Some Black mother's son. 27
He was the strongest man in the world. People drank Coca-Colas like
ambrosia and ate candy bars like Christmas. Some of the men went

behind the Store and poured white lightning in their soft-drink bottles, and a few of the bigger boys followed them. Those who were not chased away came back blowing their breath in front of themselves like proud smokers.

It would take an hour or more before the people would leave the 28 Store and head for home. Those who lived too far had made arrangements to stay in town. It wouldn't do for a Black man and his family to be caught on a lonely country road on a night when Joe Louis had proved that we were the strongest people in the world.

Meaning

1. What connection does Angelou make between the outcome of the fight and the pride of African Americans? To what degree do you think the author's view is shared by the others in the store listening to the broadcast?
2. To what extent are the statements in paragraphs 16 and 17 to be taken literally? What function do they serve in Angelou's narrative?

Purpose and Audience

1. What do you take to be the author's purpose in telling this story?
2. Primo Carnera was probably *not* the Brown Bomber's opponent on the night Maya Angelou recalls. Louis fought Carnera only once, on June 25, 1935, and it was not a title match; Angelou would have been no more than seven years old at the time. Does the author's apparent error detract from her story?

Method and Structure

1. How does Angelou build up suspense in her account of the fight? At what point were you able to predict the winner?
2. What effect does the author's use of direct quotation have on her narrative?
3. **Other Methods** Besides narration, Angelou also relies heavily on the method of description. Analyze how narration depends on description in paragraph 27 alone.

Language

1. Describe Angelou's style. How does her use of nonstandard English contribute to her narrative? (For the definition of *nonstandard English*, consult the Glossary under *diction*.)

2. Comment on the irony in Angelou's final paragraph. (If necessary, consult the Glossary for the definition of *irony*.)

Writing Topics

1. Consider groups that you belong to based on race, ethnic background, religion, sports, hobbies, politics, friendship, or any other ties. In an essay, explore your sense of membership through a narrative that tells of an incident that occurred when that sense was strong. Try to make the incident come alive for your readers with vivid details, dialogue, and tight sequencing of events.

2. Write an essay based on some childhood experience of your own, still vivid in your memory.

3. Angelou does not directly describe relations between African Americans and whites, yet her essay implies quite a lot. Write a brief essay about what you can infer from the exaggeration of paragraphs 16–17 and the obliqueness of paragraph 28. Focus on Angelou's details and the language she uses to present them.

GEORGE ORWELL

A masterful novelist, essayist, journalist, and critic, George Orwell was a highly political writer with little tolerance for authoritarianism, deceit, or pretension. He was born Eric Arthur Blair in 1903 in Bengal, India, where his father held a position in the British civil service. After attending school in England, in 1922 Orwell returned to the East as an officer with the British police in Burma. Five years later he left government service with a lasting contempt for the injustices of imperialism. He had believed since childhood that he should be a writer, so he returned to Europe to become one. His next years of wandering, odd jobs, and poverty were chronicled in Down and Out in Paris and London *(1933), his first book and the occasion for assuming his pen name. Other books followed, including* Burmese Days *(1934), a novel based on his colonial experiences, and* Homage to Catalonia *(1938), a memoir of fighting against the fascists in the Spanish Civil War in 1936. Orwell's best-known works are two satirical novels,* Animal Farm *(1945) and* Nineteen Eighty-Four *(1949), both attacks on totalitarian government. He wrote, he said, largely from political purpose, from a "desire to push the world in a certain direction, to alter other people's ideas of the kind of society that they should strive for." Orwell died in 1950, at the age of forty-six, from a lung ailment. The four-volume* Collected Essays, Journalism, and Letters of George Orwell, *coedited by his widow, Sonia Orwell, was published in 1968.*

Shooting an Elephant

In this essay, Orwell recounts a difficult decision he faced as a police officer in Burma working for the oppressive British government. The selection is from Shooting an Elephant and Other Essays *(1950).*

In Moulmein, in Lower Burma, I was hated by large numbers of 1
people—the only time in my life that I have been important enough
for this to happen to me. I was subdivisional police officer of the town,
and in an aimless, petty kind of way anti-European feeling was very
bitter. No one had the guts to raise a riot, but if a European woman

went through the bazaars alone somebody would probably spit betel juice over her dress. As a police officer I was an obvious target and was baited whenever it seemed safe to do so. When a nimble Burman tripped me up on the football field and the referee (another Burman) looked the other way, the crowd yelled with hideous laughter. This happened more than once. In the end the sneering yellow faces of young men that met me everywhere, the insults hooted after me when I was at a safe distance, got badly on my nerves. The young Buddhist priests were the worst of all. There were several thousands of them in the town and none of them seemed to have anything to do except stand on street corners and jeer at Europeans.

All this was perplexing and upsetting. For at that time I had already 2 made up my mind that imperialism was an evil thing and the sooner I chucked up my job and got out of it the better. Theoretically—and secretly, of course—I was all for the Burmese and all against the oppressors, the British. As for the job I was doing, I hated it more bitterly than I can perhaps make clear. In a job like that you see the dirty work of Empire at close quarters. The wretched prisoners huddling in the stinking cages of the lockups, the grey, cowed faces of the long-term convicts, the scarred buttocks of the men who had been flogged with bamboos—all these oppressed me with an intolerable sense of guilt. But I could get nothing into perspective. I was young and ill-educated and I had had to think out my problems in the utter silence that is imposed on every Englishman in the East. I did not even know that the British Empire is dying, still less did I know that it is a great deal better than the younger empires that are going to supplant it. All I knew was that I was stuck between my hatred of the empire I served and my rage against the evil-spirited little beasts who tried to make my job impossible. With one part of my mind I thought of the British Raj[1] as an unbreakable tyranny, as something clamped down, in *saecula saeculorum*,[2] upon the will of prostrate peoples; with another part I thought that the greatest joy in the world would be to drive a bayonet into a Buddhist priest's guts. Feelings like these are the normal by-products of imperialism; ask any Anglo-Indian official, if you can catch him off duty.

One day something happened which in a roundabout way was 3 enlightening. It was a tiny incident in itself, but it gave me a better

[1]British imperial government. *Raj* in Hindi means "reign," a word similar to *rajah*, "ruler." [Editor's note.]

[2]Latin, "world without end." [Editor's note.]

glimpse than I had had before of the real nature of imperialism — the real motives for which despotic governments act. Early one morning the subinspector at a police station the other end of town rang me up on the phone and said that an elephant was ravaging the bazaar. Would I please come and do something about it? I did not know what I could do, but I wanted to see what was happening and I got on to a pony and started out. I took my rifle, an old .44 Winchester and much too small to kill an elephant, but I thought the noise might be useful *in terrorem*.[3] Various Burmans stopped me on the way and told me about the elephant's doings. It was not, of course, a wild elephant, but a tame one which had gone "must." It had been chained up, as tame elephants always are when their attack of "must" is due, but on the previous night it had broken its chain and escaped. Its mahout,[4] the only person who could manage it when it was in that state, had set out in pursuit, but had taken the wrong direction and was now twelve hours' journey away, and in the morning the elephant had suddenly reappeared in the town. The Burmese population had no weapons and were quite helpless against it. It had already destroyed somebody's bamboo hut, killed a cow and raided some fruit stalls and devoured the stock; also it had met the municipal rubbish van and, when the driver jumped out and took to his heels, had turned the van over and inflicted violences upon it.

The Burmese subinspector and some Indian constables were   4
waiting for me in the quarter where the elephant had been seen. It was a very poor quarter, a labyrinth of squalid bamboo huts, thatched with palmleaf, winding all over a steep hillside. I remember that it was a cloudy, stuffy morning at the beginning of the rains. We began questioning the people as to where the elephant had gone and, as usual, failed to get any definite information. That is invariably the case in the East; a story always sounds clear enough at a distance, but the nearer you get to the scene of events the vaguer it becomes. Some of the people said that the elephant had gone in one direction, some said that he had gone in another, some professed not even to have heard of any elephant. I had almost made up my mind that the whole story was a pack of lies, when we heard yells a little distance away. There was a loud, scandalized cry of "Go away, child! Go away this instant!" and an old woman with a switch in her hand came round the corner of a hut, violently shooing away a crowd of naked children. Some more women followed, clicking their tongues and

3Latin, "to give warning." [Editor's note.]
4Keeper or groom, a servant of the elephant's owner. [Editor's note.]

exclaiming; evidently there was something that the children ought not to have seen. I rounded the hut and saw a man's dead body sprawling in the mud. He was an Indian, a black Dravidian coolie, almost naked, and he could not have been dead many minutes. The people said that the elephant had come suddenly upon him round the corner of the hut, caught him with its trunk, put its foot on his back and ground him into the earth. This was the rainy season and the ground was soft, and his face had scored a trench a foot deep and a couple of yards long. He was lying on his belly with arms crucified and head sharply twisted to one side. His face was coated with mud, the eyes wide open, the teeth bared and grinning with an expression of unendurable agony. (Never tell me, by the way, that the dead look peaceful. Most of the corpses I have seen looked devilish.) The friction of the great beast's foot had stripped the skin from his back as neatly as one skins a rabbit. As soon as I saw the dead man I sent an orderly to a friend's house nearby to borrow an elephant rifle. I had already sent back the pony, not wanting it to go mad with fright and throw me if it smelled the elephant.

The orderly came back in a few minutes with a rifle and five car- 5 tridges, and meanwhile some Burmans had arrived and told us that the elephant was in the paddy fields below, only a few hundred yards away. As I started forward practically the whole population of the quarter flocked out of the houses and followed me. They had seen the rifle and were all shouting excitedly that I was going to shoot the elephant. They had not shown much interest in the elephant when he was merely ravaging their homes, but it was different now that he was going to be shot. It was a bit of fun to them, as it would be to an English crowd; besides they wanted the meat. It made me vaguely uneasy. I had no intention of shooting the elephant—I had merely sent for the rifle to defend myself if necessary—and it is always unnerving to have a crowd following you. I marched down the hill, looking and feeling a fool, with the rifle over my shoulder and an ever-growing army of people jostling at my heels. At the bottom, when you got away from the huts, there was a metalled road and beyond that a miry waste of paddy fields a thousand yards across, not yet ploughed but soggy from the first rains and dotted with coarse grass. The elephant was standing eight yards from the road, his left side towards us. He took not the slightest notice of the crowd's approach. He was tearing up bunches of grass, beating them against his knees to clean them and stuffing them into his mouth.

I had halted on the road. As soon as I saw the elephant I knew with 6 perfect certainty that I ought not to shoot him. It is a serious matter to shoot a working elephant—it is comparable to destroying a huge and costly piece of machinery—and obviously one ought not to do it if it can possibly be avoided. And at that distance, peacefully eating, the elephant looked no more dangerous than a cow. I thought then and I think now that his attack of "must" was already passing off; in which case he would merely wander harmlessly about until the mahout came back and caught him. Moreover, I did not in the least want to shoot him. I decided that I would watch him for a little while to make sure that he did not turn savage again, and then go home.

But at that moment, I glanced round at the crowd that had followed 7
me. It was an immense crowd, two thousand at the least and growing every minute. It blocked the road for a long distance on either side. I looked at the sea of yellow faces above the garish clothes—faces all happy and excited over this bit of fun, all certain that the elephant was going to be shot. They were watching me as they would watch a con- juror about to perform a trick. They did not like me, but with the mag- ical rifle in my hands I was momentarily worth watching. And suddenly I realized that I should have to shoot the elephant after all. The people expected it of me and I had got to do it; I could feel their two thousand wills pressing me forward, irresistibly. And it was at this moment, as I stood there with the rifle in my hands, that I first grasped the hollowness, the futility of the white man's dominion in the East. Here was I, the white man with his gun, standing in front of the unarmed native crowd—seemingly the leading actor of the piece; but in reality I was only an absurd puppet pushed to and fro by the will of those yellow faces behind. I perceived in this moment that when the white man turns tyrant it is his own freedom that he destroys. He becomes a sort of hollow, posing dummy, the conventionalized figure of a sahib. For it is the condition of his rule that he shall spend his life in trying to impress the "natives," and so in every crisis he has got to do what the "natives" expect of him. He wears a mask, and his face grows to fit it. I had got to shoot the elephant. I had committed myself to doing it when I sent for the rifle. A sahib has got to act like a sahib; he has got to appear resolute, to know his own mind and do definite things. To come all that way, rifle in hand, with two thousand people marching at my heels, and then to trail feebly away, having done nothing—no, that was impossible. The crowd would laugh at me. And my whole life, every white man's life in the East, was one long struggle not to be laughed at.

But I did not want to shoot the elephant. I watched him beating 8
his bunch of grass against his knees, with that preoccupied grand- motherly air that elephants have. It seemed to me that it would be

murder to shoot him. At that age I was not squeamish about killing animals, but I had never shot an elephant and never wanted to. (Somehow it always seems worse to kill a *large* animal.) Besides, there was the beast's owner to be considered. Alive, the elephant was worth at least a hundred pounds; dead, he would only be worth the value of his tusks, five pounds, possibly. But I had got to act quickly. I turned to some experienced-looking Burmans who had been there when we arrived, and asked them how the elephant had been behaving. They all said the same thing: He took no notice of you if you left him alone, but he might charge if you went too close to him.

It was perfectly clear to me what I ought to do. I ought to walk up   9
to within, say, twenty-five yards of the elephant and test his behavior. If he charged, I could shoot; if he took no notice of me, it would be safe to leave him until the mahout came back. But also I knew that I was going to do no such thing. I was a poor shot with a rifle and the ground was soft mud into which one would sink at every step. If the elephant charged and I missed him, I should have about as much chance as a toad under a steamroller. But even then I was not thinking particularly of my own skin, only of the watchful yellow faces behind. For at that moment, with the crowd watching me, I was not afraid in the ordinary sense, as I would have been if I had been alone. A white man mustn't be frightened in front of "natives"; and so, in general, he isn't frightened. The sole thought in my mind was that if anything went wrong those two thousand Burmans would see me pursued, caught, trampled on, and reduced to a grinning corpse like that Indian up the hill. And if that happened it was quite probable that some of them would laugh. That would never do. There was only one alternative. I shoved the cartridges into the magazine and lay down on the road to get a better aim.

The crowd grew very still, and a deep, low, happy sigh, as of   10
people who see the theater curtain go up at last, breathed from innumerable throats. They were going to have their bit of fun after all. The rifle was a beautiful German thing with cross-hair sights. I did not then know that in shooting an elephant one would shoot to cut an imaginary bar running from ear-hole to ear-hole. I ought, therefore, as the elephant was sideways on, to have aimed straight at his ear-hole; actually I aimed several inches in front of this, thinking the brain would be further forward.

When I pulled the trigger I did not hear the bang or feel the kick—   11
one never does when a shot goes home—but I heard the devilish roar of glee that went up from the crowd. In that instant, in too

short a time, one would have thought, even for the bullet to get there, a mysterious, terrible change had come over the elephant. He neither stirred nor fell, but every line of his body had altered. He looked suddenly stricken, shrunken, immensely old, as though the frightful impact of the bullet had paralyzed him without knocking him down. At last, after what seemed a long time—it might have been five seconds, I dare say—he sagged flabbily to his knees. His mouth slobbered. An enormous senility seemed to have settled upon him. One could have imagined him thousands of years old. I fired again into the same spot. At the second shot he did not collapse but climbed with desperate slowness to his feet and stood weakly upright, with legs sagging and head drooping. I fired a third time. That was the shot that did for him. You could see the agony of it jolt his whole body and knock the last remnant of strength from his legs. But in falling he seemed for a moment to rise, for as his hind legs collapsed beneath him he seemed to tower upward like a huge rock toppling, his trunk reaching skywards like a tree. He trumpeted, for the first and only time. And then down he came, his belly towards me, with a crash that seemed to shake the ground even where I lay.

I got up. The Burmans were already racing past me across the 12 mud. It was obvious that the elephant would never rise again, but he was not dead. He was breathing very rhythmically with long rattling gasps, his great mound of a side painfully rising and falling. His mouth was wide open. I could see far down into caverns of pale pink throat. I waited a long time for him to die, but his breathing did not weaken. Finally I fired my two remaining shots into the spot where I thought his heart must be. The thick blood welled out of him like red velvet, but still he did not die. His body did not even jerk when the shots hit him, the tortured breathing continued without a pause. He was dying, very slowly and in great agony, but in some world remote from me where not even a bullet could damage him further. I felt I had got to put an end to that dreadful noise. It seemed dreadful to see the great beast lying there, powerless to move and yet powerless to die, and not even to be able to finish him. I sent back for my small rifle and poured shot after shot into his heart and down his throat. They seemed to make no impression. The tortured gasps continued as steadily as the ticking of a clock.

In the end I could not stand it any longer and went away. I heard 13 later that it took him half an hour to die. Burmans were bringing dahs and baskets even before I left, and I was told they had stripped his body almost to the bones by the afternoon.

Afterwards, of course, there were endless discussions about the   14
shooting of the elephant. The owner was furious, but he was only an
Indian and could do nothing. Besides, legally I had done the right
thing, for a mad elephant has to be killed, like a mad dog, if its owner
fails to control it. Among the Europeans opinion was divided. The
older men said I was right, the younger men said it was a damn
shame to shoot an elephant for killing a coolie, because the elephant
was worth more than any damn Coringhee coolie. And afterwards I
was very glad that the coolie had been killed; it put me legally in the
right and it gave me sufficient pretext for shooting the elephant. I
often wondered whether any of the others grasped that I had done it
solely to avoid looking a fool.

Meaning

1. Why did Orwell shoot the elephant?
2. Describe the epiphany that Orwell experiences in the course of the
   event he writes about. (An *epiphany* is a sudden realization of a truth.)
3. In the last paragraph of his essay, Orwell says he was "glad that the
   coolie had been killed." How do you account for this remark?

Purpose and Audience

1. What is the purpose of this essay? What does Orwell seem to want
   readers to think or do as a result of reading the essay?
2. What does "Shooting an Elephant" gain from having been written
   years after the events it recounts?

Method and Structure

1. In addition to serving as an introduction to Orwell's essay, what function is performed by paragraphs 1 and 2?
2. From what circumstances does the irony of Orwell's essay spring?
   (For the definition of *irony*, consult the Glossary.)
3. **Other Methods**   How do the examples in paragraphs 1 and 2 illustrate Orwell's conflict about his work as a police officer in Burma?

Language

1. What do you understand by Orwell's statement that the elephant had
   "gone 'must'" (paragraph 3)? Look up *must* or its variant *musth* in
   your dictionary.

2. How effective is Orwell's use of adjectives in describing the death of the elephant? How do these adjectives convey Orwell's feelings about his decision?

Writing Topics

1. Write a narrative essay about a time when you acted against your better judgment in order to save face in front of others. Tell the story of your action, and consider what the results were, what you might have done differently, and what you learned from the experience.

2. With what examples of governmental face saving are you familiar? If none leaps to mind, read a newspaper or watch the news on television to catch public officials in the act of covering themselves. (Not only national government but local or student government may provide examples.) In an essay, analyze two or three examples: What do you think was really going on that needed covering? Did the officials succeed in saving face, or did their efforts fail? Were the efforts harmful in any way?

3. Orwell is honest with himself and his readers in acknowledging his mistakes as a government official. Write an essay that examines the degree to which confession may, or may not, erase blameworthiness for misdeeds. Does Orwell remain just as guilty as he would have been if he had not taken responsibility for his actions? Why, or why not? Feel free to supplement your analysis of Orwell's case with examples from your own life or from the news.

Writing with the Method
Narration

Choose one of the following topics, or any other topic they suggest, for an essay developed by narration. The topic you decide on should be something you care about so that narration is a means of communicating an idea, not an end in itself.

FRIENDS AND RELATIONS
1. Gaining independence
2. A friend's generosity or sacrifice
3. A significant trip with your family
4. A wedding or funeral
5. An incident from family legend

THE WORLD AROUND YOU
6. A storm, a flood, an earthquake, or another natural event
7. The history of your neighborhood
8. The most important minutes of a particular sports game
9. A school event, such as a meeting, demonstration, or celebration
10. A time when a poem, story, film, song, or other work left you feeling changed

LESSONS OF DAILY LIFE
11. Acquiring and repaying a debt, either psychological or financial
12. A time when you confronted authority
13. A time when you had to deliver bad news
14. A time when a new, eagerly anticipated possession proved disappointing
15. Your biggest social blunder

FIRSTS
16. Your first day of school, as a child or more recently
17. The first time you met someone who became important to you
18. The first performance you gave
19. A first date

ADVENTURES

20. An episode of extrasensory perception
21. An intellectual journey, such as pursuing a new field or solving a mystery
22. A trip to an unfamiliar place

Chapter Three

EXAMPLE

USING THE METHOD

An **example** represents a general group or an abstract concept or quality. Steven Spielberg is an example of the group of movie directors. A friend's calling at 2:00 AM is an example of her inconsiderateness—or desperation. We habitually use examples to bring general and abstract statements down to earth so that listeners or readers will take an interest in them and understand them.

As this definition indicates, the chief purpose of examples is to make the general specific and the abstract concrete. Since these operations are among the most basic in writing, it is easy to see why illustration or exemplification (the use of example) is among the most common methods of writing. Examples appear frequently in essays developed by other methods. In fact, as diverse as they are, all the essays in this book employ examples for clarity, support, and liveliness. If the writers had not used examples, we might have only a vague sense of their meaning or, worse, might supply mistaken meanings from our own experiences.

While nearly indispensable in any kind of writing, examples may also serve as the dominant method of developing a thesis. For instance:

- Generalizations about trends: "The cell phone has changed the way friends relate to one another."
- Generalizations about events: "Some members of the audience at *The Rocky Horror Picture Show* were stranger than anything in the movie."

- Generalizations about institutions: "A mental hospital is no place for the mentally ill."
- Generalizations about behaviors: "The personalities of parents are sometimes visited on their children."
- Generalizations about rituals: "A funeral benefits the dead person's family and friends."

Each of the quoted ideas could form the central assertion (the thesis) of an essay, and as many examples as necessary would then support it.

How many examples are necessary? That depends on your subject, your purpose, and your intended audience. Two basic patterns are possible:

- A single **extended example** of several paragraphs or several pages fills in needed background and gives the reader a complete view of the subject from one angle. For instance, the purpose of a funeral might be made clear with a narrative and descriptive account of a particular funeral, the family and friends who attended it, and the benefits they derived from it.
- **Multiple examples,** from a few to dozens, illustrate the range covered by the generalization. The strangeness of a movie's viewers might be captured with three or four very strange examples. But supporting the generalization about mental hospitals might demand many examples of patients whose illnesses worsened in the hospital or (from a different angle) many examples of hospital practices that actually harm patients.

Sometimes a generalization merits support from both an extended example and several briefer examples, a combination that provides depth along with range. For instance, half the essay on mental hospitals might be devoted to one patient's experiences and the other half to brief summaries of the experiences of others.

DEVELOPING AN ESSAY BY EXAMPLE

Getting Started

You will need examples whenever your experiences, observations, or reading lead you to make a general statement: the examples give readers evidence for the statement, so that they see its truth. An

EXAMPLE   95

appropriate subject for an example paper is likely to be a general idea you have formed about people, things, the media, or any other feature of your life. Say, for instance, that over the past several years you have seen many made-for-television movies dealing effectively with a sensitive issue such as incest, domestic violence, or AIDS. There is your subject: some TV movies do a good job of dramatizing and explaining difficult social issues. It is a generalization about TV movies based on what you know of individual movies. This statement could serve as the thesis of an essay, the point you want readers to take away. A clear thesis is crucial for an example paper because without it readers can only guess what your illustrations are intended to show.

After arriving at your thesis, you should make a list of all the pertinent examples. This stage may take some thought and even some further reading or observation. While making the list, keep your intended readers at the front of your mind: what do they already know about your subject, and what do they need to know in order to accept your thesis? In illustrating the social value of TV movies for readers who believe television is worthless or even harmful, you might concentrate on the movies that are most relevant to readers' lives, providing enough detail about each to make readers see the relevance.

Organizing

Most example essays open with an introduction that engages readers' attention and gives them some context to relate to. You might begin the paper on TV movies, for instance, by briefly narrating the plot of one movie. The opening should lead into your thesis sentence so that readers know what to expect from the rest of the essay.

Organizing the body of the essay may not be difficult if you use a single example, for the example itself may suggest a distinct method of development (such as narration) and thus an arrangement. But an essay using multiple examples usually requires close attention to arrangement so that readers experience not a list but a pattern. Some guidelines:

- With a limited number of examples—say, four or five—use a climactic organization, arranging examples in order of increasing importance, interest, or complexity. Then the strongest and most detailed example provides a dramatic finish.
- With very many examples—ten or more—find some likenesses among examples that will allow you to treat them in groups. For instance, instead of covering fourteen TV movies in a shapeless

list, you might group them by subject into movies dealing with family relations, those dealing with illness, and the like. (This is the method of classification discussed in Chapter 5.) Covering each group in a separate paragraph or two would avoid the awkward string of choppy paragraphs that might result from covering each example independently. And arranging the groups themselves in order of increasing interest or importance would further structure your presentation.

To conclude your essay, you may want to summarize by elaborating on the generalization of your thesis now that you have supported it. But the essay may not require a conclusion at all if you believe your final example emphasizes your point and provides a strong finish.

Drafting

While you draft your essay, remember that your examples must be plentiful and specific enough to support your generalization. If you use fifteen different examples, their range should allow you to treat each one briefly, in one or two sentences. But if you use only three examples, say, you will have to describe each one in sufficient detail to make up for their small number. And, obviously, if you use only a single example, you must be as specific as possible so that readers see clearly how it illustrates your generalization.

Revising and Editing

To be sure you've met the expectations that most readers hold for examples, revise and edit your draft by considering the following questions.

- *Are all examples, or parts of a single example, obviously relevant to your generalization?* Be careful not to get sidetracked by interesting but unrelated information.
- *Are the examples specific?* Examples bring a generalization down to earth only if they are well detailed. Simply naming representative TV movies and their subjects would not demonstrate their social value. Each movie would need a plot summary that shows how the movie fits and illustrates the generalization.
- *Do the examples, or the parts of a single example, cover all the territory mapped out by your generalization?* To support your generalization, you need to present a range of instances that fairly

EXAMPLE   97

represents the whole. An essay on the social value of TV movies would be misleading if it failed to acknowledge that not *all* TV movies have social value. It would also be misleading if it presented several TV movies as representative examples of socially valuable TV when in fact they were the *only* instances of such TV.

- *Do your examples support your generalization?* You should not start with a broad statement and then try to drum up a few examples to prove it. A thesis such as "Children do poorly in school because they watch too much television" would require factual support gained from research, not the lone example of your little brother. If your little brother performs poorly in school and you attribute his performance to his television viewing, then narrow your thesis so that it accurately reflects your evidence—perhaps "In the case of my little brother, at least, the more time spent watching television the poorer the grades."

Perri Klass is a pediatrician and a writer of both fiction and nonfic-
tion. She was born in 1958 in Trinidad and grew up in New York City
and New Jersey. After obtaining a BA from Harvard University in
1979, she began graduate work in biology but then switched to med-
icine. Klass finished Harvard Medical School in 1986 and practices
pediatrics in Boston, where she also teaches at Boston University
School of Medicine. Her publications are extensive: short stories in
Mademoiselle, Antioch Review, *and other magazines; two collec-*
tions of stories, I Am Having an Adventure *(1986) and* Love and
Modern Medicine: Stories *(2001); three novels,* Recombinations
(1985), Other Women's Children *(1990), and* The Mystery of
Breathing *(2004); essays for the* New York Times, Discover, *and*
other periodicals; three collections of essays, including A Not Entirely
Benign Procedure *(1987) and* Two Sweaters for My Father *(2004);*
and the nonfiction book Quirky Kids: Understanding and Helping
Your Child Who Doesn't Fit In.

She's Your Basic
L.O.L. in N.A.D.

Most of us have felt excluded, confused, or even frightened by the jar-
gon of the medical profession—that is, by the special terminology
and abbreviations for diseases and procedures. In this essay Klass
uses examples of such language, some of it heartless, to illustrate the
pluses and minuses of becoming a doctor. The essay first appeared in
1984 as a "Hers" column in the New York Times.

"Mrs. Tolstoy is your basic L.O.L. in N.A.D., admitted for a soft rule- 1
out M.I.," the intern announces. I scribble that on my patient list. In
other words Mrs. Tolstoy is a Little Old Lady in No Apparent Distress
who is in the hospital to make sure she hasn't had a heart attack (rule
out a myocardial infarction). And we think it's unlikely that she has
had a heart attack (a *soft* rule-out).

If I learned nothing else during my first three months of working 2
in the hospital as a medical student, I learned endless jargon and

abbreviations. I started out in a state of primeval innocence, in which I didn't even know that "s̄ C.P., S.O.B., N/V" meant "without chest pain, shortness of breath, or nausea and vomiting." By the end I took the abbreviations so for granted that I would complain to my mother the English professor, "And can you believe I had to put down *three* NG tubes last night?"

"You'll have to tell me what an NG tube is if you want me to   3
sympathize properly," my mother said. NG, nasogastric—isn't it obvious?

I picked up not only the specific expressions but also the patterns   4
of speech and the grammatical conventions; for example, you never say that a patient's blood pressure fell or that his cardiac enzymes rose. Instead, the patient is always the subject of the verb: "He dropped his pressure." "He bumped his enzymes." This sort of construction probably reflects that profound irritation of the intern when the nurses come in the middle of the night to say that Mr. Dickinson has disturbingly low blood pressure. "Oh, he's gonna hurt me bad tonight," the intern may say, inevitably angry at Mr. Dickinson for dropping his pressure and creating a problem.

When chemotherapy fails to cure Mrs. Bacon's cancer, what we   5
say is, "Mrs. Bacon failed chemotherapy."

"Well, we've already had one hit today, and we're up next, but at   6
least we've got mostly stable players on our team." This means that our team (group of doctors and medical students) has already gotten one new admission today, and it is our turn again, so we'll get whoever is next admitted in emergency, but at least most of the patients we already have are fairly stable, that is, unlikely to drop their pressures or in any other way get suddenly sicker and hurt us bad. Baseball metaphor is pervasive: a no-hitter is a night without any new admissions. A player is always a patient—a nitrate player is a patient on nitrates, a unit player is a patient in the intensive-care unit, and so on, until you reach the terminal player.

It is interesting to consider what it means to be winning, or doing   7
well, in this perennial baseball game. When the intern hangs up the phone and announces, "I got a hit," that is not cause for congratulations. The team is not scoring points; rather, it is getting hit, being bombarded with new patients. The object of the game from the point of view of the doctors, considering the players for whom they are already responsible, is to get as few new hits as possible.

These special languages contribute to a sense of closeness and   8
professional spirit among people who are under a great deal of stress. As a medical student, it was exciting for me to discover that

I'd finally cracked the code, that I could understand what doctors said and wrote and could use the same formulations myself. Some people seem to become enamored of the jargon for its own sake, perhaps because they are so deeply thrilled with the idea of medicine, with the idea of themselves as doctors.

I knew a medical student who was referred to by the interns   9
on the team as Mr. Eponym because he was so infatuated with eponymous terminology,[1] the more obscure the better. He never said "capillary pulsation" if he could say "Quincke's pulses." He would lovingly tell over the multinamed syndromes—Wolff-Parkinson-White, Lown-Ganong-Levine, Henoch-Schonlein—until the temptation to suggest Schleswig-Holstein or Stevenson-Kefauver or Baskin-Robbins became irresistible to his less reverent colleagues.

And there is the jargon that you don't ever want to hear yourself   10
using. You know that your training is changing you, but there are certain changes you think would be going a little too far.

The resident was describing a man with devastating terminal   11
pancreatic cancer. "Basically he's C.T.D.," the resident concluded. I reminded myself that I had resolved not to be shy about asking when I didn't understand things. "C.T.D.?" I asked timidly.

The resident smirked at me. "Circling The Drain."   12

The images are vivid and terrible. "What happened to Mrs.   13
Melville?"

"Oh, she boxed last night." To box is to die, of course.   14

Then there are the more pompous locutions that can make the   15
beginning medical student nervous about the effects of medical training. A friend of mine was told by his resident, "A pregnant woman with sickle-cell represents a failure of genetic counseling."

Mr. Eponym, who tried hard to talk like the doctors, once explained   16
to me, "An infant is basically a brainstem preparation." A brainstem preparation, as used in neurological research, is an animal whose higher brain functions have been destroyed so that only the most primitive reflexes remain, like the sucking reflex, the startle reflex, and the rooting reflex.

The more extreme forms aside, one most important function of   17
medical jargon is to help doctors maintain some distance from their patients. By reformulating a patient's pain and problems into

---

[1]*Eponymous* means "named after"—in this case, medical terminology is named after researchers. [Editor's note.]

a language that the patient doesn't even speak, I suppose we are in some sense taking those pains and problems under our jurisdiction and also reducing their emotional impact. This linguistic separation between doctors and patients allows conversations to go on at the bedside that are unintelligible to the patient. "Naturally, we're worried about adreno-C.A.," the intern can say to the medical student, and lung cancer need never be mentioned.

I learned a new language this past summer. At times it thrills me   18 to hear myself using it. It enables me to understand my colleagues, to communicate effectively in the hospital. Yet I am uncomfortably aware that I will never again notice the peculiarities and even atrocities of medical language as keenly as I did this summer. There may be specific expressions I manage to avoid, but even as I remark them, promising myself I will never use them, I find that this language is becoming my professional speech. It no longer sounds strange in my ears — or coming from my mouth. And I am afraid that as with any new language, to use it properly you must absorb not only the vocabulary but also the structure, the logic, the attitudes. At first you may notice these new alien assumptions every time you put together a sentence, but with time and increased fluency you stop being aware of them at all. And as you lose that awareness, for better or for worse, you move closer and closer to being a doctor instead of just talking like one.

Meaning

1. What point does Klass make about medical jargon in this essay? Where does she reveal her main point explicitly?

2. What useful purposes does medical jargon serve, according to Klass? Do the examples in paragraphs 9–16 serve these purposes? Why, or why not?

Purpose and Audience

1. What does Klass imply when she states that she began her work in the hospital "in a state of primeval innocence" (paragraph 2)? What does this phrase suggest about her purpose in writing the essay?

2. From what perspective does Klass write this essay: that of a medical professional? someone outside the profession? a patient? someone else? To what extent does she expect her readers to share her perspective? What evidence in the essay supports your answer?

3. Given that she is writing for a general audience, does Klass take adequate care to define medical terms? Support your answer with examples from the essay.

Method and Structure

1. Why does Klass begin the essay with an example rather than a statement of her main idea? What effect does this example produce? How does this effect support her purpose in writing the essay?
2. Although Klass uses many examples of medical jargon, she avoids the dull effect of a list by periodically stepping back to make a general statement about her experience or the jargon—for instance, "I picked up not only the specific expressions but also the patterns of speech and the grammatical conventions" (paragraph 4). Locate other places—not necessarily at the beginnings of paragraphs—where Klass breaks up her examples with more general statements.
3. **Other Methods**   Klass uses several other methods besides example, among them classification, definition, and cause-and-effect analysis. What effects—positive and negative—does medical jargon have on Klass, other students, and doctors who use it?

Language

1. What is the tone of this essay? Is Klass trying to be humorous or tongue-in-cheek about the jargon of the profession, or is she serious? Where in the essay is the author's attitude toward her subject the most obvious?
2. Klass refers to the users of medical jargon as both *we/us* (paragraphs 1, 5, 6, 17) and *they/them* (7), and sometimes she shifts from *I* to *you* within a paragraph (4, 18). Do you think these shifts are effective or distracting? Why? Do the shifts serve any function?
3. Klass obviously experienced both positive and negative feelings about mastering medical jargon. Which words and phrases in the last paragraph reflect positive feelings, and which negative?

Writing Topics

1. Klass likens her experience learning medical jargon to that of learning a new language (paragraph 18). If you are studying or have learned a second language, write an essay in which you explain the "new alien assumptions" you must make "every time you put together a sentence." Draw your examples not just from the new language's grammar and vocabulary but from its underlying logic and attitudes.

For instance, does one speak to older people differently in the new language? make requests differently? describe love or art differently?

2. Klass's essay explores the "separation between doctors and patients" (paragraph 17). Has this separation affected you as a patient or as the relative or friend of a patient? If so, write an essay about your experiences. Did the medical professionals rely heavily on jargon? Was their language comforting, frightening, irritating? Based on your experience and on Klass's essay, do you believe that the separation between doctors and patients is desirable? Why, or why not?

3. Most groups focused on a common interest have their own jargon. If you belong to such a group—for example, runners, football fans, food servers, engineering students—spend a few days listening to yourself and others use this language and thinking about the purposes it serves. Which aspects of this language seem intended to make users feel like insiders? Which seem to serve some other purpose, and what is it? In an essay, explain what this jargon reveals about the group and its common interest, using as many specific examples as you can.

ANNA QUINDLEN

Winner of the Pulitzer Prize for commentary in 1992, Anna Quindlen writes sharp, candid columns on subjects ranging from family life to politics to September 11. She was born in 1952 in Philadelphia, where she grew up, as she puts it, "an antsy kid with a fresh mouth." After graduating from Barnard College, Quindlen began writing for the New York Post *and two years later joined the staff of the* New York Times, *where she quickly worked her way up from a city hall reporter to a regular columnist. Quindlen left the* Times *in 1995, and since 1999 she has written a biweekly column for* Newsweek *magazine. Her columns have been collected in* Living Out Loud *(1988),* Thinking Out Loud *(1993), and* Loud and Clear *(2004), and she has also authored* A Short Guide to a Happy Life *(2000) and the novels* Object Lessons *(1991),* One True Thing *(1994),* Black and Blue *(1998), and* Blessings *(2002).*

Homeless

In this essay, Quindlen uses examples to explore the importance of having a place to call "home." The selection is from her collection Living Out Loud.

Her name was Ann, and we met in the Port Authority Bus Terminal 1
several Januarys ago. I was doing a story on homeless people. She said I was wasting my time talking to her; she was just passing through, although she'd been passing through for more than two weeks. To prove to me that this was true, she rummaged through a tote bag and a manila envelope and finally unfolded a sheet of typing paper and brought out her photographs.

They were not pictures of family, or friends, or even a dog or cat, 2
its eyes brown-red in the flashbulb's light. They were pictures of a house. It was like a thousand houses in a hundred towns, not suburb, not city, but somewhere in between, with aluminum siding and a chain-link fence, a narrow driveway running up to a one-car garage and a patch of backyard. The house was yellow. I looked on the back for a date or a name, but neither was there. There was no need for discussion. I knew what she was trying to tell me, for it was something I had often felt. She was not adrift, alone, anonymous,

although her bags and her raincoat with the grime shadowing its creases had made me believe she was. She had a house, or at least once upon a time had had one. Inside were curtains, a couch, a stove, potholders. You are where you live. She was somebody.

I've never been very good at looking at the big picture, taking the global view, and I've always been a person with an overactive sense of place, the legacy of an Irish grandfather. So it is natural that the thing that seems most wrong with the world to me right now is that there are so many people with no homes. I'm not simply talking about shelter from the elements, or three square meals a day or a mailing address to which the welfare people can send the check—although I know that all these are important for survival. I'm talking about a home, about precisely those kinds of feelings that have wound up in cross-stitch and French knots on samplers over the years.

Home is where the heart is. There's no place like it. I love my home with a ferocity totally out of proportion to its appearance or location. I love dumb things about it: the hot-water heater, the plastic rack you drain dishes in, the roof over my head, which occasionally leaks. And yet it is precisely those dumb things that make it what it is—a place of certainty, stability, predictability, privacy, for me and for my family. It is where I live. What more can you say about a place than that? That is everything.

Yet it is something that we have been edging away from gradually during my lifetime and the lifetimes of my parents and grandparents. There was a time when where you lived often was where you worked and where you grew the food you ate and even where you were buried. When that era passed, where you lived at least was where your parents had lived and where you would live with your children when you became enfeebled. Then, suddenly where you lived was where you lived for three years, until you could move on to something else and something else again.

And so we have come to something else again, to children who do not understand what it means to go to their rooms because they have never had a room, to men and women whose fantasy is a wall they can paint a color of their own choosing, to old people reduced to sitting on molded plastic chairs, their skin blue-white in the lights of a bus station, who pull pictures of houses out of their bags. Homes have stopped being homes. Now they are real estate.

People find it curious that those without homes would rather sleep sitting up on benches or huddled in doorways than go to shelters. Certainly some prefer to do so because they are emotionally ill, because they have been locked in before and they are damned if they will be locked in again. Others are afraid of the violence and trouble they may find there. But some seem to want something that is not available in shelters, and they will not compromise, not for a cot, or oatmeal, or a shower with special soap that kills the bugs. "One room," a woman with a baby who was sleeping on her sister's floor, once told me, "painted blue." That was the crux of it; not size or location, but pride of ownership. Painted blue.

This is a difficult problem, and some wise and compassionate people are working hard at it. But in the main I think we work around it, just as we walk around it when it is lying on the sidewalk or sitting in the bus terminal—the problem, that is. It has been customary to take people's pain and lessen our own participation in it by turning it into an issue, not a collection of human beings. We turn an adjective into a noun: the poor, not poor people; the homeless, not Ann or the man who lives in the box or the woman who sleeps on the subway grate.   8

Sometimes I think we would be better off if we forgot about the broad strokes and concentrated on the details. Here is a woman without a bureau. There is a man with no mirror, no wall to hang it on. They are not the homeless. They are people who have no homes. No drawer that holds the spoons. No window to look out upon the world. My God. That is everything.   9

Meaning

1. What is Quindlen's thesis?
2. What distinction is Quindlen making in her conclusion with the sentences "They are not the homeless. They are people who have no homes"?

Purpose and Audience

1. What do you think is Quindlen's purpose in writing this essay? Why does she believe that having a home is important?
2. What key assumptions does the author make about her audience? Are the assumptions reasonable? Where does she specifically address an assumption that might undermine her view?

Method and Structure

1. Why do you think Quindlen begins with the story of Ann? How else might Quindlen have begun her essay?
2. What is the effect of Quindlen's examples of her own home?

3. **Other Methods**   Quindlen uses examples to support an argument. What position does she want readers to recognize and accept?

Language

1. What is the effect of "My God" in the last paragraph?

2. How might Quindlen be said to give new meaning to the old cliché "Home is where the heart is" (paragraph 4)? (If necessary, see the definition of *cliché* in the Glossary.)

3. What is meant by "crux" (paragraph 7)? Where does the word come from?

Writing Topics

1. Write an essay that gives a detailed definition of *home* by using your own home(s), hometown(s), or experiences with home(s) as supporting examples. (See Chapter 8 if you need help with definition.)

2. Have you ever moved from one place to another? What sort of experience was it? Write an essay about leaving an old home and moving to a new one. Was there an activity or a piece of furniture that helped ease the transition?

3. Address Quindlen's contention that turning homelessness into an issue avoids the problem, that we might "be better off if we forgot about the broad strokes and concentrated on the details."

4. Write a brief essay in which you agree or disagree with Quindlen's assertion that a home is "everything." Can one, for instance, be a fulfilled person without a home? In your answer, take account of the values that might underlie an attachment to home; Quindlen mentions "certainty, stability, predictability, privacy" (paragraph 4), but there are others, including some (such as fear) that are less positive.

DAVID SEDARIS

David Sedaris's hilarious yet often touching autobiographical essays have earned him both popular and critical acclaim; in 2001 he received the Thurber Prize for American Humor and was named Humorist of the Year by Time *magazine. Born in 1957, Sedaris grew up in North Carolina and attended the School of the Art Institute of Chicago, where he taught writing for several years before moving to New York City. Working odd jobs during the day and writing about them at night, Sedaris catapulted to near-overnight success in 1993 after reading on National Public Radio a piece about working as a department-store Christmas elf. Since then, he has been a frequent contributor to the* New Yorker, Esquire, *and public radio's* Morning Edition *and* This American Life. *In 1994 he published his first collection of essays,* Barrel Fever, *followed by* Naked *(1996),* Holidays on Ice *(1997),* Me Talk Pretty One Day *(2000), and* Dress Your Family in Corduroy and Denim *(2004).*

Remembering My Childhood on the Continent of Africa

When considered alongside his partner Hugh's experiences growing up in Africa, Sedaris's basically normal North Carolina childhood seems rather mundane. In this essay from Me Talk Pretty One Day, *Sedaris uses numerous examples to comically highlight that normality.*

When Hugh was in the fifth grade, his class took a field trip to an 1
Ethiopian slaughterhouse. He was living in Addis Ababa at the time, and the slaughterhouse was chosen because, he says, "it was convenient."

This was a school system in which the matter of proximity out- 2
weighed such petty concerns as what may or may not be appropriate for a busload of eleven-year-olds. "What?" I asked. "Were there no autopsies scheduled at the local morgue? Was the federal prison just a bit too far out of the way?"

Hugh defends his former school, saying, "Well, isn't that the 3
whole point of a field trip? To see something new?"

"Technically yes, but . . ."   4

"All right then," he says. "So we saw some new things."   5

One of his field trips was literally a trip to a field where the class   6
watched a wrinkled man fill his mouth with rotten goat meat and
feed it to a pack of waiting hyenas. On another occasion they were
taken to examine the bloodied bedroom curtains hanging in the
palace of the former dictator. There were tamer trips, to textile factories and sugar refineries, but my favorite is always the slaughterhouse. It wasn't a big company, just a small rural enterprise run by
a couple of brothers operating out of a low-ceilinged concrete building. Following a brief lecture on the importance of proper sanitation,
a small white piglet was herded into the room, its dainty hooves
clicking against the concrete floor. The class gathered in a circle to
get a better look at the animal, who seemed delighted with the attention he was getting. He turned from face to face and was looking up
at Hugh when one of the brothers drew a pistol from his back pocket,
held it against the animal's temple, and shot the piglet, execution-
style. Blood spattered, frightened children wept, and the man with
the gun offered the teacher and bus driver some meat from a freshly
slaughtered goat.

When I'm told such stories, it's all I can do to hold back my feel-   7
ings of jealousy. An Ethiopian slaughterhouse. Some people have all
the luck. When I was in elementary school, the best we ever got was
a trip to Old Salem or Colonial Williamsburg, one of those preserved
brick villages where time supposedly stands still and someone earns
his living as a town crier. There was always a blacksmith, a group of
wandering patriots, and a collection of bonneted women hawking
corn bread or gingersnaps made "the ol'-fashioned way." Every now
and then you might come across a doer of bad deeds serving time in
the stocks, but that was generally as exciting as it got.

Certain events are parallel, but compared with Hugh's, my child-   8
hood was unspeakably dull. When I was seven years old, my family
moved to North Carolina. When he was seven years old, Hugh's family moved to the Congo. We had a collie and a house cat. They had a
monkey and two horses named Charlie Brown and Satan. I threw
stones at stop signs. Hugh threw stones at crocodiles. The verbs are
the same, but he definitely wins the prize when it comes to nouns
and objects. An eventful day for my mother might have involved a
trip to the dry cleaner or a conversation with the potato-chip delivery-
man. Asked one ordinary Congo afternoon what she'd done with her
day, Hugh's mother answered that she and a fellow member of the
Ladies' Club had visited a leper colony on the outskirts of Kinshasa.

No reason was given for the expedition, though chances are she was staking it out for a future field trip.

Due to his upbringing, Hugh sits through inane movies never realizing that they're often based on inane television shows. There were no poker-faced sitcom martians in his part of Africa, no oil-rich hillbillies or aproned brides trying to wean themselves from the practice of witchcraft. From time to time a movie would arrive packed in a dented canister, the film scratched and faded from its slow trip around the world. The theater consisted of a few dozen folding chairs arranged before a bedsheet or the blank wall of a vacant hangar out near the airstrip. Occasionally a man would sell warm soft drinks out of a cardboard box, but that was it in terms of concessions.

When I was young, I went to the theater at the nearby shopping center and watched a movie about a talking Volkswagen. I believe the little car had a taste for mischief but I can't be certain, as both the movie and the afternoon proved unremarkable and have faded from my memory. Hugh saw the same movie a few years after it was released. His family had left the Congo by this time and were living in Ethiopia. Like me, Hugh saw the movie by himself on a weekend afternoon. Unlike me, he left the theater two hours later, to find a dead man hanging from a telephone pole at the far end of the unpaved parking lot. None of the people who'd seen the movie seemed to care about the dead man. They stared at him for a moment or two and then headed home, saying they'd never seen anything as crazy as that talking Volkswagen. His father was late picking him up, so Hugh just stood there for an hour, watching the dead man dangle and turn in the breeze. The death was not reported in the newspaper, and when Hugh related the story to his friends, they said, "You saw the movie about the talking car?"

I could have done without the flies and the primitive theaters, but I wouldn't have minded growing up with a houseful of servants. In North Carolina it wasn't unusual to have a once-a-week maid, but Hugh's family had houseboys, a word that never fails to charge my imagination. They had cooks and drivers, and guards who occupied a gatehouse, armed with machetes. Seeing as I had regularly petitioned my parents for an electric fence, the business with the guards strikes me as the last word in quiet sophistication. Having protection suggests that you are important. Having that protection paid for by the government is even better, as it suggests your safety is of interest to someone other than yourself.

Hugh's father was a career officer with the US State Department, and every morning a black sedan carried him off to the embassy. I'm told it's not as glamorous as it sounds, but in terms of fun for the entire family, I'm fairly confident that it beats the sack race at the annual IBM picnic. By the age of three, Hugh was already carrying a diplomatic passport. The rules that applied to others did not apply to him. No tickets, no arrests, no luggage search: He was officially licensed to act like a brat. Being an American, it was expected of him, and who was he to deny the world an occasional tantrum?

They weren't rich, but what Hugh's family lacked financially they 13 more than made up for with the sort of exoticism that works wonders at cocktail parties, leading always to the remark "That sounds fascinating." It's a compliment one rarely receives when describing an adolescence spent drinking Icees at the North Hills Mall. No fifteen-foot python ever wandered onto my school's basketball court. I begged, I prayed nightly, but it just never happened. Neither did I get to witness a military coup in which forces sympathetic to the colonel arrived late at night to assassinate my next-door neighbor. Hugh had been at the Addis Ababa teen club when the electricity was cut off and soldiers arrived to evacuate the building. He and his friends had to hide in the back of a jeep and cover themselves with blankets during the ride home. It's something that sticks in his mind for one reason or another.

Among my personal highlights is the memory of having my pic- 14 ture taken with Uncle Paul, the legally blind host of a Raleigh children's television show. Among Hugh's is the memory of having his picture taken with Buzz Aldrin on the last leg of the astronaut's world tour. The man who had walked on the moon placed his hand on Hugh's shoulder and offered to sign his autograph book. The man who led Wake County schoolchildren in afternoon song turned at the sound of my voice and asked, "So what's your name, princess?"

When I was fourteen years old, I was sent to spend ten days with 15 my maternal grandmother in western New York State. She was a small and private woman named Billie, and though she never came right out and asked, I had the distinct impression she had no idea who I was. It was the way she looked at me, squinting through her glasses while chewing on her lower lip. That, coupled with the fact that she never once called me by name. "Oh," she'd say, "are you still here?" She was just beginning her long struggle with Alzheimer's disease, and each time I entered the room, I felt the need to reintroduce myself and set her at ease. "Hi, it's me. Sharon's boy, David. I was just in the kitchen admiring your collection of ceramic toads." Aside from a few trips to summer camp, this was the longest I'd ever been away from home, and I like to think I was toughened by the experience.

About the same time I was frightening my grandmother, Hugh 16
and his family were packing their belongings for a move to Somalia.
There were no English-speaking schools in Mogadishu, so, after a
few months spent lying around the family compound with his pet
monkey, Hugh was sent back to Ethiopia to live with a beer enthusiast his father had met at a cocktail party. Mr. Hoyt installed security
systems in foreign embassies. He and his family gave Hugh a room.
They invited him to join them at the table, but that was as far as they
extended themselves. No one ever asked him when his birthday was,
so when the day came, he kept it to himself. There was no telephone
service between Ethiopia and Somalia, and letters to his parents
were sent to Washington and then forwarded on to Mogadishu,
meaning that his news was more than a month old by the time they
got it. I suppose it wasn't much different than living as a foreign-
exchange student. Young people do it all the time, but to me it
sounds awful. The Hoyts had two sons about Hugh's age who were
always saying things like "Hey that's *our* sofa you're sitting on" and
"Hands off that ornamental stein. It doesn't belong to you."

He'd been living with these people for a year when he overheard 17
Mr. Hoyt tell a friend that he and his family would soon be moving
to Munich, Germany, the beer capital of the world.

"And that worried me," Hugh said, "because it meant I'd have to 18
find some other place to live."

Where I come from, finding shelter is a problem the average teen- 19
ager might confidently leave to his parents. It was just something that
came with having a mom and a dad. Worried that he might be sent to
live with his grandparents in Kentucky, Hugh turned to the school's
guidance counselor, who knew of a family whose son had recently left
for college. And so he spent another year living with strangers and not
mentioning his birthday. While I wouldn't have wanted to do it myself,
I can't help but envy the sense of fortitude he gained from the experience. After graduating from college, he moved to France knowing only
the phrase "Do you speak French?"—a question guaranteed to get you
nowhere unless you also speak the language.

While living in Africa, Hugh and his family took frequent vaca- 20
tions, often in the company of their monkey. The Nairobi Hilton,
some suite of high-ceilinged rooms in Cairo or Khartoum: These are
the places his people recall when gathered at a common table. "Was
that the summer we spent in Beirut or, no, I'm thinking of the time
we sailed from Cyprus and took the *Orient Express* to Istanbul."

Theirs was the life I dreamt about during my vacations in east- 21
ern North Carolina. Hugh's family was hobnobbing with chiefs and

sultans while I ate hush puppies at the Sanitary Fish Market in Morehead City, a beach towel wrapped like a hijab[1] around my head. Someone unknown to me was very likely standing in a muddy ditch and dreaming of an evening spent sitting in a clean family restaurant, drinking iced tea and working his way through an extra-large seaman's platter, but that did not concern me, as it meant I should have been happy with what I had. Rather than surrender to my bitterness, I have learned to take satisfaction in the life that Hugh has led. His stories have, over time, become my own. I say this with no trace of a kumbaya.[2] There is no spiritual symbiosis; I'm just a petty thief who lifts his memories the same way I'll take a handful of change left on his dresser. When my own experiences fall short of the mark, I just go out and spend some of his. It is with pleasure that I sometimes recall the dead man's purpled face or the report of the handgun ringing in my ears as I studied the blood pooling beneath the dead white piglet. On the way back from the slaughterhouse, we stopped for Cokes in the village of Mojo, where the gas-station owner had arranged a few tables and chairs beneath a dying canopy of vines. It was late afternoon by the time we returned to school, where a second bus carried me to the foot of Coffeeboard Road. Once there, I walked through a grove of eucalyptus trees and alongside a bald pasture of starving cattle, past the guard napping in his gatehouse, and into the waiting arms of my monkey.

Meaning

1. What is the subject of Sedaris's comparison and contrast in this essay?
2. There is a certain amount of irony in Sedaris's envy of Hugh's childhood. What is this irony? How does Sedaris make this irony explicit in paragraph 21? (If necessary, consult the Glossary under *irony*.)

Purpose and Audience

1. What do you think is the purpose of this essay? Take into account both Sedaris's obvious envy of Hugh's childhood and Sedaris's awareness that Hugh's life was often lonely and insecure. Is the thesis stated or only implied?

[1]A headscarf worn by Muslim women. [Editor's note.]

[2]From the gospel-folk song with the line "Kumbaya, my Lord, kumbaya," meaning "Come by here." Probably because of its popularity in folk music, the word now also has negative connotations of passivity or touchy-feely spiritualism. [Editor's note.]

2. What assumptions does Sedaris make about his audience? Where in the essay do you see evidence of these assumptions?

Method and Structure

1. Why do you think Sedaris chose to examine the differences between his childhood and Hugh's through numerous examples? How do these examples help him achieve his purpose in a way that a narrative of a single example might not?
2. The first five paragraphs of the essay include a conversation between Sedaris and Hugh about Hugh's childhood. Why do you think the author opened the essay this way?
3. **Other Methods**   How does Sedaris use narration to develop his essay? How does he use comparison and contrast?

Language

1. How does Sedaris use parallelism in paragraph 8 to highlight the contrast between himself and Hugh? How does he then point up this parallelism? (For the definition of *parallelism,* consult the Glossary.)
2. Sedaris offers the image of himself as a "petty thief" in paragraph 21. What is the effect of this image?
3. Sedaris's language in this essay is notably specific and concrete. Point to examples of such language just in paragraph 6. (If necessary, consult the Glossary under *specific words* and *concrete words*.)

Writing Topics

1. Write an essay in which you compare and contrast your own experiences with those of someone whose life you've envied. Have your feelings changed over time? Why, or why not?
2. Hugh's experiences living with strangers gave him a "sense of fortitude" (paragraph 19), according to Sedaris. When have you ever gone through a difficult experience that left you somehow stronger? Write an essay about such an experience that shows how you were different before and after.
3. How seriously does Sedaris want the readers of his essay to take him? Write an essay in which you analyze his tone, citing specific passages from the text to support your conclusions. (If necessary, consult the Glossary for the definition of *tone*.)

BRENT STAPLES

Brent Staples was born in 1951 in Chester, Pennsylvania. After receiving a BA from Widener University and a PhD in psychology from the University of Chicago, he began writing on culture and politics for the New York Times *in 1985. Since 1990 he has been a member of the* Times *editorial board, and he has also contributed to publications including* Ms., Harper's Magazine, *and the* New York Times Magazine. *In 1994 Staples published a memoir,* Parallel Time: Growing Up in Black and White.

Black Men and Public Space

First published in Harper's Magazine *in 1986, this selection relates the prejudice Staples has faced as a black man walking city streets after dark. The essay also appeared in a slightly different form in* Parallel Time.

My first victim was a woman—white, well dressed, probably in her late twenties. I came upon her late one evening on a deserted street in Hyde Park, a relatively affluent neighborhood in an otherwise mean, impoverished section of Chicago. As I swung onto the avenue behind her, there seemed to be a discreet, uninflammatory distance between us. Not so. She cast back a worried glance. To her, the youngish black man—a broad six feet two inches with a beard and billowing hair, both hands shoved into the pockets of a bulky military jacket—seemed menacingly close. After a few more quick glimpses, she picked up her pace and was soon running in earnest. Within seconds she disappeared into a cross street.

That was more than a decade ago. I was twenty-two years old, a graduate student newly arrived at the University of Chicago. It was in the echo of that terrified woman's footfalls that I first began to know the unwieldy inheritance I'd come into—the ability to alter public space in ugly ways. It was clear that she thought herself the quarry of a mugger, a rapist, or worse. Suffering a bout of insomnia, however, I was stalking sleep, not defenseless wayfarers. As a softy who is scarcely able to take a knife to a raw chicken—let alone hold one to a person's throat—I was surprised, embarrassed, and dismayed all at once. Her flight made me feel like an accomplice in tyranny. It also made it clear that I was indistinguishable from the muggers who occasionally seeped into the area from the surrounding ghetto. That first encounter, and those that followed, signified that a vast, unnerving gulf lay between nighttime pedestrians—particularly women—and me. And I soon gathered that being perceived as dangerous is a hazard in itself. I only needed to turn a corner into a dicey situation, or crowd some frightened, armed person in a foyer somewhere, or make an errant move after being pulled over by a policeman. Where fear and weapons meet—and they often do in urban America—there is always the possibility of death.

In that first year, my first away from my hometown, I was to 3
become thoroughly familiar with the language of fear. At dark, shadowy intersections, I could cross in front of a car stopped at a traffic light and elicit the *thunk, thunk, thunk, thunk* of the driver—black, white, male, or female—hammering down the door locks. On less traveled streets after dark, I grew accustomed to but never comfortable with people crossing to the other side of the street rather than pass me. Then there were the standard unpleasantries with policemen, doormen, bouncers, cabdrivers, and others whose business it is to screen out troublesome individuals *before* there is any nastiness.

I moved to New York nearly two years ago and I have remained 4
an avid night walker. In central Manhattan, the near-constant crowd cover minimizes tense one-on-one street encounters. Elsewhere—in SoHo, for example, where sidewalks are narrow and tightly spaced buildings shut out the sky—things can get very taut indeed.

After dark, on the warrenlike streets of Brooklyn where I live, I 5
often see women who fear the worst from me. They seem to have set their faces on neutral, and with their purse straps strung across their chests bandolier-style, they forge ahead as though bracing themselves against being tackled. I understand, of course, that the danger they perceive is not a hallucination. Women are particularly vulnerable to street violence, and young black males are drastically overrepresented among the perpetrators of that violence. Yet these truths are no solace against the kind of alienation that comes of being ever the suspect, a fearsome entity with whom pedestrians avoid making eye contact.

It is not altogether clear to me how I reached the ripe old age 6
of twenty-two without being conscious of the lethality nighttime pedestrians attributed to me. Perhaps it was because in Chester, Pennsylvania, the small, angry industrial town where I came of age in the 1960s, I was scarcely noticeable against a backdrop of gang warfare, street knifings, and murders. I grew up one of the good

boys, had perhaps a half-dozen fistfights. In retrospect, my shyness of combat has clear sources.

As a boy, I saw countless tough guys locked away; I have since 7 buried several, too. They were babies, really—a teenage cousin, a brother of twenty-two, a childhood friend in his mid-twenties—all gone down in episodes of bravado played out in the streets. I came to doubt the virtues of intimidation early on. I chose, perhaps unconsciously, to remain a shadow—timid, but a survivor.

The fearsomeness mistakenly attributed to me in public places 8 often has a perilous flavor. The most frightening of these confusions occurred in the late 1970s and early 1980s, when I worked as a journalist in Chicago. One day, rushing into the office of a magazine I was writing for with a deadline story in hand, I was mistaken for a burglar. The office manager called security and, with an ad hoc posse, pursued me through the labyrinthine halls, nearly to my editor's door. I had no way of proving who I was. I could only move briskly toward the company of someone who knew me.

Another time I was on assignment for a local paper and killing 9 time before an interview. I entered a jewelry store on the city's affluent Near North Side. The proprietor excused herself and returned with an enormous red Doberman pinscher straining at the end of a leash. She stood, the dog extended toward me, silent to my questions, her eyes bulging nearly out of her head. I took a cursory look around, nodded, and bade her good night.

Relatively speaking, however, I never fared as badly as another 10 black male journalist. He went to nearby Waukegan, Illinois, a couple of summers ago to work on a story about a murderer who was born there. Mistaking the reporter for the killer, police officers hauled him from his car at gunpoint and but for his press credentials would probably have tried to book him. Such episodes are not uncommon. Black men trade tales like this all the time.

Over the years, I learned to smother the rage I felt at so often 11 being taken for a criminal. Not to do so would surely have led to madness. I now take precautions to make myself less threatening. I move about with care, particularly late in the evening. I give a wide berth to nervous people on subway platforms during the wee hours, particularly when I have exchanged business clothes for jeans. If I happen to be entering a building behind some people who appear skittish, I may walk by, letting them clear the lobby before I return, so as not to seem to be following them. I have been calm and extremely congenial on those rare occasions when I've been pulled over by the police.

And on late-evening constitutionals I employ what has proved to   12
be an excellent tension-reducing measure: I whistle melodies from
Beethoven and Vivaldi and the more popular classical composers.
Even steely New Yorkers hunching toward nighttime destinations
seem to relax, and occasionally they even join in the tune. Virtually
everybody seems to sense that a mugger wouldn't be warbling
bright, sunny selections from Vivaldi's *Four Seasons*. It is my equivalent of the cowbell that hikers wear when they know they are in
bear country.

Meaning

1. In paragraph 5 Staples says he understands that the danger women
   fear when they see him "is not a hallucination." Do you take this to
   mean that Staples perceives himself to be dangerous? Explain.
2. Staples says, "I chose, perhaps unconsciously, to remain a shadow—
   timid, but a survivor" (paragraph 7). What are the usual connotations
   of the word *survivor*? Is "timid" one of them? How can you explain
   this apparent discrepancy? (For the definition of *connotation*, see the
   Glossary.)

Purpose and Audience

1. What is the purpose of this essay? Do you think Staples believes that
   he (or other African American men) will cease "to alter public space
   in ugly ways" in the near future? Does he suggest any long-term solution for "the kind of alienation that comes of being ever the suspect"
   (paragraph 5)?
2. The concept of altering public space is relatively abstract. How does
   Staples convince you that this phenomenon really takes place?

Method and Structure

1. The author employs a large number of examples in a fairly small
   space. He cites three specific instances that involved him, several general situations, and one incident involving another African American
   man. How does Staples avoid having the piece sound like a list? How
   does he establish coherence among all these examples? Look, for
   example, at details and transitions. (If necessary, see the definitions of
   coherence and *transitions* in the Glossary.)
2. **Other Methods**   Many of Staples's examples are actually anecdotes—
   brief narratives. The opening paragraph is especially notable. Why is
   it so effective?

Language

1. What does the author accomplish by using the word *victim* in the essay's first paragraph? Is the word used literally? What tone does it set for the essay? (If necessary, see the Glossary under *tone*.)
2. The word *dicey* (paragraph 2) comes from British slang. Without looking it up in your dictionary, can you figure out its meaning from the context in which it appears?

Writing Topics

1. Write an essay narrating either an experience of altering public space yourself or an experience of being a witness when someone else altered public space. What changes did you observe in the behavior of the people around you? Was your behavior similarly affected? In retrospect, do you think your reactions were justified?
2. Write an essay using examples to show how a trait of your own or of someone you know well always seems to affect people, whether positively or negatively.
3. Consider, more broadly than Staples does, what it means to alter public space. Staples would rather not have the power to do so, but it *is* a power, and it could perhaps be positive in some circumstances (wielded by a street performer, for instance, or the architect of a beautiful new building on campus). Write an essay expanding on Staples's essay in which you examine the pros and cons of altering public space. Use specific examples as your evidence.

Writing with the Method
Example

Choose one of the following statements, or any other statement they suggest, and agree *or* disagree with it in an essay developed by one or more examples. The statement you decide on should concern a topic you care about so that the example or examples are a means of communicating an idea, not an end in themselves.

FAMILY
1. In happy families, talk is the main activity.
2. Grandparents relate more closely to their grandchildren than to their children.
3. Sooner or later, children take on the personalities of their parents.

BEHAVIOR AND PERSONALITY
4. Rudeness is on the rise.
5. Gestures and facial expressions often communicate what words cannot say.
6. Our natural surroundings when we are growing up contribute to our happiness or unhappiness as adults.

EDUCATION
7. The best courses are the difficult ones.
8. Education is an easy way to get ahead in life.
9. Students at schools with enforced dress codes behave better than students at schools without such codes.

POLITICS AND SOCIAL ISSUES
10. Talk radio can influence public policy.
11. Drug or alcohol addiction does not happen just to "bad" people.
12. True-life crime mimics TV and movies.
13. Unemployment is hardest on those over fifty years old.

MEDIA AND CULTURE
14. Bumper stickers are a form of conversation among Americans.
15. The Internet divides people instead of connecting them.
16. Good art can be ugly.

17. A craze or fad reveals something about the culture it arises in.
18. The best rock musicians treat social and political issues in their songs.
19. Television news programs are beauty pageants for untalented journalists.
20. The most rewarding books are always easy to read.

RULES FOR LIVING

21. Murphy's Law: If anything can go wrong, it will go wrong, and at the worst possible moment.
22. With enough motivation, a person can accomplish anything.
23. Lying may be justified by the circumstances.
24. Friends are people you can't always trust.

Chapter Four

DIVISION
OR ANALYSIS

USING THE METHOD

Division and **analysis** are interchangeable terms for the same method. *Division* comes from a Latin word meaning "to force asunder or separate." *Analysis* comes from a Greek word meaning "to undo." Using this method, we separate a whole into its elements, examine the relations of the elements to one another and to the whole, and reassemble the elements into a new whole informed by the examination. The method is essential to understanding and evaluating objects, works, and ideas.

Analysis (as we will call it) is a daily occurrence in our lives, whether we ponder our relationships with others, decide whether a certain movie was worthwhile, or try to understand a politician's campaign promises. We also use analysis throughout this book, when looking at paragraphs and essays. And it is the basic operation in at least four other methods discussed in this book: classification (Chapter 5), process analysis (Chapter 6), comparison and contrast (Chapter 7), and cause-and-effect analysis (Chapter 9).

At its most helpful, analysis builds on the separation into elements, leading to a conclusion about the meaning, significance, or value of the whole. This approach is essential to college learning, whether in discussing literature, reviewing a psychology experiment, or interpreting a business case. It is fundamental to work, from choosing a career to making sense of market research. And it informs and enriches life outside school or work, in buying a car, looking at art, or deciding whom to vote for. The method is the foundation of **critical thinking,** the ability to see beneath the surface of things, images, events, and ideas; to uncover and test assumptions; to see the importance of context; and to draw and support independent conclusions.

The subject of any analysis is usually singular — a freestanding, coherent unit, such as a bicycle or a poem, with its own unique constitution of elements. (In contrast, classification, the subject of the next chapter, usually starts with a plural subject, such as bicycles or the poems of the Civil War, and groups them according to their shared features.) You choose the subject and with it a **principle of analysis,** a framework that determines how you divide the subject and thus what elements you identify.

Sometimes the principle of analysis will be self-evident, especially when the subject is an object, such as a bicycle or a camera, that can be "undone" in only a limited number of ways. Most of the time, however, the principle you choose will depend on your view of the whole. In academic disciplines, businesses, and the professions, distinctive principles are part of what the field is about and are often the subject of debate within the field. In art, for instance, some critics see a painting primarily as a visual object and concentrate on its composition, color, line, and other formal qualities; other critics see a painting primarily as a social object and concentrate on its content and context (cultural, economic, political, and so on). Both groups use a principle of analysis that is a well-established way of looking at painting, yet each group finds different elements and thus meaning in a work.

There is, then, a great deal of flexibility in choosing a principle of analysis. But it should be appropriate for the subject and the field or discipline; it should be significant; and it should be applied thoroughly and consistently. Analysis is not done for its own sake but for a larger goal of illuminating the subject, perhaps concluding something about it, perhaps evaluating it. But even when the method culminates in evaluation — in the writer's judgment of the subject's value — the analysis should represent the subject as it actually is, in all its fullness and complexity. In analyzing a movie, for instance, a writer may emphasize one element, such as setting, and even omit some elements, such as costumes; but the characterization of the whole must still apply to *all* the elements. The writer must single out any wayward elements and explain why they do not substantially undermine the framework and thus weaken the opinion.

DEVELOPING AN ESSAY BY DIVISION OR ANALYSIS

Getting Started

Analysis is one of the readiest methods of development: almost any-thing whole can be separated into its elements, from a lemon to a play by Shakespeare to an economic theory. In college and at work, many writing assignments will demand analysis with a verb such as *analyze, criticize, discuss, evaluate, interpret,* or *review.* If you need to develop your own subject for analysis, think of something whose meaning or significance puzzles or intrigues you and whose parts you can distinguish and relate to the whole—an object such as a machine, an artwork such as a poem, a media product such as a news broadcast, an institution such as a hospital, a relation-ship such as stepparenting, a social issue such as sheltering the homeless.

If you begin by seeking meaning or significance, you will be more likely to find a workable principle of analysis and less likely to waste time on a hollow exercise. Each of the following questions suggests a distinct approach to the subject's elements—a distinct principle—that makes it easier to isolate the elements and show their connection to one another. Each question could lead to a thesis sentence that states an opinion and reveals the principle of analysis.

QUESTION   To what extent is an enormously complex hospital a com-munity in itself?

THESIS SENTENCE   The hospital encompasses such a wide range of personnel and services that it resembles a good-sized town.

QUESTION   What is the appeal of the front-page headlines in the local tabloid newspaper?

THESIS SENTENCE   The newspaper's front page routinely appeals to readers' fear of crime, anger at criminals, and sympathy for victims.

QUESTION   Why did a certain movie have such a powerful effect on you and your friends?

THESIS SENTENCE   The film is a unique and important statement of the private terrors of adolescence.

Note that all three thesis sentences imply an explanatory purpose—an effort to understand something and share that understanding with the reader. The third thesis sentence, however, conveys a persuasive purpose as well: the writer hopes that readers will accept her evaluation of the film.

Of course, the thesis must develop from and be supported by the evidence of the analysis—the elements of the subject, their interconnections, and their relation to the whole. Dissect your subject, looking at the actual, physical thing if possible, imagining it in your mind if necessary. Make detailed notes of all the elements you see, their distinguishing features, and how they help answer your starting question about meaning or significance. In analyzing someone's creation, tease out the creator's influences, assumptions, intentions, conclusions, and evidence. You may have to go outside the work for some of this information—researching an author's background, for instance, to uncover the political biases that may underlie his or her opinions. Even if you do not use all this information in your final draft, it will help you see the elements and help keep your analysis true to the subject.

At this point you should consider your readers' needs as well as the needs of your subject and your own framework:

- If the subject is familiar to readers (as, say, the newspaper's headlines might be), then your principle of analysis may not require much justification (as long as it's clear), but your details and examples must be vivid and convincing.
- If the subject is unfamiliar, then you should carefully explain your principle of analysis, define all specialized terms, distinguish parts from one another, and provide ample illustrations.
- If readers know your subject but may dispute your way of looking at it, then you should justify as well as explain your principle of analysis. You should also account for any evidence that may seem not to support your opinion by showing either why, in fact, the evidence is supportive or why it is unimportant. (If contrary evidence refuses to be dispensed with, you may have to rethink your approach.)

Organizing

In the introduction to your essay, let readers know why you are bothering to analyze your subject: Why is the subject significant? How might the essay relate to the experiences of readers or be useful to them? A subject unfamiliar to readers might be summarized or described, or part of it (an anecdote or quotation, say) might be used to tantalize readers. A familiar subject might be introduced with a surprising fact or an unusual perspective. An evaluative analysis might open with an opposing viewpoint.

In the body of the essay you'll need to explain your principle of analysis according to the preceding guidelines. The arrangement of elements and analysis should suit your subject and purpose: you can describe the elements and then offer your analysis, or you can introduce and analyze elements one by one. You can arrange the elements themselves from least to most important, least to most complex, most to least familiar, spatially, or chronologically. Devote as much space to each element as it demands: there is no requirement that all elements be given equal space and emphasis if their complexity or your framework dictates otherwise.

Most analysis essays need a conclusion that assembles the elements, returning readers to a sense of the whole subject. The conclusion can restate the thesis, summarize what the essay has contributed, consider the influence of the subject or its place in a larger picture, or (especially in an evaluation) assess the effectiveness or worth of the subject.

Drafting

If your subject or your view of it is complex, you may need at least two rough drafts of an analysis essay—one to discover what you think and one to clarify your principle, cover each element, and support your points with concrete details and vivid examples (including quotations if the subject is a written work). Plan on two drafts if you're uncertain of your thesis when you begin: you'll probably save time in the long run by attending to one goal at a time. Especially because the analysis essay says something about the subject by explaining its structure, you need to have a clear picture of the whole and relate each part to it.

Revising and Editing

When you revise and edit your essay, use the following questions to uncover any weaknesses remaining in your analysis.

- *Is your principle of analysis clear?* The significance of your analysis and your view of the subject should be apparent throughout your essay.
- *Is your analysis complete?* Have you identified all elements according to your principle of analysis and determined their relations to

one another and to the whole? If you have omitted some elements from your discussion, will the reason for their omission be clear to readers?

- *Is your analysis consistent?* Is your principle of analysis applied consistently to the entire subject (including any elements you have omitted)? Do all elements reflect the same principle, and are they clearly separate rather than overlapping? You may find it helpful to check your draft against your list of elements or your outline or to outline the draft itself.

- *Is your analysis well supported?* Is the thesis supported by clear assertions about parts of the subject, and are the assertions supported by concrete, specific evidence (sensory details, facts, quotations, and so on)? Do not rely on your readers to prove your thesis.

- *Is your analysis true to the subject?* Is your thesis unforced, your analysis fair? Is your new whole (your reassembly of the elements) faithful to the original? Be wary of leaping to a conclusion that distorts the subject.

EMILY PRAGER

An essayist and fiction writer, Emily Prager was born in 1952 and grew up in Texas, Asia, and New York City. She graduated from Barnard College. Prager has written humor, satire, and criticism for periodicals as diverse as the National Lampoon, Viva, *the* Village Voice, *and* Penthouse. *Her fiction combines a satirical wit and a lively prose style to analyze gender relations, ethnic friction, and other anxieties of contemporary life. Among other books, Prager has published* A Visit from the Footbinder and Other Stories *(1982),* Clea and Zeus Divorce *(1987),* Eve's Tattoo *(1991) and* Roger Fishbite: A Novel *(1999). Her most recent book is the memoir* Wuhu Diary: On Taking My Adopted Daughter Back to Her Hometown in China *(2002). She has also acted on a TV soap opera and in several films.*

Our Barbies, Ourselves

The Barbie doll debuted in 1959, when Prager was seven years old, and ever since has dominated the "fashion doll" market. In this essay from Interview *magazine in 1991, Prager explains how a chance bit of information changed her framework for analyzing Barbie.*

I read an astounding obituary in the *New York Times* not too long 1
ago. It concerned the death of one Jack Ryan. A former husband of Zsa Zsa Gabor, it said, Mr. Ryan had been an inventor and designer during his lifetime. A man of eclectic creativity, he designed Sparrow and Hawk missiles when he worked for the Raytheon Company, and the notice said, when he consulted for Mattel he designed Barbie.[1]

If Barbie was designed by a man, suddenly a lot of things made 2
sense to me, things I'd wondered about for years. I used to look at Barbie and wonder, What's wrong with this picture? What kind of woman designed this doll? Let's be honest: Barbie looks like someone

[1]Since Prager wrote this essay, a "biography" of Barbie and statements by a founder of Mattel have clarified Ryan's role in Barbie's creation. Barbie's prototype was a hard-edged adult doll made in Germany after World War II. At the direction of Mattel's founders, Ryan oversaw the transformation of this version into a toy for American girls. [Editor's note.]

who got her start at the Playboy Mansion. She could be a regular guest on *The Howard Stern Show*. It is a fact of Barbie's design that her breasts are so out of proportion to the rest of her body that if she were a human, she'd fall flat on her face.

If it's true that a woman didn't design Barbie, you don't know how much saner that makes me feel. Of course, that doesn't ameliorate the damage. There are millions of women who are subliminally sure that a thirty-nine-inch bust and a twenty-three-inch waist are the epitome of lovability. Could this account for the popularity of breast implant surgery? 3

I don't mean to step on anyone's toes here. I loved my Barbie. Secretly, I still believe that neon pink and turquoise are the only colors in which to decorate a duplex condo. And like many others of my generation, I've never married, simply because I cannot find a man who looks as good in clam diggers as Ken. 4

The question that comes to mind is, of course, Did Mr. Ryan design Barbie as a weapon? Because it *is* odd that Barbie appeared about the same time in my consciousness as the feminist movement—a time when women sought equality and small breasts were king. Or is Barbie the dream date of weapons designers? Or perhaps it's simpler than that: perhaps Barbie is Zsa Zsa if she were eleven inches tall. No matter what, my discovery of Jack Ryan confirms what I have always felt: there is something indescribably masculine about Barbie— dare I say it, phallic. For all her giant breasts and high-heeled feet, she lacks a certain softness. If you asked a little girl what kind of doll she wanted for Christmas, I just don't think she'd reply, "Please, Santa, I want a hard-body." 5

On the other hand, you could say that Barbie, in feminist terms, is definitely her own person. With her condos and fashion plazas and pools and beauty salons, she is definitely a liberated woman, a gal on the move. And she has always been sexual, even totemic. Before Barbie, American dolls were flat-footed and breastless, and ineffably dignified. They were created in the image of little girls or babies. Madame Alexander was the queen of doll makers in the '50s, and her dollies looked like Elizabeth Taylor in *National Velvet*. They repre-sented the kind of girls who looked perfect in jodhpurs, whose hair was never out of place, who grew up to be Jackie Kennedy—before she married Onassis. Her dolls' boyfriends were figments of the imag-ination, figments with large portfolios and three-piece suits and presidential aspirations, figments who could keep dolly in the style to which little girls of the '50s were programmed to become accus-tomed, a style that spasmed with the '60s, and the appearance of 6

Barbie. And perhaps what accounts for Barbie's vast popularity is that she was also a '60s woman: into free love and fun colors, anti-class, and possessed of a real, molded boyfriend, Ken, with whom she could chant a mantra.

But there were problems with Ken. I always felt weird about him. He had no genitals, and, even at age ten, I found that ominous. I mean, here was Barbie with these humongous breasts, and that was O.K. with the toy company. And then, there was Ken with that truncated, unidentifiable lump at his groin. I sensed injustice at work. Why, I wondered, was Barbie designed with such obvious sexual equipment and Ken not? Why was his treated as if it were more mysterious than hers? Did the fact that it was treated as such indicate that somehow his equipment, his essential maleness, was considered more powerful than hers, more worthy of the dignity of concealment? And if the issue in the mind of the toy company was obscenity and its possible damage to children, I still object. How do they think I felt, knowing that no matter how many water beds they slept in, or hot tubs they romped in, or swimming pools they lounged by under the stars, Barbie and Ken could never make love? No matter how much sexuality Barbie possessed, she would never turn Ken on. He would be forever withholding, forever detached. There was a loneliness about Barbie's situation that was always disturbing. And twenty-five years later, movies and videos are still filled with topless women and covered men. As if we're all trapped in Barbie's world and can never escape.

Meaning

1. "If Barbie was designed by a man," Prager writes in her second paragraph, "suddenly a lot of things make sense to me." What are these "things," and how do they relate to Prager's main idea? What is that idea?

2. In paragraph 5 Prager asks, "Did Mr. Ryan design Barbie as a weapon?" What do you think she means here? A weapon against what?

Purpose and Audience

1. Why do you think Prager wrote this essay? What did she hope her readers would gain?

2. In her next-to-last sentence, Prager states that "twenty-five years later, movies and videos are still filled with topless women and covered men." What does this statement reveal about Prager's biases and the assumptions she makes about her audience?

Method and Structure

1. What elements of Barbie does Prager analyze, and how does she reassemble these elements into a new whole? Support your answer with evidence from the essay.

2. Why is division or analysis essential for Prager to make her claims about Barbie? Is an analysis of Barbie's features important even to readers already familiar with the doll?

3. Prager waits until the end of her essay to make the connection between Barbie and today's movies featuring "topless women and covered men." What is the effect of this decision? How might the essay be different if she had opened with a straightforward thesis statement such as "The Barbie doll is partly responsible for the double standards regarding male and female nudity in the movies today"?

4. **Other Methods**   In addition to analysis, Prager uses description in her essay to create a clear, concrete image of Barbie. In paragraph 6 she also uses comparison and contrast, comparing Barbie to the American dolls who came before her. How did these dolls differ from Barbie, and what does this comparison contribute to Prager's overall purpose?

Language

1. Prager's diction includes some words and phrases that are colloquial ("condo," "dream date," "gal," "humongous," "turn . . . on") and others that are more formal ("ameliorate," "subliminally," "epitome," "totemic," "ineffably"). What purpose do these different levels of language serve? (If necessary, see *colloquial language* in the Glossary.)

2. In paragraph 6 Prager says of Barbie, "With her condos and fashion plazas and pools and beauty salons, she is definitely a liberated woman, a gal on the move." How would you characterize the tone of this statement? Where else in the essay can you locate this tone?

Writing Topics

1. Think of a toy or game that you played with as a child (G.I. Joe, *Star Wars* action figures, Risk, Monopoly, Life) that may have had other meanings besides pure entertainment. For example, Monopoly could be seen as teaching children the values of capitalism. Using Prager's essay as a model, write an analysis of the toy or game, making sure to examine each element for its contribution to the intentional or unintentional meanings you identified. Your essay may be serious or humorous, but it should include plenty of description to make the elements clear and support your analysis.

2. Defend Barbie or Ken: write an essay analyzing the positive lessons about women and men that children might learn from either or both of these dolls. Your essay may, but need not, directly challenge Prager's essay.

3. As explained in the footnote on page 128, Barbie was adapted from a German adult doll into a doll specifically for American girls. What characteristics of Barbie and Ken strike you as especially American? How might the dolls be different in other cultures? Write an essay analyzing Barbie and Ken in which you answer these questions. The characteristics you identify may come from Prager's analysis, but be sure to explain why you think they are distinctly American.

MARGARET VISSER

Born in 1940 in South Africa, Margaret Visser was raised in Zambia and lived in England, France, Iraq, and the United States before settling in Toronto, Canada. (She is a naturalized citizen of Canada.) Visser was educated at the University of Toronto, where she earned a BA (1970), an MA (1973), and a PhD in classics (1980). She taught classics at York University in Toronto and has published articles in scholarly and popular periodicals. Visser also appears on television and radio, discussing her discoveries about the history and social mythology of everyday life. "The extent to which we take everyday objects for granted," she says, "is the precise extent to which they govern and inform our lives." Four books illuminate this important territory: Much Depends on Dinner *(1986),* The Rituals of Dinner *(1991),* The Way We Are *(1994), and* The Geometry of Love *(2001).*

The Ritual of Fast Food

In this excerpt from The Rituals of Dinner, *an investigation of table manners, Visser analyzes the fast-food restaurant. What do we seek when we visit such a place? How does the management oblige us? Success hinges on predictability.*

An early precursor of the restaurant meal was dinner served to the public at fixed times and prices at an eating house or tavern. Such a meal was called, because of its predetermined aspects, an "ordinary," and the place where it was eaten came to be called an "ordinary," too. When a huge modern business conglomerate offers fast food to travellers on the highway, it knows that its customers are likely to desire No Surprises. They are hungry, tired, and not in a celebratory mood; they are happy to pay—provided that the price looks easily manageable—for the safely predictable, the convenient, the fast and ordinary.

Ornamental formalities are pruned away (tables and chairs are bolted to the floor, for instance, and "cutlery" is either nonexistent or not worth stealing); but rituals, in the sense of behaviour and expectations that conform to preordained rules, still inform the proceedings. People who stop for a hamburger—at a Wendy's, a Harvey's, a McDonald's, or a Burger King—know exactly what the building that

133

houses the establishment should look like; architectural variations merely ring changes on rigidly imposed themes. People want, perhaps even need, to *recognize* their chain store, to feel that they know it and its food in advance. Such an outlet is designed to be a "home away from home," on the highway, or anywhere in the city, or for Americans abroad.

Words and actions are officially laid down, learned by the staff   3
from handbooks and teaching sessions, and then picked up by customers in the course of regular visits. Things have to be called by their correct names ("Big Mac," "large fries"); the McDonald's rubric in 1978 required servers to ask "Will that be with cheese, sir?" "Will there be any fries today, sir?" and to close the transaction with "Have a nice day." The staff wear distinctive garments; menus are always the same, and even placed in the same spot in every outlet in the chain; prices are low and predictable; and the theme of cleanliness is proclaimed and tirelessly reiterated. The company attempts also to play the role of a lovable host, kind and concerned, even parental: it knows that blunt and direct confrontation with a huge faceless corporation makes us suspicious, and even badly behaved. So it stresses its love of children, its nostalgia for cozy warmth and for the past (cottage roofs, warm earth tones), or its clean, brisk modernity (glass walls, smooth surfaces, red trim). It responds to social concerns — when they are insistent enough, sufficiently widely held, and therefore "correct." McDonald's for example, is at present busy showing how much it cares about the environment.

Fast-food chains know that they are ordinary. They *want* to be   4
ordinary, and for people to think of them as almost inseparable from the idea of everyday food consumed outside the home. They are happy to allow their customers time off for feasts — on Thanksgiving, Christmas, and so on — to which they do not cater. Even those comparatively rare holiday times, however, are turned to a profit, because the companies know that their favourite customers — law-abiding families — are at home together then, watching television, where carefully placed commercials will spread the word concerning new fast-food products, and re-imprint the image of the various chain stores for later, when the long stretches of ordinary times return.

Families are the customers the fast-food chains want: solid citi-   5
zens in groups of several at a time, the adults hovering over their children, teaching them the goodness of hamburgers, anxious to bring them up to behave typically and correctly. Customers usually

maintain a clean, restrained, considerate, and competent demeanour as they swiftly, gratefully, and informally eat. Fast-food operators have recently faced the alarming realization that crack addicts, craving salt and fat, have spread the word among their number that French fries deliver these substances easily, ubiquitously, cheaply, and at all hours. Dope addicts at family "ordinaries"! The unacceptability of such a thought was neatly captured by a news story in *The Economist* (1990) that spelled out the words a fast-food proprietor can least afford to hear from his faithful customers, the participants in his polite and practiced rituals: the title of the story was "Come on Mabel, let's leave." The plan to counter this threat included increasing the intensity of the lighting in fast-food establishments — drug addicts, apparently, prefer to eat in the dark.

The formality of eating at a restaurant belonging to a fast-food   6 chain depends upon the fierce regularity of its product, its simple but carefully observed rituals, and its environment. Supplying a hamburger that adheres to perfect standards of shape, weight, temperature, and consistency, together with selections from a pre-set list of trimmings, to a customer with fiendishly precise expectations is an enormously complex feat. The technology involved in performing it has been learned through the expenditure of huge sums on research, and after decades of experience — not to mention the vast political and economic ramifications involved in maintaining the supplies of cheap beef and cheap buns. But these costs and complexities are, with tremendous care, hidden from view. We know of course that, say, a Big Mac is a cultural construct: the careful control expended upon it is one of the things we are buying. But McDonald's manages — it must do so if it is to succeed in being ordinary — to provide a "casual" eating experience. Convenient, innocent simplicity is what the technology, the ruthless politics, and the elaborate organization serve to the customer.

Meaning

1. In paragraph 6 Visser writes, "Supplying a hamburger that adheres to perfect standards of shape, weight, temperature, and consistency . . . to a customer with fiendishly precise expectations is an enormously complex feat." How does this statement illustrate Visser's main idea?

2. What do you think Visser means by the statement that "a Big Mac is a cultural construct" (paragraph 6)?

Purpose and Audience

1. What is Visser's purpose in writing this essay: to propose more interesting surroundings and menus at fast-food restaurants? to argue that the patrons of these establishments are too demanding? to explain how these chains manage to satisfy so many customers? something else?

2. Whom does Visser seem to imagine as her audience? Is she writing for sociologists? for managers at corporations such as McDonald's and Burger King? for diners who patronize fast-food restaurants? What evidence in the essay supports your answer?

Method and Structure

1. How does Visser's analysis, breaking the fast-food experience down into its elements, help her achieve her purpose?

2. Into what elements does Visser divide the fast-food restaurant? Be specific, supporting your answer with examples from the text.

3. **Other Methods**   In paragraph 5 Visser uses cause-and-effect analysis to explain both why crack addicts began to frequent chain restaurants and why these restaurants couldn't risk including addicts among their clientele. What does this cause-and-effect analysis add to the analysis of fast-food restaurants? How would addicts, whose money is presumably as good as anyone else's, interfere with the operation of these restaurants?

Language

1. What is Visser's tone? How seriously does she take her subject?

2. Visser writes that McDonald's used to require its servers to ask patrons, depending on their order, "Will that be with cheese, sir?" or "Will there be any fries today, sir?" (paragraph 3). What would be the purpose of such questions? How would you characterize this use of language?

3. According to Visser, people who patronize fast-food restaurants "want, perhaps even need, to *recognize* their chain store" (paragraph 2); they are looking for "the safely predictable, the convenient, the fast and ordinary" (1). Find other instances in the essay where Visser describes the people who eat in these restaurants. What portrait emerges of these customers? How does this portrait contribute to Visser's overall message?

Writing Topics

1. What kinds of junk food do you regularly consume? Think about when and where and why you eat it, and then write an essay in which you analyze your behavior as a consumer of junk food. Make a list of all the

elements that constitute this activity and the setting in which it occurs. In your essay, examine each element to show what it contributes to the whole. Be sure your principle of analysis is clear to readers.

2. In her last paragraph, Visser writes that the "costs and complexities" of providing "a 'casual' eating experience" in a fast-food restaurant are "hidden from view." Does this seem appropriate to you, or would you rather know what the corporation feeding you puts into its operation, such as the "economic ramifications involved in maintaining the supplies of cheap beef and cheap buns"? Write an essay exploring the issues this question raises for you.

3. All of us have probably experienced a particular moment (or perhaps many moments) when we were willing to dine out on anything *but* fast food. What, at these moments, do you think we are seeking? Following Visser's example, write an essay analyzing the "culture" of a particular *non*chain restaurant. How does the management deliver what the customer wants?

SCOTT RUSSELL SANDERS

Scott Russell Sanders was born in Memphis, Tennessee, in 1945. After attending Brown University and Columbia University, he went on to teach English at Indiana University in Bloomington. Throughout his career, he has published novels, collections of short stories, and children's books, but he is best known for his essay collections, including Secrets of the Universe *(1991),* Staying Put: Making a Home in a Restless World *(1993),* Writing from the Center *(1995),* Hunting for Hope: A Father's Journey *(1998), and* The Country of Language *(1999). He won a Lannan Literary Award for his most recent book,* The Force of Spirit *(2000), in which he examines the sacred connections among family, community, and the land.*

The Men We Carry in Our Minds

"The Men We Carry in Our Minds" first appeared in Milkweed Chronicle *in 1984. Looking back at the men he knew as a child, Sanders compellingly analyzes his own mixed feelings toward feminism.*

"This must be a hard time for women," I say to my friend Anneke. 1
"They have so many paths to choose from, and so many voices calling them."

"I think it's a lot harder for men," she replies. 2

"How do you figure that?" 3

"The women I know feel excited, innocent, like crusaders in a just 4
cause. The men I know are eaten up with guilt."

We are sitting at the kitchen table drinking sassafras tea, our 5
hands wrapped around the mugs because this April morning is cool
and drizzly. "Like a Dutch morning," Anneke told me earlier. She is
Dutch herself, a writer and midwife and peacemaker, with the round
face and sad eyes of a woman in a Vermeer[1] painting who might be

---

[1]The Dutch painter Jan Vermeer (1632–75) is best known for his realistic portrayals of quiet domestic scenes. [Editor's note.]

waiting for the rain to stop, for a door to open. She leans over to sniff a sprig of lilac, pale lavender, that rises from a vase of cobalt blue.

"Women feel such pressure to be everything, do everything," I say. 6 "Career, kids, art, politics. Have their babies and get back to the office a week later. It's as if they're trying to overcome a million years' worth of evolution in one lifetime."

"But we help one another. We don't try to lumber on alone, like so 7 many wounded grizzly bears, the way men do." Anneke sips her tea. I gave her the mug with owls on it, for wisdom. "And we have this deep-down sense that we're in the *right*—we've been held back, passed over, used—while men feel they're in the wrong. Men are the ones who've been discredited, who have to search their souls."

I search my soul. I discover guilty feelings aplenty—toward the 8 poor, the Vietnamese, Native Americans, the whales, an endless list of debts—a guilt in each case that is as bright and unambiguous as a neon sign. But toward women I feel something more confused, a snarl of shame, envy, wary tenderness, and amazement. This muddle troubles me. To hide my unease I say, "You're right, it's tough being a man these days."

"Don't laugh." Anneke frowns at me, mournful-eyed, through the 9 sassafras steam. "I wouldn't be a man for anything. It's much easier being the victim. All the victim has to do is break free. The persecutor has to live with his past."

How deep is this past? I find myself wondering after Anneke has 10 left. How much of an inheritance do I have to throw off? Is it just the beliefs I breathed in as a child? Do I have to scour memory back through father and grandfather? Through St. Paul? Beyond Stonehenge and into the twilit caves? I'm convinced the past we must contend with is deeper even than speech. When I think back on my childhood, on how I learned to see men and women, I have a sense of ancient, dizzying depths. The back roads of Tennessee and Ohio where I grew up were probably closer, in their sexual patterns, to the campsites of Stone Age hunters than to the genderless cities of the future into which we are rushing.

The first men, besides my father, I remember seeing were black 11 convicts and white guards, in the cottonfield across the road from our farm on the outskirts of Memphis. I must have been three or four. The prisoners wore dingy gray-and-black zebra suits, heavy as canvas, sodden with sweat. Hatless, stooped, they chopped weeds in the fierce heat, row after row, breathing the acrid dust of boll-weevil poison. The overseers wore dazzling white shirts and broad shadowy hats. The oiled barrels of their shotguns flashed in the sunlight. Their faces in memory are utterly blank. Of course those men, white and black, have become for me an emblem of racial hatred. But they have also come to stand for the twin poles of my early vision of manhood—the brute toiling animal and the boss.

When I was a boy, the men I knew labored with their bodies. They were marginal farmers, just scraping by, or welders, steelworkers, carpenters; they swept floors, dug ditches, mined coal, or drove trucks, their forearms ropy with muscle; they trained horses, stoked furnaces, built tires, stood on assembly lines wrestling parts onto cars and refrigerators. They got up before light, worked all day long whatever the weather, and when they came home at night they looked as though somebody had been whipping them. In the evenings and on weekends they worked on their own places, tilling gardens that were lumpy with clay, fixing broken-down cars, hammering on houses that were always too drafty, too leaky, too small.

The bodies of the men I knew were twisted and maimed in ways visible and invisible. The nails of their hands were black and split, the hands tattooed with scars. Some had lost fingers. Heavy lifting had given many of them finicky backs and guts weak from hernias. Racing against conveyor belts had given them ulcers. Their ankles and knees ached from years of standing on concrete. Anyone who had worked for long around machines was hard of hearing. They squinted, and the skin of their faces was creased like the leather of old work gloves. There were times, studying them, when I dreaded growing up. Most of them coughed, from dust or cigarettes, and most of them drank cheap wine or whiskey, so their eyes looked bloodshot and bruised. The fathers of my friends always seemed older than the mothers. Men wore out sooner. Only women lived into old age.

As a boy I also knew another sort of men, who did not sweat and break down like mules. They were soldiers, and so far as I could tell they scarcely worked at all. During my early school years we lived on a military base, an arsenal in Ohio, and every day I saw GIs in the guardshacks, on the stoops of barracks, at the wheels of olive drab Chevrolets. The chief fact of their lives was boredom. Long after I left the arsenal I came to recognize the sour smell the soldiers gave off as that of souls in limbo. They were all waiting—for wars, for transfers, for leaves, for promotions, for the end of their hitch—like so many braves waiting for the hunt to begin. Unlike the warriors of older tribes, however, they would have no say about when the battle would start or how it would be waged. Their waiting was broken only when they practiced for war. They fired guns at targets, drove tanks across the churned-up fields of the military reservation, set off bombs in the

12

13

14

wrecks of old fighter planes. I knew this was all play. But I also felt certain that when the hour for killing arrived, they would kill. When the real shooting started, many of them would die. This was what soldiers were *for*, just as a hammer was for driving nails.

Warriors and toilers: those seemed, in my boyhood vision, to be 15 the chief destinies for men. They weren't the only destinies, as I learned from having a few male teachers, from reading books, and from watching television. But the men on television—the politicians, the astronauts, the generals, the savvy lawyers, the philosophical doctors, the bosses who gave orders to both soldiers and laborers— seemed as remote and unreal to me as the figures in tapestries. I could no more imagine growing up to become one of these cool, potent creatures than I could imagine becoming a prince.

A nearer and more hopeful example was that of my father, who 16 had escaped from a red-dirt farm to a tire factory, and from the assembly line to the front office. Eventually he dressed in a white shirt and tie. He carried himself as if he had been born to work with his mind. But his body, remembering the early years of slogging work, began to give out on him in his fifties, and it quit on him entirely before he turned sixty-five. Even such a partial escape from man's fate as he had accomplished did not seem possible for most of the boys I knew. They joined the army, stood in line for jobs in the smoky plants, helped build highways. They were bound to work as their fathers had worked, killing themselves or preparing to kill others.

A scholarship enabled me not only to attend college, a rare 17 enough feat in my circle, but even to study in a university meant for children of the rich. Here I met for the first time young men who had assumed from birth that they would lead lives of comfort and power. And for the first time I met women who told me that men were guilty of having kept all the joys and privileges of the earth for themselves. I was baffled. What privileges? What joys? I thought about the maimed dismal lives of most of the men back home. What had they stolen from their wives and daughters? The right to go five days a week, twelve months a year, for thirty or forty years to a steel mill or a coal mine? The right to drop bombs and die in war? The right to feel every leak in the roof, every gap in the fence, every cough in the engine, as a wound they must mend? The right to feel, when the lay-off comes or the plant shuts down, not only afraid but ashamed?

I was slow to understand the deep grievances of women. This was 18 because, as a boy, I had envied them. Before college, the only people I had ever known who were interested in art or music or literature, the only ones who read books, the only ones who ever seemed to enjoy a sense of ease and grace were the mothers and daughters. Like the menfolk, they fretted about money, they scrimped and made-do. But, when the pay stopped coming in, they were not the ones who had failed. Nor did they have to go to war, and that seemed to me a blessed fact. By comparison with the narrow, ironclad days of fathers, there was an expansiveness, I thought, in the days of mothers. They went to see neighbors, to shop in town, to run errands at school, at the library, at church. No doubt, had I looked harder at their lives, I would have envied them less. It was not my fate to become a woman, so it was easier for me to see the graces. Few of them held jobs outside the home, and those who did filled thankless roles as clerks and waitresses. I didn't see, then, what a prison a house could be, since houses seemed to me brighter, handsomer places than any factory. I did not realize—because such things were never spoken of—how often women suffered from men's bullying. I did learn about the wretchedness of abandoned wives, single mothers, widows; but I also learned about the wretchedness of lone men. Even then I could see how exhausting it was for a mother to cater all day to the needs of young children. But if I had been asked, as a boy, to choose between tending a baby and tending a machine, I think I would have chosen the baby. (Having now tended both, I know I would choose the baby.)

So I was baffled when the women at college accused me and my 19 sex of having cornered the world's pleasure. I think something like my bafflement has been felt by other boys (and by girls as well) who grew up in dirt-poor farm country, in mining country, in black ghettos, in Hispanic barrios,[2] in the shadows of factories, in third world nations—any place where the fate of men is as grim and bleak as the fate of women. Toilers and warriors. I realize now how ancient these identities are, how deep the tug they exert on men, the undertow of a thousand generations. The miseries I saw, as a boy, in the lives of nearly all men I continue to see in the lives of many—the body-breaking toil, the tedium, the call to be tough, the humiliating power-lessness, the battle for a living and for territory.

When the women I met at college thought about the joys and priv- 20 ileges of men, they did not carry in their minds the sort of men I had known in my childhood. They thought of their fathers, who were bankers, physicians, architects, stockbrokers, the big wheels of the big cities. These fathers rode the train to work or drove cars that cost more than any of my childhood houses. They were attended from morning to night by female helpers, wives and nurses and secretaries.

---

[2]A Spanish-speaking community. [Editor's note.]

They were never laid off, never short of cash at month's end, never lined up for welfare. These fathers made decisions that mattered. They ran the world.

The daughters of such men wanted to share in this power, this 21 glory. So did I. They yearned for a say over their future, for jobs worthy of their abilities, for the right to live at peace, unmolested, whole. Yes, I thought, yes yes. The difference between me and these daughters was that they saw me, because of my sex, as destined from birth to become like their fathers, and therefore an enemy to their desires. But I knew better. I wasn't an enemy, in fact or in feeling. I was an ally. If I had known, then, how to tell them so, would they have believed me? Would they now?

Meaning

1. Sanders's opening (paragraphs 1–10) relates a conversation he had with a female friend about the relative positions of men and women in the early 1980s when the essay was written. How did Sanders's opinion differ from his friend's? How do Sanders's thoughts here illustrate the main idea of the essay? How is this central idea reinforced by the essay's two concluding paragraphs?

2. What employment options does Sanders say were available to the men he knew when he was growing up? What other responsibilities made the lives of such men difficult?

3. When he went to college in the mid-1960s, Sanders was "baffled" that women there believed "men were guilty of having kept all the joys and privileges of the earth for themselves" (paragraph 17). Why was he so baffled? How did his image of women from his childhood contribute to his lack of understanding?

Purpose and Audience

1. What would you say is Sanders's purpose in this essay? Is he simply sharing his own experiences, trying to change readers' minds about the status of men and women in contemporary society, or attempting something else? Why do you think so?

2. Sanders ends his essay with two questions. What do these questions suggest to you about his imagined audience?

Method and Structure

1. What are the elements of Sanders's childhood vision of manhood? What does his analysis reveal about his feelings toward feminism?

2. In terms of subject and focus, this essay can be divided into three main sections. What are these sections, and what is each section's primary focus?

3. **Other Methods** Sanders relies on comparison and contrast throughout this essay. Note some specific instances of comparison and contrast, and explain what these contribute to Sanders's larger point.

Language

1. Analyze paragraph 12 to consider Sanders's use of verbs (such as *swept* and *dug*) and verb forms (such as *tilling* and *fixing*). What is the effect of the verbs and verb forms in this passage?

2. What might be the significance of Sanders's use of the verb *carry* in the title of the essay? How would the effect differ if Sanders had titled the essay "The Men We Remember"?

Writing Topics

1. In his essay Sanders focuses on the two main social classes he recognized as a child: the laboring class that included "warriors and toilers" and the professional class that represented "power" and "glory." Many would argue, though, that class distinctions in the United States are more complex than this, consisting of various hierarchies of social class. Develop an essay that analyzes your own views on social class in the United States today, describing clearly and fully the characteristics of each class you distinguish. Take a humorous approach to the subject if you wish.

2. Write an essay focusing on the images of men that you carry in your mind, beginning with your childhood observations of men. Be sure that, like Sanders, you support your analysis with specific examples. Alternatively, you could write an essay focusing on the women you carry in your mind.

3. Writing in the mid-1980s, Sanders refers to the "genderless cities of the future into which we are rushing" (paragraph 10). To what extent have the distinctions between women and men decreased over the past twenty years? To what extent have they stayed the same—or even increased? In an essay, consider the current state of women and men in relation to each other and to society.

Writing with the Method
Division or Analysis

Choose one of the following topics, or any other topic they suggest, for an essay developed by analysis. The topic you decide on should be something you care about so that analysis is a means of communicating an idea, not an end in itself.

PEOPLE, ANIMALS, OBJECTS
1. The personality of a friend or relative
2. The personality of a typical politician, teacher, or other professional
3. An animal such as a cat, dog, horse, cow, spider, or bat
4. A machine or appliance such as a car engine, harvesting combine, laptop computer, hair dryer, toaster, or sewing machine
5. A nonmotorized vehicle such as a skateboard, an in-line skate, a bicycle, or a snowboard
6. A building such as a hospital, theater, or sports arena

IDEAS
7. The perfect city
8. The perfect crime
9. A theory or concept in a field such as psychology, sociology, economics, biology, physics, engineering, or astronomy
10. The evidence in a political argument (written, spoken, or reported in the news)
11. A liberal arts education

ASPECTS OF CULTURE
12. A style of dress or "look" such as that associated with the typical businessperson, jock, rap musician, or outdoors enthusiast
13. A typical hero or villain in science fiction, romance novels, war movies, or movies or novels about adolescents
14. A television or film comedy
15. A literary work: short story, novel, poem, essay
16. A visual work: painting, sculpture, building
17. A musical work: song, concerto, symphony, opera
18. A performance: sports, acting, dance, music, speech
19. The slang of a particular group or occupation

Chapter Five

CLASSIFICATION

USING THE METHOD

We **classify** when we sort things into groups: kinds of cars, styles of writing, types of psychotherapy. Because it creates order, classification helps us make sense of our physical and mental experience. With it, we see the correspondences among like things and distinguish them from unlike things. We can name things, remember them, discuss them.

Writers classify primarily to explain a pattern in a subject that might not have been noticed before: for instance, a sportswriter might observe that basketball players tend to fall into one of three groups based on the aggressiveness of their play. Sometimes, writers also classify to persuade readers that one group is superior: the sportswriter might argue that one style of basketball play is more effective than the other two.

Classification is a three-step process:

- Separate things into their elements, using the method of division or analysis (previous chapter).
- Isolate the similarities among the elements.
- Group or classify the things based on those similarities, matching like with like.

The following diagram illustrates a classification essay that appears later in this chapter, "The Plot Against People" by Russell Baker (p. 151). Baker's subject is inanimate objects, and he sees three distinct kinds:

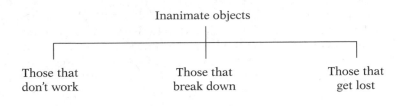

Inanimate objects

| Those that | Those that | Those that |
| don't work | break down | get lost |

All the members of Baker's overall group share at least one characteristic: they are inanimate objects. The members of each subgroup also share at least one characteristic: they break down, for instance, or get lost. The objects in each subgroup are independent of each other, and none of them is essential to the existence of the subgroup: the subgroup "things that break down" would continue to exist even if at the moment Baker's car was running just fine.

The number of groups in a classification scheme depends entirely on the basis for establishing the classes in the first place. There are two systems:

- In a complex classification, each thing or person fits firmly into one class because of at least one distinguishing feature shared with all members of that class but not with any members of any other classes.

- In a binary or two-part classification, two classes are in opposition to each other. Often, one group has a certain characteristic that the other group lacks. For instance, objects could be classified into those that are mechanical and those that aren't. A binary scheme is useful to emphasize the possession of a particular characteristic, but it is limited if it specifies nothing about the members of the "other" class except that they lack the trait. (An old joke claims that there are two kinds of people in the world—those who classify, and all others.)

Sorting items demands a **principle of classification** that determines the groups by distinguishing them. For instance, Baker's principle in identifying three groups of objects is the way they attempt to "defeat" their human owners. Principles for sorting a year's movies might be genre (action-adventures, comedies, dramas); place of origin (domestic, foreign); or cost of production (low-budget, medium-priced, high-budget). Your choice of a principle depends on your interest.

Although you may emphasize one class over the others, the classification itself must be complete and consistent. A classification of movies by genre would be incomplete if it omitted comedies. It would be inconsistent if it included action-adventures, comedies, dramas, low-budget films, and foreign films: such a system mixes *three* principles (genre, cost, origin); it omits whole classes (what of high-budget domestic dramas?); and it overlaps other classes (a low-budget foreign action-adventure would fit in three different groups).

DEVELOPING AN ESSAY BY CLASSIFICATION

Getting Started

Classification essays are often assigned in college courses. When you need to develop your own subject for a classification essay, think of one large class of things whose members you've noticed fall into subclasses, such as study habits, midnight grocery shoppers, or political fund-raising appeals. Be sure that your general subject forms a class in its own right—that all its members share at least one important quality. Then look for your principle of classification, the quality or qualities that distinguish some members from others, providing poles for the members to group themselves around. One such principle for political fund-raising appeals might be the different methods of delivery, including letters, telephone calls, advertisements, telethons, social gatherings, and rallies.

Your principle of classification may suggest a thesis sentence, but be sure the sentence also conveys a *reason* for the classification so that the essay does not become a dull list of categories. The following tentative thesis sentence is mechanical; the revision is more interesting.

> TENTATIVE THESIS SENTENCE   Political fund-raising appeals are delivered in any of six ways.

> REVISED THESIS SENTENCE   Of the six ways to deliver political fund-raising appeals, the three that rely on personal contact are generally the most effective.

(Note that the revised thesis sentence implies a further classification based on whether the appeals involve personal contact or not.)

While generating ideas for your classification, keep track of them in a list, diagram, or outline to ensure that your principle is applied thoroughly (all classes) and consistently (each class relating to the principle). Fill in the list, diagram, or outline with the distinguishing features of each class and with examples that will clarify your scheme. Be sure to consider your readers' needs. The principle for classifying a familiar subject such as study habits might need little justification, although the classes themselves would need to be enlivened with vivid examples. An unfamiliar subject, in contrast, might require considerable care in explaining the principle of classification as well as attention to the details.

Organizing

The introduction to a classification essay should make clear why the classification is worthwhile: What situation prompted the essay? What do readers already know about the subject? What use might they make of the information you will provide? Unless your principle of classification is self-evident, you may want to explain it briefly—though save extensive explanation for the body of the essay. Do state your principle in a thesis sentence, so that readers know where you're taking them.

In the body of the essay the classes may be arranged in order of decreasing familiarity or increasing importance or size—whatever pattern provides the emphasis you want and clarifies your scheme for readers. You should at least mention each class, but some classes may demand considerable space and detail.

A classification essay often ends with a conclusion that restores the wholeness of the subject. Among other uses, the conclusion might summarize the classes, comment on the significance of one particular class in relation to the whole, or point out a new understanding of the whole subject gained from the classification.

Drafting

For the first draft of your classification, your main goal will be to establish your scheme: spelling out the purpose and principle of classification and defining the groups so that they are complete and consistent, covering the subject without mixing principles or overlapping. The more you've planned your scheme, the less difficult the draft will be. If you can also fill in the examples and other details needed to develop the groups, do so, but you may want to save this important work for revision.

Revising and Editing

The following questions can help your revise and edit your classification.

- *Will readers see the purpose of your classification?* Let readers know early why you are troubling to classify your subject, and keep this purpose evident throughout the essay.

- *Is your classification complete?* Your principle of classification should create categories that encompass every representative of the general subject. If some representatives will not fit the scheme, you may have to create a new category or revise the existing categories to include them.

- *Is your classification consistent?* Consistency is essential to save readers from confusion or irritation. Make sure all the classes reflect the same principle and that they do not overlap. Remedy flaws by adjusting the classes or creating new ones.

RUSSELL BAKER

A distinguished journalist, prize-winning memoirist, and treasured humorist, Russell Baker has informed and amused readers for more than fifty years. He was born in 1925 in Baltimore, served as a flyer during World War II, and graduated from Johns Hopkins University in 1947. That same year he began his journalism career at the Baltimore Sun *and in 1954 he moved to the* New York Times, *covering the president, the State Department, and Congress. In 1962 he launched a regular column for the* Times *titled "Observer," which appeared twice weekly on the op-ed page until 1998. Baker has received two Pulitzer Prizes, one for distinguished commentary in 1979 and one for his memoir,* Growing Up *(1982). His most recent book is another memoir,* Looking Back *(2002). Baker is a television star as well, hosting PBS's* Masterpiece Theatre *since 1993.*

The Plot Against People

Classifying inanimate objects, Baker here provides a funny take on how we relate to our cars, keys, flashlights, and other things. The essay was first published in 1968 in the New York Times.

1   Inanimate objects are classified scientifically into three major categories—those that don't work, those that break down and those that get lost.

2   The goal of all inanimate objects is to resist man and ultimately to defeat him, and the three major classifications are based on the method each object uses to achieve its purpose. As a general rule, any object capable of breaking down at the moment when it is most needed will do so. The automobile is typical of the category.

3   With the cunning typical of its breed, the automobile never breaks down while entering a filling station with a large staff of idle mechanics. It waits until it reaches a downtown intersection in the middle of the rush hour, or until it is fully loaded with family and luggage on the Ohio turnpike.

4   Thus it creates maximum misery, inconvenience, frustration and irritability among its human cargo, thereby reducing its owner's life span.

Washing machines, garbage disposals, lawn mowers, light bulbs, 5
automatic laundry dryers, water pipes, furnaces, electrical fuses, television tubes, hose nozzles, tape recorders, slide projectors all are in
league with the automobile to take their turn at breaking down
whenever life threatens to flow smoothly for their human enemies.

Many inanimate objects, of course, find it extremely difficult to 6
break down. Pliers, for example, and gloves and keys are almost
totally incapable of breaking down. Therefore, they have had to evolve
a different technique for resisting man.

They get lost. Science has still not solved the mystery of how they 7
do it, and no man has ever caught one of them in the act of getting
lost. The most plausible theory is that they have developed a secret
method of locomotion which they are able to conceal the instant a
human eye falls upon them.

It is not uncommon for a pair of pliers to climb all the way from 8
the cellar to the attic in its single-minded determination to raise its
owner's blood pressure. Keys have been known to burrow three feet
under mattresses. Women's purses, despite their great weight, frequently travel through six or seven rooms to find hiding space under
a couch.

Scientists have been struck by the fact that things that break down 9
virtually never get lost, while things that get lost hardly ever break
down.

A furnace, for example, will invariably break down at the depth of 10
the first winter cold wave, but it will never get lost. A woman's purse,
which after all does have some inherent capacity for breaking down,
hardly ever does; it almost invariably chooses to get lost.

Some persons believe this constitutes evidence that inanimate 11
objects are not entirely hostile to man, and that a negotiated peace
is possible. After all, they point out, a furnace could infuriate a man
even more thoroughly by getting lost than by breaking down, just as
a glove could upset him far more by breaking down than by getting
lost.

Not everyone agrees, however, that this indicates a conciliatory 12
attitude among inanimate objects. Many say it merely proves that
furnaces, gloves and pliers are incredibly stupid.

The third class of objects—those that don't work—is the most 13
curious of all. These include such objects as barometers, car clocks,
cigarette lighters, flashlights and toy-train locomotives. It is inaccurate, of course, to say that they never work. They work once, usually
for the first few hours after being brought home, and then quit.
Thereafter, they never work again.

In fact, it is widely assumed that they are built for the purpose of not 14 working. Some people have reached advanced ages without ever seeing some of these objects—barometers, for example—in working order.

Science is utterly baffled by the entire category. There are many 15 theories about it. The most interesting holds that the things that don't work have attained the highest state possible for an inanimate object, the state to which things that break down and things that get lost can still only aspire.

They have truly defeated man by conditioning him never to expect 16 anything of them, and in return they have given man the only peace he receives from inanimate society. He does not expect his barometer to work, his electric locomotive to run, his cigarette lighter to light or his flashlight to illuminate, and when they don't it does not raise his blood pressure.

He cannot attain that peace with furnaces and keys, and cars and 17 women's purses as long as he demands that they work for their keep.

Meaning

1. What is Baker's thesis? How is it ironic? (See *irony* in the Glossary.)
2. How have things that don't work "defeated man" (paragraph 16)?

Purpose and Audience

1. How can we tell that Baker intends to entertain us with his essay? What are some of the elements of his humor?
2. What assumptions does Baker make about the readers of his essay? Are the assumptions correct in your case?

Method and Structure

1. How does Baker use the method of classification for comic effect? In what ways does classification lend itself particularly well to a humorous subject such as this one?
2. What is Baker's principle of classification?
3. Where in the essay does Baker take pains to distinguish his classes of objects?
4. How does Baker make the transition between his discussion of objects that break down and his discussion of objects that get lost?
5. **Other Methods** For each of his classes, Baker offers specific examples. What functions do these examples serve? Can you think of other objects that would fit in each class?

Language

1. Baker's tone is often quite serious, from the abrupt opening assertion to the concluding statement about spiritual "peace." How do you account for such seriousness in a humorous essay?

2. Find three places where Baker uses hyperbole (see the Glossary for a definition). What is the effect of this figure of speech?

3. What does the word *cunning* mean (paragraph 3)? What are its connotations? In what way does the word set a pattern for Baker's use of words to describe objects?

Writing Topics

1. Can you think of other ways to classify inanimate objects? For instance, a scheme centering on student life might include objects no student can live without, objects no student would be caught dead with, objects that cause students problems, and perhaps other categories as well. Write a brief, humorous essay based on the classification scheme that you develop. To achieve humor, you might want to draw on some of Baker's techniques, such as a mock-serious tone, exaggeration, attributing human qualities to things, and appeals to science. But make your scheme thorough and consistent at the same time.

2. Are we the helpless victims of our things, as Baker holds, or can we get the upper hand? What advice would you give Baker for taming his things? Write him a letter in which you offer this advice, either seriously or mock-seriously.

3. What can you infer from the examples used in this essay about Baker's age and economic status? Does he seem to assume his audience is similar? (Remember, this essay first appeared in the *New York Times*.) Are readers who don't match those assumptions (perhaps you yourself) likely to enjoy Baker's essay as much as those who do match? Write an essay in which you analyze Baker's apparent assumptions, explaining whether and how they strengthen the essay, weaken it, or don't affect it.

DEBORAH TANNEN

Well known for her books on how men and women communicate, Deborah Tannen is a linguist with a knack for popular writing. She was born in 1945 in Brooklyn, New York, and attended Hunter College High School in Manhattan. She received a BA in 1966 from Harpur College (now the State University of New York at Binghamton), MA degrees in 1970 from Wayne State University and in 1976 from the University of California at Berkeley, and a linguistics PhD in 1979 from Berkeley. Tannen attributes her interest in linguistics partly to a childhood hearing impairment that, she says, schooled her in "tone of voice, attitude, and all the other conversational signals" in addition to the words themselves. She has been teaching linguistics since 1979 at Georgetown University, has published extensively in scholarly and popular periodicals, and has lectured widely. Her best-selling books, all concerning communication breakdowns and how to repair them, include That's Not What I Meant! *(1986),* You Just Don't Understand *(1990),* Talking 9 to 5 *(1994),* The Argument Culture *(1998), and* I Only Say This Because I Love You *(2001).*

But What Do You Mean?

Tannen's most popular books examine differences in the ways men and women talk to each other. In this essay, excerpted in Redbook *magazine from Tannen's book* Talking from 9 to 5, *she examines seven areas of miscommunication between genders.*

Conversation is a ritual. We say things that seem obviously the thing   1
to say, without thinking of the literal meaning of our words, any more than we expect the question "How are you?" to call forth a detailed account of aches and pains.

Unfortunately, women and men often have different ideas about   2
what's appropriate, different ways of speaking. Many of the conversational rituals common among women are designed to take the other person's feelings into account, while many of the conversational rituals common among men are designed to maintain the one-up position, or at least avoid appearing one-down. As a result, when men and women interact — especially at work — it's often

women who are at the disadvantage. Because women are not trying to avoid the one-down position, that is unfortunately where they may end up.

Here, the biggest areas of miscommunication.   3

1. APOLOGIES

Women are often told they apologize too much. The reason they're   4
told to stop doing it is that, to many men, apologizing seems syn-
onymous with putting oneself down. But there are many times when
"I'm sorry" isn't self-deprecating, or even an apology; it's an automatic
way of keeping both speakers on an equal footing. For example, a
well-known columnist once interviewed me and gave me her phone
number in case I needed to call her back. I misplaced the number and
had to go through the newspaper's main switchboard. When our
conversation was winding down and we'd both made ending-type
remarks, I added, "Oh, I almost forgot—I lost your direct number,
can I get it again?" "Oh, I'm sorry," she came back instantly, even
though she had done nothing wrong and *I* was the one who'd lost the
number. But I understood she wasn't really apologizing; she was just
automatically reassuring me she had no intention of denying me her
number.

Even when "I'm sorry" *is* an apology, women often assume it will   5
be the first step in a two-step ritual: I say "I'm sorry" and take half
the blame, then you take the other half. At work, it might go something like this:

A: When you typed this letter, you missed this phrase I inserted.
B: Oh, I'm sorry. I'll fix it.
A: Well, I wrote it so small it was easy to miss.

When both parties share blame, it's a mutual face-saving device.   6
But if one person, usually the woman, utters frequent apologies and
the other doesn't, she ends up looking as if she's taking the blame for
mishaps that aren't her fault. When she's only partially to blame, she
looks entirely in the wrong.

I recently sat in on a meeting at an insurance company where the   7
sole woman, Helen, said "I'm sorry" or "I apologize" repeatedly. At
one point she said, "I'm thinking out loud. I apologize." Yet the meeting was intended to be an informal brainstorming session, and *everyone* was thinking out loud.

The reason Helen's apologies stood out was that she was the only   8
person in the room making so many. And the reason I was concerned
was that Helen felt the annual bonus she had received was unfair.
When I interviewed her colleagues, they said that Helen was one of
the best and most productive workers—yet she got one of the smallest bonuses. Although the problem might have been outright sexism,
I suspect her speech style, which differs from that of her male colleagues, masks her competence.

Unfortunately, not apologizing can have its price too. Since so   9
many women use ritual apologies, those who don't may be seen as
hard-edged. What's important is to be aware of how often you say
you're sorry (and why), and to monitor your speech based on the
reaction you get.

2. CRITICISM

A woman who cowrote a report with a male colleague was hurt   10
when she read a rough draft to him and he leapt into a critical
response—"Oh, that's too dry! You have to make it snappier!" She
herself would have been more likely to say, "That's a really good
start. Of course, you'll want to make it a little snappier when you
revise."

Whether criticism is given straight or softened is often a matter   11
of convention. In general, women use more softeners. I noticed this
difference when talking to an editor about an essay I'd written.
While going over changes she wanted to make, she said, "There's
one more thing. I know you may not agree with me. The reason I
noticed the problem is that your other points are so lucid and elegant." She went on hedging for several more sentences until I put
her out of her misery: "Do you want to cut that part?" I asked—and
of course she did. But I appreciated her tentativeness. In contrast,
another editor (a man) I once called summarily rejected my idea for
an article by barking, "Call me when you have something new to
say."

Those who are used to ways of talking that soften the impact of   12
criticism may find it hard to deal with the right-between-the-eyes
style. It has its own logic, however, and neither style is intrinsically
better. People who prefer criticism given straight are operating on an
assumption that feelings aren't involved: "Here's the dope. I know
you're good; you can take it."

3. THANK-YOUS

A woman manager I know starts meetings by thanking everyone for   13
coming, even though it's clearly their job to do so. Her "thank-you"
is simply a ritual.

A novelist received a fax from an assistant in her publisher's office;   14
it contained suggested catalog copy for her book. She immediately
faxed him her suggested changes and said, "Thanks for running this
by me," even though her contract gave her the right to approve all
copy. When she thanked the assistant, she fully expected him to reciprocate: "Thanks for giving me such a quick response." Instead, he
said, "You're welcome." Suddenly, rather than an equal exchange of
pleasantries, she found herself positioned as the recipient of a favor.
This made her feel like responding, "Thanks for nothing!"

Many women use "thanks" as an automatic conversation starter   15
and closer; there's nothing literally to say thank you for. Like many
rituals typical of women's conversation, it depends on the goodwill
of the other to restore the balance. When the other speaker doesn't
reciprocate, a woman may feel like someone on a seesaw whose
partner abandoned his end. Instead of balancing in the air, she has
plopped to the ground, wondering how she got there.

4. FIGHTING

Many men expect the discussion of ideas to be a ritual fight—   16
explored through verbal opposition. They state their ideas in the
strongest possible terms, thinking that if there are weaknesses someone will point them out, and by trying to argue against those objections, they will see how well their ideas hold up.

Those who expect their own ideas to be challenged will respond   17
to another's ideas by trying to poke holes and find weak links—as a
way of *helping*. The logic is that when you are challenged you will
rise to the occasion: Adrenaline makes your mind sharper; you get
ideas and insights you would not have thought of without the spur
of battle.

But many women take this approach as a personal attack. Worse,   18
they find it impossible to do their best work in such a contentious
environment. If you're not used to ritual fighting, you begin to hear
criticism of your ideas as soon as they are formed. Rather than making you think more clearly, it makes you doubt what you know.
When you state your ideas, you hedge in order to fend off potential

attacks. Ironically, this is more likely to *invite* attack because it makes you look weak.

Although you may never enjoy verbal sparring, some women find 19 it helpful to learn how to do it. An engineer who was the only woman among four men in a small company found that as soon as she learned to argue she was accepted and taken seriously. A doctor attending a hospital staff meeting made a similar discovery. She was becoming more and more angry with a male colleague who'd loudly disagreed with a point she'd made. Her better judgment told her to hold her tongue, to avoid making an enemy of this powerful senior colleague. But finally she couldn't hold it in any longer, and she rose to her feet and delivered an impassioned attack on his position. She sat down in a panic, certain she had permanently damaged her relationship with him. To her amazement, he came up to her afterward and said, "That was a great rebuttal. I'm really impressed. Let's go out for a beer after work and hash out our approaches to this problem."

5. PRAISE

A manager I'll call Lester had been on his new job six months when 20 he heard that the women reporting to him were deeply dissatisfied. When he talked to them about it, their feelings erupted; two said they were on the verge of quitting because he didn't appreciate their work, and they didn't want to wait to be fired. Lester was dumbfounded: He believed they were doing a fine job. Surely, he thought, he had said nothing to give them the impression he didn't like their work. And indeed he hadn't. That was the problem. He had said *nothing* — and the women assumed he was following the adage "If you can't say something nice, don't say anything." He thought he was showing confidence in them by leaving them alone.

Men and women have different habits in regard to giving praise. 21 For example, Deirdre and her colleague William both gave presentations at a conference. Afterward, Deirdre told William, "That was a great talk!" He thanked her. Then she asked, "What did you think of mine?" and he gave her a lengthy and detailed critique. She found it uncomfortable to listen to his comments. But she assured herself that he meant well, and that his honesty was a signal that she, too, should be honest when he asked for a critique of his performance. As a matter of fact, she had noticed quite a few ways in which he could have improved his presentation. But she never got a chance to tell him because he never asked—and she felt put down. The worst part was that it seemed she had only herself to blame, since she *had* asked what he thought of her talk.

But had she really asked for his critique? The truth is, when   22 she asked for his opinion, she was expecting a compliment, which she felt was more or less required following anyone's talk. When he responded with criticism, she figured, "Oh, he's playing 'Let's critique each other'"—not a game she'd initiated, but one which she was willing to play. Had she realized he was going to criticize her and not ask her to reciprocate, she would never have asked in the first place.

It would be easy to assume that Deirdre was insecure, whether she   23 was fishing for a compliment or soliciting a critique. But she was simply talking automatically, performing one of the many conversational rituals that allow us to get through the day. William may have sincerely misunderstood Deirdre's intention—or may have been unable to pass up a chance to one-up her when given the opportunity.

6. COMPLAINTS

"Troubles talk" can be a way to establish rapport with a colleague.   24 You complain about a problem (which shows that you are just folks) and the other person responds with a similar problem (which puts you on equal footing). But while such commiserating is common among women, men are likely to hear it as a request to *solve* the problem.

One woman told me she would frequently initiate what she   25 thought would be pleasant complaint-airing sessions at work. She'd talk about situations that bothered her just to talk about them, maybe to understand them better. But her male office mate would quickly tell her how she could improve the situation. This left her feeling condescended to and frustrated. She was delighted to see this very impasse in a section in my book *You Just Don't Understand*, and showed it to him. "Oh," he said, "I see the problem. How can we solve it?" Then they both laughed, because it had happened again: He short-circuited the detailed discussion she'd hoped for and cut to the chase of finding a solution.

Sometimes the consequences of complaining are more serious: A   26 man might take a woman's lighthearted griping literally, and she can get a reputation as a chronic malcontent. Furthermore, she may be seen as not up to solving the problems that arise on the job.

7. JOKES

I heard a man call in to a talk show and say, "I've worked for two 27
women and neither one had a sense of humor. You know, when you
work with men, there's a lot of joking and teasing." The show's host
and the guest (both women) took his comment at face value and
assumed the women this man worked for were humorless. The
guest said, "Isn't it sad that women don't feel comfortable enough
with authority to see the humor?" The host said, "Maybe when more
women are in authority roles, they'll be more comfortable with
power." But although the women this man worked for *may* have
taken themselves too seriously, it's just as likely that they each had a
terrific sense of humor, but maybe the humor wasn't the type he was
used to. They may have been like the woman who wrote to me:
"When I'm with men, my wit or cleverness seems inappropriate (or
lost!) so I don't bother. When I'm with my women friends, however,
there's no hold on puns or cracks and my humor is fully appreciated."

The types of humor women and men tend to prefer differ. Research 28
has shown that the most common form of humor among men is
razzing, teasing, and mock-hostile attacks, while among women it's
self-mocking. Women often mistake men's teasing as genuinely hostile. Men often mistake women's mock self-deprecation as truly putting themselves down.

Women have told me they were taken more seriously when they 29
learned to joke the way the guys did. For example, a teacher who
went to a national conference with seven other teachers (mostly
women) and a group of administrators (mostly men) was annoyed
that the administrators always found reasons to leave boring semi-
nars, while the teachers felt they had to stay and take notes. One evening, when the group met at a bar in the hotel, the principal asked
her how one such seminar had turned out. She retorted, "As soon as
you left, it got much better." He laughed out loud at her response.
The playful insult appealed to the men—but there was a trade-off.
The women seemed to back off from her after this. (Perhaps they
were put off by her using joking to align herself with the bosses.)

There is no "right" way to talk. When problems arise, the culprit 30
may be style differences—and *all* styles will at times fail with others
who don't share or understand them, just as English won't do you
much good if you try to speak to someone who knows only French.
If you want to get your message across, it's not a question of being
"right"; it's a question of using language that's shared—or at least
understood.

Meaning

1. What does Tannen mean when she writes, "Conversation is a ritual" (paragraph 1)?
2. What does Tannen see as the fundamental difference between men's and women's conversational strategies?
3. Why is "You're welcome" not always an appropriate response to "Thank you"?

Purpose and Audience

1. What is Tannen's purpose in writing this essay? What does she hope it will accomplish?
2. Whom does Tannen see as her primary audience? Analyze her use of the pronoun *you* in paragraphs 9 and 19. Whom does she seem to be addressing here? Why?

Method and Structure

1. This essay has a large cast of characters: twenty-three to be exact. What function do these characters serve? How does Tannen introduce them to the reader? Does she describe them in sufficient detail?
2. How does Tannen's description of a columnist as "well-known" (paragraph 4) contribute to the effectiveness of her example?
3. **Other Methods**   For each of her seven areas of miscommunication, Tannen compares and contrasts male and female communication styles and strategies. Summarize the main source of misunderstanding in each area.

Language

1. What is the effect of "I put her out of her misery" (paragraph 11)? What does this phrase usually mean?
2. What does Tannen mean by a "right-between-the-eyes style" (paragraph 12)? What is the figure of speech involved here? (If necessary, see the Glossary under *figures of speech*.)
3. What is the effect of Tannen's use of figurative verbs, such as "barking" (paragraph 11) and "erupted" (20)? Find at least one other example of the use of a verb in a nonliteral sense.

Writing Topics

1. Write an essay classifying unconscious patterns of speech into categories of your own devising. For example, when someone says "Have

a good trip," do you answer "You too," even if the other person isn't going anywhere? Do you find yourself overusing certain words or phrases such as "like" or "you know"? You might sort out the examples by context ("phone blunders," "faulty farewells"), by purpose ("nervous tics," "space fillers"), or by some other principle of classification. Given your subject matter, you might want to adopt a humorous tone.

2. How well does your style of communication conform to that of your gender as described by Tannen? Write a short essay about a specific communication problem or misunderstanding you have had with someone of the opposite sex (sibling, friend, parent, significant other). How well does Tannen's differentiation of male and female communication styles account for your particular problem?

3. How true do you find Tannen's assessment of miscommunication between the sexes? Consider the conflicts you have observed between your parents, among fellow students or coworkers, in fictional portrayals in books and movies. Are Tannen's conclusions confirmed or called into question by your own observations and experiences? Write an essay confirming or questioning Tannen's generalizations, using your own examples.

STEPHANIE ERICSSON

Stephanie Ericsson was born in 1953 and grew up in San Francisco, California. Much of her writing draws on personal experience and reflection to examine love, loss, and grief. Her book Companion Through the Darkness: Inner Dialogues on Grief *(1993) began as a series of journal entries she wrote following the unexpected death of her husband. She lives in Minneapolis, Minnesota, and works as a screenwriter and advertising copywriter. Her most recent book is* Companion into the Dawn: Inner Dialogues on Loving *(1994).*

The Ways We Lie

"The Ways We Lie," which Ericsson wrote from her notes for Companion into the Dawn, *first appeared in the* Utne Reader *in 1992. The essay examines the destructive potential of various types of lies, including those that seem necessary and even beneficial.*

The bank called today and I told them my deposit was in the mail, 1
even though I hadn't written a check yet. It'd been a rough day. The baby I'm pregnant with decided to do aerobics on my lungs for two hours, our three-year-old daughter painted the living-room couch with lipstick, the IRS put me on hold for an hour, and I was late to a business meeting because I was tired.

I told my client that traffic had been bad. When my partner came 2
home, his haggard face told me his day hadn't gone any better than mine, so when he asked, "How was your day?" I said, "Oh, fine," knowing that one more straw might break his back. A friend called and wanted to take me to lunch. I said I was busy. Four lies in the course of a day, none of which I felt the least bit guilty about.

We lie. We all do. We exaggerate, we minimize, we avoid con- 3
frontation, we spare people's feelings, we conveniently forget, we keep secrets, we justify lying to the big-guy institutions. Like most people, I indulge in small falsehoods and still think of myself as an honest person. Sure I lie, but it doesn't hurt anything. Or does it?

I once tried going a whole week without telling a lie, and it was 4
paralyzing. I discovered that telling the truth all the time is nearly impossible. It means living with some serious consequences: The

bank charges me $60 in overdraft fees, my partner keels over when I tell him about my travails, my client fires me for telling her I didn't feel like being on time, and my friend takes it personally when I say I'm not hungry. There must be some merit to lying.

But if I justify lying, what makes me any different from slick   5 politicians or the corporate robbers who raided the S&L industry? Saying it's okay to lie one way and not another is hedging. I cannot seem to escape the voice deep inside me that tells me: When someone lies, someone loses.

What far-reaching consequences will I, or others, pay as a result   6 of my lie? Will someone's trust be destroyed? Will someone else pay *my* penance because I ducked out? We must consider the *meaning of our actions*. Deception, lies, capital crimes, and misdemeanors all carry meanings. *Webster's* definition of *lie* is specific:

1: a false statement or action especially made with the intent to deceive;

2: anything that gives or is meant to give a false impression.

A definition like this implies that there are many, many ways to   7 tell a lie. Here are just a few.

THE WHITE LIE

A man who won't lie to a woman has very little consideration for her feelings. — BERGEN EVANS

The white lie assumes that the truth will cause more damage than a   8 simple, harmless untruth. Telling a friend he looks great when he looks like hell can be based on a decision that the friend needs a compliment more than a frank opinion. But, in effect, it is the liar deciding what is best for the lied to. Ultimately, it is a vote of no confidence. It is an act of subtle arrogance for anyone to decide what is best for someone else.

Yet not all circumstances are quite so cut-and-dried. Take, for   9 instance, the sergeant in Vietnam who knew one of his men was killed in action but listed him as missing so that the man's family would receive indefinite compensation instead of the lump-sum pittance the military gives widows and children. His intent was honorable. Yet for twenty years this family kept their hopes alive, unable to move on to a new life.

FAÇADES

Et tu, Brute? —CAESAR

We all put up façades to one degree or another. When I put on a suit   10
to go to see a client, I feel as though I am putting on another face,
obeying the expectation that serious businesspeople wear suits
rather than sweatpants. But I'm a writer. Normally, I get up, get the
kid off to school, and sit at my computer in my pajamas until four in
the afternoon. When I answer the phone, the caller thinks I'm wearing a suit (though the UPS man knows better).

But façades can be destructive because they are used to seduce   11
others into an illusion. For instance, I recently realized that a former
friend was a liar. He presented himself with all the right looks and
the right words and offered lots of new consciousness theories, fab-
ulous books to read, and fascinating insights. Then I did some business with him, and the time came for him to pay me. He turned out
to be all talk and no walk. I heard a plethora of reasonable excuses,
including in-depth descriptions of the big break around the corner.
In six months of work, I saw less than a hundred bucks. When I confronted him, he raised both eyebrows and tried to convince me that
I'd heard him wrong, that he'd made no commitment to me. A
simple investigation into his past revealed a crowded graveyard of
disenchanted former friends.

IGNORING THE PLAIN FACTS

Well, you must understand that Father Porter is only human.
          —A MASSACHUSETTS PRIEST

In the '60s, the Catholic Church in Massachusetts began hearing   12
complaints that Father James Porter was sexually molesting children. Rather than relieving him of his duties, the ecclesiastical
authorities simply moved him from one parish to another between
1960 and 1967, actually providing him with a fresh supply of unsus-
pecting families and innocent children to abuse. After treatment in
1967 for pedophilia, he went back to work, this time in Minnesota.
The new diocese was aware of Father Porter's obsession with children, but they needed priests and recklessly believed treatment had
cured him. More children were abused until he was relieved of his

duties a year later. By his own admission, Porter may have abused as many as a hundred children.

Ignoring the facts may not in and of itself be a form of lying, but 13 consider the context of this situation. If a lie is *a false action done with the intent to deceive*, then the Catholic Church's conscious covering for Porter created irreparable consequences. The church became a co-perpetrator with Porter.

DEFLECTING

When you have no basis for an argument, abuse the plaintiff.

— CICERO

I've discovered that I can keep anyone from seeing the true me by 14 being selectively blatant. I set a precedent of being up-front about intimate issues, but I never bring up the things I truly want to hide; I just let people assume I'm revealing everything. It's an effective way of hiding.

Any good liar knows that the way to perpetuate an untruth is to 15 deflect attention from it. When Clarence Thomas exploded with accusations that the Senate hearings were a "high-tech lynching," he simply switched the focus from a highly charged subject to a radioactive subject.[1] Rather than defending himself, he took the offensive and accused the country of racism. It was a brilliant maneuver. Racism is now politically incorrect in official circles—unlike sexual harassment, which still rewards those who can get away with it.

Some of the most skilled deflectors are passive-aggressive people 16 who, when accused of inappropriate behavior, refuse to respond to the accusations. This you-don't-exist stance infuriates the accuser, who, understandably, screams something obscene out of frustration. The trap is sprung and the act of deflection successful, because now the passive-aggressive person can indignantly say, "Who can talk to someone as unreasonable as you?" The real issue is forgotten and the sins of the original victim become the focus. Feeling guilty of name-calling, the victim is fully tamed and crawls into a hole, ashamed. I have watched this fighting technique work thousands of times in disputes between men and women, and what I've learned is that the real culprit is not necessarily the one who swears the loudest.

[1]Ericsson refers to the 1991 hearings to confirm Thomas for the Supreme Court, at which Anita Hill accused Thomas of sexual harassment. [Editor's note.]

OMISSION

The cruelest lies are often told in silence. —R. L. STEVENSON

Omission involves telling most of the truth minus one or two key   17
facts whose absence changes the story completely. You break a pair
of glasses that are guaranteed under normal use and get a new pair,
without mentioning that the first pair broke during a rowdy game of
basketball. Who hasn't tried something like that? But what about
omission of information that could make a difference in how a person lives his or her life?

For instance, one day I found out that rabbinical legends tell of   18
another woman in the Garden of Eden before Eve. I was stunned.
The omission of the Sumerian goddess Lilith from Genesis—as well
as her demonization by ancient misogynists as an embodiment of
female evil—felt like spiritual robbery. I felt like I'd just found out
my mother was really my stepmother. To take seriously the tradition
that Adam was created out of the same mud as his equal counterpart, Lilith, redefines all of Judeo-Christian history.

Some renegade Catholic feminists introduced me to a view of   19
Lilith that had been suppressed during the many centuries when this
strong goddess was seen only as a spirit of evil. Lilith was a proud
goddess who defied Adam's need to control her, attempted negotia-
tions, and when this failed, said adios and left the Garden of Eden.

This omission of Lilith from the Bible was a patriarchal strategy   20
to keep women weak. Omitting the strong-woman archetype of
Lilith from Western religions and starting the story with Eve the Rib
has helped keep Christian and Jewish women believing they were
the lesser sex for thousands of years.

STEREOTYPES AND CLICHÉS

Where opinion does not exist, the status quo becomes stereotyped
and all originality is discouraged. —BERTRAND RUSSELL

Stereotype and cliché serve a purpose as a form of shorthand. Our   21
need for vast amounts of information in nanoseconds has made the
stereotype vital to modern communication. Unfortunately, it often
shuts down original thinking, giving those hungry for the truth a candy
bar of misinformation instead of a balanced meal. The stereotype
explains a situation with just enough truth to seem unquestionable.

All the "isms"—racism, sexism, ageism, et al.—are founded on 22
and fueled by the stereotype and the cliché, which are lies of exaggeration, omission, and ignorance. They are always dangerous. They
take a single tree and make it a landscape. They destroy curiosity.
They close minds and separate people. The single mother on welfare
is assumed to be cheating. Any black male could tell you how much
of his identity is obliterated daily by stereotypes. Fat people, ugly
people, beautiful people, old people, large-breasted women, short
men, the mentally ill, and the homeless all could tell you how much
more they are like us than we want to think. I once admitted to a
group of people that I had a mouth like a truck driver. Much to my
surprise, a man stood up and said, "I'm a truck driver, and I never
cuss." Needless to say, I was humbled.

GROUPTHINK

*Who is more foolish, the child afraid of the dark, or the man afraid
of the light?* —MAURICE FREEHILL

Irving Janis, in *Victims of Group Think*, defines this sort of lie as a 23
psychological phenomenon within decision-making groups in which
loyalty to the group has become more important than any other
value, with the result that dissent and the appraisal of alternatives
are suppressed. If you've ever worked on a committee or in a corporation, you've encountered groupthink. It requires a combination of
other forms of lying—ignoring facts, selective memory, omission,
and denial, to name a few.

The textbook example of groupthink came on December 7, 24
1941. From as early as the fall of 1941, the warnings came in, one
after another, that Japan was preparing for a massive military operation. The navy command in Hawaii assumed Pearl Harbor was
invulnerable—the Japanese weren't stupid enough to attack the
United States' most important base. On the other hand, racist stereotypes said the Japanese weren't smart enough to invent a torpedo effective in less than 60 feet of water (the fleet was docked in 30 feet); after
all, US technology hadn't been able to do it.

On Friday, December 5, normal weekend leave was granted to all 25
the commanders at Pearl Harbor, even though the Japanese con-
sulate in Hawaii was busy burning papers. Within the tight, good-
ole-boy cohesiveness of the US command in Hawaii, the myth of

invulnerability stayed well entrenched. No one in the group considered the alternatives. The rest is history.

OUT-AND-OUT LIES

The only form of lying that is beyond reproach is lying for its own sake. — OSCAR WILDE

Of all the ways to lie, I like this one the best, probably because I get   26
tired of trying to figure out the real meanings behind things. At least
I can trust the bald-faced lie. I once asked my five-year-old nephew,
"Who broke the fence?" (I had seen him do it.) He answered, "The
murderers." Who could argue?

At least when this sort of lie is told it can be easily confronted. As   27
the person who is lied to, I know where I stand. The bald-faced lie
doesn't toy with my perceptions—it argues with them. It doesn't try
to refashion reality, it tries to refute it. *Read my lips.* . . . No sleight of
hand. No guessing. If this were the only form of lying, there would be
no such things as floating anxiety or the adult-children-of-alcoholics
movement.

DISMISSAL

Pay no attention to that man behind the curtain!
I am the Great Oz! — THE WIZARD OF OZ

Dismissal is perhaps the slipperiest of all lies. Dismissing feelings,   28
perceptions, or even the raw facts of a situation ranks as a kind of lie
that can do as much damage to a person as any other kind of lie.

The roots of many mental disorders can be traced back to the dis-   29
missal of reality. Imagine that a person is told from the time she is a
tot that her perceptions are inaccurate. *"Mommy, I'm scared."* "No
you're not, darling." *"I don't like that man next door, he makes me feel
icky."* "Johnny, that's a terrible thing to say, of course you like him.
You go over there right now and be nice to him."

I've often mused over the idea that madness is actually a sane reac-   30
tion to an insane world. Psychologist R. D. Laing supports this
hypothesis in *Sanity, Madness and the Family*, an account of his investigation into the families of schizophrenics. The common thread that
ran through all of the families he studied was a deliberate, staunch

dismissal of the patient's perceptions from a very early age. Each of the patients started out with an accurate grasp of reality, which, through meticulous and methodical dismissal, was demolished until the only reality the patient could trust was catatonia.

Dismissal runs the gamut. Mild dismissal can be quite handy for 31 forgiving the foibles of others in our day-to-day lives. Toddlers who have just learned to manipulate their parents' attention sometimes are dismissed out of necessity. Absolute attention from the parents would require so much energy that no one would get to eat dinner. But we must be careful and attentive about how far we take our "necessary" dismissals. Dismissal is a dangerous tool, because it's nothing less than a lie.

DELUSION

We lie loudest when we lie to ourselves. —ERIC HOFFER

I could write the book on this one. Delusion, a cousin of dismissal, is 32 the tendency to see excuses as facts. It's a powerful lying tool because it filters out information that contradicts what we want to believe. Alcoholics who believe that the problems in their lives are legitimate reasons for drinking rather than results of the drinking offer the classic example of deluded thinking. Delusion uses the mind's ability to see things in myriad ways to support what it wants to be the truth.

But delusion is also a survival mechanism we all use. If we were 33 to fully contemplate the consequences of our stockpiles of nuclear weapons or global warming, we could hardly function on a day-to-day level. We don't want to incorporate that much reality into our lives because to do so would be paralyzing.

Delusion acts as an adhesive to keep the status quo intact. It 34 shamelessly employs dismissal, omission, and amnesia, among other sorts of lies. Its most cunning defense is that it cannot see itself.

• • •

The liar's punishment . . . is that he cannot believe anyone else.
—GEORGE BERNARD SHAW

These are only a few of the ways we lie. Or are lied to. As I said 35 earlier, it's not easy to entirely eliminate lies from our lives. No matter how pious we may try to be, we will still embellish, hedge, and omit to lubricate the daily machinery of living. But there is a world of difference between telling functional lies and living a lie. Martin Buber once said, "The lie is the spirit committing treason against itself." Our acceptance of lies becomes a cultural cancer that eventually shrouds and reorders reality until moral garbage becomes as invisible to us as water is to a fish.

How much do we tolerate before we become sick and tired of 36 being sick and tired? When will we stand up and declare our *right* to trust? When do we stop accepting that the real truth is in the fine print? Whose lips do we read this year when we vote for president? When will we stop being so reticent about making judgments? When do we stop turning over our personal power and responsibility to liars?

Maybe if I don't tell the bank the check's in the mail I'll be less 37 tolerant of the lies told me every day. A country song I once heard said it all for me: "You've got to stand for something or you'll fall for anything."

Meaning

1. What is Ericsson's thesis?
2. Does Ericsson think it's possible to eliminate lies from our lives? What evidence does she offer?
3. If it were possible to eliminate lies from our lives, why would that be desirable?

Purpose and Audience

1. What is this essay's purpose?
2. Identify instances where Ericsson directly addresses her audience. What does she accomplish by using the pronoun *we* throughout the essay?

Method and Structure

1. Ericsson starts out by recounting her own four-lie day (paragraphs 1–2). What is the effect of this introduction?
2. At the beginning of each kind of lie, Ericsson provides an epigraph, a short quotation that forecasts a theme. Which of these epigraphs work best, do you think? What are your criteria for judgment?
3. What is the message of Ericsson's conclusion? Does the conclusion work well? Why, or why not?

4. **Other Methods**   Examine the way Ericsson uses definition and example to support her classification. Which definitions are clearest? Which examples are the most effective? Why?

Language

1. In paragraph 35 Ericsson writes, "Our acceptance of lies becomes a cultural cancer that eventually shrouds and reorders reality until moral garbage becomes as invisible to us as water is to a fish." How do the two figures of speech in this sentence—cancer and garbage—relate to each other? (If necessary, see *figures of speech* in the Glossary.)
2. Occasionally Ericsson's anger shows through, as in paragraphs 12–13 and 18–20. Is the tone appropriate in these cases? Why, or why not?

Writing Topics

1. Consider some lies that you have told, whether large or seemingly harmless. Develop one or more of these lies into an essay. You may choose to elaborate on your lies by classifying according to some principle or by narrating the story of a particular lie and its outcome. Try to give your reader a sense of your motivation for lying in the first place.
2. Ericsson writes, "All the 'isms'—racism, sexism, ageism, et al.—are founded on and fueled by the stereotype and the cliché, which are lies of exaggeration, omission, and ignorance. They are always dangerous. They take a single tree and make it a landscape" (paragraph 22). Write an essay discussing stereotypes and how they work to encourage prejudice. Use Ericsson's definition as a base, and expand it to include stereotypes you find particularly injurious. How do these stereotypes oversimplify? How are they "dangerous"?
3. Evaluate the success of Ericsson's essay, considering especially how effectively her evidence supports her generalizations. Are there important categories she overlooks, exceptions she neglects to account for, gaps in definitions or examples? Offer specific evidence for your own view, whether positive or negative.

Writing with the Method
Classification

Choose one of the following topics, or any other topic they suggest, for an essay developed by classification. The topic you decide on should be something you care about so that classification is a means of communicating an idea, not an end in itself.

PEOPLE
1. People you like (or dislike)
2. Boring people
3. Teachers or students
4. Friends or coworkers
5. Mothers or fathers

PSYCHOLOGY AND BEHAVIOR
6. Friendships
7. Ways of disciplining children
8. Ways of practicing religion
9. Obsessions
10. Diets
11. Dreams

THINGS
12. Buildings on campus
13. Junk foods
14. Computer games
15. Cars or trucks

SPORTS AND PERFORMANCE
16. Styles of baseball pitching, football tackling, or another sports skill
17. Runners
18. Styles of dance, guitar playing, acting, or another performance art

COMMUNICATIONS MEDIA

19. Young male or female movie stars
20. Talk-show hosts
21. Television programs
22. Radio stations
23. Magazines or newspapers

Chapter Six

PROCESS ANALYSIS

USING THE METHOD

Game rules, car-repair manuals, cookbooks, science textbooks—
these and many other familiar works are essentially process analyses. They explain how to do something (play Monopoly, tune a
car), how to make something (a carrot cake), or how something
happens (how our hormones affect our behavior, how a computer
stores and retrieves data). That is, they explain a sequence of
actions with a specified result (the **process**) by dividing it into its
component steps (the **analysis**). Almost always, the purpose of
process analysis is to explain, but sometimes a parallel purpose is
to prove something about the process or to evaluate it: to show
how easy it is to change a tire, for instance, or to urge dieters to
follow a weight-loss plan on the grounds of its safety and effectiveness.

Process analysis overlaps several other methods discussed in this
book. The analysis is actually the method examined in Chapter 4—
dividing a thing or concept into its elements. And we analyze a process much as we analyze causes and effects (Chapter 9), except that
cause-and-effect analysis asks mainly *why* something happens or
why it has certain results, whereas process analysis asks mainly *how*
something happens. Process analysis also overlaps narration
(Chapter 2), for the steps of the process are almost always presented
in chronological sequence. But narration recounts a unique sequence
of events with a unique result, whereas process analysis explains a
series of steps with the same predictable result. You might narrate

a particularly exciting baseball game, but you would analyze the process—the rules—of any baseball game.

Processes occur in several varieties, including mechanical (a car engine), natural (cell division), psychological (acquisition of sex roles), and political (the electoral process). Process analyses generally fall into one of two types:

- In a **directive** process analysis, you tell how to do or make something: bake a cake, repair a bicycle, negotiate a deal, write a process analysis. You outline the steps in the process completely so that the reader who follows them can achieve the specified result. Generally, you address the reader directly, using the second-person *you* ("You should concentrate on the words that tell you what to do") or the imperative (commanding) mood of verbs ("Add one egg yolk and stir vigorously").

- In an **explanatory** process analysis, you provide the information necessary for readers to understand the process, but more to satisfy their curiosity than to teach them how to perform it. You may address the reader directly, but the third-person *he, she, it*, and *they* are more common.

Whether directive or explanatory, process analyses usually follow a chronological sequence. Most processes can be divided into phases or stages, and these in turn can be divided into steps. The stages of changing a tire, for instance, may be jacking up the car, removing the flat, putting on the spare, and lowering the car. The steps within, say, jacking up the car may be setting the emergency brake, blocking the other wheels, loosening the bolts, positioning the jack, and raising the car. Following a chronological order, you cover the stages in sequence and, within each stage, cover the steps in sequence.

To ensure that the reader can duplicate the process or understand how it unfolds, you must fully detail each step and specify the reasons for it. In addition, you must be sure that the reader grasps the sequence of steps, their duration, and where they occur. To this end, transitional expressions that signal time and place—such as *after five minutes, meanwhile, to the left*, and *below*—can be invaluable in process analysis.

Though a chronological sequence is usual for process analysis, you may have to interrupt or modify it to suit your material. You may need to pause in the sequence to provide definitions of specialized terms or to explain why a step is necessary or how it relates to the preceding and following steps. In an essay on how to change a tire, for instance, you might stop briefly to explain that the bolts should be slightly loosened *before* the car is jacked up in order to prevent the wheel from spinning afterward.

DEVELOPING AN ESSAY BY PROCESS ANALYSIS

Getting Started

You'll find yourself writing process analyses for your courses in school (for instance, explaining how a drug affects brain chemistry), in memos at work (recommending a new procedure for approving cost estimates), or in life outside work (giving written directions to your home). To find a subject when an assignment doesn't make one obvious, examine your interests or hobbies or think of something whose workings you'd like to research in order to understand them better. Explore the subject by listing chronologically all the necessary stages and steps.

While you are exploring your subject, decide on the point of your analysis and express it in a thesis sentence that will guide your writing and tell your readers what to expect. The simplest thesis states what the process is and its basic stages. For instance:

> Building a table is a three-stage process of cutting, assembling, and finishing.

But you can increase your readers' interest in the process by also conveying your reason for writing about it. You might assert that a seemingly difficult process is actually quite simple, or vice versa:

> Changing a tire does not require a mechanic's skill or strength; on the contrary, a ten-year-old child can do it.

> Windsurfing may look easy, but it demands the knowledge of an experienced sailor and the balance of an acrobat.

You might show how the process demonstrates a more general principle:

> The process of getting a bill through Congress illustrates majority rule at work.

Or you might assert that a process is inefficient or unfair:

> The overly complicated registration procedure forces students to waste two days each semester standing in line.

Remember your readers while you are generating ideas and formulating your thesis. Consider how much background information they need, where specialized terms must be defined, and where examples must be given. Especially if you are providing directions, consider what special equipment readers will need, what hitches they may encounter, and what the interim results should be. To build a table, for instance, what tools will readers need? What should they do if the table wobbles even after the corners are braced? What should the table feel like after the first sanding or the first varnishing?

Organizing

Many successful process analyses begin with an overview of the process to which readers can relate each step. In such an introduction you can lead up to your thesis sentence by specifying when or where the process occurs, why it is useful or interesting or controversial, what its result is, and the like. Especially if you are providing directions, you can also use the introduction (perhaps a separate paragraph) to provide essential background information, such as the materials readers will need.

After the introduction, you should present the stages distinctly, perhaps one or two paragraphs for each, and usually in chronological order. Within each stage, also chronologically, you then cover the necessary steps. This chronological sequence helps readers see how a process unfolds or how to perform it themselves. Try not to deviate from it unless you have good reason to—perhaps because your process requires you to group simultaneous steps or your readers need definitions of terms, reasons for steps, connections between separated steps, and other explanations.

A process essay may end simply with the result. Or you might conclude with a summary of the major stages, with a comment on the significance or usefulness of the process, or with a recommendation for changing a process you have criticized. For an essay providing directions, you might state the standards by which readers can measure their success or give an idea of how much practice may be necessary to master the process.

Drafting

While drafting your process analysis, concentrate on getting in as many details as you can: every step, how each relates to the one before and after, how each contributes to the result. In revising you can always delete unnecessary details and connective tissue if they seem cumbersome, but in the first draft it's better to overexplain than underexplain.

Drafting a process analysis is a good occasion to practice a straightforward, concise writing style, because clarity is more important than originality of expression. Stick to plain language and uncomplicated sentences. If you want to dress up your style a bit, you can always do so after you have made yourself clear.

Revising and Editing

When you've finished your draft, ask a friend to read it. If you have explained a process, he or she should be able to understand it. If you have given directions, he or she should be able to follow them, or imagine following them. Then examine the draft yourself against the following questions.

- *Have you adhered to a chronological sequence?* Unless there is a compelling and clear reason to use some other arrangement, the stages and steps of your analysis should proceed in chronological order. If you had to depart from that order — to define or explain or to sort out simultaneous steps — the reasons should be clear to your readers.
- *Have you included all necessary steps and omitted any unnecessary digressions?* The explanation should be as complete as possible but not cluttered with information, however interesting, that contributes nothing to the readers' understanding of the process.
- *Have you accurately gauged your readers' need for information?* You don't want to bore readers with explanations and details they don't need. But erring in the other direction is even worse, for your essay will achieve little if readers cannot understand it.
- *Have you shown readers how each step fits into the whole process and relates to the other steps?* If your analysis seems to break down into a multitude of isolated steps, you may need to organize them more clearly into stages.
- *Have you used plenty of informative transitions?* Transitions such as *at the same time* and *on the other side of the machine* indicate when steps start and stop, how long they last, and where

they occur. (A list of such expressions appears in the Glossary under *transitions*.) The expressions should be as informative as possible; signals such as *first . . . second . . . third . . . fourteenth* and *next . . . next* do not help indicate movement in space or lapses in time, and they quickly grow tiresome.

LARS EIGHNER

An essayist and fiction writer, Lars Eighner was born in 1948 in Texas and attended the University of Texas at Austin. He has contributed essays to Threepenny Review *and stories to that periodical as well as to* Advocate Men, *the* Guide, *and* Inches. *His volumes of stories include* Bayou Boy and Other Stories *(1985),* American Prelude *(1994), and* Whispered in the Dark *(1995). In 1988 Eighner became homeless after leaving a job he had held for ten years as an attendant in a mental hospital. He now lives in an apartment in Austin and supports himself as a writer. His memoir about homelessness,* Travels with Lizbeth, *was published in 1993.*

Dumpster Diving

This essay from a 1992 Utne Reader *was abridged from a prize-winning piece published first in* Threepenny Review *and then in Eighner's* Travels with Lizbeth *(1993). Eighner explains a process that you probably do not want to learn: how to subsist on what you can scavenge from trash. But, as Eighner observes, scavenging has lessons to teach about value.*

I began Dumpster diving about a year before I became homeless. 1

I prefer the term *scavenging.* I have heard people, evidently mean- 2
ing to be polite, use the word *foraging,* but I prefer to reserve that word for gathering nuts and berries and such, which I also do, according to the season and opportunity.

I like the frankness of the word *scavenging.* I live from the refuse 3
of others. I am a scavenger. I think it a sound and honorable niche, although if I could I would naturally prefer to live the comfortable consumer life, perhaps—and only perhaps—as a slightly less wasteful consumer owing to what I have learned as a scavenger.

Except for jeans, all my clothes come from Dumpsters. Boom 4
boxes, candles, bedding, toilet paper, medicine, books, a typewriter, a virgin male love doll, coins sometimes amounting to many dollars: all came from Dumpsters. And, yes, I eat from Dumpsters, too.

There is a predictable series of stages that a person goes through   5
in learning to scavenge. At first the new scavenger is filled with dis-
gust and self-loathing. He is ashamed of being seen.

This stage passes with experience. The scavenger finds a pair of   6
running shoes that fit and look and smell brand-new. He finds a pocket
calculator in perfect working order. He finds pristine ice cream, still
frozen, more than he can eat or keep. He begins to understand: people
do throw away perfectly good stuff, a lot of perfectly good stuff.

At this stage he may become lost and never recover. All the   7
Dumpster divers I have known come to the point of trying to acquire
everything they touch. Why not take it, they reason, it is all free. This
is of course, hopeless, and most divers come to realize that they must
restrict themselves to items of relatively immediate utility.

The finding of objects is becoming something of an urban art.   8
Even respectable, employed people will sometimes find something
tempting sticking out of a Dumpster or standing beside one. Quite a
number of people, not all of them of the bohemian type, are willing
to brag that they found this or that piece in the trash.

But eating from Dumpsters is the thing that separates the dilet-   9
tanti from the professionals. Eating safely involves three principles:
using the senses and common sense to evaluate the condition of the
found materials; knowing the Dumpsters of a given area and check-
ing them regularly; and seeking always to answer the question "Why
was this discarded?"

Yet perfectly good food can be found in Dumpsters. Canned   10
goods, for example, turn up fairly often in the Dumpsters I frequent.
I also have few qualms about dry foods such as crackers, cookies,
cereal, chips, and pasta if they are free of visible contaminants and
still dry and crisp. Raw fruits and vegetables with intact skins seem
perfectly safe to me, excluding, of course, the obviously rotten. Many
are discarded for minor imperfections that can be pared away.

A typical discard is a half jar of peanut butter—though nonor-   11
ganic peanut butter does not require refrigeration and is unlikely to
spoil in any reasonable time. One of my favorite finds is yogurt—
often discarded, still sealed, when the expiration date has passed—
because it will keep for several days, even in warm weather.

No matter how careful I am I still get dysentery at least once a   12
month, oftener in warm weather. I do not want to paint too roman-
tic a picture. Dumpster diving has serious drawbacks as a way of life.

I find from the experience of scavenging two rather deep lessons.   13
The first is to take what I can use and let the rest go. I have come to

think that there is no value in the abstract. A thing I cannot use or make useful, perhaps by trading, has no value, however fine or rare it may be.

The second lesson is the transience of material being. I do not 14 suppose that ideas are immortal, but certainly they are longer-lived than material objects.

The things I find in Dumpsters, the love letters and rag dolls of so 15 many lives, remind me of this lesson. Now I hardly pick up a thing without envisioning the time I will cast it away. This, I think, is a healthy state of mind. Almost everything I have now has already been cast out at least once, proving that what I own is valueless to someone.

I find that my desire to grab for the gaudy bauble has been largely 16 sated. I think this is an attitude I share with the very wealthy—we both know there is plenty more where whatever we have came from. Between us are the rat-race millions who have confounded their selves with the objects they grasp and who nightly scavenge the cable channels for they know not what.

I am sorry for them. 17

Meaning

1. Eighner ends his essay with the statement "I am sorry for them." Whom is he sorry for, and why? How does this statement relate to the main point of Eighner's essay?
2. How does Eighner decide what to keep when he digs through Dumpsters? How does he decide a thing's value? What evidence in the essay supports your answer?

Purpose and Audience

1. How does paragraph 2 reveal that Eighner's purpose is not simply to explain how to scavenge but also to persuade his readers to examine any stereotypes they may hold about scavengers?
2. In paragraphs 10 and 11 Eighner goes into considerable detail about the food he finds in Dumpsters. Why do you think he does this?

Method and Structure

1. Eighner identifies three main stages "a person goes through in learning to scavenge" (paragraph 5). What are these stages, and do all scavengers experience each one? Support your answer with evidence from the essay.

2. **Other Methods**   In paragraph 2 Eighner uses definition to distinguish "foraging" from "scavenging." What is the distinction he makes? How does it relate to the overall meaning of the essay?

Language

1. Eighner says of his life as a scavenger, "I think it a sound and honorable niche, although if I could I would naturally prefer to live the comfortable consumer life" (paragraph 3). How would you characterize the tone of this statement? Where else in the essay do you find this tone?

2. Eighner's style is often formal: consider the word choice and order in such phrases as "I think it a sound and honorable niche" (paragraph 3) and "who nightly scavenge the cable channels for they know not what" (16). Find at least three other instances of formal style. What is the effect of this language, and how does it further Eighner's purpose? (If necessary, consult *style* in the Glossary.)

Writing Topics

1. Eighner writes that since he became a scavenger he hardly "pick[s] up a thing without envisioning the time I will cast it away. This, I think, is a healthy state of mind." Do you agree? What associations do you have with material objects that cause you to support or deny Eighner's claim? Do you own things that matter a great deal to you, or would it be relatively easy to cast many of your possessions away? Write an essay arguing either for or against Eighner's position, making sure to provide your own illustrations to support your argument.

2. Eighner writes that he and the very wealthy share the attitude that "there is plenty more where whatever we have came from." In your experience, how true is this statement? Do you agree that one needs to be very poor or very rich to feel this way? Is this state of mind a response to the amount of money a person has, or can it be developed independently, regardless of one's wealth or lack of it? Write an essay describing how you think people arrive at the belief that "there is plenty more" of whatever they have available.

3. Eighner attempts to teach his readers how to scavenge, certainly, but he also attempts to persuade his audience to examine their stereotypes about the homeless. Write an essay in which you examine your stereotypes about homeless people. Describe any personal encounters you have had and the images you have seen in the media, and discuss how these experiences led you to the beliefs you hold. Finally, consider the extent to which "Dumpster Diving" changed your perspective.

ANNE LAMOTT

Anne Lamott is a well-known writing teacher and author of novels and best-selling nonfiction, including Bird by Bird *(1994),* Traveling Mercies *(1999),* All New People *(1999), and* Blue Shoe *(2002). She has taught at the University of California, Davis, and at writing workshops across the country. Lamott's biweekly diary in the online magazine* Salon, *"Word by Word," which ran from 1996 to 1999, was voted "The Best of the Web" by* Time *magazine.* Bird by Bird with Annie *(1999) documents a year of Lamott's life, which Amazon.com characterizes as that of "your run-of-the-mill recovering alcoholic and drug addict, born-again Christian, left-wing liberal, and single mother who just so happens to have written* New York Times–*best-selling books." Lamott lives in northern California with her son.*

The Crummy First Draft

Lamott's Bird by Bird *is an inspiring and often very funny guide to writing. In this excerpt from the book, Lamott advises others how to begin writing by silencing their noisy inner critics.*

For me and most of the other writers I know, writing is not rapturous. In fact, the only way I can get anything written at all is to write really, really crummy first drafts.

The first draft is the child's draft, where you let it all pour out and then let it romp all over the place, knowing that no one is going to see it and that you can shape it later. You just let this childlike part of you channel whatever voices and visions come through and onto the page. If one of the characters wants to say "Well, so what, Mr. Poopy Pants?" you let her. No one is going to see it. If the kid wants to get into really sentimental, weepy, emotional territory, you let him. Just get it all down on paper, because there may be something great in those six crazy pages that you would never have gotten to by more rational, grown-up means. There may be something in the very last line of the very last paragraph on page six that you just love, that is so beautiful or wild that you now know what you're supposed to be writing about, more or less, or in what direction you might go—but there was no way to get to this without first getting through the first five and a half pages.

I used to write food reviews for *California* magazine before it folded. 3 (My writing food reviews had nothing to do with the magazine folding, although every single review did cause a couple of canceled subscriptions. Some readers took umbrage at my comparing mounds of vegetable puree with various ex-presidents' brains.) These reviews always took two days to write. First I'd go to a restaurant several times with a few opinionated, articulate friends in tow. I'd sit there writing down everything anyone said that was at all interesting or funny. Then on the following Monday I'd sit down at my desk with my notes, and try to write the review. Even after I'd been doing this for years, panic would set in. I'd try to write a lead, but instead I'd write a couple of dreadful sentences, xx them out, try again, xx everything out, and then feel despair and worry settle on my chest like an x-ray apron. It's over, I'd think, calmly. I'm not going to be able to get the magic to work this time. I'm ruined. I'm through. I'm toast. Maybe, I'd think, I can get my old job back as a clerk-typist. But probably not. I'd get up and study my teeth in the mirror for a while. Then I'd stop, remember to breathe, make a few phone calls, hit the kitchen and chow down. Eventually I'd go back and sit down at my desk, and sigh for the next ten minutes. Finally I would pick up my one-inch picture frame, stare into it as if for the answer, and every time the answer would come: all I had to do was to write a really crummy first draft of, say, the opening paragraph. And no one was going to see it.

So I'd start writing without reining myself in. It was almost just 4 typing, just making my fingers move. And the writing would be *terrible*. I'd write a lead paragraph that was a whole page, even though the entire review could only be three pages long, and then I'd start writing up descriptions of the food, one dish at a time, bird by bird, and the critics would be sitting on my shoulders, commenting like cartoon characters. They'd be pretending to snore, or rolling their eyes at my overwrought descriptions, no matter how hard I tried to tone those descriptions down, no matter how conscious I was of what a friend said to me gently in my early days of restaurant reviewing. "Annie," she said, "it is just a piece of *chick*en. It is just a bit of *cake*."

But because by then I had been writing for so long, I would eventu- 5 ally let myself trust the process—sort of, more or less. I'd write a first draft that was maybe twice as long as it should be, with a self-indulgent and boring beginning, stupefying descriptions of the meal, lots of quotes from my black-humored friends that made them sound more like the Manson girls[1] than food lovers, and no ending to speak of. The whole thing would be so long and incoherent and hideous that for the rest of the day I'd obsess about getting creamed by a car before I could write a decent second draft. I'd worry that people would read what I'd written and believe that the accident had really been a suicide, that I had panicked because my talent was waning and my mind was shot.

The next day, though, I'd sit down, go through it all with a colored   6 pen, take out everything I possibly could, find a new lead somewhere on the second page, figure out a kicky place to end it, and then write a second draft. It always turned out fine, sometimes even funny and weird and helpful. I'd go over it one more time and mail it in.

Then, a month later, when it was time for another review, the   7 whole process would start again, complete with the fears that people would find my first draft before I could rewrite it.

Almost all good writing begins with terrible first efforts. You need   8 to start somewhere. Start by getting something—anything—down on paper. A friend of mine says that the first draft is the down draft—you just get it down. The second draft is the up draft—you fix it up. You try to say what you have to say more accurately. And the third draft is the dental draft, where you check every tooth, to see if it's loose or cramped or decayed, or even, God help us, healthy.

What I've learned to do when I sit down to work on a crummy first   9 draft is to quiet the voices in my head. First there's the vinegar-lipped Reader Lady, who says primly, "Well, *that's* not very interesting, is it?" And there's the emaciated German male who writes these Orwellian[2] memos detailing your thought crimes. And there are your parents, agonizing over your lack of loyalty and discretion; and there's William Burroughs,[3] dozing off or shooting up because he finds you as bold and articulate as a houseplant; and so on. And there are also the dogs: let's not forget the dogs, the dogs in their pen who will surely hurtle

---

[1]The Manson girls were young, troubled members of the cult led by Charles Manson (born 1934). In 1969 Manson and some of his followers were convicted of murder in California. [Editor's note.]

[2]In his novel *1984*, the British writer George Orwell (1903–50) depicts a futuristic world in which a totalitarian government controls citizens' behavior and thoughts. [Editor's note.]

[3]The American novelist William Burroughs (1914–97) wrote experimental and often surreal works on drug addiction and other aspects of contemporary life. [Editor's note.]

and snarl their way out if you ever *stop* writing, because writing is, for some of us, the latch that keeps the door of the pen closed, keeps those crazy, ravenous dogs contained. . . .

Close your eyes and get quiet for a minute, until the chatter starts 10 up. Then isolate one of the voices and imagine the person speaking as a mouse. Pick it up by the tail and drop it into a mason jar. Then isolate another voice, pick it up by the tail, drop it in the jar. And so on. Drop in any high-maintenance parental units, drop in any contractors, lawyers, colleagues, children, anyone who is whining in your head. Then put the lid on, and watch all these mouse people clawing at the glass, jabbering away, trying to make you feel crummy because you won't do what they want—won't give them more money, won't be more successful, won't see them more often. Then imagine that there is a volume-control button on the bottle. Turn it all the way up for a minute, and listen to the stream of angry, neglected, guilt-mongering voices. Then turn it all the way down and watch the frantic mice lunge at the glass, trying to get to you. Leave it down, and get back to your crummy first draft.

A writer friend of mine suggests opening the jar and shooting 11 them all in the head. But I think he's a little angry, and I'm sure nothing like this would ever occur to you.

Meaning

1. What is Lamott's thesis? Which sentences best convey her main idea?
2. According to Lamott, what role can other people, real or imaginary, play in the writing process? Are they helpful?
3. Review the comment by Lamott's friend (paragraph 8) that "the first draft is the down draft. . . . The second draft is the up draft. . . . And the third draft is the dental draft. . . ." What do you think is the difference in the writer's approach and focus at each stage? In what ways, if any, do these stages relate to your own approach to writing?
4. What do you think Lamott means when she says that "writing is, for some of us, the latch that keeps the door of the pen closed, keeps those crazy, ravenous dogs contained" (paragraph 9). What might the dogs and control of them stand for in this image?

Purpose and Audience

1. What is the purpose of Lamott's piece? To advise inexperienced writers? To relate her own difficulties with writing? Both, or something else? How do you know?

2. Lamott's book *Bird by Bird*, the source of this piece, is subtitled *Some Instructions on Writing and Life*. Who do you believe would find Lamott's advice most useful? Will it be useful to you? Why, or why not?

Method and Structure

1. In paragraph 4 Lamott says that she wrote food reviews "one dish at a time" and "bird by bird" (a metaphor from earlier in her book, meaning one step at a time). What steps does her process analysis outline for overcoming obstacles?

2. Process analysis can be directive or explanatory (see p. 177), and Lamott's piece has good examples of both types. In which paragraphs does Lamott use each type or combine them? What does each type contribute? Is the mixture effective? Why, or why not?

3. What transitions does Lamott use to guide the reader through the steps of her process analysis? Is her use of transitions effective?

4. **Other Methods**   Paragraphs 3–7 narrate Lamott's experience writing food reviews for a magazine. What is the effect of this story?

Language

1. Although trying to be encouraging, Lamott uses many negative adjectives to describe her own first efforts: for example, "terrible" (paragraph 4) and "incoherent" (5). Find some other examples of negative adjectives. Why do you think Lamott uses so many of them?

2. What is Lamott's tone? How seriously does she take the difficulties facing the writer? (If necessary, see the Glossary for the definition of *tone*.)

3. Lamott uses several original images, such as the "vinegar-lipped Reader Lady" (paragraph 9). List some images that made a particular impression on you, and explain their effect.

Writing Topics

1. Write an essay that explains your own writing process (in general or on a specific project) as you progress from idea to final draft. Enliven the process with specific methods and incidents—techniques of procrastination, ripping up draft after draft, listening to and silencing (or not) your own imagined voices, and so on. Try to draw some conclusions about what the writing process means to you.

2. Writing is, of course, only one way to communicate ideas. Other forms of communication can also be difficult: speaking up in class, making

a presentation to a group of people, meeting with a teacher, interviewing for a job, making an important telephone call. Write a process analysis in which you first examine an oral encounter that was particularly difficult for you and then offer advice about how best to tackle such a situation.

3. We are usually taught to respect our parents and other authority figures, but Lamott advises writers to ignore them while composing. Is her advice justified in your view? Are there times when we can, even should, disregard authority? Write an essay about a time when you felt you could accomplish something only by disregarding the advice of someone you would normally listen to — or, in contrast, when you heeded advice even though it held you back or ignored advice and eventually regretted doing so. How difficult was your action? How did the situation turn out? Looking back, do you believe you did the right thing?

JESSICA MITFORD

Tough-minded, commonsensical, and witty, Jessica Mitford was described by Time *magazine as the "Queen of Muckrakers." She was born in England in 1917, the sixth of Lord and Lady Redesdale's seven children, and was educated entirely at home. Her highly eccentric family is the subject of novels by her sister Nancy Mitford and of her own autobiographical* Daughters and Rebels *(1960). In 1939, a few years after she left home, Mitford took up permanent residence in the United States, becoming a naturalized American citizen in 1944. Shortly afterward, moved by her long-standing antifascism and the promise of equality in a socialist society, she joined the American Communist party; her years as a "Red Menace" are recounted in* A Fine Old Conflict *(1977). In the late 1950s she turned to investigative journalism, researching and exposing numerous instances of deception, greed, and foolishness in American society. Her articles appeared in the* Nation, Esquire, *the* Atlantic, *and other magazines, and many of them are collected in* Poison Penmanship: The Gentle Art of Muckraking *(1979). Her book-length exposés include* The Trial of Dr. Spock *(1969),* Kind and Usual Punishment: The Prison Business *(1973), and* The American Way of Birth *(1992). Mitford died in 1996.*

Embalming Mr. Jones

In 1963 Mitford published The American Way of Death, *a daring and influential look at the standard practices of the American funeral industry. (*The American Way of Death Revisited, *nearly complete at Mitford's death, was published in 1998.) Mitford pegs the modern American funeral as "the most irrational and weirdest" custom of our affluent society, in which "the trappings of Gracious Living are transformed, as in a nightmare, into the trappings of Gracious Dying." This excerpt from the book, an analysis of the process of embalming a corpse and restoring it for viewing, demonstrates Mitford's sharp eye for detail, commanding style, and caustic wit.*

The drama begins to unfold with the arrival of the corpse at the   1
mortuary.

Alas, poor Yorick![1] How surprised he would be to see how his   2
counterpart of today is whisked off to a funeral parlor and is in short
order, sprayed, sliced, pierced, pickled, trussed, trimmed, creamed,
waxed, painted, rouged, and neatly dressed—transformed from a common corpse into a Beautiful Memory Picture. This process is known
in the trade as embalming and restorative art, and is so universally
employed in the United States and Canada that the funeral director
does it routinely, without consulting corpse or kin. He regards as
eccentric those few who are hardy enough to suggest that it might be
dispensed with. Yet no law requires embalming, no religious doctrine
commends it, nor is it dictated by considerations of health, sanitation, or even of personal daintiness. In no part of the world but in
Northern America is it widely used. The purpose of embalming is to
make the corpse presentable for viewing in a suitably costly container;
and here too the funeral director routinely, without first consulting
the family, prepares the body for public display.

Is all this legal? The processes to which a dead body may be sub-   3
jected are after all to some extent circumscribed by law. In most
states, for instance, the signature of next of kin must be obtained
before an autopsy may be performed, before the deceased may be
cremated, before the body may be turned over to a medical school for
research purposes; or such provision must be made in the decedent's
will. In the case of embalming, no such permission is required nor is
it ever sought.[2] A textbook, *The Principles and Practices of Embalming*,
comments on this: "There is some question regarding the legality of
much that is done within the preparation room." The author points
out that it would be most unusual for a responsible member of a

[1]A line from Shakespeare's *Hamlet*, spoken by Hamlet in a graveyard as he
contemplates the skull of the former jester in his father's court. [Editor's note.]

[2]In 1982, nineteen years after this was written, the Federal Trade Commission
issued comprehensive regulations on the funeral industry, including the requirement that funeral providers prepare an itemized price list for their goods and services. The list must include a notice that embalming is not required by law, along
with an indication of the charge for embalming and an explanation of the alternatives. Consumers must give permission for embalming before they may be
charged for it. Shortly before her death, however, Mitford wrote that thirteen
years after the ruling the FTC had "watered down" the regulations and "routinely
ignored" consumer complaints against the funeral industry, enforcing the regulations only forty-two times. [Editor's note.]

bereaved family to instruct the mortician, in so many words, to *"embalm"* the body of a deceased relative. The very term *embalming* is so seldom used that the mortician must rely upon custom in the matter. The author concludes that unless the family specifies otherwise, the act of entrusting the body to the care of a funeral establishment carries with it an implied permission to go ahead and embalm.

Embalming is indeed a most extraordinary procedure, and one   4
must wonder at the docility of Americans who each year pay hundreds of millions of dollars for its perpetuation, blissfully ignorant of what it is all about, what is done, how it is done. Not one in ten thousand has any idea of what actually takes place. Books on the subject are extremely hard to come by. They are not to be found in most libraries or bookshops.

In an era when huge television audiences watch surgical operations   5
in the comfort of their living rooms, when, thanks to the animated cartoon, the geography of the digestive system has become familiar territory even to the nursery school set, in a land where the satisfaction of curiosity about all matters is a national pastime, the secrecy surrounding embalming can, surely, hardly be attributed to the inherent gruesomeness of the subject. Custom in this regard has within this century suffered a complete reversal. In the early days of American embalming, when it was performed in the home of the deceased, it was almost mandatory for some relative to stay by the embalmer's side and witness the procedure. Today, family members who might wish to be in attendance would certainly be dissuaded by the funeral director. All others, except apprentices, are excluded by law from the preparation room.

A close look at what does actually take place may explain in large   6
measure the undertaker's intractable reticence concerning a procedure that has become his major *raison d'être*.[3] Is it possible he fears that public information about embalming might lead patrons to wonder if they really want this service? If the funeral men are loath to discuss the subject outside the trade, the reader may, understandably, be equally loath to go on reading at this point. For those who have the stomach for it, let us part the formaldehyde curtain. . . .

The body is first laid out in the undertaker's morgue — or rather,   7
Mr. Jones is reposing in the preparation room — to be readied to bid the world farewell.

The preparation room in any of the better funeral establish-   8
ments has the tiled and sterile look of a surgery, and indeed the embalmer–restorative artist who does his chores there is beginning

---

[3]French, meaning "reason for being." [Editor's note.]

to adopt the term "dermasurgeon" (appropriately corrupted by some mortician-writers as "demisurgeon") to describe his calling. His equipment, consisting of scalpels, scissors, augers, forceps, clamps, needles, pumps, tubes, bowls and basins, is crudely imitative of the surgeon's, as is his technique, acquired in a nine- or twelve-month post–high-school course in an embalming school. He is supplied by an advanced chemical industry with a bewildering array of fluids, sprays, pastes, oils, powders, creams, to fix or soften tissue, shrink or distend it as needed, dry it here, restore the moisture there. There are cosmetics, waxes, and paints to fill and cover features, even plaster of Paris to replace entire limbs. There are ingenious aids to prop and stabilize the cadaver: a Vari-Pose Head Rest, the Edwards Arm and Hand Positioner, the Repose Block (to support the shoulders during the embalming), and the Throop Foot Positioner, which resembles an old-fashioned stocks.

Mr. John H. Eckels, president of the Eckels College of Mortuary   9
Science, thus describes the first part of the embalming procedure: "In the hands of a skilled practitioner, this work may be done in a comparatively short time and without mutilating the body other than by slight incision—so slight that it scarcely would cause serious inconvenience if made upon a living person. It is necessary to remove the blood, and doing this not only helps in the disinfecting, but removes the principal cause of disfigurements due to discoloration."

Another textbook discusses the all-important time element: "The   10
earlier this is done, the better, for every hour that elapses between death and embalming will add to the problems and complications encountered. . . ." Just how soon should one get going on the embalming? The author tells us, "On the basis of such scanty information made available to this profession through its rudimentary and haphazard system of technical research, we must conclude that the best results are to be obtained if the subject is embalmed before life is completely extinct—that is, before cellular death has occurred. In the average case, this would mean within an hour after somatic death." For those who feel that there is something a little rudimentary, not to say haphazard, about this advice, a comforting thought is offered by another writer. Speaking of fears entertained in early days of premature burial, he points out, "One of the effects of embalming by chemical injection, however, has been to dispel fears of live burial." How true; once the blood is removed, chances of live burial are indeed remote.

To return to Mr. Jones, the blood is drained out through the veins   11
and replaced by embalming fluid pumped in through the arteries. As noted in *The Principles and Practices of Embalming*, "every operator

has a favorite injection and drainage point—a fact which becomes a handicap only if he fails or refuses to forsake his favorites when conditions demand it." Typical favorites are the carotid artery, femoral artery, jugular vein, subclavian vein. There are various choices of embalming fluid. If Flextone is used, it will produce a "mild, flexible rigidity. The skin retains a velvety softness, the tissues are rubbery and pliable. Ideal for women and children." It may be blended with B. and G. Products Company's Lyf-Lyk tint, which is guaranteed to reproduce "nature's own skin texture . . . the velvety appearance of living tissue." Suntone comes in three separate tints: Suntan; Special Cosmetic Tint, a pink shade "especially indicated for young female subjects"; and Regular Cosmetic Tint, moderately pink.

About three to six gallons of a dyed and perfumed solution of   12 formaldehyde, glycerin, borax, phenol, alcohol, and water is soon circulating through Mr. Jones, whose mouth has been sewn together with a "needle directed upward between the upper lip and gum and brought out through the left nostril," with the corners raised slightly "for a more pleasant expression." If he should be bucktoothed, his teeth are cleaned with Bon Ami and coated with colorless nail polish. His eyes, meanwhile, are closed with flesh-tinted eye caps and eye cement.

The next step is to have at Mr. Jones with a thing called a trocar.   13 This is a long, hollow needle attached to a tube. It is jabbed into the abdomen, poked around the entrails and chest cavity, the contents of which are pumped out and replaced with "cavity fluid." This done, and the hole in the abdomen sewn up, Mr. Jones's face is heavily creamed (to protect the skin from burns which may be caused by leakage of the chemicals), and he is covered with a sheet and left unmolested for a while. But not for long—there is more, much more, in store for him. He has been embalmed, but not yet restored, and the best time to start the restorative work is eight to ten hours after embalming, when the tissues have become firm and dry.

The object of all this attention to the corpse, it must be remem-   14 bered, is to make it presentable for viewing in an attitude of healthy repose. "Our customs require the presentation of our dead in the semblance of normality . . . unmarred by the ravages of illness, disease or mutilation," says Mr. J. Sheridan Mayer in his *Restorative Art*. This is a rather large order since few people die in the full bloom of health, unravaged by illness and unmarked by some disfigurement. The funeral industry is equal to the challenge: "In some cases the gruesome appearance of a mutilated or disease-ridden subject may be quite discouraging. The task of restoration may seem impossible and shake the confidence of the embalmer. This is the time for intestinal fortitude and determination. Once the formative work is begun and affected tissues are cleaned or removed, all doubts of success vanish. It is surprising and gratifying to discover the results which may be obtained."

The embalmer, having allowed an appropriate interval to elapse, 15 returns to the attack, but now he brings into play the skill and equipment of sculptor and cosmetician. Is a hand missing? Casting one in plaster of Paris is a simple matter. "For replacement purposes, only a cast of the back of the hand is necessary; this is within the ability of the average operator and is quite adequate." If a lip or two, a nose or an ear should be missing, the embalmer has at hand a variety of restorative waxes with which to model replacements. Pores and skin texture are simulated by stippling with a little brush, and over this cosmetics are laid on. Head off? Decapitation cases are rather routinely handled. Ragged edges are trimmed, and head joined to torso with a series of splints, wires and sutures. It is a good idea to have a little something at the neck—a scarf or high collar—when time for viewing comes. Swollen mouth? Cut out tissue as needed from inside the lips. If too much is removed, the surface contour can easily be restored by padding with cotton. Swollen necks and cheeks are reduced by removing tissue through vertical incisions made down each side of the neck. "When the deceased is casketed, the pillow will hide the suture incisions . . . as an extra precaution against leakage, the suture may be painted with liquid sealer."

The opposite condition is more likely to present itself—that of 16 emaciation. His hypodermic syringe now loaded with massage cream, the embalmer seeks out and fills the hollowed and sunken areas by injection. In this procedure the backs of the hands and fingers and the under-chin area should not be neglected.

Positioning the lips is a problem that recurrently challenges the 17 ingenuity of the embalmer. Closed too tightly they tend to give a stern, even disapproving expression. Ideally, embalmers feel, the lips should give the impression of being ever so slightly parted, the upper lip protruding slightly for a more youthful appearance. This takes some engineering, however, as the lips tend to drift apart. Lip drift can sometimes be remedied by pushing one or two straight pins through the inner margin of the lower lip and then inserting them between the two upper front teeth. If Mr. Jones happens to have no teeth, the pins can just as easily be anchored in his Armstrong Face Former and Denture Replacer. Another method to maintain lip closure is to dislocate the lower jaw, which is then held in its new position by a wire run through holes which have been drilled through the upper and lower jaws at the midline. As the French are fond of saying, *il faut souffrir pour être belle*.[4]

If Mr. Jones has died of jaundice, the embalming fluid will very 18 likely turn him green. Does this deter the embalmer? Not if he has intestinal fortitude. Masking pastes and cosmetics are heavily laid on, burial garments and casket interiors are color-correlated with particular care, and Jones is displayed beneath rose-colored lights. Friends will say, "How *well* he looks." Death by carbon monoxide, on the other hand, can be rather a good thing from the embalmer's viewpoint: "One advantage is the fact that this type of discoloration is an exaggerated form of a natural pink coloration." This is nice because the healthy glow is already present and needs but little attention.

The patching and filling completed, Mr. Jones is now shaved, 19 washed, and dressed. Cream-based cosmetic, available in pink, flesh, suntan, brunette, and blond, is applied to his hands and face, his hair is shampooed and combed (and, in the case of Mrs. Jones, set), his hands manicured. For the horny-handed son of toil special care must be taken; cream should be applied to remove ingrained grime, and the nails cleaned. "If he were not in the habit of having them manicured in life, trimming and shaping is advised for better appearance—never questioned by kin."

Jones is now ready for casketing (this is the present participle of 20 the verb "to casket"). In this operation his right shoulder should be depressed slightly "to turn the body a bit to the right and soften the appearance of lying flat on the back." Positioning the hands is a matter of importance, and special rubber positioning blocks may be used. The hands should be cupped slightly for a more lifelike, relaxed appearance. Proper placement of the body requires a delicate sense of balance. It should lie as high as possible in the casket, yet not so high that the lid, when lowered, will hit the nose. On the other hand, we are cautioned, placing the body too low "creates the impression that the body is in a box."

Jones is next wheeled into the appointed slumber room where a 21 few last touches may be added—his favorite pipe placed in his hand or, if he was a great reader, a book propped into position. (In the case of little Master Jones a Teddy bear may be clutched.) Here he will hold open house for a few days, visiting hours 10 AM to 9 PM.

[4]French, meaning "It is necessary to suffer in order to be beautiful." [Editor's note.]

Meaning

1. According to Mitford, what is the purpose of embalming and restoration (see paragraphs 2 and 14)? If they are not required by law or religion or "considerations of health, sanitation, or even of personal daintiness," why are they routinely performed?
2. Why do Americans know so little about embalming (paragraphs 3–6)? Does Mitford blame Americans themselves, the funeral industry, or both?

Purpose and Audience

1. What does Mitford reveal about her purpose when she questions whether the undertaker "fears that public information about embalming might lead patrons to wonder if they really want this service" (paragraph 6)?
2. Mitford's chief assumption about her readers is evident in paragraph 4. What is it?
3. Most readers find Mitford's essay humorous. Assuming you did, too, which details or comments struck you as especially amusing? How does Mitford use humor to achieve her purpose?

Method and Structure

1. Why do you think Mitford chose the method of process analysis to explore this particular social custom? What does the method allow her to convey about the custom? How does this information help her achieve her purpose?
2. Despite the fact that her purpose goes beyond mere explanation, does Mitford explain the process of embalming and restoration clearly enough for you to understand how it's done and what the reasons for each step are? Starting at paragraph 7, what are the main steps in the process?
3. Mitford interrupts the sequence of steps in the process several times. What information does she provide in paragraphs 8, 10, and 14 to make the interruptions worthwhile?
4. **Other Methods**   Mitford occasionally uses other methods to develop her process analysis—for instance, in paragraph 8 she combines description and classification to present the embalmer's preparation room and tools; and in paragraph 5 she uses contrast to note changes in the family's knowledge of embalming. What does this contrast suggest about our current attitudes toward death and the dead?

Language

1. How would you characterize Mitford's tone? Support your answer with specific details, sentence structures, and words in the essay. (See the Glossary for a discussion of *tone*.)

2. Mitford is more than a little ironic—that is, she often says one thing when she means another or deliberately understates her meaning. Here are two examples from paragraph 10: "the all-important time element" in the embalming of a corpse; "How true; once the blood is removed, chances of live burial are indeed remote." What additional examples do you find? What does this persistent irony contribute to Mitford's tone? (For a fuller explanation of *irony*, consult the Glossary.)

3. Mitford's style in this essay is often informal, even conversational, as in "The next step is to have at Mr. Jones with a thing called a trocar" (paragraph 13). But equally often she seems to imitate the technical, impersonal style of the embalming textbooks she quotes so extensively, as in "Another method to maintain lip closure is to dislocate the lower jaw" (17). What other examples of each style do you find? What does each style contribute to Mitford's purpose? Is the contrast effective, or would a consistent style, one way or the other, be more effective? Why?

Writing Topics

1. Think of a modern custom or practice that you find ridiculous, barbaric, tedious, or otherwise objectionable. Write an essay that analyzes the process by which your chosen custom or practice unfolds. Following Mitford's model, explain the process clearly while also conveying your attitude toward it.

2. Elsewhere in her book *The American Way of Death*, Mitford notes that the open casket at funerals, which creates the need for embalming and restoration, is "a custom unknown in other parts of the world. Foreigners are astonished by it." Write an essay in which you explore the possible reasons for the custom in the United States. Or, if you have strong feelings about closed or open caskets at funerals— derived from religious beliefs, family tradition, or some other source— write an essay agreeing or disagreeing with Mitford's treatment of embalming and restoration.

3. Read about funeral customs in another country. Write an essay in which you analyze the process covered in your sources and use it as the basis for agreeing or disagreeing with Mitford's opinion of embalming and restoration.

Writing with the Method
Process Analysis

Choose one of the following topics, or any other topic they suggest, for an essay developed by process analysis. The topic you decide on should be something you care about so that process analysis is a means of communicating an idea, not an end in itself.

TECHNOLOGY AND THE ENVIRONMENT
1. How an engine or other machine works
2. How the Internet works
3. Setting up a recycling program in a home or an office
4. How solar energy can be converted into electricity

EDUCATION AND CAREER
5. How children learn to dress themselves, play with others, read, or write
6. Interviewing for a job
7. Succeeding in biology, history, computer science, or another course
8. Learning a foreign language
9. Coping with a bad boss

ENTERTAINMENT AND HOBBIES
10. Keeping a car in good shape
11. Throwing a really *bad* party
12. Playing a sport or a musical instrument
13. Making great chili or some other dish

HEALTH AND APPEARANCE
14. Getting physically fit
15. Climbing a mountain
16. Dieting
17. Cutting or coloring one's own hair

FAMILY AND FRIENDS
18. Offering constructive criticism to a friend
19. Driving your parents, brother, sister, friend, or roommate crazy
20. Minimizing sibling rivalry
21. Making new friends in a new place

Chapter Seven

COMPARISON AND CONTRAST

USING THE METHOD

An insomniac watching late-night television faces a choice between two World War II movies broadcasting at the same time. To make up his mind, he uses the dual method of comparison and contrast.

- **Comparison** shows the similarities between two or more subjects: the similar broadcast times and topics of the two movies force the insomniac to choose between them.
- **Contrast** shows the differences between subjects: the different actors, locations, and reputations of the two movies make it possible for the insomniac to choose one.

As in this example, comparison and contrast usually work together because any subjects that warrant side-by-side examination usually resemble each other in some respects and differ in others. (Since comparison and contrast are so closely related, the terms *comparison* and *compare* will be used from now on to designate both.)

You'll generally write a comparison for one of two purposes:

- To explain the similarities and differences between subjects so as to make either or both of them clear—an explanatory comparison.
- To evaluate subjects so as to establish their advantages and disadvantages, strengths and weaknesses—an evaluative comparison.

The explanatory comparison does not take a position on the relative merits of the subjects; the evaluative comparison does, and it usually concludes with a preference or a suggested course of action. In an explanatory comparison you might show how new income-tax laws differ from old laws. In an evaluative comparison on the same subject, you might argue that the old laws were more equitable than the new ones are.

Whether explanatory or evaluative, comparisons treat two or more subjects in the same general class or group: tax laws, religions, attitudes toward marriage, diseases, advertising strategies, diets, contact sports, friends. You may define the class to suit your interest—for instance, you might focus on Tuesday night's television shows, on network news programs, or on old situation comedies. The class likeness ensures that the subjects share enough features to make comparison worthwhile. With subjects from different classes, such as an insect and a tree, the similarities are so few and differences so numerous—and both are so obvious—that explaining them would be pointless.

In writing a comparison, you not only select subjects from the same class but also, using division or analysis, identify the features shared by the subjects. These **points of comparison** are the attributes of the class and thus of the subjects within the class. For instance, the points of comparison for diets may be forbidden foods, allowed foods, speed of weight loss, and nutritional quality; for air pollutants they may be sources and dangers to plants, animals, and humans. These points help you arrange similarities and differences between subjects, and, more important, they ensure direct comparison rather than a random listing of unrelated characteristics.

In an effective comparison, a thesis or controlling idea governs the choice of class, points of comparison, and specific similarities and differences, while also making the comparison worthwhile for the reader. The thesis of an evaluative comparison generally emerges naturally because it coincides with the writer's purpose of supporting a preference for one subject over another:

THESIS SENTENCE (EVALUATION)   The two diets result in similarly rapid weight loss, but Harris's requires much more self-discipline and is nutritionally much riskier than Marconi's.

In an explanatory comparison, however, the thesis does more than merely reflect the general purpose of explaining. It should go beyond the obvious and begin to identify the points of comparison. For example:

TENTATIVE THESIS SENTENCE (EXPLANATION)   Rugby and American football are the same in some respects and different in others.

REVISED THESIS SENTENCE (EXPLANATION)   Though rugby requires less strength and more stamina than American football, the two games are very much alike in their rules and strategies.

These examples suggest other decisions you must make when writing a comparison:

- Should the subjects be treated in equal detail, or should one be emphasized over the others? Generally, give the subjects equal emphasis when they are equally familiar or are being evaluated (as the diets are in the previous example). Stress one subject over the others when it is less familiar (as rugby is in this country).
- Should the essay focus on similarities or differences, or both? Generally, stress them equally when all the points of comparison are equally familiar or important. Stress the differences between subjects usually considered similar (such as diets) or the similarities between subjects usually considered different (such as rugby and American football).

With two or more subjects, several points of comparison, many similarities and differences, and a particular emphasis, comparison clearly requires a firm organizational hand. You have two options for arranging a comparison:

- **Subject-by-subject,** in which you group the points of comparison under each subject so that the *subjects* are covered one at a time.
- **Point-by-point,** in which you group the subjects under each point of comparison so that the *points* are covered one at a time.

The following brief outlines illustrate the different arrangements as they might be applied to diets:

Subject-by-subject	*Point-by-point*
Harris's diet	Speed of weight loss
Speed of weight loss	Harris's diet
Required self-discipline	Marconi's diet
Nutritional risk	
	Required self-discipline
Marconi's diet	Harris's diet
Speed of weight loss	Marconi's diet
Required self-discipline	
Nutritional risk	Nutritional risk
	Harris's diet
	Marconi's diet

Because the subject-by-subject arrangement presents each subject as a coherent unit, it is particularly useful for comparing impressions of subjects: the dissimilar characters of two friends, for instance. However, covering the subjects one at a time can break an essay into discrete pieces and strain readers' memories, so this arrangement is usually confined to essays that are short or that compare several subjects briefly. For longer papers requiring precise treatment of the individual points of comparison—say, an evaluation of two proposals for a new student-aid policy—the point-by-point arrangement is more useful. Its chief disadvantage is that the reader can get lost in details and fail to see any subject as a whole. Because each arrangement has its strengths and weaknesses, you may sometimes combine the two in a single work, using the divided arrangement to introduce or summarize overall impressions of the subjects and using the alternating arrangement to deal specifically with the points of comparison.

DEVELOPING AN ESSAY BY COMPARISON AND CONTRAST

Getting Started

Whenever you observe similarities or differences between two or more members of the same general class—activities, people, ideas, things, places—you have a possible subject for comparison and contrast. Just be sure that the subjects are worth comparing and that you can do the job in the space and time allowed. For instance, if you have a week to complete a three-page paper, don't try to show all the similarities and differences between country-and-western music and rhythm-and-blues. The effort can only frustrate you and irritate your readers. Instead, limit the subjects to a manageable size—for instance, the lyrics of a representative song in each type of music—so that you can develop the comparisons completely and specifically.

To generate ideas for a comparison, explore each subject separately to pick out its characteristics, and then explore the subjects together to see what characteristics one suggests for the other. Look for points of comparison. Early on, you can use division or analysis (Chapter 4) to identify points of comparison by breaking the subjects' general class into its elements. A song lyric, for instance, could be divided into story line or plot, basic emotion, and special language such as dialect or slang. After you have explored your subjects fully, you can use classification (Chapter 5) to group your characteristics under the points of comparison. For instance, you might classify characteristics of two proposals for a new student-aid policy into qualifications for aid, minimum and maximum amounts to be made available, and repayment terms.

While you are shaping your ideas, you should begin formulating your controlling idea, your thesis. As discussed on pages 203–4, the thesis should reflect your answers to these questions:

- Do the ideas suggest an explanatory or evaluative comparison?
- If explanatory, what point will the comparison make so that it does not merely recite the obvious?
- If evaluative, what preference or recommendation will you express?
- Will you emphasize both subjects equally or stress one over the other?
- Will you emphasize differences or similarities, or both?

As you gain increasing control over your material, consider also the needs of your readers:

- Do they know your subjects well, or should you take special care to explain one or both of them?
- Will your readers be equally interested in similarities and differences, or will they find one more enlightening than the other?
- If your essay is evaluative, are your readers likely to be biased against your preference? If so, you will need to support your case with plenty of specific reasons.

Most readers know intuitively how a comparison works, so they will expect you to balance your comparison feature for feature. In other words, all the features you mention for the first subject should be mentioned as well for the second, and any features not mentioned for the first subject should not suddenly materialize for the second.

Organizing

Your readers' needs and expectations can also help you plan your essay's organization. An effective introduction to a comparison essay often provides some context for readers—the situation that prompts the comparison, for instance, or the need for the comparison. Placing your thesis sentence in the introduction also informs readers of your purpose and point, and it may help keep you focused while you write.

For the body of the essay, choose the arrangement that will present your material most clearly and effectively. Remember that the subject-by-subject arrangement suits brief essays that compare dominant impressions of the subjects, whereas the point-by-point arrangement suits longer essays that require emphasis on the individual points of comparison. If you are torn between the two—wanting both to sum up each subject and to show the two side by side—then a combined arrangement may be your wisest choice.

A rough outline like the models on page 204 can help you plan the basic arrangement of your essay and also the order of the subjects and points of comparison. If your subjects are equally familiar to your readers and equally important to you, then it may not matter which subject you treat first, even in a subject-by-subject arrangement. But if one subject is less familiar or if you favor one, then that one should probably come second. You can also arrange the points themselves to reflect their importance and your readers' knowledge: from least to most significant or complex, from most to least familiar. Be sure to use the same order for both subjects.

The conclusion to a comparison essay can help readers see the whole picture: the chief similarities and differences between two subjects compared in a divided arrangement, or the chief characteristics of subjects compared in an alternating arrangement. In addition, you may want to comment on the significance of your comparison, advise readers on how they can use the information you have provided, or recommend a specific course of action for them to follow. As with all other methods of development, the choice of conclusion should reflect the impression you want to leave with readers.

Drafting

Drafting your essay gives you the chance to spell out your comparison so that it supports your thesis or, if your thesis is still tentative, to find your idea by writing into it. You can use paragraphs to help manage the comparison as it unfolds:

- In a subject-by-subject arrangement, if you devote two paragraphs to the first subject, try to do the same for the second subject. For both subjects, try to cover the points of comparison in the same order and group the same ones in paragraphs.
- In a point-by-point arrangement, balance the paragraphs as you move back and forth between subjects. If you treat several points

of comparison for the first subject in one paragraph, do the same for the second subject. If you apply a single point of comparison to both subjects in one paragraph, do the same for the next point of comparison.

This way of drafting will help you achieve balance in your comparison and see where you may need more information to flesh out your subjects and your points. If the finished draft seems to march too rigidly in its pattern, you can always loosen things up when revising (see the next section).

Revising and Editing

When you are revising and editing your draft, use the following questions to be certain that your essay meets the principal requirements of the comparative method.

- *Are your subjects drawn from the same class?* The subjects must have notable differences *and* notable similarities to make comparison worthwhile—though, of course, you may stress one group over the other.
- *Does your essay have a clear purpose and say something significant about the subject?* Your purpose of explaining or evaluating and the point you are making should be evident in your thesis *and* throughout the essay. A vague, pointless comparison will quickly bore readers.
- *Do you apply all points of comparison to both subjects?* Even if you emphasize one subject, the two subjects must match feature for feature. An unmatched comparison may leave readers with unanswered questions or weaken their confidence in your authority.
- *Does the pattern of comparison suit readers' needs and the complexity of the material?* Although readers will appreciate a clear organization and roughly equal treatment of your subjects and points of comparison, they will also appreciate some variety in the way you move back and forth. You don't have to devote a sentence to each point, first for one subject and then for the other, or alternate subjects sentence by sentence through several paragraphs. Instead, you might write a single sentence on one point or subject but four sentences on the other—if that's what your information requires.

Suzanne Britt has contributed essays and articles to the New York Times, Newsweek, *and the* Boston Globe, *and she has published two collections of essays,* Skinny People Are Dull and Crunchy Like Carrots *(1982) and* Show and Tell *(1983). She has also authored two college English textbooks and published her poetry in literary magazines such as* Denver Quarterly *and* Southern Poetry Review. *Born in Winston-Salem, North Carolina, Britt teaches part-time at Meredith College in North Carolina.*

Neat People
vs.
Sloppy People

In "Neat People vs. Sloppy People," from Show and Tell, *Britt explores the fundamental differences underlying these two kinds of people. She uses humor in her comparison to challenge the way we think about our habits.*

I've finally figured out the difference between neat people and 1 sloppy people. The distinction is, as always, moral. Neat people are lazier and meaner than sloppy people.

Sloppy people, you see, are not really sloppy. Their sloppiness is 2 merely the unfortunate consequence of their extreme moral rectitude. Sloppy people carry in their mind's eye a heavenly vision, a precise plan, that is so stupendous, so perfect, it can't be achieved in this world or the next.

Sloppy people live in Never-Never Land. Someday is their métier. 3 Someday they are planning to alphabetize all their books and set up home catalogs. Someday they will go through their wardrobes and mark certain items for tentative mending and certain items for passing on to relatives of similar shape and size. Someday sloppy people will make family scrapbooks into which they will put newspaper clippings, postcards, locks of hair, and the dried corsage from their senior prom. Someday they will file everything on the surface of their desks, including the cash receipts from coffee purchases at the snack shop. Someday they will sit down and read all the back issues of the *New Yorker*.

For all these noble reasons and more, sloppy people never get neat.   4
They aim too high and wide. They save everything, planning someday to file, order, and straighten out the world. But while these ambitious plans take clearer and clearer shape in their heads, the books spill from the shelves onto the floor, the clothes pile up in the hamper and closet, the family mementos accumulate in every drawer, the surface of the desk is buried under mounds of paper, and the unread magazines threaten to reach the ceiling.

Sloppy people can't bear to part with anything. They give loving   5
attention to every detail. When sloppy people say they're going to tackle the surface of a desk, they really mean it. Not a paper will go unturned; not a rubber band will go unboxed. Four hours or two weeks into the excavation, the desk looks exactly the same, primarily because the sloppy person is meticulously creating new piles of papers with new headings and scrupulously stopping to read all the old book catalogs before he throws them away. A neat person would just bulldoze the desk.

Neat people are bums and clods at heart. They have cavalier atti-   6
tudes toward possessions, including family heirlooms. Everything is just another dust-catcher to them. If anything collects dust, it's got to go and that's that. Neat people will toy with the idea of throwing the children out of the house just to cut down on the clutter.

Neat people don't care about process. They like results. What they   7
want to do is get the whole thing over with so they can sit down and watch the rasslin' on TV. Neat people operate on two unvarying principles: Never handle any item twice, and throw everything away.

The only thing messy in a neat person's house is the trash can. The   8
minute something comes to a neat person's hand, he will look at it, try to decide if it has immediate use and, finding none, throw it in the trash.

Neat people are especially vicious with mail. They never go through   9
their mail unless they are standing directly over a trash can. If the trash can is beside the mailbox, even better. All ads, catalogs, pleas for charitable contributions, church bulletins, and money-saving coupons go straight into the trash can without being opened. All letters from home, postcards from Europe, bills, and paychecks are opened, immediately responded to, then dropped in the trash can. Neat people keep their receipts only for tax purposes. That's it. No

sentimental salvaging of birthday cards or the last letter a dying relative ever wrote. Into the trash it goes.

Neat people place neatness above everything, even economics. 10 They are incredibly wasteful. Neat people throw away several toys every time they walk through the den. I knew a neat person once who threw away a perfectly good dish drainer because it had mold on it. The drainer was too much trouble to wash. And neat people sell their furniture when they move. They will sell a La-Z-Boy recliner while you are reclining in it.

Neat people are no good to borrow from. Neat people buy every- 11 thing in expensive little single portions. They get their flour and sugar in two-pound bags. They wouldn't consider clipping a coupon, saving a leftover, reusing plastic nondairy whipped cream containers, or rinsing off tin foil and draping it over the unmoldy dish drainer. You can never borrow a neat person's newspaper to see what's playing at the movies. Neat people have the paper all wadded up and in the trash by 7:05 AM.

Neat people cut a clean swath through the organic as well as the 12 inorganic world. People, animals, and things are all one to them. They are so insensitive. After they've finished with the pantry, the medicine cabinet, and the attic, they will throw out the red geranium (too many leaves), sell the dog (too many fleas), and send the children off to boarding school (too many scuff-marks on the hardwood floors).

Meaning

1. "Suzanne Britt believes that neat people are lazy, mean, petty, callous, wasteful, and insensitive." How do you respond to this statement?
2. What is meant by "as always" in the sentence "The distinction is, as always, moral" (paragraph 1)? Does the author seem to be suggesting that any and all distinctions between people are moral?

Purpose and Audience

1. Is the author's main purpose to make fun of neat people, to assess the habits of neat and sloppy people, to help neat and sloppy people get along better, to defend sloppy people, to amuse and entertain, or to prove that neat people are morally inferior to sloppy people? Discuss.
2. Is Britt writing primarily to neat people, to sloppy people, or to both? How do you think each group would react to the essay? What is *your* reaction?

Method and Structure

1. Britt mentions no similarities between neat and sloppy people. Does that mean this is not a good comparison and contrast essay? Why might a writer deliberately focus on differences and give very little or no time to similarities?

2. Consider the following generalizations: "For all these noble reasons and more, sloppy people never get neat" (paragraph 4) and "The only thing messy in a neat person's house is the trash can" (8). How can you tell that these statements are generalizations? Look for other generalizations in the essay. What is the effect of using so many?

3. **Other Methods**   Although filled with generalizations, Britt's essay does not lack for examples. Study the examples in paragraph 11 and explain how they do and don't work the way examples should: to bring the generalizations about people down to earth.

Language

1. What is the general tone of this essay? What words and phrases help you determine that tone? (If necessary, see *tone* in the Glossary.)

2. How do you understand the use of the word *noble* in the first sentence of paragraph 4? Is it meant literally? Are there other words in the essay that appear to be written in a similar tone?

Writing Topics

1. What oppositions do you use to evaluate people? Smart versus dumb? Hip versus clueless? Fun versus dull? Choose your favorite opposition for evaluating people, and write an essay in which you compare and contrast those who pass your "test" with those who fail it. You may choose to write your essay tongue-in-cheek, as Britt does, or seriously.

2. Write an essay in which you compare and contrast two apparently dissimilar groups of people: for example, blue-collar workers and white-collar workers, runners and football players, readers and TV watchers, or any other variation you choose. Your approach may be either light-hearted or serious, but make sure you come to some conclusion about your subjects. Which group do you favor? Why?

3. Analyze the similarities and differences between two characters in your favorite novel, story, film, or television show. Which aspects of their personalities make them work well together, within the context in which they appear? Which characteristics work against each other, and therefore provide the necessary conflict to hold the reader's or viewer's attention?

4. Britt's essay is remarkable for its exaggeration of the two types. Write a brief essay analyzing and contrasting the ways Britt characterizes sloppy people and neat people. Be sure to consider the connotations of the words, such as "moral rectitude" for sloppy people (paragraph 2) and "cavalier" for neat people (6). (If necessary, see *connotation* in the Glossary.)

BRUCE CATTON

As a leading historian of the American Civil War, Bruce Catton was always guided by his sense that "history ought to be a good yarn." He was born in 1899 in Petoskey, Michigan, and attended Oberlin College. After reporting for newspapers in Cleveland, Boston, and Washington, DC, he worked in the federal government from 1942 to 1948 before turning full-time to writing. In 1951 Catton published Mr. Lincoln's Army, *his first book on the Civil War and the first volume in a trilogy on the Union army that also included* Glory Road *(1952) and* A Stillness at Appomattox *(1953). The last book won both the Pulitzer Prize and the National Book Award and reignited popular interest in the Civil War. Catton was the founding editor of* American Heritage *magazine and wrote ten more books on the Civil War, including a three-volume centennial history:* The Coming Fury *(1961),* Terrible Swift Sword *(1963), and* Never Call Retreat *(1965). His autobiography,* Waiting for the Morning Train: An American Boyhood, *was published four years before his death in 1978.*

Grant and Lee:
A Study in Contrasts

Like all good historians, Catton searched not just for the facts but for the life that lay behind them. In this famous essay, he treats the two great antagonists of the Civil War and in doing so provides an exceptional model of development by comparison and contrast. The piece first appeared in The American Story *(1956), a collection of essays by noted historians on colorful and significant people and events in our nation's past.*

When Ulysses S. Grant and Robert E. Lee met in the parlor of a mod- 1
est house at Appomattox Court House, Virginia, on April 9, 1865, to work out the terms for the surrender of Lee's Army of Northern Virginia, a great chapter in American life came to a close, and a great new chapter began.

These men were bringing the Civil War to its virtual finish. To be 2
sure, other armies had yet to surrender, and for a few days the fugitive

Confederate government would struggle desperately and vainly, trying to find some way to go on living now that its chief support was gone. But in effect it was all over when Grant and Lee signed the papers. And the little room where they wrote out the terms was the scene of one of the poignant, dramatic contrasts in American history.

They were two strong men, these oddly different generals, and they   3
represented the strengths of two conflicting currents that, through them, had come into final collision.

Back of Robert E. Lee was the notion that the old aristocratic con-   4
cept might somehow survive and be dominant in American life.

Lee was tidewater Virginia, and in his background were family,   5
culture, and tradition . . . the age of chivalry transplanted to a New World which was making its own legends and its own myths. He embodied a way of life that had come down through the age of knighthood and the English country squire. America was a land that was beginning all over again, dedicated to nothing much more complicated than the rather hazy belief that all men had equal rights and should have an equal chance in the world. In such a land Lee stood for the feeling that it was somehow of advantage to human society to have a pronounced inequality in the social structure. There should be a leisure class, backed by ownership of land; in turn, society itself should be keyed to the land as the chief source of wealth and influence. It would bring forth (according to this ideal) a class of men with a strong sense of obligation to the community; men who lived not to gain advantage for themselves, but to meet the solemn obligations which had been laid on them by the very fact that they were privileged. From them the country would get its leadership; to them it could look for the higher values—of thought, of conduct, of personal deportment—to give it strength and virtue.

Lee embodied the noblest elements of this aristocratic ideal.   6
Through him, the landed nobility justified itself. For four years, the Southern states had fought a desperate war to uphold the ideals for which Lee stood. In the end, it almost seemed as if the Confederacy fought for Lee; as if he himself was the Confederacy . . . the best thing that the way of life for which the Confederacy stood could ever have to offer. He had passed into legend before Appomattox. Thousands of tired, underfed, poorly clothed Confederate soldiers, long since past the simple enthusiasm of the early days of the struggle, somehow considered Lee the symbol of everything for which they had been willing to die. But they could not quite put this feeling into words. If the Lost Cause, sanctified by so much heroism and so many deaths, had a living justification, its justification was General Lee.

Grant, the son of a tanner on the Western frontier, was everything   7
Lee was not. He had come up the hard way and embodied nothing
in particular except the eternal toughness and sinewy fiber of the
men who grew up beyond the mountains. He was one of a body of
men who owed reverence and obeisance to no one, who were self-
reliant to a fault, who cared hardly anything for the past but who
had a sharp eye for the future.

These frontier men were the precise opposites of the tidewater   8
aristocrats. Back of them, in the great surge that had taken people
over the Alleghenies and into the opening Western country, there
was a deep, implicit dissatisfaction with a past that had settled into
grooves. They stood for democracy, not from any reasoned conclusion about the proper ordering of human society, but simply because
they had grown up in the middle of democracy and knew how it
worked. Their society might have privileges, but they would be privileges each man had won for himself. Forms and patterns meant
nothing. No man was born to anything, except perhaps to a chance
to show how far he could rise. Life was competition.

Yet along with this feeling had come a deep sense of belonging to a   9
national community. The Westerner who developed a farm, opened a
shop, or set up in business as a trader could hope to prosper only as his
own community prospered—and his community ran from the Atlantic
to the Pacific and from Canada down to Mexico. If the land was settled,
with towns and highways and accessible markets, he could better himself. He saw his fate in terms of the nation's own destiny. As its horizons
expanded, so did his. He had, in other words, an acute dollars-and-
cents stake in the continued growth and development of his country.

And that, perhaps, is where the contrast between Grant and Lee   10
becomes most striking. The Virginia aristocrat, inevitably, saw himself
in relation to his own region. He lived in a static society which could
endure almost anything except change. Instinctively, his first loyalty
would go to the locality in which that society existed. He would fight
to the limit of endurance to defend it, because in defending it he was
defending everything that gave his own life its deepest meaning.

The Westerner, on the other hand, would fight with an equal tenac-   11
ity for the broader concept of society. He fought so because everything he lived by was tied to growth, expansion, and a constantly
widening horizon. What he lived by would survive or fall with the
nation itself. He could not possibly stand by unmoved in the face of
an attempt to destroy the Union. He would combat it with everything he had, because he could only see it as an effort to cut the
ground out from under his feet.

So Grant and Lee were in complete contrast, representing two 12
diametrically opposed elements in American life. Grant was the
modern man emerging; beyond him, ready to come on the stage, was
the great age of steel and machinery, of crowded cities and a restless
burgeoning vitality. Lee might have ridden down from the old age of
chivalry, lance in hand, silken banner fluttering over his head. Each
man was the perfect champion of his cause, drawing both his strengths
and his weaknesses from the people he led.

Yet it was not all contrast, after all. Different as they were—in 13
background, in personality, in underlying aspiration—these two
great soldiers had much in common. Under everything else, they
were marvelous fighters. Furthermore, their fighting qualities were
really very much alike.

Each man had, to begin with, the great virtue of utter tenacity and 14
fidelity. Grant fought his way down the Mississippi Valley in spite of
acute personal discouragement and profound military handicaps. Lee
hung on in the trenches at Petersburg after hope itself had died. In each
man there was an indomitable quality . . . the born fighter's refusal to
give up as long as he can still remain on his feet and lift his two fists.

Daring and resourcefulness they had, too: the ability to think faster 15
and move faster than the enemy. These were the qualities which gave
Lee the dazzling campaigns of Second Manassas and Chancellorsville
and won Vicksburg for Grant.

Lastly, and perhaps greatest of all, there was the ability, at the end, 16
to turn quickly from war to peace once the fighting was over. Out of
the way these two men behaved at Appomattox came the possibility
of a peace of reconciliation. It was a possibility not wholly realized,
in the years to come, but which did, in the end, help the two sections
to become one nation again . . . after a war whose bitterness might
have seemed to make such a reunion wholly impossible. No part of
either man's life became him more than the part he played in their
brief meeting in the McLean house at Appomattox. Their behavior
there put all succeeding generations of Americans in their debt. Two
great Americans, Grant and Lee—very different, yet under everything
very much alike. Their encounter at Appomattox was one of the great
moments of American history.

Meaning

1. What is the main idea of Catton's essay? Besides the fact that it signaled
   the end of the Civil War, why was the meeting between Grant and Lee
   significant? Did its significance derive from the men's differences, their

similarities, or both? Where in the essay does Catton make the main idea clear?

2. Briefly, what traditions and ideals does Catton see Grant and Lee, respectively, as representing? What characteristics do they share? Do you think Catton means these shared characteristics to represent something as well? If so, what?

3. Catton does not say precisely how Grant and Lee "behaved" at Appomattox (paragraph 16), but what can you infer about their behavior from what he *does* say?

Purpose and Audience

1. Would you say the purpose of Catton's comparison is primarily to explain his two subjects or to evaluate their relative merits? What passages in the essay support your answer?

2. What assumptions does Catton seem to make about his readers' knowledge of the Civil War? Why, for instance, does he explain the reasons for the meeting at Appomattox (paragraphs 1–2), while not specifying either Grant's or Lee's roles in the Civil War? How familiar with the Civil War must readers be in order to understand the points Catton is making?

3. Catton says that "Lee embodied the noblest elements of [the] aristocratic ideal" of the South (paragraph 6). Catton does not mention the institution of slavery, which was an ignoble part of that ideal that Lee did not support. Given his main idea, why do you think Catton ignores slavery?

Method and Structure

1. Catton's essay illustrates both ways of organizing a comparison. Paragraphs 4–9 are arranged subject-by-subject, and the points made in these paragraphs are then sharpened and summarized in paragraphs 10–12. Paragraphs 13–16 are then arranged point-by-point. Why does Catton's focus in paragraphs 4–9 make a subject-by-subject arrangement effective? How does the focus of paragraphs 13–16 shift to merit a point-by-point arrangement?

2. Why does Catton devote more space to the differences between the two men than to their similarities? And why does he position the similarities at the end of the essay instead of at the beginning? How do these choices relate to Catton's main idea?

3. **Other Methods** In identifying "two conflicting currents" (paragraph 3), Catton uses classification to sort Civil War–era Americans into two groups represented by Lee and Grant. Catton then uses analysis to

tease out the characteristics of each current, each type. How do both classification and analysis serve Catton's comparison and contrast?

Language

1. What is Catton's attitude toward his two subjects? How is it revealed in Catton's choice of words, especially in paragraphs 12–16?

2. Paragraphs 4–11 depend largely on abstract words such as "aristocratic" (4), "obligation" (5), and "reverence" (7) rather than on concrete and specific examples of these qualities. Is this abstraction a flaw in Catton's essay, or is it justified by his purpose in these paragraphs? Why? (If necessary, consult the Glossary under *abstract and concrete words*.)

3. Catton uses many metaphors—for instance, calling two American traditions "conflicting currents," as if the traditions were rivers. How many other metaphors do you see? What does each one contribute to Catton's meaning? (If necessary, consult the Glossary under *figures of speech*.)

Writing Topics

1. Think of two people (say, two friends, or two teachers, or two characters in fiction or movies) whose personal traits strike you as remarkable. Write an essay in which you compare the two, focusing on similarities or differences or both as seems most appropriate. If you like, you might also explain the differences or similarities with reference to your subjects' backgrounds and attitudes.

2. In the early West, Catton tells us, "Life was competition" (paragraph 8). Does that statement still apply to most parts of American life today? Is competition essential to a democratic society? Are there ways in which competition conflicts with democratic ideals? Using these questions as a starting point, develop an essay that applies Catton's statement to the United States today. Support your ideas with specific examples from your own observations or reading.

3. In paragraphs 13–16 Catton notes several qualities that Lee and Grant shared as fighters. Write an essay explaining why you would or would not value those same qualities in a president or other national leader charged with establishing and carrying out our defense policy. Support your main idea with reasons, examples, and details.

NANCY MAIRS

Nancy Mairs was born in 1943 in Long Beach, California, and grew up in Boston. After earning a BA from Wheaton College, she taught writing to high school and college students while working toward graduate degrees in creative writing and English literature from the University of Arizona. Due to multiple sclerosis, Mairs has used a wheelchair since 1993. Her essays, memoirs, and poetry candidly explore, as she has put it, "issues charged with personal significance," including death, disability, and feminism. Her essay collections include Plaintext *(1986),* Carnal Acts *(1990),* Waist High in the World: A Life Among the Nondisabled *(1996), and, most recently,* A Troubled Guest *(2001).*

Disability

In this essay, Mairs compares the media's depiction of disability with the reality that she experiences firsthand as a person afflicted with multiple sclerosis. "Disability" was first published in the New York Times *in 1987 and later included in* Carnal Acts.

For months now I've been consciously searching for representation of myself in the media, especially television. I know I'd recognize this self because of certain distinctive, though not unique, features: I am a forty-three-year-old woman crippled with multiple sclerosis; although I can still totter short distances with the aid of a brace and a cane, more and more of the time I ride in a wheelchair. Because of these appliances and my peculiar gait, I'm easy to spot even in a crowd. So when I tell you I haven't noticed any women like me on television, you can believe me.

Actually, last summer I did see a woman with multiple sclerosis portrayed on one of those medical dramas that offer an illness-of-the-week like the daily special at your local diner. In fact, that was the whole point of the show: that this poor young woman had MS. She was terribly upset (understandably, I assure you) by the diagnosis, and her response was to plan a trip to Kenya while she was still physically capable of making it, against the advice of the young, fit, handsome doctor who had fallen in love with her. And she almost did it. At least, she got as far as a taxi to the airport, hotly pursued by the doctor. But at the last she succumbed to his blandishments and fled the taxi into his manly protective embrace. No escape to Kenya for this cripple.

Capitulation into the arms of a man who uses his medical powers 3 to strip one of even the urge toward independence is hardly the sort of representation I had in mind. But even if the situation had been sensitively handled, according to the woman her right to her own adventures, it wouldn't have been what I'm looking for. Such a television show, as well as films like *Duet for One* and *Children of a Lesser God*, in taking disability as its major premise, excludes the complexities that round out a character and make her whole. It's not about a woman who happens to be physically disabled; it's about physical disability and the determining factor of a woman's existence.

Take it from me, physical disability looms pretty large in one's life. 4 But it doesn't devour one wholly. I'm not, for instance, Ms. MS, a walking, talking embodiment of a chronic incurable degenerative disease. In most ways I'm just like every other woman of my age, nationality, and socioeconomic background. I menstruate, so I have to buy tampons. I worry about smoker's breath, so I buy mouthwash. I smear my wrinkling skin with lotions. I put bleach in the washer so my family's undies won't be dingy. I drive a car, talk on the telephone, get runs in my pantyhose, eat pizza. In most ways, that is, I'm the advertisers' dream: Ms. Great American Consumer. And yet the advertisers, who determine nowadays who will get represented publicly and who will not, deny the existence of me and my kind absolutely.

I once asked a local advertiser why he didn't include disabled peo- 5 ple in his spots. His response seemed direct enough: "We don't want to give people the idea that our product is just for the handicapped." But tell me truly now: If you saw me pouring out puppy biscuits, would you think these kibbles were only for the puppies of the cripples? If you saw my blind niece ordering a Coke, would you switch to Pepsi lest you be struck sightless? No, I think the advertiser's excuse masked a deeper and more anxious rationale: To depict disabled people in the ordinary activities of daily life is to admit that there is something ordinary about disability itself, that it may enter anybody's life. If it is effaced completely, or at least isolated as a separate "problem," so that it remains at a safe distance from other human issues, then the viewer won't feel threatened by her or his own physical vulnerability.

This kind of effacement or isolation has painful, even dangerous 6 consequences, however. For the disabled person, these include self-degradation and a subtle kind of self-alienation not unlike that experienced by other minorities. Socialized human beings love to conform, to study others and then mold themselves to the contours of those whose images, for good reasons or bad, they come to love. Imagine a life in which feasible others—others you can hope to be like— don't exist. At the least you might conclude that there is something queer about you, something ugly or foolish or shameful. In the extreme, you might feel as though you don't exist, in any meaningful social sense, at all. Everyone else is "there," sucking breath mints and splashing cologne and swigging wine coolers. You're "not there." And if not there, nowhere.

But this denial of disability imperils even you who are able-bodied,   7 and not just by shrinking your insight into the physically and emotionally complex world you live in. Some disabled people call you TAPs, or Temporarily Abled Persons. The fact is that ours is the only minority you can join involuntarily, without warning, at any time. And if you live long enough, as you're increasingly likely to do, you may well join it. The transition will probably be difficult from a physical point of view no matter what. But it will be a good bit easier psychologically if you are accustomed to seeing disability as a normal characteristic, one that complicates but does not ruin human existence. Achieving this integration, for disabled and able-bodied people alike, requires that we insert disability daily into our field of vision: quietly, naturally, in the small and common scenes of our ordinary lives.

Meaning

1. Why does Mairs object to the TV movie about the woman with multiple sclerosis (paragraphs 2–3)?
2. What does Mairs mean by the phrase "Ms. Great American Consumer" (paragraph 4)?
3. Why, according to Mairs, should there be images of people with disabilities on television?
4. What is Mairs's thesis? Restate it in your own words.

Purpose and Audience

1. What is this essay's purpose?
2. What lessons might both people with disabilities and people without disabilities take from this essay?

Method and Structure

1. What does Mairs compare and contrast in this essay? How does the comparison help her achieve her purpose?

2. What key generalizations does Mairs make to support her thesis? Do you find them valid? Why, or why not?

3. How does Mairs use her introduction to lay the groundwork for her essay? How does she make the transition from her introduction into the TV drama?

4. **Other Methods**   Discuss how Mairs uses example to help build her case. What kinds of examples does she select? What are their effects?

Language

1. How would you characterize Mairs's tone in this essay? Point out specific sentences and words that establish it. What is the effect? (If necessary, see *tone* in the Glossary.)

2. What is the function of irony in this essay (for example, "If you saw my blind niece ordering a Coke, would you switch to Pepsi lest you be struck sightless?")? (If necessary, consult the Glossary for the definition of *irony*.)

3. What are the connotations of the words "crippled," "totter," "appliances," and "peculiar gait" (paragraph 1)? What is the effect of these words in the essay's introduction? (For the definition of *connotation*, consult the Glossary.)

Writing Topics

1. Write an essay that explains how your own responses to people with disabilities lead you to accept or dispute Mairs's call for depicting "disabled people in the ordinary activities of daily life."

2. Choose another group you think has been "effaced" in television advertising and programming—a racial, ethnic, or religious group, for instance. Write an essay detailing how and why that group is overlooked. How could representations of the group be incorporated into the media? What effects might such representation have?

3. Write an essay discussing how people with disabilities are treated in our society. You could narrate a day in the life of someone with a disability; you could compare and contrast the access and facilities your school provides physically average versus disabled students; you could classify social attitudes toward disabilities, with examples of each type.

4. Reread Mairs's essay carefully. Mairs tells us about herself through details and through tone (for example, through irony, intensity, and humor). Write an essay on how Mairs's self-revelations do or do not help further her thesis.

RICHARD RODRIGUEZ

*Born in 1944 in San Francisco to Spanish-speaking Mexican immi-
grants, Richard Rodriguez entered school speaking essentially no
English and left it with a PhD in English literature. In between, his
increasing assimilation into the mainstream of American society
meant increasing alienation from his parents and their culture—a
simultaneous gain and loss that he often writes about. Rodriguez was
educated in the Catholic schools of Sacramento, California; graduated
from Stanford University; and earned a PhD from the University of
California at Berkeley. A lecturer and writer, he is an editor at* Pacific
News Service *and a contributing editor for* Harper's Magazine, US
News & World Report, *and the* Los Angeles Times. *His books include*
Days of Obligation: An Argument with My Mexican Father *(1993)
and* Brown: The Last Discovery of America *(2002). Rodriguez's work
frequently addresses the controversial programs of affirmative action
and bilingual education, both of which his own experiences have led
him to oppose. On bilingual education he says, "To me,
public educators in a public schoolroom have an obligation to teach
a public language. . . . The imperative is to get children away from
those languages that increase their sense of alienation from the public
society."*

Private Language,
Public Language

In this excerpt from his memoir Hunger of Memory *(1982), Rodriguez
tells of shuttling between the private language of family and the public
language of society. His family spoke Spanish, his society English, but
the distinction between an intimate private language and an alienating
public language is experienced, he believes, by all children.*

I remember to start with that day in Sacramento—a California now   1
nearly thirty years past—when I first entered a classroom, able to
understand some fifty stray English words.

The third of four children, I had been preceded to a neighborhood   2
Roman Catholic school by an older brother and sister. But neither of

them had revealed very much about their classroom experiences. Each afternoon they returned, as they left in the morning, always together, speaking in Spanish as they climbed the five steps of the porch. And their mysterious books, wrapped in shopping-bag paper, remained on the table next to the door, closed firmly behind them.

An accident of geography sent me to a school where all my class- 3 mates were white, many the children of doctors and lawyers and business executives. All my classmates certainly must have been uneasy on that first day of school—as most children are uneasy—to find themselves apart from their families in the first institution of their lives. But I was astonished.

The nun said, in a friendly but oddly impersonal voice, "Boys and 4 girls, this is Richard Rodriguez." (I heard her sound out: *Rich-heard Road-ree-guess*.) It was the first time I had heard anyone name me in English. "Richard," the nun repeated more slowly, writing my name down in her black leather book. Quickly I turned to see my mother's face dissolve in a watery blur behind the pebbled glass door.

Many years later there is something called bilingual education— 5 a scheme proposed in the late 1960s by Hispanic American social activists, later endorsed by a congressional vote. It is a program that seeks to permit non-English-speaking children, many from lower-class homes, to use their family language as the language of school. (Such is the goal its supporters announce.) I hear them and am forced to say no: it is not possible for a child—any child—ever to use his family's language in school. Not to understand this is to misunderstand the public uses of schooling and to trivialize the nature of intimate life—a family's "language."

Memory teaches me what I know of these matters; the boy 6 reminds the adult. I was a bilingual child, a certain kind—socially disadvantaged—the son of working-class parents, both Mexican immigrants.

In the early years of my boyhood, my parents coped very well in 7 America. My father had steady work. My mother managed at home. They were nobody's victims. Optimism and ambition led them to a house (our home) many blocks from the Mexican south side of town. We lived among *gringos*[1] and only a block from the biggest, whitest houses. It never occurred to my parents that they couldn't live wherever they chose. Nor was the Sacramento of the fifties bent on teaching them a contrary lesson. My mother and father were

[1]Spanish for "foreigners," especially Americans and the English. [Editor's note.]

more annoyed than intimidated by those two or three neighbors who tried initially to make us unwelcome. ("Keep your brats away from my sidewalk!") But despite all they achieved, perhaps because they had so much to achieve, any deep feeling of ease, the confidence of "belonging" in public was withheld from them both. They regarded the people at work, the faces in crowds, as very distant from us. They were the others, *los gringos*. That term was interchangeable in their speech with another, even more telling, *los americanos*. . . .

In public, my father and mother spoke a hesitant, accented, not   8
always grammatical English. And they would have to strain—their bodies tense—to catch the sense of what was rapidly said by *los gringos*. At home they spoke Spanish. The language of their Mexican past sounded in counterpoint to the English of public society. The words would come quickly, with ease. Conveyed through those sounds was the pleasing, soothing, consoling reminder of being at home.

During those years when I was first conscious of hearing, my   9
mother and father addressed me only in Spanish; in Spanish I learned to reply. By contrast, English (*inglés*), rarely heard in the house, was the language I came to associate with *gringos*. I learned my first words of English overhearing my parents speak to strangers. At five years of age, I knew just enough English for my mother to trust me on errands to stores one block away. No more.

I was a listening child, careful to hear the very different sounds of   10
Spanish and English. Wide-eyed with learning, I'd listen to sounds more than words. First, there were English (*gringo*) sounds. So many words were still unknown that when the butcher or the lady at the drugstore said something to me, exotic polysyllabic sounds would bloom in the midst of their sentences. Often the speech of people in public seemed to me very loud, booming with confidence. The man behind the counter would literally ask, "What can I do for you?" But by being so firm and so clear, the sound of his voice said that he was a *gringo*; he belonged in public society.

I would also hear then the high nasal tones of middle-class   11
American speech. The air stirred with sound. Sometimes, even now, when I have been traveling abroad for several weeks, I will hear what I heard as a boy. In hotel lobbies or airports, in Turkey or Brazil, some Americans will pass, and suddenly I will hear it again—the high sound of American voices. For a few seconds I will hear it with pleasure, for it is now the sound of my society—a reminder of home. But inevitably—already on the flight headed for home—the sound fades with repetition. I will be unable to hear it anymore.

When I was a boy, things were different. The accent of *los gringos* 12
was never pleasing nor was it hard to hear. Crowds at Safeway or at
bus stops would be noisy with sound. And I would be forced to edge
away from the chirping chatter above me.

I was unable to hear my own sounds, but I knew very well that I 13
spoke English poorly. My words could not stretch far enough to form
complete thoughts. And the words I did speak I didn't know well
enough to make into distinct sounds. (Listeners would usually lower
their heads, better to hear what I was trying to say.) But it was one
thing for *me* to speak English with difficulty. It was more troubling
for me to hear my parents speak in public: their high-whining vow-
els and guttural consonants; their sentences that got stuck with "eh"
and "ah" sounds; the confused syntax; the hesitant rhythm of sounds
so different from the way *gringos* spoke. I'd notice, moreover, that
my parents' voices were softer than those of *gringos* we'd meet. . . .

There were many times like the night at a brightly lit gasoline sta- 14
tion (a blaring white memory) when I stood uneasily, hearing my
father. He was talking to a teenaged attendant. I do not recall what
they were saying, but I cannot forget the sounds my father made as
he spoke. At one point his words slid together to form one word—
sounds as confused as the threads of blue and green oil in the puddle
next to my shoes. His voice rushed through what he had left to say.
And, toward the end, reached falsetto notes, appealing to his listen-
er's understanding. I looked away to the lights of passing automobiles. I tried not to hear anymore. But I heard only too well the calm,
easy tones in the attendant's reply. Shortly afterward, walking
toward home with my father, I shivered when he put his hand on my
shoulder. The very first chance that I got, I evaded his grasp and ran
on ahead into the dark, skipping with feigned boyish exuberance.

But then there was Spanish. *Español*: my family's language. 15
Español: the language that seemed to me a private language. I'd hear
strangers on the radio and in the Mexican Catholic church across
town speaking Spanish, but I couldn't really believe that Spanish was
a public language, like English. Spanish speakers, rather, seemed
related to me, for I sensed that we shared—through our language—
the experience of feeling apart from *los gringos*. It was thus a ghetto
Spanish that I heard and I spoke. Like those whose lives are bound
by a barrio, I was reminded by Spanish of my separateness from *los
otros*,[2] *los gringos* in power. But more intensely than for most barrio
children—because I did not live in a barrio—Spanish seemed to me

---

[2]Spanish: "the others." [Editor's note.]

the language of home. (Most days it was only at home that I'd hear it.) It became the language of joyful return.

A family member would say something to me and I would feel 16
myself specially recognized. My parents would say something to me and I would feel embraced by the sounds of their words. Those sounds said: *I am speaking with ease in Spanish. I am addressing you in words I never use with* los gringos. *I recognize you as someone special, close, like no one outside. You belong with us. In the family.*

(*Ricardo.*) 17

At the age of five, six, well past the time when most other children 18
no longer easily notice the difference between sounds uttered at home and words spoken in public, I had a different experience. I lived in a world magically compounded of sounds. I remained a child longer than most; I lingered too long, poised at the edge of language—often frightened by the sounds of *los gringos*, delighted by the sounds of Spanish at home. I shared with my family a language that was startlingly different from that used in the great city around us.

For me there were none of the gradations between public and 19
private society so normal to a maturing child. Outside the house was public society; inside the house was private. Just opening or closing the screen door behind me was an important experience. I'd rarely leave home all alone or without reluctance. Walking down the sidewalk, under the canopy of tall trees, I'd warily notice the—suddenly—silent neighborhood kids who stood warily watching me. Nervously, I'd arrive at the grocery store to hear there the sounds of the *gringo*—foreign to me—reminding me that in this world so big, I was a foreigner. But then I'd return. Walking back toward our house, climbing the steps from the sidewalk, when the front door was open in summer, I'd hear voices beyond the screen door talking in Spanish. For a second or two, I'd stay, linger there, listening. Smiling, I'd hear my mother call out, saying in Spanish (words), "Is that you, Richard?" All the while her sounds would assure me: *You are home now; come closer; inside. With us.*

"*Sí,*" I'd reply. 20

Once more inside the house I would resume (assume) my place in 21
the family. The sounds would dim, grow harder to hear. Once more at home, I would grow less aware of that fact. It required, however, no more than the blurt of the doorbell to alert me to listen to sounds all over again. The house would turn instantly still while my mother went to the door. I'd hear her hard English sounds. I'd wait to hear her voice return to soft-sounding Spanish, which assured me, as surely as did the clicking tongue of the lock of the door, that the stranger was gone.

Plainly, it is not healthy to hear such sounds so often. It is not 22
healthy to distinguish public words from private sounds so easily. I
remained cloistered by sounds, timid and shy in public, too dependent on voices at home. And yet it needs to be emphasized: I was an
extremely happy child at home. I remember many nights when my
father would come back from work, and I'd hear him call out to my
mother in Spanish, sounding relieved. In Spanish, he'd sound light
and free notes he never could manage in English. Some nights I'd
jump up just at hearing his voice. With *mis hermanos*[3] I would come
running into the room where he was with my mother. Our laughing
(so deep was the pleasure!) became screaming. Like others who
know pain of public alienation, we transformed the knowledge of
our public separateness and made it consoling—the reminder of
intimacy. Excited, we joined our voices in a celebration of sounds.
*We are speaking now the way we never speak out in public. We are
alone—together*, voices sounded, surrounded to tell me. Some nights,
no one seemed willing to loosen the hold sound had on us. At dinner,
we invented new words. (Ours sounded Spanish, but made sense
only to us.) We pieced together new words by taking, say, an English
verb and giving it Spanish endings. My mother's instructions at bed-
time would be lacquered with mock-urgent tones. Or a word like *sí*
would become, in several notes, able to convey added measures of
feeling. Tongues explored the edges of words, especially the fat vow-
els. And we happily sounded that military drum roll, the twirling roar
of the Spanish *r*. Family language: my family's sounds. The voices of
my parents and sisters and brothers. Their voices insisting: *You
belong here. We are family members. Related. Special to one another.
Listen!* Voices singing and sighing, rising, straining, then surging,
teeming with pleasure that burst syllables into fragments of laughter.
At times it seemed there was steady quiet only when, from another
room, the rustling whispers of my parents faded and I moved closer
to sleep.

Meaning

1. What is Rodriguez's main idea about public and private language?
2. What did language apparently represent for the young Rodriguez? In
   answering, consider both his contrasting perceptions of the sounds of
   English and of Spanish and his contrasting feelings among *los gringos* and among his family.

[3]Spanish: "my siblings"—Rodriguez's brothers and sisters. [Editor's note.]

3. What explanation does Rodriguez give for why his transition from private to public language took longer than most children's (paragraphs 18–19)? Given his characterization of himself as a child (especially in paragraph 10), does his slow transition seem attributable solely to his bilingual environment? Why?

Purpose and Audience

1. What seems to be Rodriguez's purpose in this piece? Is he primarily expressing his memories of childhood, explaining something about childhood in a bilingual environment and about childhood in general, or arguing against bilingual education? What passages support your answer?

2. Since he writes in English, Rodriguez is presumably addressing English-speaking readers. Why, then, does he occasionally use Spanish words (such as *gringos*, paragraph 7) without translating them? What do these words contribute to the essay?

Method and Structure

1. Rodriguez's comparison of private and public language includes smaller comparisons between himself and other children (paragraphs 3, 15, 18–19), himself as an adult and a child (11–12), and himself and his parents (13). What does each of these smaller comparisons contribute to Rodriguez's portrayal of himself and to his main idea?

2. Where does Rodriguez shift his focus from public language to private language? Why does he treat private language second? What effect does he achieve with the last paragraph?

3. **Other Methods**   Rodriguez uses narration in paragraphs 3–4, 10, 14, and 22. Do you think the experiences and the feelings Rodriguez either expresses or implies are shared by children in one-language environments? What do these narratives contribute to Rodriguez's main idea?

Language

1. Why does Rodriguez spell out his name to reflect its pronunciation with an American accent (paragraph 4)? What does the contrast between this form of his name and the Spanish form (17) contribute to his comparison?

2. Compare the words Rodriguez uses to describe *los gringos* and their speech (paragraphs 4, 7, 10, 12, 14, 19) with those he uses to describe his family and their speech (paragraphs 7, 8, 13, 14, 16, 21, 22). What does his word choice tell you about his childhood attitudes toward each group of people?

3. Notice the figures of speech Rodriguez uses: for instance, "My words could not stretch far enough to form complete thoughts" (paragraph 13); "a blaring white memory" (14). What do these and other figures convey about Rodriguez's feelings? (If necessary, consult the Glossary under *figures of speech*.)

Writing Topics

1. Rodriguez has said, "What I know about language—the movement between private and public society, the distance between sound and words—is a universal experience." Consider a "private" group you feel a part of—for instance, your family, friends, fellow athletes, people who share the same hobby. How do the language, behaviors, and attitudes of the group distinguish it from "public" society? Write an essay in which you compare your perceptions of and feelings toward the two worlds.

2. Many books and articles have been written on the subject of bilingual education in American schools. Locate an article, book, or Web site that presents a variety of opinions on the issue. Or read what Rodriguez says about it in the rest of *Hunger of Memory*. Then write an essay in which you state and support your opinion on whether children whose first language is not English should be taught in English or in their native language.

3. Recall any difficulties you have had with language—learning English as a second language, learning any other second language, learning to read, overcoming a speech impediment, improving your writing in freshman composition. Write an essay in which you explain the circumstances and their significance for you.

Writing with the Method
Comparison and Contrast

Choose one of the following topics, or any other topic they suggest, for an essay developed by comparison and contrast. The topic you decide on should be something you care about so that the comparison and contrast is a means of communicating an idea, not an end in itself.

EXPERIENCE
1. Two jobs you have held
2. Two experiences with discrimination
3. Your own version of an event you witnessed or participated in and someone else's view of the same event
4. A good and a bad job interview

PEOPLE
5. Your relationships with two friends
6. Someone before and after marriage or the birth of a child
7. Two or more candidates for public office
8. Two relatives

PLACES AND THINGS
9. A place as it is now and as it was years ago
10. Two cars
11. Two towns or cities
12. Nature in the city and in the country

ART AND ENTERTAINMENT
13. The work of two artists or writers, or two works by the same person
14. Two or more forms of jazz, classical music, or rock music
15. Movies or television today and when you were a child
16. A novel and a movie or television show on which it's based
17. A high school sports game and a professional game in the same sport
18. The advertisements during two very different television programs or in two very different magazines

EDUCATION AND IDEAS
19. Talent and skill
20. Two styles of teaching
21. Two religions
22. A passive student and an active student

Chapter Eight

DEFINITION

USING THE METHOD

Definition sets the boundaries of a thing, a concept, an emotion, or a value. In answering "What is it?" and also "What is it *not*?" definition specifies the main qualities of the subject and its essential nature. Because words are only symbols, pinning down their precise meanings is essential for us to understand ourselves and one another. Thus we use definition constantly, whether we are explaining a slang word like *dis* to someone who has never heard it or explaining what *culture* means on an essay examination.

There are several kinds of definition, each with different uses. One is the **formal definition,** usually a statement of the general class of things to which the word belongs, followed by the distinction(s) between it and other members of the class. For example:

	General Class	*Distinction(s)*
A submarine is	a seagoing vessel	that operates underwater.
A parable is	a brief, simple story	that illustrates a moral or religious principle.
Pressure is	the force	applied to a given surface.
Insanity is	a mental condition	in which a defendant does not know right from wrong.

A formal definition usually gives a standard dictionary meaning of the word (as in the first two examples) or a specialized meaning agreed to by the members of a profession or discipline (as in the last two examples, from physics and criminal law, respectively). It is most useful to explain the basic meaning of a term that readers need to know in order to understand the rest of a discussion. Occasionally, you might also use a formal definition as a springboard to a more elaborate, detailed exploration of a word. For instance, you might define *pride* simply as "a sense of self-respect" before probing the varied meanings of the word as people actually understand it and then settling on a fuller and more precise meaning of your own devising.

This more detailed definition of *pride* could fall into one of two other types of definition: stipulative and extended. A **stipulative definition** clarifies the particular way you are using a word: you stipulate, or specify, a meaning to suit a larger purpose; the definition is part of a larger whole. For example, if you wanted to show how pride can destroy personal relationships, you might first stipulate a meaning of *pride* that ties in with that purpose. Though a stipulative definition may sometimes take the form of a brief formal definition, most require several sentences or even paragraphs. In a physics textbook, for instance, the physicist's definition of *pressure* quoted earlier probably would not suffice to give readers a good sense of the term and eliminate all the other possible meanings they may have in mind.

Whereas you use a formal or stipulative definition for some larger purpose, you write an **extended definition** for the sake of defining— that is, for the purpose of exploring a thing, quality, or idea in its full complexity and drawing boundaries around it until its meaning is complete and precise. Extended definitions usually treat subjects so complex, vague, or laden with emotions or values that people misunderstand or disagree over their meanings. The subject may be an abstract concept like *patriotism*, a controversial phrase like *beginnings of life*, a colloquial or slang expression like *hype*, a thing like *microcomputer*, a scientific idea like *natural selection*, even an everyday expression like *nagging*. Besides defining, your purpose may be to persuade readers to accept a definition (for instance, that life begins at conception, or at birth), to explain (what is natural selection?), or to amuse (nagging as exemplified by great nags).

As the variety of possible subjects and purposes may suggest, an extended definition may draw on whatever methods will best accomplish the goal of specifying what the subject encompasses and distinguishing it from similar things, qualities, or concepts. Several strategies are unique to definition:

- **Synonyms,** or words of similar meaning, can convey the range of the word's meanings. For example, you could equate *misery* with *wretchedness* and *distress*.
- **Negation,** or saying what a word does not mean, can limit the meaning, particularly when you want to focus on only one sense of an abstract term, such as *pride*, that is open to diverse interpretations.
- The **etymology** of a word—its history—may illuminate its meaning, perhaps by showing the direction and extent of its change (*pride*, for instance, comes from a Latin word meaning "to be beneficial or useful") or by uncovering buried origins that remain implicit in the modern meaning (*patriotism* comes from the Greek word for "father"; *happy* comes from the Old Norse word for "good luck").

You may use these strategies of definition alone or together, and they may occupy whole paragraphs is an essay-length definition; but they rarely provide enough range to surround the subject completely. To do that, you'll need to draw on the other methods discussed in this book. One or two methods may predominate: an essay on nagging, for instance, might be developed with brief narratives. Or several methods may be combined: a definition of *patriotism* could compare it with *nationalism*, analyze its effects (such as the actions people take on its behalf), and give examples of patriotic individuals. The goal is not to employ every method in a sort of catalog of methods but to use those which best illuminate the subject. By drawing on the appropriate methods, you define and clarify your perspective on the subject so that the reader understands the meaning exactly.

DEVELOPING AN ESSAY BY DEFINITION

Getting Started

You'll sometimes be asked to write definition essays, as when a psychology exam asks for a discussion of *schizophrenia* or a political science assignment calls for an explanation of the term *totalitarianism*. To come up with a subject on your own, consider words that have complex meanings and are either unfamiliar to readers or open to varied interpretations. The subject should be something you know and care enough about to explore in great detail and surround completely. An idea for a subject may come from an overheard conversation (for instance, a reference to someone as "too patriotic"), a personal experience (a broken marriage you think attributable to one spouse's pride), or something you've seen or read (another writer's definition of *jazz*).

Begin exploring your subject by examining and listing its conventional meanings (consulting an unabridged dictionary may help here, and the dictionary will also give you synonyms and etymology). Also examine the differences of opinion about the word's meanings — the different ways, wrong or right, that you have heard or seen it used. Run through the other methods to see what fresh approaches to the subject they open up:

- How can the subject be described?
- What are some examples?
- Can the subject be divided into qualities or characteristics?
- Can its functions help define it?
- Will comparing and contrasting it with something else help sharpen its meaning?
- Do its causes or effects help clarify its sense?

Some of the questions may turn up nothing, but others may open your eyes to meanings you had not seen.

When you have generated a good list of ideas about your subject, settle on the purpose of your definition. Do you mostly want to explain a word that is unfamiliar to readers? Do you want to express your own view so that readers see a familiar subject from a new angle? Do you want to argue in favor of a particular definition or perhaps persuade readers to look more critically at themselves or their surroundings? Try to work your purpose into a tentative thesis sentence that asserts something about the subject. For example:

> Though generally considered entirely positive in meaning, *patriotism* also reflects childlike, self-centered feelings that have no place in a global society, even one threatened by terrorism.

With a thesis sentence formulated, reevaluate your ideas in light of it and pause to consider the needs of your readers:

- What do readers already know about your subject, and what do they need to be told in order to understand it as you do?
- Are your readers likely to be biased for or against your subject? If you were defining *patriotism*, for example, you might assume that

your readers see the word as representing a constructive, even essential value that contributes to the strength of the country. If your purpose were to contest this view, as implied by the thesis above, you would have to build your case carefully to win readers to your side.

Organizing

The introduction to a definition essay should provide a base from which to expand and at the same time explain to readers why the forthcoming definition is useful, significant, or necessary. You may want to report the incident that prompted you to define, say, why the subject itself is important, or specify the common understandings, or misunderstandings, about its meaning. Several devices can serve as effective beginnings: the etymology of the word; a quotation from another writer supporting or contradicting your definition; or an explanation of what the word does *not* mean (negation). (Try to avoid the overused opening that cites a dictionary: "According to *The American Heritage Dictionary*, _____ means . . ." Your readers have probably seen this opening many times before.) If it is not implied in the rest of your introduction, you may want to state your thesis so that readers know precisely what your purpose and point are.

The body of the essay should then proceed, paragraph by paragraph, to refine the characteristics or qualities of the subject, using the arrangement and methods that will distinguish it from anything similar and provide your perspective. For instance:

- You might draw increasingly tight boundaries around the subject, moving from broader, more familiar meanings to the one you have in mind.
- You might arrange your points in order of increasing drama.
- You might begin with your own experience of the subject and then show how you see it operating in your surroundings.

The conclusion to a definition essay is equally a matter of choice. You might summarize your definition, indicate its superiority to other definitions of the same subject, quote another writer whose view supports your own, or recommend that readers make some use of the information you have provided. The choice depends—as it does in any kind of essay—on your purpose and the impression you want to leave with readers.

Drafting

While drafting your extended definition, keep your subject vividly in mind. Say too much rather than too little about it to ensure that you capture its essence; you can always cut when you revise. And be sure to provide plenty of details and examples to support your view. Such evidence is particularly important when, as in the earlier example of patriotism, you seek to change readers' perceptions of your subject.

In definition the words you use are especially important. Abstractions and generalities cannot draw precise boundaries around a subject, so your words must be as concrete and specific as you can make them. You'll have chances during revising and editing to work on your words, but try during drafting to pin down your meanings. Use words and phrases that appeal directly to the senses and experiences of readers. When appropriate, use figures of speech to make meaning inescapably clear; instead of "Patriotism can be childlike," for example, you might say, "Some self-described patriots seem to see their country as a child sees a parent, all-knowing, always right." The connotations of words — the associations called up in readers' minds by words like *home, ambitious*, and *generous* — can contribute to your definition as well. But be sure that connotative words trigger associations suited to your purpose. And when you are trying to explain something precisely, rely most heavily on words with generally neutral meanings. (For further discussion, consult the following entries in the Glossary: *concrete words, specific words, figures of speech*, and *connotation and denotation*.)

Revising and Editing

When you are satisfied that your draft is complete, revise and edit it using the following questions.

- *Have you surrounded your subject completely and tightly?* Your definition should not leave gaps, nor should the boundaries be so broadly drawn that the subject overlaps something else. For instance, a definition of *hype* that focused on exaggerated and deliberately misleading claims should include all such claims (some political speeches, say, as well as some advertisements), and it should exclude appeals that do not fit the basic definition (some public-service advertising, for instance).
- *Does your definition reflect the conventional meanings of the word?* Even if you are providing a fresh slant on your subject, you can't

change its meaning entirely or you will confuse your readers and perhaps undermine your own credibility. *Patriotism*, for example, could not be defined from the first as "hatred of foreigners," for that definition strays into an entirely different realm. The conventional meaning of "love of country" would have to serve as the starting point, though your essay might interpret the meaning in an original way.

JUDY BRADY

Judy Brady was born in 1937 in San Francisco. She attended the University of Iowa and graduated with a bachelor's degree in painting in 1962. Married in 1960, by the mid-1960s she was raising two daughters. She began working in the women's movement in 1969 and through it developed an ongoing concern with political and social issues, especially women's rights. She believes that "as long as women continue to tolerate a society which places profits above the needs of people, we will continue to be exploited as workers and as wives." In addition to the essay reprinted here, Brady has written articles for various magazines and edited 1 in 3: Women with Cancer Confront an Epidemic *(1991), motivated by her own struggle with the disease. Divorced from her husband, Judy Brady is cofounder of the Toxic Links Coalition and a volunteer at the Women's Cancer Resource Center in Berkeley, California.*

I Want a Wife

Writing after eleven years of marriage, and before separating from her husband, Brady here pins down the meaning of the word wife *from the perspective of one person who lives the role. This essay was published in the first issue of* Ms. *magazine in December 1971, and it has since been reprinted widely. Is its harsh portrayal still relevant today?*

I belong to that classification of people known as wives. I am A Wife. 1
And, not altogether incidentally, I am a mother.

Not too long ago a male friend of mine appeared on the scene 2
fresh from a recent divorce. He had one child, who is, of course, with his ex-wife. He is looking for another wife. As I thought about him while I was ironing one evening, it suddenly occurred to me that I, too, would like to have a wife. Why do I want a wife?

I would like to go back to school so that I can become econom- 3
ically independent, support myself, and, if need be, support those dependent upon me. I want a wife who will work and send me to school. And while I am going to school I want a wife to take care of my children. I want a wife to keep track of the children's doctor and

dentist appointments. And to keep track of mine, too. I want a wife to make sure my children eat properly and are kept clean. I want a wife who will wash the children's clothes and keep them mended. I want a wife who is a good nurturant attendant to my children, who arranges for their schooling, makes sure that they have an adequate social life with their peers, takes them to the park, the zoo, etc. I want a wife who takes care of the children when they are sick, a wife who arranges to be around when the children need special care, because, of course, I cannot miss classes at school. My wife must arrange to lose time at work and not lose the job. It may mean a small cut in my wife's income from time to time, but I guess I can tolerate that. Needless to say, my wife will arrange and pay for the care of the children while my wife is working.

I want a wife who will take care of *my* physical needs. I want a 4 wife who will keep my house clean. A wife who will pick up after my children, a wife who will pick up after me. I want a wife who will keep my clothes clean, ironed, mended, replaced when need be, and who will see to it that my personal things are kept in their proper place so that I can find what I need the minute I need it. I want a wife who cooks the meals, a wife who is a *good* cook. I want a wife who will plan the menus, do the necessary grocery shopping, prepare the meals, serve them pleasantly, and then do the cleaning up while I do my studying. I want a wife who will care for me when I am sick and sympathize with my pain and loss of time from school. I want a wife to go along when our family takes a vacation so that someone can continue to care for me and my children when I need a rest and change of scene.

I want a wife who will not bother me with rambling complaints 5 about a wife's duties. But I want a wife who will listen to me when I feel the need to explain a rather difficult point I have come across in my course of studies. And I want a wife who will type my papers for me when I have written them.

I want a wife who will take care of the details of my social life. 6 When my wife and I are invited out by friends, I want a wife who will take care of the babysitting arrangements. When I meet people at school that I like and want to entertain, I want a wife who will have the house clean, will prepare a special meal, serve it to me and my friends, and not interrupt when I talk about things that interest me and my friends. I want a wife who will have arranged that the children are fed and ready for bed before my guests arrive so that the children do not bother us. I want a wife who takes care of the needs of my guests so that they feel comfortable, who makes sure that they have an ashtray, that they are passed the hors d'oeuvres, that they are offered a second helping of the food, that their wine glasses are replenished when necessary, that their coffee is served to them as they like it. And I want a wife who knows that sometimes I need a night out by myself.

I want a wife who is sensitive to my sexual needs, a wife who   7
makes love passionately and eagerly when I feel like it, a wife who makes sure that I am satisfied. And, of course, I want a wife who will not demand sexual attention when I am not in the mood for it. I want a wife who assumes the complete responsibility for birth control, because I do not want more children. I want a wife who will remain sexually faithful to me so that I do not have to clutter up my intellectual life with jealousies. And I want a wife who understands that *my* sexual needs may entail more than strict adherence to monogamy. I must, after all, be able to relate to people as fully as possible.

If, by chance, I find another person more suitable as a wife than   8
the wife I already have, I want the liberty to replace my present wife with another one. Naturally, I will expect a fresh, new life; my wife will take the children and be solely responsible for them so that I am left free.

When I am through with school and have a job, I want my wife to   9
quit working and remain at home so that my wife can more fully and completely take care of a wife's duties.

My God, who *wouldn't* want a wife?   10

Meaning

1. In one or two sentences, summarize Brady's definition of a wife. Consider not only the functions she mentions but also the relationship she portrays.

2. Brady provides many instances of a double standard of behavior and responsibility for the wife and the wife's spouse. What are the wife's chief responsibilities and expected behaviors? What are the spouse's?

Purpose and Audience

1. Why do you think Brady wrote this essay? Was her purpose to explain a wife's duties, to complain about her own situation, to poke fun at men, to attack men, to attack society's attitudes toward women, or something else? Was she trying to provide a realistic and fair definition of *wife*? What passages in the essay support your answers?

2. What does Brady seem to assume about her readers' gender (male or female) and their attitudes toward women's roles in society, relations between the sexes, and work inside and outside the home? Does she seem to write from the perspective of a particular age group or social and economic background? In answering these questions, cite specific passages from the essay.

3. Brady clearly intended to provoke a reaction from readers. What is *your* reaction to this essay: do you think it is realistic or exaggerated, fair or unfair to men, relevant or irrelevant to the present time? Why?

Method and Structure

1. Why would anybody need to write an essay defining a term like *wife*? Don't we know what a wife is already? How does Brady use definition in an original way to achieve her purpose?

2. Analyze Brady's essay as a piece of definition, considering its thoroughness, its specificity, and its effectiveness in distinguishing the subject from anything similar.

3. Analyze the introduction to Brady's essay. What function does paragraph 1 serve? In what way does paragraph 2 confirm Brady's definition? How does the question at the end of the introduction relate to the question at the end of the essay?

4. **Other Methods**   Brady develops her definition primarily by classification. What does she classify, and what categories does she form? What determines her arrangement of these categories? What does the classification contribute to the essay?

Language

1. How would you characterize Brady's tone: whining, amused, angry, contemptuous, or what? What phrases in the essay support your answer? (If necessary, consult the Glossary under *tone*.)

2. Why does Brady repeat "I want a wife" in almost every sentence, often at the beginning of the sentence? What does this stylistic device convey about the person who wants a wife? How does it fit in with Brady's main idea and purpose?

3. Why does Brady never substitute the personal pronoun "she" for "my wife"? Does the effect gained by repeating "my wife" justify the occasionally awkward sentences, such as the last one in paragraph 3?

4. What effect does Brady achieve with the expressions "of course" (paragraphs 3, 7), "Needless to say" (3), "after all" (7), and "Naturally" (8)?

Writing Topics

1. Analyze a role that is defined by gender, such as that of a wife or husband, mother or father, sister or brother, daughter or son. First write down the responsibilities, activities, and relationships that define that role, and then elaborate your ideas into an essay defining this role as you see it. You could, if appropriate, follow Brady's model by showing how the role is influenced by the expectations of another person or people.

2. Combine the methods of definition and comparison in an essay that compares a wife or a husband you know with Brady's definition of either role. Be sure that the point of your comparison is clear and that you use specific examples to illustrate the similarities or differences you see.

3. Brady's essay was written in the specific cultural context of 1971. Undoubtedly, many cultural changes have taken place since then, particularly changes in gender roles. However, one could also argue that much remains the same. Write an essay in which you compare the stereotypical role of a wife now with the role Brady defines. In addition to your own observations and experiences, consider contemporary images of wives that the media present—for instance, in television advertising or sitcoms.

NOEL PERRIN

Noel Perrin was born in 1927 in New York City. He received degrees from Williams College, Duke University, and Cambridge University. The author of many books dealing with themes of nature, ecology, and New England, Perrin is well known for Giving Up the Gun: Japan's Reversion to the Sword, 1543–1879 *and four collections of essays in the "First Person Rural" series. Recent publications include an article in* Vermont Life *about electric cars; a guide, in the* Chronicle of Higher Education, *to colleges focused on environmental protection; and book reviews in the* Washington Post *and the* Los Angeles Times. *Perrin is a former chair of the English department at Dartmouth.*

The Androgynous Man

"The Androgynous Man" first appeared in the New York Times *Sunday magazine as part of a series called "About Men." In the essay Perrin explores his idea of "spiritual androgyny": a crossing over in spirit between the masculine and feminine realms, freeing the self from limiting expectations and roles.*

The summer I was sixteen, I took a train from New York to Steamboat 1 Springs, Colorado, where I was going to be assistant horse wrangler at a camp. The trip took three days, and since I was much too shy to talk to strangers, I had quite a lot of time for reading. I read all of *Gone with the Wind*. I read all the interesting articles in a couple of magazines I had, and then I went back and read all the dull stuff. I also took all the quizzes, a thing of which magazines were even fuller then than now.

The one that held my undivided attention was called "How 2 Masculine/Feminine Are You?" It consisted of a large number of inkblots. The reader was supposed to decide which of the four objects each blot most resembled. The choices might be a cloud, a steam engine, a caterpillar and a sofa.

When I finished the test, I was shocked to find that I was barely 3 masculine at all. On a scale of 1 to 10, I was about a 1.2. Me, the horse wrangler? (And not just wrangler, either. That summer, I had to skin a couple of horses that died—the camp owner wanted the hides.)

246

The results of the test were so terrifying to me that for the first
time in my life I did a piece of original analysis. Having unlimited
time on the train, I looked at the "masculine" answers over and over,
trying to find what it was that distinguished real men from people
like me—and eventually I discovered two very simple patterns. It
was "masculine" to think the blots looked like man-made objects and
"feminine" to think they looked like natural objects. It was masculine to think they looked like things capable of causing harm, and
feminine to think of innocent things.

Even at sixteen, I had the sense to see that the compilers of the
test were using rather limited criteria—maleness and femaleness
are both more complicated than *that*—and I breathed a huge sigh of
relief. I wasn't necessarily a wimp, after all.

That the test did reveal something other than the superficiality of
its makers I realized only many years later. What it revealed was that
there is a large class of men and women both, to which I belong, who
are essentially androgynous. That doesn't mean we're gay, or low in
the appropriate hormones, or uncomfortable performing the jobs
traditionally assigned our sexes. (A few years after that summer, I
was leading troops in combat and, unfashionable as it now is to
admit this, having a very good time. War is exciting. What a pity the
twentieth century went and spoiled it with high-tech weapons.)

What it does mean to be spiritually androgynous is a kind of freedom. Men who are all-male, or he-man, or 100 percent red-blooded
Americans, have a little biological set that causes them to be attracted
to physical power, and probably also to dominance. Maybe even to
watching football. I don't say this to criticize them. Completely masculine men are quite often wonderful people: good husbands, good
(although sometimes overwhelming) fathers, good members of society. Furthermore, they are often so unselfconsciously at ease in the
world that other men seek to imitate them. They just aren't as free as
us androgynes. They pretty nearly have to be what they are; we have
a range of choices open.

The sad part is that many of us never discover that. Men who are
not 100 percent red-blooded Americans—say, those who are only
75 percent red-blooded—often fail to notice their freedom. They
are too busy trying to copy the he-men ever to realize that men, like
women, come in a wide variety of acceptable types. Why this frantic imitation? My answer is mere speculation, but not casual. I have
speculated on this for a long time.

Partly they're just envious of the he-man's unconscious ease.
Mostly they're terrified of finding that there may be something

wrong with them deep down, some weakness at the heart. To avoid discovering that, they spend their lives acting out the role that the he-man naturally lives. Sad.

One thing that men owe to the women's movement is that this 10 kind of failure is less common than it used to be. In releasing themselves from the single ideal of the dependent woman, women have more or less incidentally released a lot of men from the single ideal of the dominant male. The one mistake the feminists have made, I think, is in supposing that *all* men need this release, or that the world would be a better place if all men achieved it. It wouldn't. It would just be duller.

So far I have been pretty vague about just what the freedom of an 11 androgynous man is. Obviously it varies with the case. In the case I know best, my own, I can be quite specific. It has freed me most as a parent. I am, among other things, a fairly good natural mother. I like the nurturing role. It makes me feel good to see a child eat — and it turns me to mush to see a four-year-old holding a glass with both small hands, in order to drink. I even enjoyed sewing patches on the knees of my daughter Amy's Dr. Dentons when she was at the crawling stage. All that pleasure I would have lost if I had made myself stick to the notion of the paternal role that I started with.

Or take a smaller and rather ridiculous example. I feel free to kiss 12 cats. Until recently it never occurred to me that I would want to, though my daughters have been doing it all their lives. But my elder daughter is now twenty-two, and in London. Of course, I get to look after her cat while she is gone. He's a big, handsome farm cat named Petrushka, very unsentimental, though used from kittenhood to being kissed on the top of the head by Elizabeth. I've gotten very fond of him (he's the adventurous kind of cat who likes to climb hills with you), and one night I simply felt like kissing him on the top of the head, and did. Why did no one tell me sooner how silky cat fur is?

Then there's my relation to cars. I am completely unembarrassed 13 by my inability to diagnose even minor problems in whatever object I happen to be driving, and don't have to make some insider's remark to mechanics to try to establish that I, too, am a "Man with His Machine."

The same ease extends to household maintenance. I do it, of 14 course. Service people are expensive. But for the last decade my house has functioned better than it used to because I've had the aid of a volume called *Home Repairs Any Woman Can Do*, which is pitched just right for people at my technical level. As a youth, I'd as soon have touched such a book as I would have become a transvestite. Even though common sense says there is really nothing sexual whatsoever about fixing sinks.

Or take public emotion. All my life I have easily been moved by 15 certain kinds of voices. The actress Siobhan McKenna's,[1] to take a notable case. Give her an emotional scene in a play, and within ten words my eyes are full of tears. In boyhood, my great dread was that someone might notice. I struggled manfully, you might say, to suppress this weakness. Now, of course, I don't see it was a weakness at all, but as a kind of fulfillment. I even suspect that the true he-men feel the same way, or one kind of them does, at least, and it's only the poor imitators who have to struggle to repress themselves.

Let me come back to the inkblots, with their assumption that mas- 16 culine equates with machinery and science, and feminine with art and nature. I have no idea whether the right pronoun for God is He, She or It. But this I'm pretty sure of. If God could somehow be induced to take that test, God would not come out macho, and not feminismo, either, but right in the middle. Fellow androgynes, it's a nice thought.

Meaning

1. In paragraph 6 Perrin writes that "there is a large class of men and women both, to which I belong, who are essentially androgynous." What does *androgynous* mean? Is Perrin at ease with his androgynous identity?

2. In paragraphs 7–9 Perrin defines *manhood* across a kind of range or spectrum. What is this spectrum, and how does it relate to the inkblot test he describes in his opening paragraphs?

3. In paragraph 10 Perrin claims that men owe a debt to the women's movement. Explain what he believes feminists have contributed to society's understanding of manhood.

Purpose and Audience

1. Why do you think Perrin wrote this essay? Was he trying to justify or come to terms with his own masculinity? If not, what was he trying to do?

2. In his conclusion (paragraph 16), Perrin speaks directly to his "Fellow androgynes." What does this suggest about Perrin's vision of his readers?

---

[1]Siobhan McKenna (1923–86) was an Irish stage and movie actress. [Editor's note.]

3. How do you think Perrin expects his audience to react to this essay? Does he seem to assume his audience's agreement, does he write defensively to forestall criticism, or does he assume some other response? What in the essay makes you think as you do?

Method and Structure

1. Why is definition an appropriate method for Perrin to use in developing his ideas? What specific features of this method serve him?
2. In developing his definition, Perrin relies heavily on personal anecdotes. What do the anecdotes contribute to his essay? Do they weaken his case in any way?
3. **Other Methods**   In what ways does Perrin use comparison and contrast as part of his definition? Why is this method important in developing his point?

Language

1. Perrin's vocabulary in this essay ranges from relatively formal to highly informal. For example, in paragraph 5 he uses the phrase "rather limited criteria" as well as the word "wimp." What does this range of vocabulary suggest about Perrin's role as a writer here?
2. In paragraph 8 Perrin writes that the point he is making is "mere speculation, but not casual." What does he mean?
3. Point out some examples that show Perrin appealing to his readers' sense of humor. What is the effect of these examples?

Writing Topics

1. In an essay, define *manhood* or *womanhood*. Does your definition correspond to traditional assumptions about gender or is it more like Perrin's? What characteristics does your definition *not* include?
2. Based on your own experience, write an essay in which you define a stereotype you have encountered, not necessarily a gender stereotype. Examples include assumptions about jocks, techies, persons in wheelchairs, persons who are thin or heavy or have other physical characteristics, or racial differences.
3. Despite the societal changes Perrin refers to, many gender-related issues continue to be a source of controversy and debate: coeducation versus gender-specific classrooms, discrepancies between men's and women's earnings, what constitutes sexual harassment, parental roles within the family, gender stereotypes in the media, and so on. Choose one such controversy that interests you, and in an essay explore its various sides as well as your own position.

GLORIA NAYLOR

An American novelist and essayist, Gloria Naylor was born in 1950 in New York City. She served as a missionary for Jehovah's Witnesses from 1967 to 1975 and then worked as a hotel telephone operator until 1981. That year she graduated from Brooklyn College of the City of New York with a BA and went on to do graduate work in African American studies at Yale University. Since receiving an MA from Yale, Naylor has published five novels dealing with the varied histories and life-styles often lumped together as "the black experience": The Women of Brewster Place *(1982), about the lives of eight black women, which won the American Book Award for fiction and was made into a television movie;* Linden Hills *(1985), about a black middle-class neighborhood;* Mama Day *(1988), about a Georgian woman with visionary powers;* Bailey's Cafe *(1992), about a group of people whose lives are at crossroads; and* The Men of Brewster Place *(1997), about the men whose lives intersect those of the women of Brewster Place.*

The Meanings of a Word

Recalling an experience as a third-grader leads Naylor to probe the meanings of a highly sensitive word. At the same time she explores how words acquire their meanings from use. This essay first appeared in the New York Times *in 1986.*

Language is the subject. It is the written form with which I've managed to keep the wolf away from the door and, in diaries, to keep my sanity. In spite of this, I consider the written word inferior to the spoken, and much of the frustration experienced by novelists is the awareness that whatever we manage to capture in even the most transcendent passages falls far short of the richness of life. Dialogue achieves its power in the dynamics of a fleeting moment of sight, sound, smell, and touch. 1

I'm not going to enter the debate here about whether it is language that shapes reality or vice versa. The battle is doomed to be waged whenever we seek intermittent reprieve from the chicken and egg dispute. I will simply take the position that the spoken word, like the written word, amounts to a nonsensical arrangement of sounds 2 or letters without a consensus that assigns "meaning." And building from the meanings of what we hear, we order reality. Words themselves are innocuous; it is the consensus that gives them true power.

I remember the first time I heard the word *nigger*. In my third-grade class, our math tests were being passed down the rows, and as I handed the papers to a little boy in back of me, I remarked that once again he had received a much lower mark than I did. He snatched his test from me and spit out that word. Had he called me a nymphomaniac or a necrophiliac, I couldn't have been more puzzled. I didn't know what a nigger was, but I knew that whatever it meant, it was something he shouldn't have called me. This was verified when I raised my hand, and in a loud voice repeated what he had said and watched the teacher scold him for using a "bad" word. I was later to go home and ask the inevitable question that every black parent must face—"Mommy, what does *nigger* mean?"

And what exactly did it mean? Thinking back, I realize that this could not have been the first time the word was used in my presence. I was part of a large extended family that had migrated from the rural South after World War II and formed a close-knit network that gravitated around my maternal grandparents. Their ground-floor apartment in one of the buildings they owned in Harlem was a weekend mecca for my immediate family, along with countless aunts, uncles, and cousins who brought along assorted friends. It was a bustling and open house with assorted neighbors and tenants popping in and out to exchange bits of gossip, pick up an old quarrel, or referee the ongoing checkers game in which my grandmother cheated shamelessly. They were all there to let down their hair and put up their feet after a week of labor in the factories, laundries, and shipyards of New York.

Amid the clamor, which could reach deafening proportions—two or three conversations going on simultaneously, punctuated by the sound of a baby's crying somewhere in the back rooms or out on the street—there was still a rigid set of rules about what was said and how. Older children were sent out of the living room when it was time to get into the juicy details about "you-know-who" up on the third floor who had gone and gotten herself "p-r-e-g-n-a-n-t!" But my parents, knowing that I could spell well beyond my years, always demanded that I follow the others out to play. Beyond sexual misconduct and death, everything else was considered harmless for our young ears. And so among the anecdotes of the triumphs and disappointments in the various workings of their lives, the word *nigger* was used in my presence, but it was set within contexts and inflections that caused it to register in my mind as something else.

In the singular, the word was always applied to a man who had   6
distinguished himself in some situation that brought their approval for his strength, intelligence, or drive:

"Did Johnny *really* do that?"   7

"I'm telling you, that nigger pulled in $6,000 of overtime last year.   8
Said he got enough for a down payment on a house."

When used with a possessive adjective by a woman—"my nigger"—   9
it became a term of endearment for her husband or boyfriend. But it could be more than just a term applied to a man. In their mouths it became the pure essence of manhood—a disembodied force that channeled their past history of struggle and present survival against the odds into a victorious statement of being: "Yeah, that old foreman found out quick enough—you don't mess with a nigger."

In the plural, it became a description of some group within the   10
community that had overstepped the bounds of decency as my family defined it. Parents who neglected their children, a drunken couple who fought in public, people who simply refused to look for work, those with excessively dirty mouths or unkempt households were all "trifling niggers." This particular circle could forgive hard times, unemployment, the occasional bout of depression—they had gone through all of that themselves—but the unforgivable sin was a lack of self-respect.

A woman could never be a "nigger" in the singular, with its con-   11
notation of confirming worth. The noun *girl* was its closest equivalent in that sense, but only when used in direct address and regardless of the gender doing the addressing. *Girl* was a token of respect for a woman. The one-syllable word was drawn out to sound like three in recognition of the extra ounce of wit, nerve, or daring that the woman had shown in the situation under discussion.

"G-i-r-l, stop. You mean you said that to his face?"   12

But if the word was used in a third-person reference or shortened   13
so that it almost snapped out of the mouth, it always involved some element of communal disapproval. And age became an important factor in these exchanges. It was only between individuals of the same generation, or from any older person to a younger (but never the other way around), that *girl* would be considered a compliment.

I don't agree with the argument that use of the word *nigger* at this   14
social stratum of the black community was an internalization of racism. The dynamics were the exact opposite: the people in my grandmother's living room took a word that whites used to signify

worthlessness or degradation and rendered it impotent. Gathering there together, they transformed *nigger* to signify the varied and complex human beings they knew themselves to be. If the word was to disappear totally from the mouths of even the most liberal of white society, no one in that room was naive enough to believe it would disappear from white minds. Meeting the word head-on, they proved it had absolutely nothing to do with the way they were determined to live their lives.

So there must have been dozens of times that *nigger* was spoken 15 in front of me before I reached the third grade. But I didn't "hear" it until it was said by a small pair of lips that had already learned it could be a way to humiliate me. That was the word I went home and asked my mother about. And since she knew that I had to grow up in America, she took me in her lap and explained.

Meaning

1. Naylor writes that "the spoken word, like the written word, amounts to a nonsensical arrangement of sounds or letters without a consensus that assigns 'meaning'" (paragraph 2). Explain this statement in your own words. How did this statement apply to the word *nigger* for the young Naylor?
2. What is Naylor's main idea? Where does she express it?
3. In paragraph 14 Naylor disagrees with those who claim that the African American community's use of the term *nigger* constitutes "an internalization of racism." What alternative explanation does she offer? Do you agree with her interpretation? Why, or why not?

Purpose and Audience

1. What is Naylor's purpose or purposes in writing this essay: to express herself? to explain something? to convince readers of something? Support your answer by referring to passages from the essay.
2. Naylor's essay first appeared in the *New York Times*, a daily newspaper whose readers are largely middle-class whites. In what ways does she seem to consider and address this audience?

Method and Structure

1. Why is Naylor's choice of the method of definition especially appropriate given the point she is trying to make about language?
2. Naylor supports her main idea by defining two words, *nigger* and *girl*. What factors influence the various meanings of each word?

3. Naylor's essay is divided into sections, each contributing something different to the whole. Identify the sections and their functions.

4. **Other Methods**   Like many writers of definition, Naylor employs a number of other methods of development: for instance, in paragraphs 4 and 5 she describes the atmosphere of her grandparents' apartment; in 8, 9, and 12 she cites examples of speech; and in 11–13 she compares and contrasts the two uses of *girl*. At two points in the essay Naylor relies on a narrative of the same incident. Where, and for what purpose?

Language

1. How would you describe the tone of Naylor's essay? Steady and reasoned, or impassioned? Is the style more academic or more informal? Do you find Naylor's tone and style appropriate given her subject matter? Why?

2. In paragraph 3 Naylor uses language to convey a child's perspective. For example, she seems to become the arrogant little girl who "remarked that once again he had received a much lower mark than I did." Locate three or four other uses of language in the essay that emphasize her separation from the world of adults. How does this perspective contribute to the effect of the essay?

3. In paragraph 14 Naylor concludes that her family used *nigger* "to signify the varied and complex human beings they knew themselves to be." This variety and complexity is demonstrated through the words and expressions she uses to describe life in her grandparents' home — "a weekend mecca," "a bustling and open house" (4). Cite five or six other examples of concrete, vivid language in this description.

Writing Topics

1. Using your own experiences for examples, write an essay modeled on Naylor's in which you define "the meanings of a word" (or words). The word you choose might be a stereotype based on ethnicity, gender, appearance, or income, for example. Have you found, like Naylor, that meaning varies with context? If so, make the variations clear.

2. A recent grassroots movement tried but failed to have the word *nigger* removed from dictionaries. Are there some words so hateful that they should be banned from the language? Or is such an attempt to control language even more objectionable? Write an essay that states and supports your answers, giving plenty of examples.

3. About African Americans' use of the word *nigger*, Naylor writes that "the people in my grandmother's living room took a word that whites used to signify worthlessness or degradation and rendered it impotent"

(paragraph 14). Write an essay in which you discuss a symbol, a trait, or another word that has been used negatively by one group toward another but has been transformed by the targeted group into a positive meaning. Examples include the gay community's use of the word *queer* and the Jewish community's reclaiming of the Star of David after the Nazis used the symbol to stigmatize Jews. How did the definition of the symbol, trait, or word change from one community to another? Like Naylor, provide readers with examples that clarify your definitions.

AMY TAN

Amy Tan was born in 1952 in Oakland, California, the daughter of Chinese immigrants. She grew up in northern California and majored in English and linguistics at San Jose State University, where she received a BA and an MA. Tan's first career was as a business writer, crafting corporate reports and executives' speeches. Dissatisfied with her work, she began writing fiction. Her first book, The Joy Luck Club *(1989), a critical and popular success, is a series of interrelated stories about the bonds between immigrant Chinese mothers and their American-born daughters. Since* The Joy Luck Club *was published, she has written three more novels:* The Kitchen God's Wife *(1991),* The Hundred Secret Senses *(1995), and* The Bonesetter's Daughter *(2001).*

Mother Tongue

In this essay, Tan defines her sense of a mother tongue, exploring the versions of English that she has used as a daughter, a student, and a writer. The essay was first published in Threepenny Review *in 1990.*

I am not a scholar of English or literature. I cannot give you much 1
more than personal opinions on the English language and its variations in this country or others.

I am a writer. And by that definition, I am someone who has always 2
loved language. I am fascinated by language in daily life. I spend a great deal of my time thinking about the power of language — the way it can evoke an emotion, a visual image, a complex idea, or a simple truth. Language is the tool of my trade. And I use them all — all the Englishes I grew up with.

Recently, I was made keenly aware of the different Englishes I do 3
use. I was giving a talk to a large group of people, the same talk I had already given to half a dozen other groups. The nature of the talk was about my writing, my life, and my book, *The Joy Luck Club*. The talk was going along well enough, until I remembered one major difference that made the whole talk sound wrong. My mother was in the room. And it was perhaps the first time she had heard me give a lengthy speech, using the kind of English I have never used with her.

I was saying things like, "The intersection of memory upon imagination" and "There is an aspect of my fiction that relates to thusand-thus" — a speech filled with carefully wrought grammatical phrases, burdened, it suddenly seemed to me, with nominalized forms, past perfect tenses, conditional phrases, all the forms of Standard English that I had learned in school and through books, the forms of English I did not use at home with my mother.

Just last week, I was walking down the street with my mother, and   4
I again found myself conscious of the English I was using, and the English I do use with her. We were talking about the price of new and used furniture and I heard myself saying this: "Not waste money that way." My husband was with us as well, and he didn't notice any switch in my English. And then I realized why. It's because over the twenty years we've been together I've often used that same kind of English with him, and sometimes he even uses it with me. It has become our language of intimacy, a different sort of English that relates to family talk, the language I grew up with.

So you'll have some idea of what this family talk I heard sounds   5
like, I'll quote what my mother said during a recent conversation which I videotaped and then transcribed. During this conversation, my mother was talking about a political gangster in Shanghai who had the same last name as her family's, Du, and how the gangster in his early years wanted to be adopted by her family, which was rich by comparison. Later, the gangster became more powerful, far richer than my mother's family, and one day showed up at my mother's wedding to pay his respects. Here's what she said in part:

"Du Yusong having business like fruit stand. Like off the street   6
kind. He is like Du Zong — but not Tsung-ming Island people. The local people call putong, the river east side, he belong to that side local people. That man want to ask Du Zong father take him in like become own family. Du Zong father wasn't look down on him, but didn't take seriously, until that man big like become a mafia. Now important person, very hard to inviting him. Chinese way, came only to show respect, don't stay for dinner. Respect for making big celebration, he shows up. Mean gives lots of respect. Chinese custom. Chinese social life that way. If too important won't have to stay too long. He come to my wedding. I didn't see, I heard it. I gone to boy's side, they have YMCA dinner. Chinese age I was nineteen."

You should know that my mother's expressive command of En   7
glish belies how much she actually understands. She reads the *Forbes* report, listens to *Wall Street Week*, converses daily with her stockbroker, reads all of Shirley MacLaine's books with ease — all

kinds of things I can't begin to understand. Yet some of my friends tell me they understand fifty percent of what my mother says. Some say they understand eighty to ninety percent. Some say they understand none of it, as if she were speaking pure Chinese. But to me, my mother's English is perfectly clear, perfectly natural. It's my mother tongue. Her language, as I hear it, is vivid, direct, full of observation and imagery. That was the language that helped shape the way I saw things, expressed things, made sense of the world.

Lately, I've been giving more thought to the kind of English my 8 mother speaks. Like others, I have described it to people as "broken" or "fractured" English. But I wince when I say that. It has always bothered me that I can think of no way to describe it other than "broken," as if it were damaged and needed to be fixed, as if it lacked a certain wholeness and soundness. I've heard other terms used, "limited English," for example. But they seem just as bad, as if everything is limited, including people's perceptions of the limited English speaker.

I know this for a fact, because when I was growing up, my mother's 9 "limited" English limited *my* perception of her. I was ashamed of her English. I believed that her English reflected the quality of what she had to say. That is, because she expressed them imperfectly her thoughts were imperfect. And I had plenty of empirical evidence to support me: the fact that people in department stores, at banks, and at restaurants did not take her seriously, did not give her good service, pretended not to understand her, or even acted as if they did not hear her.

My mother has long realized the limitations of her English as 10 well. When I was fifteen, she used to have me call people on the phone to pretend I was she. In this guise, I was forced to ask for information or even to complain and yell at people who had been rude to her. One time it was a call to her stockbroker in New York. She had cashed out her small portfolio and it just so happened we were going to go to New York the next week, our very first trip outside California. I had to get on the phone and say in an adolescent voice that was not very convincing, "This is Mrs. Tan."

And my mother was standing in the back whispering loudly, "Why 11 he don't send me check, already two weeks late. So mad he lie to me, losing me money."

And then I said in perfect English, "Yes, I'm getting rather con- 12 cerned. You had agreed to send the check two weeks ago, but it hasn't arrived."

Then she began to talk more loudly. "What he want, I come to New 13 York tell him front of his boss, you cheating me?" And I was trying to calm her down, make her be quiet, while telling the stockbroker, "I can't tolerate any more excuses. If I don't receive the check immediately, I am going to have to speak to your manager when I'm in New York next week." And sure enough, the following week there we were in front of this astonished stockbroker, and I was sitting there red-faced and quiet, and my mother, the real Mrs. Tan, was shouting at his boss in her impeccable broken English.

We used a similar routine just five days ago, for a situation that was far less humorous. My mother had gone to the hospital for an appointment, to find out about a benign brain tumor a CAT scan had revealed a month ago. She said she had spoken very good English, her best English, no mistakes. Still, she said, the hospital did not apologize when they said they had lost the CAT scan and she had come for nothing. She said they did not seem to have any sympathy when she told them she was anxious to know the exact diagnosis, since her husband and son had both died of brain tumors. She said they would not give her any more information until the next time and she would have to make another appointment for that. So she said she would not leave until the doctor called her daughter. She wouldn't budge. And when the doctor finally called her daughter, me, who spoke in perfect English—lo and behold—we had assurances the CAT scan would be found, promises that a conference call on Monday would be held, and apologies for any suffering my mother had gone through for a most regrettable mistake. 14

I think my mother's English almost had an effect on limiting my possibilities in life as well. Sociologists and linguists probably will tell you that a person's developing language skills are more influenced by peers. But I think that the language spoken in the family, especially in immigrant families which are more insular, plays a large role in shaping the language of the child. And I believe that it affected my results on achievement tests, IQ tests, and the SAT. While my English skills were never judged as poor, compared to math, English could not be considered my strong suit. In grade school I did moderately well, getting perhaps B's, sometimes B-pluses, in English and scoring perhaps in the sixtieth or seventieth percentile on achievement tests. But those scores were not good enough to override the opinion that my true abilities lay in math and science, because in those areas I achieved A's and scored in the ninetieth percentile or higher. 15

This was understandable. Math is precise; there is only one correct answer. Whereas, for me at least, the answers on English tests were always a judgment call, a matter of opinion and personal experience. 16

Those tests were constructed around items like fill-in-the-blank sentence completion, such as, "Even though Tom was ____, Mary thought he was ____." And the correct answer always seemed to be the most bland combinations of thoughts, for example, "Even though Tom was shy, Mary thought he was charming," with the grammatical structure "even though" limiting the correct answer to some sort of semantic opposites, so you wouldn't get answers like, "Even though Tom was foolish, Mary thought he was ridiculous." Well, according to my mother, there were very few limitations as to what Tom could have been and what Mary might have thought of him. So I never did well on tests like that.

The same was true with word analogies, pairs of words in which you were supposed to find some sort of logical, semantic relationship—for example, "*Sunset* is to *nightfall* as ____ is to ____." And here you would be presented with a list of four possible pairs, one of which showed the same kind of relationship: *red* is to *stoplight, bus* is to *arrival, chills* is to *fever, yawn* is to *boring.* Well, I could never think that way. I knew what the tests were asking, but I could not block out of my mind the images already created by the first pair, "*sunset* is to *nightfall*"—and I would see a burst of colors against a darkening sky, the moon rising, the lowering of a curtain of stars. And all the other pairs of words—*red, bus, stoplight, boring*—just threw up a mass of confusing images, making it impossible for me to sort out something as logical as saying: "A sunset precedes nightfall" is the same as "a chill precedes a fever." The only way I would have gotten that answer right would have been to imagine an associative situation, for example, my being disobedient and staying out past sunset, catching a chill at night, which turns into feverish pneumonia as punishment, which indeed did happen to me. 17

I have been thinking about all this lately, about my mother's English, about achievement tests. Because lately I've been asked, as a writer, why there are not more Asian Americans enrolled in creative writing programs. Why do so many Chinese students go into engineering? Well, these are broad sociological questions I can't begin to answer. But I have noticed in surveys—in fact, just last week—that Asian students, as a whole, always do significantly better on math achievement tests than in English. And this makes me think that there are other Asian American students whose English spoken in the home might also be described as "broken" or "limited." And perhaps they also have teachers who are steering them away from writing and into math and science, which is what happened to me. 18

Fortunately, I happen to be rebellious in nature and enjoy the   19
challenge of disproving assumptions made about me. I became an
English major my first year in college, after being enrolled as pre-
med. I started writing nonfiction as a freelancer the week after I was
told by my former boss that writing was my worst skill and I should
hone my talents toward account management.

But it wasn't until 1985 that I finally began to write fiction. And at   20
first I wrote using what I thought to be wittily crafted sentences, sentences that would finally prove I had mastery over the English language. Here's an example from the first draft of a story that later
made its way into *The Joy Luck Club*, but without this line: "That was
my mental quandary in its nascent state." A terrible line, which I can
barely pronounce.

Fortunately, for reasons I won't get into today, I later decided I   21
should envision a reader for the stories I would write. And the
reader I decided upon was my mother, because these were stories
about mothers. So with this reader in mind—and in fact she did
read my early drafts—I began to write stories using all the Englishes I grew up with: the English I spoke to my mother, which for
lack of a better term might be described as "simple"; the English
she used with me, which for lack of a better term might be
described as "broken"; my translation of her Chinese, which could
certainly be described as "watered down"; and what I imagined to
be her translation of her Chinese if she could speak in perfect English, her internal language, and for that I sought to preserve the
essence, but neither an English nor a Chinese structure. I wanted
to capture what language ability tests can never reveal: her intent,
her passion, her imagery, the rhythms of her speech, and the
nature of her thoughts.

Apart from what any critic had to say about my writing, I knew I   22
had succeeded where it counted when my mother finished reading
my book and gave me her verdict: "So easy to read."

Meaning

1. For Tan the phrase "mother tongue" has a special meaning. How
   would you summarize this meaning? Why does Tan feel so deeply
   about her "mother tongue"?
2. In what ways does the English that Tan's mother speaks affect how
   people outside the Chinese American community think of her?
   What examples does Tan give to demonstrate this fact of her mother's
   life?

3. In paragraph 15, Tan writes, "[M]y mother's English almost had an effect on limiting my possibilities in life as well." What does she mean? Why does she use the qualifier "almost"?

Purpose and Audience

1. Why do you suppose Tan wrote this essay? Does she have a purpose beyond changing readers' perceptions of her mother's "broken" English? What passages support your answer?

2. How can you tell that Tan is not writing primarily to an audience of Asian Americans? If Asian Americans were her primary audience, how might the essay be different?

Method and Structure

1. How does Tan develop her definition of her "mother tongue"? That is, how does she best help readers understand her mother's speech?

2. Tan divides her essay into three sections, the second beginning in paragraph 8 and the third beginning in paragraph 18. What is the focus of each section? Why do think Tan divided the essay like this?

3. **Other Methods**   In paragraph 2 and again in paragraph 21, Tan refers to "all the Englishes I grew up with." How does she classify these various "Englishes"?

Language

1. What troubles Tan about the labels "broken," "fractured," and "limited" for her mother's English (paragraph 8)? How do these labels contrast with the way she views her mother's speech?

2. In paragraphs 16 and 17, Tan writes about the kinds of vocabulary items that appear on standardized English tests. In contrast to the precision of the answers to mathematical questions, why were the answers to vocabulary questions "always a judgment call, a matter of opinion and personal experience" for her?

Writing Topics

1. Think about the language you speak with close friends or family members. What are some characteristics of this language that outsiders might find difficult to understand? Write an essay that focuses on the idea of "personal" language—that is, language that creates or reflects closeness among people. In developing your essay, you may call on your own experiences, your observations of others, and your

reading (of both fiction and nonfiction). Be sure to provide as many specific examples of language use as you can.

2. How do you define "standard English"? To what extent do you believe that nonstandard English marks people as "limited"? On what occasions is standard English absolutely required? Are there any occasions when nonstandard English is entirely appropriate? In an essay, explain and illustrate both the drawbacks and the benefits of standard and nonstandard English. (If necessary, consult the Glossary under *nonstandard English*.)

3. Tan writes that as a student she didn't do well on standardized English tests. In recent years, such standardized testing has grown increasingly prominent in evaluating students' achievement. In an essay, discuss your ideas about standardized tests. How accurately do you think they assess students' academic abilities? How do you respond to the claim that many such tests are biased in favor of affluent white students? How, in your experience, have they affected classroom teaching strategies? You can consider any of these questions or other related ones that interest you.

Writing with the Method
Definition

Choose one of the following topics, or any other topic they suggest, for an essay developed by definition. The topic you decide on should be something you care about so that definition is a means of communicating an idea, not an end in itself.

PERSONAL QUALITIES
1. Ignorance
2. Selflessness or selfishness
3. Loyalty or disloyalty
4. Responsibility
5. A good sport

EXPERIENCES AND FEELINGS
6. A nightmare
7. A good teacher, coach, parent, or friend
8. Religious faith

ASPIRATIONS
9. The Good Life
10. Success or failure
11. A good job

SOCIAL CONCERNS
12. Poverty
13. Education
14. Domestic violence
15. Substance abuse
16. Prejudice
17. An American ethnic group such as Italians, WASPs, or Chinese

ART AND ENTERTAINMENT
18. Jazz or some other kind of music
19. A good novel, movie, or television program
20. Impressionist painting or some other school of art

IDEAS

21. Freedom
22. Feminism
23. A key concept in a course you're taking

Chapter Nine

CAUSE-AND-EFFECT ANALYSIS

USING THE METHOD

Why did free agency become so important in professional baseball, and how has it affected the sport? What caused the recent warming of the Pacific Ocean, and how did the warming affect the earth's weather? We answer questions like these with **cause-and-effect analysis,** the method of dividing occurrences into their elements to find relationships among them. Cause-and-effect analysis is a specific kind of analysis, the method discussed in Chapter 4.

When we analyze **causes,** we discover which of the events preceding a specified outcome actually made it happen:

What caused Adolf Hitler's rise in Germany?

Why have herbal medicines become so popular?

When we analyze **effects,** we discover which of the events following a specified occurrence actually resulted from it:

What do we do for (or to) drug addicts when we imprison them?

What happens to our foreign policy when the president's advisers disagree over its conduct?

These are existing effects of past or current situations, but effects are often predicted for the future:

How would a cure for cancer affect the average life expectancy of men and women?

How might your decision to major in history affect your job prospects?

Causes and effects can also be analyzed together, as the questions opening this chapter illustrate.

Cause-and-effect analysis is found in just about every discipline and occupation, including history, social science, natural science, engineering, medicine, law, business, and sports. In any of these fields, as well as in writing done for college courses, your purpose in analyzing may be to explain or to persuade. In explaining why something happened or what its outcome was or will be, you try to order experience and pin down the connections in it. In arguing with cause-and-effect analysis, you try to demonstrate why one explanation of causes is more accurate than another or how a proposed action will produce desirable or undesirable consequences.

The possibility of arguing about causes and effects points to the main challenge of this method. Related events sometimes overlap, sometimes follow one another immediately, and sometimes connect over gaps in time. They vary in their duration and complexity. They vary in their importance. Analyzing causes and effects thus requires not only identifying them but also discerning their relationships accurately and weighing their significance fairly.

Causes and effects often do occur in a sequence, each contributing to the next in what is called a **causal chain.** For instance, an unlucky man named Jones ends up in prison, and the causal chain leading to his imprisonment can be outlined as follows: Jones's neighbor, Smith, dumped trash on Jones's lawn. In reprisal, Jones set a small brushfire in Smith's yard. A spark from the fire accidentally ignited Smith's house. Jones was prosecuted for the fire and sent to jail. In this chain, each event is the cause of an effect, which in turn is the cause of another effect, and so on to the unhappy conclusion.

Identifying a causal chain partly involves sorting out events in time:

- **Immediate** causes or effects occur nearest an event. For instance, the immediate cause of a town's high unemployment rate may be the closing of a large manufacturing plant where many townspeople work.
- **Remote** causes or effects occur further away in time. The remote cause of the town's unemployment rate may be a drastic decline in the company's sales or (more remote) a weak regional or national economy.

Analyzing causes also requires distinguishing their relative importance in the sequence:

- **Major** causes are directly and primarily responsible for the outcome. For instance, if a weak economy is responsible for low sales, it is a major cause of the manufacturing plant's closing.
- **Minor** causes (also called **contributory** causes) merely contribute to the outcome. The manufacturing plant may have closed for the additional reason that the owners could not afford to make repairs to its machines.

As these examples illustrate, time and significance can overlap in cause-and-effect analysis: a weak economy, for instance, is both a remote and a major cause; the lack of funds for repairs is both an immediate and a minor cause.

Because most cause-and-effect relationships are complex, you should take care to avoid several pitfalls in analyzing and presenting them. One is a confusion of coincidence and cause—that is, an assumption that because one event preceded another, it must have caused the other. This error is nicknamed **post hoc,** from the Latin *post hoc, ergo propter hoc,* meaning "after this, therefore because of this." Superstitions often illustrate post hoc: a basketball player believes that a charm once ended her shooting slump, so she now wears the charm whenever she plays. But post hoc also occurs in more serious matters. For instance, the office of a school administrator is vandalized, and he blames the incident on a recent speech by the student-government president criticizing the administration. But the administrator has no grounds for his accusation unless he can prove that the speech incited the vandals. In the absence of proof, the administrator commits the error of post hoc by asserting that the speech caused the vandalism simply because the speech preceded the vandalism.

Another potential problem in cause-and-effect writing is **oversimplification.** You must consider not just the causes and effects that seem obvious or important but all the possibilities: remote as well as immediate, minor as well as major. One form of oversimplification confuses a necessary cause with a sufficient cause:

- A **necessary** cause, as the term implies, is one that must happen in order for an effect to come about; an effect can have more than one necessary cause. For example, if emissions from a factory cause a high rate of illness in a neighborhood, the emissions are a necessary cause.

- A **sufficient** cause, in contrast, is one that brings about the effect *by itself*. The emissions are not a sufficient cause of the illness rate unless all other possible causes — such as water pollution or infection—can be eliminated.

Oversimplification can also occur if you allow opinions or emotions to cloud the interpretation of evidence. Suppose that you are examining the reasons why a gun-control bill you opposed was passed by the state legislature. Some of your evidence strongly suggests that a member of the legislature, a vocal supporter of the bill, was unduly influenced by lobbyists. But if you attributed the passage of the bill solely to this legislator, you would be exaggerating the significance of a single legislator and you would be ignoring the opinions of the many others who also voted for the bill. To achieve a balanced analysis, you would have to put aside your own feelings and consider all possible causes for the bill's passage.

DEVELOPING AN ESSAY BY CAUSE-AND-EFFECT ANALYSIS

Getting Started

Assignments in almost any course or line of work ask for cause-and-effect analysis: What caused the Vietnam War? In the theory of sociobiology, what are the effects of altruism on the survival of the group? Why did costs exceed the budget last month? You can find your own subject for cause-and-effect analysis from your experiences, from observation of others, from your course work, or from your reading outside school. Anytime you find yourself wondering what happened or why or what if, you may be onto an appropriate subject.

Remember that your treatment of causes or effects or both must be thorough; thus your subject must be manageable within the constraints of time and space imposed on you. Broad subjects like those following must be narrowed to something whose complexities you can cover adequately.

BROAD SUBJECT	Causes of the increase in American industrial productivity
NARROWER SUBJECT	Causes of increasing productivity on one assembly line

BROAD SUBJECT   Effects of cigarette smoke
NARROWER SUBJECT   Effects of parents' secondhand smoke on
                      small children

Whether your subject suggests a focus on causes or effects or both, list as many of them as you can from memory or from further reading. If the subject does not suggest a focus, then ask yourself questions to begin exploring it:

- Why did it happen?
- What contributed to it?
- What were or are its results?
- What might its consequences be?

One or more of these questions should lead you to a focus and, as you explore further, to a more complete list of ideas.

But you cannot stop with a simple list, for you must arrange the causes or effects in sequence and weigh their relative importance: Do the events sort out into a causal chain? Besides the immediate causes and effects, are there also less obvious, more remote ones? Besides the major causes or effects, are there also minor ones? At this stage, you may find that diagramming relationships helps you see them more clearly. The following diagram illustrates the earlier example of the plant closing:

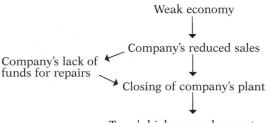

Though uncomplicated, the diagram does sort out the causes and effects and shows their relationships and sequence.

While you are developing a clear picture of your subject, you should also be anticipating the expectations and needs of your readers. As with the other methods of essay development, consider especially what your readers already know about your subject and what they need to be told:

- Do readers require background information?
- Are they likely to be familiar with some of the causes or effects you are analyzing, or should you explain every one completely?
- Which causes or effects might readers already accept?
- Which ones might they disagree with? If, for instance, the plant closing affected many of your readers—putting them or their relatives out of work—they might blame the company's owners rather than economic forces beyond the owners' control. You would have to address these preconceptions and provide plenty of evidence for your own interpretation.

To help manage your ideas and information, try to develop a thesis sentence that states your subject, your perspective on it, and your purpose. The thesis sentence should reflect your judgments about the relative significance of possible causes or effects. For instance:

EXPLANATORY THESIS SENTENCE   Being caught in the middle of a family quarrel has affected not only my feelings about my family but also my relations with friends.

PERSUASIVE THESIS SENTENCE   Contrary to local opinion, the many people put out of work by the closing of Windsor Manufacturing were victims not of the owners' incompetence but of the nation's weak economy.

Organizing

The introduction to a cause-and-effect essay can pull readers in by describing the situation whose causes or effects you plan to analyze, such as the passage of a bill in the legislature or a town's high unemployment rate. The introduction may also provide background, such as a brief narrative of a family quarrel; or it may summarize the analysis of causes or effects that the essay disputes, such as the townspeople's blaming the owners for a plant's closing. If your thesis is not already apparent in the introduction, stating it explicitly can tell readers exactly what your purpose is and which causes or effects or both you plan to highlight. If you anticipate that readers will oppose your thesis, however, you may want to delay stating it until the end of the essay, after you have provided the evidence to support it.

The arrangement of the body of the essay depends primarily on your material and your emphasis. If events unfold in a causal chain with each effect becoming the cause of another effect, and if stressing these links coincides with your purpose, then a simple chronological sequence will probably be clearest. But if events overlap and vary in significance, their organization will require more planning. Probably the most effective way to arrange either causes or effects is in order of increasing importance. Such an arrangement helps readers see which causes or effects you consider minor and which major, while it also reserves your most significant (and probably most detailed) point for last. The groups of minor or major events may then fit into a chronological framework.

To avoid being preoccupied with organization while you are drafting your essay, prepare some sort of outline before you start writing. The outline need not be detailed so long as you have written the details elsewhere or can retrieve them easily from your mind. But it should show all the causes or effects you want to discuss and the order in which you will cover them.

To conclude your essay, you may want to restate your thesis—or state it, if you deliberately withheld it for the end—so that readers are left with the point of your analysis. If your analysis is complex, readers may also benefit from a summary of the relationships you have identified. And depending on your purpose, you may want to specify why your analysis is significant, what use your readers can make of it, or what action you hope they will take.

Drafting

While drafting your essay, strive primarily for clarity—sharp details, strong examples, concrete explanations. To make readers see not only *what* you see but also *why* you see it, you can draw on just about any method of writing discussed in this book. For instance, you might narrate the effect of a situation on one person, analyze a process, or compare and contrast two interpretations of cause. Particularly if your thesis is debatable (like the earlier example asserting the owners' blamelessness for the plant's closing), you will need accurate, representative facts to back up your interpretation, and you may also need quotations from experts such as witnesses and scholars. If you do not support your assertions specifically, your readers will have no reason to believe them. (For more on evidence in persuasive writing, see pp. 308 and 313–14.)

Revising and Editing

While revising and editing your draft, consider the following questions to be sure your analysis is sound and clear.

- *Have you explained causes or effects clearly and specifically?* Readers will need to see the pattern of causes or effects—their sequence and relative importance. And readers will need facts, examples, and other evidence to understand and accept your analysis.

- *Have you demonstrated that causes are not merely coincidences?* Avoid the error of post hoc—of assuming that one event caused another just because it preceded the other. To be convincing, a claim that one event caused another must be supported with ample evidence.

- *Have you considered all the possible causes or effects?* Your analysis should go beyond what is most immediate or obvious so that you do not oversimplify the cause-and-effect relationships. Your readers will expect you to present the relationships in all their complexity.

- *Have you represented the cause-and-effect relationships honestly?* Don't deliberately ignore or exaggerate causes or effects in a misguided effort to strengthen your essay. If a cause fails to support your thesis but still does not invalidate it, mention the cause and explain why you believe it to be unimportant. If a change you are proposing will have bad effects as well as good, mention the bad effects and explain how they are outweighed by the good. As long as your reasoning and evidence are sound, such admissions will not weaken your essay; on the contrary, readers will appreciate your fairness.

- *Have you used transitions to signal the sequence and relative importance of events?* Transitions between sentences can help you pinpoint causes or effects (*for this reason, as a result*), show the steps in a sequence (*first, second, third*), link events in time (*in the same month*), specify duration (*a year later*), and indicate the weights you assign events (*equally important, even more crucial*). (See also *transitions* in the Glossary.)

MALCOLM GLADWELL

Born in England in 1963 to an English father and a West Indian mother, Malcolm Gladwell immigrated with his parents to Canada as a child. After receiving his bachelor's degree in history from the University of Toronto, Gladwell worked for the Washington Post *as a science and medicine reporter and later as chief of the* Post's *New York bureau. Gladwell is currently a staff writer at the* New Yorker, *where he is known for highly readable articles that synthesize complex research in the sciences and social sciences. In 2000 he published the best-selling book* The Tipping Point: How Little Things Can Make a Big Difference, *an examination of why change occurs. As he writes the book's introduction, "The best way to understand the dramatic transformation of unknown books into bestsellers, or the rise of teenage smoking, or the phenomena of word of mouth, or any number of the other mysterious changes that mark everyday life is to think of them as epidemics. Ideas and products and messages and behaviors spread just like viruses do." The title of the book—and of this selection—comes from epidemiology. As Gladwell defined it in a recent interview, the* tipping point *is "the name given to that moment in an epidemic when a virus reaches critical mass."*

The Tipping Point

In this chapter from The Tipping Point, *Gladwell focuses on the dramatic decrease in New York City's violent crime rate during the 1990s. The decrease, Gladwell explains, was fueled in large part by strict policing of more minor crimes.*

During the 1990s violent crime declined across the United States   1 for a number of fairly straightforward reasons. The illegal trade in crack cocaine, which had spawned a great deal of violence among gangs and drug dealers, began to decline. The economy's dramatic recovery meant that many people who might have been lured into crime got legitimate jobs instead, and the general aging of the population meant that there were fewer people in the age range— males between eighteen and twenty-four—that is responsible for the majority of all violence. The question of why crime declined in

New York City, however, is a little more complicated. In the period when the New York epidemic tipped down, the city's economy hadn't improved. It was still stagnant. In fact, the city's poorest neighborhoods had just been hit hard by the welfare cuts of the early 1990s. The waning of the crack cocaine epidemic in New York was clearly a factor, but then again, it had been in steady decline well before crime dipped. As for the aging of the population, because of heavy immigration to New York in the 1980s, the city was getting younger in the 1990s, not older. In any case, all of these trends are long-term changes that one would expect to have gradual effects. In New York the decline was anything but gradual. Something else clearly played a role in reversing New York's crime epidemic.

The most intriguing candidate for that "something else" is called 2 the Broken Windows theory. Broken Windows was the brainchild of the criminologists James Q. Wilson and George Kelling. Wilson and Kelling argued that crime is the inevitable result of disorder. If a window is broken and left unrepaired, people walking by will conclude that no one cares and no one is in charge. Soon, more windows will be broken, and the sense of anarchy will spread from the building to the street on which it faces, sending a signal that anything goes. In a city, relatively minor problems like graffiti, public disorder, and aggressive panhandling, they write, are all the equivalent of broken windows, invitations to more serious crimes:

> Muggers and robbers, whether opportunistic or professional, believe they reduce their chances of being caught or even identified if they operate on streets where potential victims are already intimidated by prevailing conditions. If the neighborhood cannot keep a bothersome panhandler from annoying passersby, the thief may reason, it is even less likely to call the police to identify a potential mugger or to interfere if the mugging actually takes place.

This is an epidemic theory of crime. It says that crime is contagious—just as a fashion trend is contagious—that it can start with a broken window and spread to an entire community. The Tipping Point in this epidemic, though, isn't a particular kind of person—a Connector like Lois Weisberg or a Maven like Mark Alpert.[1] It's something physical like

---

[1]In an earlier chapter of *The Tipping Point*, Gladwell discusses personality types who trigger major changes in society. Connectors have unusually large social circles, and Mavens are particularly knowledgeable about products, services, and prices. Lois Weisberg and Mark Alpert are two typical Americans whom Gladwell interviewed to illustrate these types. [Editor's note.]

graffiti. The impetus to engage in a certain kind of behavior is not coming from a certain kind of person but from a feature of the environment.

In the mid-1980s Kelling was hired by the New York Transit   3
Authority as a consultant, and he urged them to put the Broken
Windows theory into practice. They obliged, bringing in a new subway director by the name of David Gunn to oversee a multibillion-
dollar rebuilding of the subway system. Many subway advocates, at
the time, told Gunn not to worry about graffiti, to focus on the larger
questions of crime and subway reliability, and it seemed like reasonable advice. Worrying about graffiti at a time when the entire
system was close to collapse seems as pointless as scrubbing the
decks of the *Titanic* as it headed toward the icebergs. But Gunn
insisted. "The graffiti was symbolic of the collapse of the system,"
he says. "When you looked at the process of rebuilding the organization and morale, you had to win the battle against graffiti. Without
winning that battle, all the management reforms and physical
changes just weren't going to happen. We were about to put out new
trains that were worth about ten million bucks apiece, and unless we
did something to protect them, we knew just what would happen.
They would last one day and then they would be vandalized."

Gunn drew up a new management structure and a precise set of   4
goals and timetables aimed at cleaning the system line by line, train
by train. He started with the number seven train that connects Queens
to midtown Manhattan, and began experimenting with new techniques to clean off the paint. On stainless-steel cars, solvents were
used. On the painted cars, the graffiti were simply painted over. Gunn
made it a rule that there should be no retreat, that once a car was
"reclaimed" it should never be allowed to be vandalized again. "We
were religious about it," Gunn said. At the end of the number one line
in the Bronx, where the trains stop before turning around and going
back to Manhattan, Gunn set up a cleaning station. If a car came in
with graffiti, the graffiti had to be removed during the changeover, or
the car was removed from service. "Dirty" cars, which hadn't yet been
cleansed of graffiti, were never to be mixed with "clean" cars. The idea
was to send an unambiguous message to the vandals themselves.

"We had a yard up in Harlem on One hundred thirty-fifth Street   5
where the trains would lay up over night," Gunn said. "The kids
would come the first night and paint the side of the train white. Then
they would come the next night, after it was dry, and draw the outline. Then they would come the third night and color it in. It was a
three-day job. We knew the kids would be working on one of the dirty
trains, and what we would do is wait for them to finish their mural.

Then we'd walk over with rollers and paint it over. The kids would be in tears, but we'd just be going up and down, up and down. It was a message to them. If you want to spend three nights of your time vandalizing a train, fine. But it's never going to see the light of day."

Gunn's graffiti cleanup took from 1984 to 1990. At that point, the 6 Transit Authority hired William Bratton to head the transit police, and the second stage of the reclamation of the subway system began. Bratton was, like Gunn, a disciple of Broken Windows. He describes Kelling, in fact, as his intellectual mentor, and so his first step as police chief was as seemingly quixotic as Gunn's. With felonies—serious crimes—on the subway system at an all-time high, Bratton decided to crack down on fare-beating. Why? Because he believed that, like graffiti, fare-beating could be a signal, a small expression of disorder that invited much more serious crimes. An estimated 170,000 people a day were entering the system, by one route or another, without paying a token. Some were kids, who simply jumped over the turnstiles. Others would lean backward on the turnstiles and force their way through. And once one or two or three people began cheating the system, other people—who might never otherwise have considered evading the law—would join in, reasoning that if some people weren't going to pay, they shouldn't either, and the problem would snowball. The problem was exacerbated by the fact fare-beating was not easy to fight. Because there was only $1.25 at stake, the transit police didn't feel it was worth their time to pursue it, particularly when there were plenty of more serious crimes happening down on the platform and in the trains.

Bratton is a colorful, charismatic man, a born leader, and he 7 quickly made his presence felt. His wife stayed behind in Boston, so he was free to work long hours, and he would roam the city on the subway at night, getting a sense of what the problems were and how best to fight them. First, he picked stations where fare-beating was the biggest problem, and put as many as ten policemen in plain-clothes at the turnstiles. The team would nab fare-beaters one by one, handcuff them, and leave them standing, in a daisy chain, on the platform until they had a "full catch." The idea was to signal, as publicly as possible, that the transit police were now serious about cracking down on fare-beaters. Previously, police officers had been wary of pursuing fare-beaters because the arrest, the trip to the station house, the filling out of necessary forms, and the waiting for those forms to be processed took an entire day—all for a crime that usually merited no more than a slap on the wrist. Bratton retrofitted a city bus and turned it into a rolling station house, with its own fax machines, phones, holding pen, and fingerprinting facilities. Soon the turnaround time on an arrest was down to an hour. Bratton also insisted that a check be run on all those arrested. Sure enough, one out of seven arrestees had an outstanding warrant for a previous crime, and one out of twenty was carrying a weapon of some sort. Suddenly it wasn't hard to convince police officers that tackling fare-beating made sense. "For the cops it was a bonanza," Bratton writes. "Every arrest was like opening a box of Cracker Jack. What kind of toy am I going to get? Got a gun? Got a knife? Got a warrant? Do we have a murderer here? . . . After a while the bad guys wised up and began to leave their weapons home and pay their fares." Under Bratton, the number of ejections from subway stations—for drunkenness, or improper behavior—tripled within his first few months in office. Arrests for misdemeanors, for the kind of minor offenses that had gone unnoticed in the past, went up fivefold between 1990 and 1994. Bratton turned the transit police into an organization focused on the smallest infractions, on the details of life underground.

After the election of Rudolph Giuliani as mayor of New York in 1994, Bratton was appointed head of the New York City Police Department, and he applied the same strategies to the city at large. He instructed his officers to crack down on quality-of-life crimes: on the "squeegee men" who came up to drivers at New York City intersections and demanded money for washing car windows, for example, and on all the other above-ground equivalents of turnstile-jumping and graffiti. "Previous police administration had been handcuffed by restrictions," Bratton says. "We took the handcuffs off. We stepped up enforcement of the laws against public drunkenness and public urination and arrested repeat violators, including those who threw empty bottles on the street or were involved in even relatively minor damage to property. . . . If you peed in the street, you were going to jail." When crime began to fall in the city—as quickly and dramatically as it had in the subways—Bratton and Giuliani pointed to the same cause. Minor, seemingly insignificant quality-of-life crimes, they said, were Tipping Points for violent crime.

Meaning

1. What is the Broken Windows theory? How does it explain increases or decreases in crime in particular communities?
2. As director of New York City's subways, why did David Gunn crack down on grafitti? What was the result?

3. How did William Bratton, first as chief of the transit police and later as chief of the New York City police, continue to apply Gunn's methods? Again, what was the result? What is the lesson to be drawn?

Purpose and Audience

1. Do you think that Gladwell achieves his purpose here? Is his explanation for the dramatic reduction of crime in New York City convincing? Why, or why not?
2. Throughout his essay, Gladwell includes quotations from David Gunn and William Bratton. What effect do you suppose he hoped these quotations would have on readers?

Method and Structure

1. Given its subject and purpose, why is cause-and-effect analysis the most appropriate method for this essay?
2. Gladwell opens his essay by showing why the decrease in New York City crime is "more complicated" than the national decline in crime. Why do you think he chose to begin in this way?
3. **Other Methods**   Why is Gladwell's early definition of the Broken Window theory (paragraph 2) crucial to the development of his essay as a whole?

Language

1. In paragraph 2, Gladwell writes that "crime is contagious—just as a fashion trend is contagious." In what way is the word *contagious* appropriate in this context?
2. Gladwell generally maintains a reporter's neutral tone throughout the essay. In paragraph 3, however, he writes, "Worrying about graffiti at a time when the entire system was close to collapse seems as pointless as scrubbing the decks of the *Titanic* as it headed toward the icebergs." Why do you think Gladwell made this shift in tone?

Writing Topics

1. It is clear that Gladwell agrees with James Q. Wilson and George Kelling that bad behavior, if left unchecked, spreads among people—that "once one or two or three people began cheating the system, other people—who might never otherwise have considered evading the law—would join in" (paragraph 6). Drawing on your own experiences and observations, write an essay that considers how widespread you

believe this phenomenon to be. Be sure to include examples that support your point.

2. Do you agree with William Bratton that even minor infractions of the law deserve harsh penalties? For example, should subway fare-beaters be handcuffed and arrested? Should teenagers who engage in minor vandalism, such as graffiti, be treated as criminals? In an essay, consider the extent to which you believe that minor crimes should have major consequences.

3. Gladwell notes in his opening paragraph that "males between eighteen and twenty-four" are responsible for most violent crime in the United States. Brainstorm some reasons why you think this might be the case. Then analyze your reasons, and develop them with brief explanations. Finally, draft an essay in which you explain the possible causes of high crime rates among young men. (If you wish, you may do some research to augment your own ideas, but be sure to acknowledge your sources.)

BARBARA EHRENREICH

Barbara Ehrenreich was born in 1941 in Butte, Montana. She graduated from Reed College, received a PhD from Rockefeller University, and taught for a while at the State University of New York. Her feature articles, reviews, and essays have appeared in a wide range of publications, including the New York Times Magazine, *the* Washington Post Magazine, *the* Wall Street Journal, Esquire, *the* Atlantic, Harper's Magazine, *the* New Republic, Social Policy, Vogue, *and* Z Magazine. *She is currently a contributing writer at the* Nation. *Ehrenreich's books include* The Sexual Politics of Sickness *(1973),* Fear of Falling: The Inner Life of the Middle Class *(1989),* The Worst Years of Our Lives *(1990),* The Snarling Citizen *(1995), and* Nickel and Dimed *(2001).*

Cultural Baggage

After struggling to identify her "ethnic genes," Ehrenreich looks to the spirit of her parents, whose unofficial motto was "new things [are] better than old." This essay from The Snarling Citizen *presents an unorthodox understanding of cultural heritage: a celebration of lineage free from the shackles of "poverty, superstition, and grief."*

An acquaintance was telling me about the joys of rediscovering her 1 ethnic and religious heritage. "I know exactly what my ancestors were doing 2,000 years ago," she said, eyes gleaming with enthusiasm, "and *I can do the same things now*." Then she leaned forward and inquired politely, "And what is your ethnic background, if I may ask?"

"None," I said, that being the first word in line to get out of my 2 mouth. Well, not "none," I backtracked. Scottish, English, Irish— that was something, I supposed. Too much Irish to qualify as a WASP; too much of the hated English to warrant a "Kiss Me, I'm Irish" button; plus there are a number of dead ends in the family tree due to adoptions, missing records, failing memories and the like. I was blushing by this time. Did "none" mean I was rejecting my heritage out of Anglo-Celtic self-hate? Or was I revealing a hidden ethnic chauvinism in which the Britannically derived served as a kind of neutral standard compared with the ethnic "others"?

Throughout the 60s and 70s, I watched one group after another— 3
African-Americans, Latinos, Native Americans—stand up and proudly
reclaim their roots while I just sank back ever deeper into my seat. All
this excitement over ethnicity stemmed, I uneasily sensed, from a
past in which *their* ancestors had been trampled upon by *my* ancestors, or at least by people who looked very much like them. In addition, it had begun to seem almost un-American not to have some sort
of hyphen at hand, linking one to more venerable times and locales.

But the truth is, I was raised with none. We'd eaten ethnic foods 4
in my childhood home, but these were all borrowed, like the pasties,
or Cornish meat pies, my father had picked up from his fellow min-
ers in Butte, Montana. If my mother had one rule, it was militant
ecumenism in all matters of food and experience. "Try new things,"
she would say, meaning anything from sweetbreads to clams, with
an emphasis on the "new."

As a child, I briefly nourished a craving for tradition and roots. I 5
immersed myself in the works of Sir Walter Scott.[1] I pretended to
believe that the bagpipe was a musical instrument. I was fascinated
to learn from a grandmother that we were descended from certain
Highland clans and longed for a pleated skirt in one of their distinctive tartans.

But in *Ivanhoe*, it was the dark-eyed "Jewess" Rebecca I identified 6
with, not the flaxen-haired bimbo Rowena. As for clans: Why not call
them "tribes," those bands of half-clad peasants and warriors whose
idea of cuisine was stuffed sheep gut washed down with whisky?
And then there was the sting of Disraeli's[2] remark—which I came
across in my early teens—to the effect that his ancestors had been
leading orderly, literate lives when my ancestors were still rampag-
ing through the Highlands daubing themselves with blue paint.

Motherhood put the screws on me, ethnicity-wise. I had hoped that 7
by marrying a man of Eastern European–Jewish ancestry I would
acquire for my descendants the ethnic genes that my own forebears so
sadly lacked. At one point, I even subjected the children to a seder[3] of

[1]Scott (1771–1832) was a Scottish poet and novelist. His novel *Ivanhoe* (next
paragraph) is a historical romance set in medieval times. The Jewish Rebecca
falls in love with the Christian Ivanhoe, but it is Lady Rowena, the upper-class
Saxon, who wins Ivanhoe's love. [Editor's note.]

[2]Benjamin Disraeli (1804–81), British statesman, writer, and prime minister,
was of Jewish descent. [Editor's note.]

[3]A Jewish ceremonial meal, eaten on the first or second day of Passover, that
celebrates the release of the Jews from captivity in Egypt. [Editor's note.]

my own design, including a little talk about the flight from Egypt and its relevance to modern social issues. But the kids insisted on buttering their matzohs and snickering through my talk. "Give me a break, Mom," the older one said. "You don't even believe in God."

After the tiny pagans had been put to bed, I sat down to brood   8 over Elijah's wine.[4] What had I been thinking? The kids knew that their Jewish grandparents were secular folks who didn't hold seders themselves. And if ethnicity eluded me, how could I expect it to take root in my children, who are not only Scottish-English-Irish, but Hungarian-Polish-Russian to boot?

But, then, on the fumes of Manischewitz,[5] a great insight took   9 form in my mind. It was true, as the kids said, that I didn't "believe in God." But this could be taken as something very different from an accusation—a reminder of a genuine heritage. My parents had not believed in God either, nor had my grandparents or any other progenitors going back to the great-great level. They had become disillusioned with Christianity generations ago—just as, on the in-law side, my children's other ancestors had shaken off their Orthodox Judaism. This insight did not exactly furnish me with an "identity," but it was at least something to work with: we are the kind of people, I realized—whatever our distant ancestors' religions—who do *not* believe, who do not carry on traditions, who do not do things just because someone has done them before.

The epiphany went on: I recalled that my mother never intro-   10 duced a procedure for cooking or cleaning by telling me, "Grandma did it this way." What did Grandma know, living in the days before vacuum cleaners and disposable toilet mops? In my parents' general view, new things were better than old, and the very fact that some ritual had been performed in the past was a good reason for abandoning it now. Because what was the past, as our forebears knew it? Nothing but poverty, superstition and grief. "Think for yourself," Dad used to say. "Always ask why."

In fact, this may have been the ideal cultural heritage for my par-   11 ticular ethnic strain—bounced as it was from the Highlands of Scotland across the sea, out to the Rockies, down into the mines and finally spewed out into high-tech, suburban America. What better philosophy, for a race of migrants, than "Think for yourself"? What

[4]A special cup of wine placed on the Seder table as an offering to the Hebrew prophet Elijah. [Editor's note.]

[5]The brand name of a kosher wine often served during Passover. [Editor's note.]

better maxim, for people whose whole world was rudely inverted every thirty years or so, than "Try new things"?

The more tradition-minded, the newly enthusiastic celebrants of 12 Purim and Kwanzaa and Solstice,[6] may see little point to survival if the survivors carry no cultural freight—religion, for example, or ethnic tradition. To which I would say that skepticism, curiosity and wide-eyed ecumenical tolerance are also worthy elements of the human tradition and are at least as old as such notions as "Serbian" or "Croatian," "Scottish" or "Jewish." I make no claims for my personal line of progenitors except that they remained loyal to the values that may have induced all of our ancestors, long, long ago, to climb down from the trees and make their way into the open plains.

A few weeks ago, I cleared my throat and asked the children, now 13 mostly grown and fearsomely smart, whether they felt any stirrings of ethnic or religious identity, etc., which might have been, ahem, insufficiently nourished at home. "None," they said, adding firmly, "and the world would be a better place if nobody else did, either." My chest swelled with pride, as would my mother's, to know that the race of "none" marches on.

Meaning

1. What personal heritage does Ehrenreich embrace? How does she feel this heritage was passed down to her?
2. At the end of paragraph 2, Ehrenreich asks herself whether, by claiming no ethnic background, she was "revealing a hidden ethnic chauvinism in which the Britannically derived served as a kind of neutral standard compared with the ethnic 'others.'" What does she mean? Why might this make her feel guilty?
3. In what ways did Ehrenreich attempt to assert an ethnic identity for herself? Why did her efforts fail?

Purpose and Audience

1. Ehrenreich's thesis does not become clear until paragraphs 12 and 13. What is her thesis?
2. What seems to be Ehrenreich's main purpose in this essay? To defend her lack of ethnic identity? To persuade her readers that some traditions

---

[6]Purim is a Jewish festival also known as the Feast of Lots. Kwanzaa is a holiday that celebrates the cultural heritage of African Americans. Solstice, occurring on the shortest day of the year, is an ancient pagan celebration welcoming the return of the sun. [Editor's note.]

are more important than ethnic traditions? To explore the evolution of her own sense of tradition and cultural identity? Something else? Why do you think so?

3. Is Ehrenreich writing primarily for those with a strong ethnic identity, for those—like herself—without one, or for both? How can you tell? What other assumptions does she seem to make about her audience?

Method and Structure

1. What are the two main cause-and-effect relationships that Ehrenreich explores in this essay? How are these central to her purpose for writing?

2. Ehrenreich opens and closes her essay with two anecdotes. How is the dialogue in these anecdotes connected?

3. Ehrenreich poses a number of questions (for example, in paragraphs 2, 8, 10, 11, and 13). Why are such questions particularly appropriate in this essay?

4. **Other Methods**   In paragraphs 3 and 12, Ehrenreich brings in comparison and contrast. What are her subjects in each case? What point does comparison and contrast help her make?

Language

1. How would you describe Ehrenreich's tone in this essay? Is it consistent throughout?

2. Why does Ehrenreich italicize the words "I can do the same things now" when quoting her friend in paragraph 1? Does this phrase have a larger point in the essay?

3. Why does Ehrenreich link "Purim and Kwanzaa and Solstice" in paragraph 12? What is her point?

4. In her final sentence Ehrenreich refers to "the race of 'none.'" Why does she use the word "race" in this context?

Writing Topics

1. Write an essay in which you evaluate the importance you assign to any outward symbols of your heritage: food, music, holidays, customs, religious services, clothing, and the like. For example, do such signs serve to strengthen your cultural identity? If you don't have such signs, how important is their absence?

2. By referring in paragraph 12 to Serbs and Croats—two ethnic groups that fought each other in the 1990s—Ehrenreich just suggests the potentially negative consequences of ethnic pride or religious zeal. In

an essay, consider when people's cultural identity can be a source of conflict, even violence. Is there any way such conflicts can be avoided or resolved? You may wish to think globally about this issue, but be sure to bring your essay down to earth by focusing primarily on what you've experienced or witnessed closer to home.

3. The United States is a country of immigrants, and each group has made an indelible mark on American identity. For example, consider just foods: salsa outsells ketchup, tacos are to be found everywhere, and cappuccino and sushi are now everyday food items for many Americans who have no Italian or Japanese heritage. Write an essay about the effects of immigration on your daily life: the food you consume, the music you listen to, the dress styles you prefer, and so forth. Include personal examples to bring your ideas to life.

K. C. COLE

K. C. Cole is a journalist and essayist who writes mainly about science and women's issues. She was born in 1946 in Detroit, Michigan, and received a BA in 1968 from Columbia University. She began her journalism career as a specialist in Eastern European affairs, working as a reporter in Czechoslovakia, Hungary, and the former Soviet Union. In the early 1970s, back in the United States, she began writing about science for the Exploratorium, a science museum in San Francisco. Currently a science writer for the Los Angeles Times, *Cole has also held editorial and writing posts with* Saturday Review *and* Newsday *and has published articles on education, science, and women in those periodicals and in the* New York Times, Lear's, *and others. Her collections of essays include* Between the Lines *(1982),* The Universe and the Teacup: The Mathematics of Truth and Beauty *(1998), and* Mind over Matter: Conversations with the Cosmos *(2003). She has held fellowships to teach science writing at Yale and Wesleyan universities, and she currently teaches at the University of California, Los Angeles.*

Women in Science

In this essay Cole joins her primary writing interests, science and women, as she explores the causes of a troubling effect: many fewer women than men choose science as a career. The essay first appeared in the New York Times *in 1981.*

1 I know few other women who do what I do. What I do is write about science, mainly physics. And to do that, I spend a lot of time reading about science, talking to scientists, and struggling to understand physics. In fact, most of the women (and men) I know think me quite queer for actually liking physics. "How can you write about that stuff?" they ask, always somewhat askance. "I could never understand that in a million years." Or more simply, "I hate science."

2 I didn't realize what an odd creature a woman interested in physics was until a few years ago when a science magazine sent me to Johns Hopkins University in Baltimore for a conference on an electrical phenomenon known as the Hall effect. We sat in a huge

lecture hall and listened as physicists talked about things engineers didn't understand, and engineers talked about things physicists didn't understand. What *I* didn't understand was why, out of several hundred young students of physics and engineering in the room, less than a handful were women.

Sometime later, I found myself at the California Institute of Technology reporting on the search for the origins of the universe. I interviewed physicist after physicist, man after man. I asked one young administrator why none of the physicists were women. And he answered: "I don't know, but I suppose it must be something innate. My seven-year-old daughter doesn't seem to be much interested in science." 3

It was with that experience fresh in my mind that I attended a conference in Cambridge, Massachusetts, on science literacy, or rather the worrisome lack of it in this country today. We three women—a science teacher, a young chemist, and myself—sat surrounded by a company of august men. The chemist, I think, first tentatively raised the issue of science illiteracy in women. It seemed like an obvious point. After all, everyone had agreed over and over again that scientific knowledge these days was a key factor in economic power. But as soon as she made the point, it became clear that we women had committed a grievous social error. Our genders were suddenly showing; we had interrupted the serious talk with a subject unforgivably silly. 4

For the first time, I stopped being puzzled about why there weren't any women in science and began to be angry. Because if science is a search for answers to fundamental questions then it hardly seems frivolous to find out why women are excluded. Never mind the economic consequences. 5

A lot of the reasons women are excluded are spelled out by the Massachusetts Institute of Technology experimental physicist Vera Kistiakowsky in a recent article in *Physics Today* called "Women in Physics: Unnecessary, Injurious, and Out of Place?" The title was taken from a nineteenth-century essay written in opposition to the appointment of a female mathematician to a professorship at the University of Stockholm. "As decidedly as two and two make four," a woman in mathematics is a "monstrosity," concluded the writer of the essay. 6

Dr. Kistiakowsky went on to discuss the factors that make women in science today, if not monstrosities, at least oddities. Contrary to much popular opinion, one of those is *not* an innate difference in the scientific ability of boys and girls. But early conditioning does play 7 a stubborn and subtle role. A recent *Nova* program, "The Pinks and the Blues," documented how girls and boys are treated differently from birth—the boys always encouraged in more physical kinds of play, more active explorations of their environments. Sheila Tobias, in her book, *Math Anxiety*, showed how the games boys play help them to develop an intuitive understanding of speed, motion, and mass.

The main sorting out of the girls from the boys in science seems to happen in junior high school. As a friend who teaches in a science museum said, "By the time we get to electricity, the boys already have had some experience with it. But it's unfamiliar to the girls." Science books draw on boys' experiences. "The examples are all about throwing a baseball at such and such a speed," said my stepdaughter, who barely escaped being a science drop-out.   8

The most obvious reason there are not many more women in science is that women are discriminated against as a class, in promotions, salaries, and hirings, a conclusion reached by a recent analysis by the National Academy of Sciences.   9

Finally, said Dr. Kistiakowsky, women are simply made to feel out of place in science. Her conclusion was supported by a Ford Foundation study by Lynn H. Fox on the problems of women in mathematics. When students were asked to choose among six reasons accounting for girls' lack of interest in math, the girls rated this statement second: "Men do not want girls in the mathematical occupations."   10

A friend of mine remembers winning a Bronxwide mathematics competition in the second grade. Her friends—both boys and girls— warned her that she shouldn't be good at math: "You'll never find a boy who likes you." My friend continued nevertheless to excel in math and science, won many awards during her years at the Bronx High School of Science, and then earned a full scholarship to Harvard. After one year of Harvard science, she decided to major in English.   11

When I asked her why, she mentioned what she called the "macho mores" of science. "It would have been O.K. if I'd had someone to talk to," she said. "But the rules of comportment were such that you never admitted you didn't understand. I later realized that even the boys didn't get everything clearly right away. You had to stick with it until it had time to sink in. But for the boys, there was a payoff in suffering through the hard times, and a kind of punishment—a shame—if they didn't. For the girls it was O.K. not to get it, and the only payoff for sticking it out was that you'd be considered a freak."   12

Science is undeniably hard. Often, it can seem quite boring. It is unfortunately too often presented as laws to be memorized instead   13 of mysteries to be explored. It is too often kept a secret that science, like art, takes a well-developed esthetic sense. Women aren't the only ones who say, "I hate science."

That's why everyone who goes into science needs a little help from 14 friends. For the past ten years, I have been getting more than a little help from a friend who is a physicist. But my stepdaughter—who earned the highest grades ever recorded in her California high school on the math Scholastic Aptitude Test—flunked calculus in her first year at Harvard. When my friend the physicist heard about it, he said, "Harvard should be ashamed of itself."

What he meant was that she needed that little extra encourage- 15 ment that makes all the difference. Instead, she got that little extra discouragement that makes all the difference.

"In the first place, all the math teachers are men," she explained. 16 "In the second place, when I met a boy I liked and told him I was tak- ing chemistry, he immediately said: 'Oh, you're one of those science types.' In the third place, it's just a kind of a social thing. The math clubs are full of boys and you don't feel comfortable joining."

In other words, she was made to feel unnecessary, injurious, and 17 out of place.

A few months ago, I accompanied a male colleague from the 18 science museum where I sometimes work to a lunch of the his- tory of science faculty at the University of California. I was the only woman there, and my presence for the most part was obviously and rudely ignored. I was so surprised and hurt by this that I made an extra effort to speak knowledgeably and well. At the end of the lunch, one of the professors turned to me in all seriousness and said: "Well, K. C., what do the women think of Carl Sagan?" I replied that I had no idea what "the women" thought about any- thing. But now I know what I should have said: I should have told him that his comment was unnecessary, injurious, and out of place.

Meaning

1. Explain in a sentence what Cole sees as the basic cause of women's not entering science. To what extent does this basic cause underlie the specific causes she mentions in the essay? Why do you think she does not state this basic cause directly?

2. Why was it "a grievous social error" to ask specifically about science illiteracy among women (paragraph 4)? What male attitudes did this experience make Cole aware of?

Purpose and Audience

1. What seems to be Cole's primary purpose in this essay: to encourage more women to become scientists? to make men ashamed of their attitudes? to express her anger? to make readers aware of this kind of sexism? Do you think Cole accomplishes her purpose? Why, or why not?

2. Cole admits that "science is undeniably hard" (paragraph 13) and that she spends "a lot of time . . . struggling to understand physics" (1). Why does she admit this difficulty? Do you think her emphasis on the difficulty of science weakens her case? Why, or why not?

3. In the conclusion of the essay, quoting a conversation between herself and a male professor, Cole writes: "I replied that I had no idea what 'the women' thought about anything." What does her response reveal about her ultimate goals? What does her last sentence suggest as a way of reaching these goals?

Method and Structure

1. List several causes Cole identifies as contributing to the exclusion of women from science. How does she arrange these causes?

2. Cole borrows much of her analysis from Vera Kistiakowsky's article in *Physics Today* (paragraphs 6–10). Which of the points made in this section of the essay are Kistiakowsky's? What does Cole contribute to the analysis? What does she gain by citing Kistiakowsky?

3. **Other Methods**   In addition to cause-and-effect analysis, Cole relies mainly on narration and example. Analyze the contributions made to the essay by the narrative passages (paragraphs 2, 3, 4, 11–12, 18) and by the examples of her stepdaughter (8, 14–16) and her friend from the Bronx (11–12).

Language

1. At the conference on science literacy, Cole reports, she became angry about the problem of women in science (paragraph 5). What kind of anger does Cole express through her words and sentence structures: rage? irritation? bitterness? sarcasm? controlled anger? impatience? something else? How and to what extent did her anger affect your response to the essay?

2. Why did Cole write this essay in the first person, using *I*? How would the essay have differed if she had avoided *I*?

Writing Topics

1. Write a narrative account of your most significant experiences with science and mathematics, in an attempt to discover why you have the attitudes you do about them. To help focus on significant experiences, consider the following questions: Who encouraged or discouraged your study of science? To what extent was science related to the real world in your elementary and high school education? What measures were taken to help students through the hard parts? Was there a science club? If so, who belonged and what kinds of activities did it sponsor? Did you encounter science anywhere besides school—in a museum program, for instance, or at summer camp?

2. Think of ways in which experience with sports could contribute to the study of science. Cole mentions "an intuitive understanding of speed, motion, and mass" (paragraph 7); other contributions might include patience and perseverance, an appreciation for method and technique, or a liking for statistics. Using as many specific examples as you can, develop an essay explaining the positive effect of sports participation on the study of science. Your purpose may be explanatory or persuasive—for instance, you might argue for expanding your school's sports programs for women.

3. Ask the reference librarian at your library to help you find information (statistics and opinions) about the changing role of women in some profession other than science (business or medicine, for example). Write an essay explaining when, how, and to what extent women have participated in that profession; to what extent women have been accepted by men; and to what extent sexual discrimination still remains in the profession. (Be sure to use current sources.) Alternatively, you could explore minority participation in the profession, addressing the same questions about the roles of, say, African Americans, Hispanic Americans, or Asian Americans.

STEPHEN JAY GOULD

One of the best-known science writers of the twentieth century, Stephen Jay Gould was born in New York City in 1941 and attended Antioch College and Columbia University. Though he wrote scholarly articles and taught biology, geology, and history of science courses at Harvard, his essays, including a long-running column for Natural History *magazine, made science accessible to a popular audience. He won the National Book Award for* The Panda's Thumb *(1980) and the National Book Critics Circle Award for* The Mismeasure of Man *(1981). His essays were collected in many books, including* The Panda's Thumb *(1980),* Dinosaur in a Haystack *(1995), and* I Have Landed *(2002). His last book,* The Structure of Evolutionary Theory *(2002), is the culmination of his more than twenty years of writing and thinking on Darwinism. Gould died in 2002 at the age of sixty.*

Sex, Drugs, Disasters, and the Extinction of Dinosaurs

This essay originally appeared in Discover *magazine and was republished in Gould's collection* The Flamingo's Smile. *Gould attempts to explain why dinosaurs disappeared, speculating on the chain of events that most likely led to their extinction.*

Science, in its most fundamental definition, is a fruitful mode of inquiry, not a list of enticing conclusions. The conclusions are the consequence, not the essence. 1

My greatest unhappiness with most popular presentations of science concerns their failure to separate fascinating claims from the methods that scientists use to establish the facts of nature. Journalists, and the public, thrive on controversial and stunning statements. But science is, basically, a way of knowing—in P. B. Medawar's apt words, "the art of the soluble." If the growing corps of popular science writers would focus on *how* scientists develop and defend those fascinating claims, they would make their greatest possible contribution to public understanding. 2

Consider three ideas, proposed in perfect seriousness to explain   3
that greatest of all titillating puzzles—the extinction of dinosaurs.
Since these three notions invoke the primally fascinating themes of
our culture—sex, drugs, and violence—they surely reside in the
category of fascinating claims. I want to show why two of them rank
as silly speculation, while the other represents science at its grand-
est and most useful.

Science works with testable proposals. If, after much compilation   4
and scrutiny of data, new information continues to affirm a hypothesis, we may accept it provisionally and gain confidence as further
evidence mounts. We can never be completely sure that a hypothesis
is right, though we may be able to show with confidence that it is
wrong. The best scientific hypotheses are also generous and expansive: They suggest extensions and implications that enlighten related,
and even far distant, subjects. Simply consider how the idea of evolution has influenced virtually every intellectual field.

Useless speculation, on the other hand, is restrictive. It generates   5
no testable hypothesis, and offers no way to obtain potentially
refuting evidence. Please note that I am not speaking of truth or fal-
sity. The speculation may well be true; still, if it provides, in principle, no material for affirmation or rejection, we can make nothing
of it. It must simply stand forever as an intriguing idea. Useless
speculation turns in on itself and leads nowhere; good science, containing both seeds for its potential refutation and implications for
more and different testable knowledge, reaches out. But, enough
preaching. Let's move on to dinosaurs, and the three proposals for
their extinction.

1. *Sex.*   Testes function only in a narrow range of temperature (those
   of mammals hang externally in a scrotal sac because internal body
   temperatures are too high for their proper function). A worldwide
   rise in temperature at the close of the Cretaceous period caused
   the testes of dinosaurs to stop functioning and led to their extinction by sterilization of males.
2. *Drugs.*   Angiosperms (flowering plants) first evolved toward the
   end of the dinosaurs' reign. Many of these plants contain psychoactive agents, avoided by mammals today as a result of their
   bitter taste. Dinosaurs had neither means to taste the bitterness
   nor livers effective enough to detoxify the substances. They died of
   massive overdoses.
3. *Disasters.*   A large comet or asteroid struck the earth some 65 million years ago, lofting a cloud of dust into the sky and blocking
   sunlight, thereby suppressing photosynthesis and so drastically

lowering world temperatures that dinosaurs and hosts of other creatures became extinct.

Before analyzing these three tantalizing statements, we must establish a basic ground rule often violated in proposals for the dinosaurs' demise. *There is no separate problem of the extinction of dinosaurs.* Too often we divorce specific events from their wider contexts and systems of cause and effect. The fundamental fact of dinosaur extinction is its synchrony with the demise of so many other groups across a wide range of habitats, from terrestrial to marine.

The history of life has been punctuated by brief episodes of mass   6 extinction. A recent analysis by University of Chicago paleontologists Jack Sepkoski and Dave Raup, based on the best and most exhaustive tabulation of data ever assembled, shows clearly that five episodes of mass dying stand well above the "background" extinctions of normal times (when we consider all mass extinctions, large and small, they seem to fall in a regular 26-million-year cycle). The Cretaceous debacle, occurring 65 million years ago and separating the Mesozoic and Cenozoic eras of our geological time scale, ranks prominently among the five. Nearly all the marine plankton (single-celled floating creatures) died with geological suddenness; among marine invertebrates, nearly 15 percent of all families perished, including many previously dominant groups, especially the ammonites (relatives of squids in coiled shells). On land, the dinosaurs disappeared after more than 100 million years of unchallenged domination.

In this context, speculations limited to dinosaurs alone ignore the   7 larger phenomenon. We need a coordinated explanation for a system of events that includes the extinction of dinosaurs as one component. Thus it makes little sense, though it may fuel our desire to view mammals as inevitable inheritors of the earth, to guess that dinosaurs died because small mammals ate their eggs (a perennial favorite among untestable speculations). It seems most unlikely that some disaster peculiar to dinosaurs befell these massive beasts—and that the debacle happened to strike just when one of history's five great dyings had enveloped the earth for completely different reasons.

The testicular theory, an old favorite from the 1940s, had its root   8 in an interesting and thoroughly respectable study of temperature tolerances in the American alligator, published in the staid *Bulletin of the American Museum of Natural History* in 1946 by three experts on living and fossil reptiles—E. H. Colbert, my own first teacher in paleontology; R. B. Cowles; and C. M. Bogert.

The first sentence of their summary reveals a purpose beyond   9
alligators: "This report describes an attempt to infer the reactions of
extinct reptiles, especially the dinosaurs, to high temperatures as
based upon reactions observed in the modern alligator." They studied, by rectal thermometry, the body temperatures of alligators
under changing conditions of heating and cooling. (Well, let's face it,
you wouldn't want to try sticking a thermometer under a 'gator's
tongue.) The predictions under test go way back to an old theory first
stated by Galileo in the 1630s—the unequal scaling of surfaces and
volumes. As an animal, or any object, grows (provided its shape
doesn't change), surface areas must increase more slowly than
volumes—since surfaces get larger as length squared, while volumes
increase much more rapidly, as length cubed. Therefore, small animals have high ratios of surface to volume, while large animals cover
themselves with relatively little surface.

Among cold-blooded animals lacking any physiological mecha-   10
nism for keeping their temperatures constant, small creatures have
a hell of a time keeping warm—because they lose so much heat
through their relatively large surfaces. On the other hand, large animals, with their relatively small surfaces, may lose heat so slowly
that, once warm, they may maintain effectively constant temperatures against ordinary fluctuations of climate. (In fact, the resolution
of the "hot-blooded dinosaur" controversy that burned so brightly a
few years back may simply be that, while large dinosaurs possessed
no physiological mechanism for constant temperature, and were not
therefore warm-blooded in the technical sense, their large size and
relatively small surface area kept them warm.)

Colbert, Cowles, and Bogert compared the warming rates of   11
small and large alligators. As predicted, the small fellows heated up
(and cooled down) more quickly. When exposed to a warm sun, a tiny
50-gram (1.76-ounce) alligator heated up one degree Celsius every
minute and a half, while a large alligator, 260 times bigger at 13,000
grams (28.7 pounds), took seven and a half minutes to gain a degree.
Extrapolating up to an adult 10-ton dinosaur, they concluded that a
one-degree rise in body temperature would take eighty-six hours. If
large animals absorb heat so slowly (through their relatively small
surfaces), they will also be unable to shed any excess heat gained
when temperatures rise above a favorable level.

The authors then guessed that large dinosaurs lived at or near   12
their optimum temperatures; Cowles suggested that a rise in global
temperatures just before the Cretaceous extinction caused the
dinosaurs to heat up beyond their optimal tolerance—and, being so

large, they couldn't shed the unwanted heat. (In a most unusual statement within a scientific paper, Colbert and Bogert then explicitly disavowed this speculative extension of their empirical work on alligators.) Cowles conceded that this excess heat probably wasn't enough to kill or even to enervate the great beasts, but since testes often function only within a narrow range of temperature, he proposed that this global rise might have sterilized all the males, causing extinction by natural contraception.

The overdose theory has recently been supported by UCLA psy-   13
chiatrist Ronald K. Siegel. Siegel has gathered, he claims, more than 2,000 records of animals who, when given access, administer various drugs to themselves — from a mere swig of alcohol to massive doses of the big H. Elephants will swill the equivalent of twenty beers at a time, but do not like alcohol in concentrations greater than 7 percent. In a silly bit of anthropocentric speculation, Siegel states that "elephants drink, perhaps, to forget [. . .] the anxiety produced by shrinking rangeland and the competition for food."

Since fertile imaginations can apply almost any hot idea to the   14
extinction of dinosaurs, Siegel found a way. Flowering plants did not evolve until late in the dinosaurs' reign. These plants also produced an array of aromatic, amino-acid-based alkaloids — the major group of psychoactive agents. Most mammals are "smart" enough to avoid these potential poisons. The alkaloids simply don't taste good (they are bitter); in any case, we mammals have livers happily supplied with the capacity to detoxify them. But, Siegel speculates, perhaps dinosaurs could neither taste the bitterness nor detoxify the substances once ingested. He recently told members of the American Psychological Association: "I'm not suggesting that all dinosaurs OD'd on plant drugs, but it certainly was a factor." He also argued that death by overdose may help explain why so many dinosaur fossils are found in contorted positions. (Do not go gently into that good night.)

Extraterrestrial catastrophes have long pedigrees in the popular   15
literature of extinction, but the subject exploded again in 1979, after a long lull, when the father-son, physicist-geologist team of Luis and Walter Alvarez proposed that an asteroid, some 10 km in diameter, struck the earth 65 million years ago. (Comets, rather than asteroids, have since gained favor. Good science is self-corrective.)

The force of such a collision would be immense, greater by far   16
than the megatonnage of all the world's nuclear weapons. In trying

to reconstruct a scenario that would explain the simultaneous dying of dinosaurs on land and so many creatures in the sea, the Alvarezes proposed that a gigantic dust cloud, generated by particles blown aloft in the impact, would so darken the earth that photosynthesis would cease and temperatures drop precipitously. (Rage, rage against the dying of the light.) The single-celled photosynthetic oceanic plankton, with life cycles measured in weeks, would perish outright, but land plants might survive through the dormancy of their seeds (land plants were not much affected by the Cretaceous extinction, and any adequate theory must account for the curious pattern of differential survival). Dinosaurs would die by starvation and freezing; small, warm-blooded mammals, with more modest requirements for food and better regulation of body temperature, would squeak through. "Let the bastards freeze in the dark," as bumper stickers of our chauvinistic neighbors in sunbelt states proclaimed several years ago during the Northeast's winter oil crisis.

All three theories, testicular malfunction, psychoactive overdosing, and asteroidal zapping, grab our attention mightily. As pure phenomenology, they rank about equally high on any hit parade of primal fascination. Yet one represents expansive science, the others restrictive and untestable speculation. The proper criterion lies in evidence and methodology; we must probe behind the superficial fascination of particular claims. 17

How could we possibly decide whether the hypothesis of testicular frying is right or wrong? We would have to know things that the fossil record cannot provide. What temperatures were optimal for dinosaurs? Could they avoid the absorption of excess heat by staying in the shade, or in caves? At what temperatures did their testicles cease to function? Were late Cretaceous climates ever warm enough to drive the internal temperatures of dinosaurs close to this ceiling? Testicles simply don't fossilize, and how could we infer their temperature tolerances even if they did? In short, Cowles's hypothesis is only an intriguing speculation leading nowhere. The most damning statement against it appeared right in the conclusion of Colbert, Cowles, and Bogert's paper, when they admitted: "It is difficult to advance any definite arguments against this hypothesis." My statement may seem paradoxical—isn't a hypothesis really good if you can't devise any arguments against it? Quite the contrary. It is simply untestable and unusable. 18

Siegel's overdosing has even less going for it. At least Cowles extrapolated his conclusion from some good data on alligators. 19

And he didn't completely violate the primary guideline of siting dinosaur extinction in the context of a general mass dying—for rise in temperature could be the root cause of a general catastrophe, zapping dinosaurs by testicular malfunction and different groups for other reasons. But Siegel's speculation cannot touch the extinction of ammonites or oceanic plankton (diatoms make their own food with good sweet sunlight; they don't OD on the chemicals of terrestrial plants). It is simply a gratuitous, attention-grabbing guess. It cannot be tested, for how can we know what dinosaurs tasted and what their livers could do? Livers don't fossilize any better than testicles.

The hypothesis doesn't even make any sense in its own context. 20 Angiosperms were in full flower ten million years before dinosaurs went the way of all flesh. Why did it take so long? As for the pains of a chemical death recorded in contortions of fossils, I regret to say (or rather I'm pleased to note for the dinosaurs' sake) that Siegel's knowledge of geology must be a bit deficient: Muscles contract after death and geological strata rise and fall with motions of the earth's crust after burial—more than enough reason to distort a fossil's pristine appearance.

The impact story, on the other hand, has a sound basis in evi- 21 dence. It can be tested, extended, refined, and, if wrong, disproved. The Alvarezes did not just construct an arresting guess for public consumption. They proposed their hypothesis after laborious geochemical studies with Frank Asaro and Helen Michael had revealed a massive increase of iridium in rocks deposited right at the time of extinction. Iridium, a rare metal of the platinum group, is virtually absent from indigenous rocks of the earth's crust; most of our iridium arrives on extraterrestrial objects that strike the earth.

The Alvarez hypothesis bore immediate fruit. Based originally on 22 evidence from two European localities, it led geochemists throughout the world to examine other sediments of the same age. They found abnormally high amounts of iridium everywhere—from continental rocks of the western United States to deep sea cores from the South Atlantic.

Cowles proposed his testicular hypothesis in the mid-1940s. 23 Where has it gone since then? Absolutely nowhere, because scientists can do nothing with it. The hypothesis must stand as a curious appendage to a solid study of alligators. Siegel's overdose scenario will also win a few press notices and fade into oblivion. The Alvarezes' asteroid falls into a different category altogether, and much of the popular commentary has missed this essential distinction by focusing on the impact and its attendant results, and forgetting what really matters to a scientist—the iridium. If you talk just about asteroids, dust, and darkness, you tell stories no better and no more entertaining than fried testicles or terminal trips. It is the iridium—the source of testable evidence—that counts and forges the crucial distinction between speculation and science.

The proof, to twist a phrase, lies in the doing. Cowles's hypothesis 24 has generated nothing in thirty-five years. Since its proposal in 1979, the Alvarez hypothesis has spawned hundreds of studies, a major conference, and attendant publications. Geologists are fired up. They are looking for iridium at all other extinction boundaries. Every week exposes a new wrinkle in the scientific press. Further evidence that the Cretaceous iridium represents extraterrestrial impact and not indigenous volcanism continues to accumulate. As I revise this essay in November 1984 (this paragraph will be out of date when [it] is published), new data include chemical "signatures" of other isotopes indicating unearthly provenance, glass spherules of a size and sort produced by impact and not by volcanic eruptions, and high-pressure varieties of silica formed (so far as we know) only under the tremendous shock of impact.

My point is simply this: Whatever the eventual outcome (I sus- 25 pect it will be positive), the Alvarez hypothesis is exciting, fruitful science because it generates tests, provides us with things to do, and expands outward. We are having fun, battling back and forth, moving toward a resolution, and extending the hypothesis beyond its original scope.

As just one example of the unexpected, distant cross-fertilization 26 that good science engenders, the Alvarez hypothesis made a major contribution to a theme that has riveted public attention in the past few months—so-called nuclear winter. In a speech delivered in April 1982, Luis Alvarez calculated the energy that a ten-kilometer asteroid would release on impact. He compared such an explosion with a full nuclear exchange and implied that all-out atomic war might unleash similar consequences.

This theme of impact leading to massive dust clouds and falling 27 temperatures formed an important input to the decision of Carl Sagan and a group of colleagues to model the climatic consequences of nuclear holocaust. Full nuclear exchange would probably generate the same kind of dust cloud and darkening that may have wiped out the dinosaurs. Temperatures would drop precipitously and agriculture might become impossible. Avoidance of nuclear war is fundamentally an ethical and political imperative, but we must know the factual consequences to make firm judgments. I am heartened by a final link across disciplines and deep concerns—another criterion, by the way, of science at its best: A recognition of the very phenomenon that made our evolution possible by exterminating the previously dominant dinosaurs and clearing a way for the evolution of large mammals, including us, might actually help to save us from joining those magnificent beasts in contorted poses among the strata of the earth.

Meaning

1. According to Gould, what constitutes a scientific hypothesis? What constitutes useless speculation? Where in the essay do you find his definitions of these terms?
2. State, in your own words, the thesis of this essay.
3. What does Gould perceive to be the major flaws in the testicular malfunction and drug overdose theories about the extinction of dinosaurs? Cite his specific reasons for discrediting each theory.
4. What is the connection between nuclear holocaust and the extinction of dinosaurs? (See the essay's last paragraph.)

Purpose and Audience

1. Overall, do you find Gould's essay effective in explaining a specialized subject to an audience of nonspecialists? Why, or why not?
2. Paragraphs 14 and 16 contain references to Dylan Thomas's poem "Do Not Go Gentle into That Good Night." (The poem's title is used in paragraph 14; "Rage, rage against the dying of the light," one of the poem's refrains, appears in paragraph 16.) If you are not familiar with the poem, look it up. Is it necessary to know the poem to understand Gould's use of these lines? What is the effect of these allusions? (If necessary, see the Glossary under *allusion*.)

Method and Structure

1. In explaining the Alvarezes' hypothesis about the causes of the dinosaurs' extinction, Gould outlines a causal chain. Draw a diagram to illustrate this chain.
2. **Other Methods**   How does the process analysis in paragraphs 4–5, 9–12, 14, and 16 help Gould analyze the possible causes of dinosaur extinction? What would the essay lack without these paragraphs?

Language

1. How do you understand the phrases "hit parade of primal fascination" (paragraph 17) and "the hypothesis of testicular frying" (18)? Is the tone here somber, silly, whimsical, ironic, or what? (If necessary, see the definition of *tone* in the Glossary.)

2. What do you take the following sentence to mean: "There is no separate problem of the extinction of dinosaurs" (paragraph 5)? Separate from what? According to Gould, then, what *is* the problem being discussed?

Writing Topics

1. In an essay, explore the causes of a situation that affects you directly—a breakup with a close friend or significant other, a course you are having difficulties with, a problem you face at work, or the like. Make sure to give your audience a clear sense of the situation. You may want to rely on narration, telling the story of the circumstances.

2. As Gould himself predicts (paragraph 24), his summary of the research into the Alvarez hypothesis is now dated: more data have accumulated; the hypothesis has been challenged, tested, revised. Do research in the library or on the Web to find articles written over the past several years about the extinction of the dinosaurs. Write an essay updating Gould's in which you summarize the significant evidence for and against the Alvarez hypothesis.

3. Apply Gould's distinction between hypothesis and speculation (paragraphs 1 5) in an area you know well — for instance, Civil War battles, dance, basketball, waste recycling, carpentry, nursing. What, in your area, is the equivalent of the useful hypothesis? What is the equivalent of the useless speculation? Be as specific as possible so that a reader outside the field can understand you.

Writing with the Method
Cause-and-Effect Analysis

Choose one of the following questions, or any other question they suggest, and answer it in an essay developed by analyzing causes or effects. The question you decide on should concern a topic you care about so that your analysis of causes or effects is a means of communicating an idea, not an end in itself.

PEOPLE AND THEIR BEHAVIOR

1. Why is a past or present politician, athlete, police officer, or fire fighter considered a hero?
2. Why did one couple you know marry or divorce?
3. Why is a particular friend or relative always getting into trouble?
4. Why do people root for the underdog?
5. How does a person's alcohol or drug dependency affect others in his or her family?

WORK

6. At what age should a person start working for pay, and why?
7. What effects do you expect your education to have on your choice of career and your performance in it?
8. What effect has the job market had on you and your friends?

ART AND ENTERTAINMENT

9. Why do teenagers like rock music?
10. What makes a professional sports team succeed in a new city?
11. Why is (or was) a particular television show or movie so popular?

CONTEMPORARY ISSUES

12. Why does the United States spend so much money on defense?
13. What are the possible effects of rising college tuitions?
14. How can a long period of involuntary unemployment affect a person?
15. Why is a college education important?
16. Why do marriages between teenagers fail more often than marriages between people in other age groups?
17. Why might someone resort to a public act of violence, such as bombing a building?

Chapter Ten

ARGUMENT AND PERSUASION

USING THE METHOD

We argue all the time—with relatives, with friends, with the auto mechanic or the shop clerk—so a chapter devoted to argument and persuasion may at first seem unnecessary. But arguing with an auto mechanic over the cost of repairs is quite a different process from arguing with readers over a complex issue. In both cases we are trying to find common ground with our audience, perhaps to change its views or even to compel it to act as we wish. But the mechanic is in front of us; we can shift our tactics in response to his or her gestures, expressions, and words. The reader, in contrast, is "out there"; we have to anticipate those gestures, expressions, and words in the way we structure the argument, the kinds of evidence we use to support it, even the way we conceive of the subject.

A great many assertions that are worth making are debatable at some level—whether over the facts on which the assertions are based or over the values they imply. Two witnesses to an accident cannot agree on what they saw; two scientists cannot agree on what an experiment shows; two economists cannot agree on what measures will reduce unemployment; two doctors cannot agree on what constitutes life or death. Making an effective case for our opinions requires upholding certain responsibilities and attending to several established techniques of argumentation, most of them dating back to ancient Greece.

305

Technically, argument and persuasion are two different processes:

- **Argument** appeals mainly to an audience's sense of reason in order to negotiate a common understanding or to win agreement with a claim. It is the method of a columnist who defends a president's foreign policy on the grounds of economics and defense strategy.
- **Persuasion** appeals mainly to an audience's feelings and values in order to compel some action, or at least to win support for an action. It is the method of a mayoral candidate who urges voters to support her because she is sensitive to the poor.

But argument and persuasion so often mingle that we will use the one term *argument* to mean a deliberate appeal to an audience's reason and emotions in order to create compromise, win agreement, or compel action.

The Elements of Argument

All arguments share certain elements:

- The core of the argument is an **assertion** or **proposition,** a debatable claim about the subject. Generally, you express this assertion as your thesis statement. It may defend or attack a position, suggest a solution to a problem, recommend a change in policy, or challenge a value or belief. Here are a few examples:

  > The college should give first priority for on-campus jobs to students who need financial aid.
  >
  > School prayer has been rightly declared unconstitutional and should not be reinstituted in any form.
  >
  > Smokers who wish to poison themselves should be allowed to do so, but not in any place where their smoke will poison others.

- You break down the central assertion into subclaims, each one supported by evidence.
- You raise significant opposing arguments and dispense with them, again with the support of evidence.
- You organize the parts of the argument into a clear, logical structure that pushes steadily toward the conclusion.

You may draw on classification, comparison, or any other rhetorical method to develop the entire argument or to introduce evidence or strengthen your conclusion. For instance, in a paper arguing for raising a college's standards of admission, you might contrast the existing standards with the proposed standards, analyze a process for raising the standards over a period of years, and predict the effects of the new standards on future students' preparedness for college work.

Appeals to Readers

In arguing you are appealing to readers: you want them to listen to what you have to say, judge your words fairly, and, as much as they can, agree with you. Most arguments combine three kinds of appeals to readers: ethical, emotional, and rational.

Ethical Appeal

The **ethical appeal** is often not explicit in an argument, yet it pervades the whole. It is the sense you convey of your expertise and character, projected by the reasonableness of the argument, by the use of evidence, and by tone. A rational argument shows readers that you are thinking logically and fairly. Strong evidence establishes your credibility. And a sincere, reasonable tone demonstrates your balance and goodwill.

Emotional Appeal

The **emotional appeal** in argument aims directly for readers' hearts — for the complex of beliefs, values, and feelings deeply embedded in all of us. We are just as often motivated by these ingrained ideas and emotions as by our intellects. Even scientists, who stress the rational interpretation of facts above all else, are sometimes influenced in their interpretations by emotions deriving from, say, competition with other scientists. And the willingness of a nation's citizens to go to war may result more from their fear and pride than from their reasoned considerations of risks and gains. An emotional appeal in argument attempts to tap such feelings for any of several reasons:

- To heighten the responsiveness of readers
- To inspire readers to new beliefs
- To compel readers to act
- To assure readers that their values remain unchallenged

An emotional appeal may be explicit, as when an argument against capital punishment appeals to readers' religious values by citing the Bible's Sixth Commandment, "Thou shalt not kill." But an emotional appeal may also be less obvious, because individual words may have connotations that elicit emotional responses from readers. For instance, one writer may characterize an environmental group as "a well-organized team representing diverse interests," while another may call the same group "a hodgepodge of nature lovers and irresponsible businesspeople." The first appeals to readers' preference for order and balance, the second to readers' fear of extremism and disdain for unsound business practices. (See the Glossary for more on *connotation*.)

The use of emotional appeals requires care:

- The appeal must be directed at the audience's actual beliefs and feelings.
- The appeal must be presented dispassionately enough so that readers have no reason to doubt your fairness in the rest of the argument.
- The appeal must be appropriate to the subject and to the argument. For instance, in arguing against a pay raise for city councilors, you might be tempted to appeal to readers' resentment and distrust of wealthy people by pointing out that two of the councilors are rich enough to work for no pay. But such an appeal would divert attention from the issue of whether the pay raise is justified for all councilors on the basis of the work they do and the city's ability to pay the extra cost.

Carefully used, emotional appeals have great force, particularly when they contribute to an argument based largely on sound reasoning and evidence. The appropriate mix of emotion and reason in a given essay is entirely dependent on the subject, your purpose, and the audience. Emotional appeals are out of place in most arguments in the natural and social sciences, where rational interpretations of factual evidence are all that will convince readers of the truth of an assertion. But emotional appeals may be essential when you want an audience to support or take an action, for emotion is a stronger motivator than reason.

Rational Appeal

A **rational appeal** is one that, as the name implies, addresses the rational faculties of readers—their capacity to reason logically about a problem. You establish the truth of a proposition or claim by moving through a series of related subclaims, each supported by evidence. In doing so, you follow processes of reasoning that are natural to all of us and thus are expected by readers. These processes are induction and deduction.

Inductive reasoning moves from the particular to the general, from evidence to a generalization or conclusion about the evidence. It is a process we begin learning in infancy and use daily throughout our lives: a child burns herself the three times she touches a stove, so she concludes that stoves burn; we have liked four movies directed by Oliver Stone, so we form the generalization that Oliver Stone makes good movies. Inductive reasoning is also very common in argument: you might offer facts showing that chronic patients in the state's mental hospitals receive only drugs as treatment, and then you conclude that the state's hospitals rely exclusively on drugs to treat chronic patients.

The movement from particular to general is called an **inductive leap** because you must make something of a jump to conclude that what is true of some instances (the chronic patients whose records were available) is also true of all other instances in the class (the rest of the chronic patients). In an ideal world we could perhaps avoid the inductive leap by pinning down every conceivable instance, but in the real world such thoroughness is usually impractical and often impossible. Instead, we gather enough evidence to make our generalizations probable.

The evidence for induction may be of several kinds:

- Facts: statistics or other hard data that are verifiable or, failing that, attested to by reliable sources (for instance, the number of drug doses per chronic patient, derived from hospital records).

- The opinions of recognized experts on the subject, opinions that are themselves conclusions based on research and observation (for instance, the testimony of an experienced hospital doctor).

- Examples illustrating the evidence (for instance, the treatment history of one patient).

A sound inductive generalization can form the basis for the second reasoning process, **deductive reasoning.** Working from the general to the particular, you start with such a generalization and apply it to a new situation in order to draw a conclusion about that situation. Like induction, deduction is a process we use constantly to order our experience. The child who learns from three experiences that all stoves burn then sees a new stove and concludes that this stove also will burn. The child's thought process can be written in the form of a **syllogism,** a three-step outline of deductive reasoning:

All stoves burn me.
This is a stove.
Therefore, this stove will burn me.

The first statement, the generalization derived from induction, is called the **major premise.** The second statement, a more specific assertion about some element of the major premise, is called the **minor premise.** And the third statement, an assertion of the logical connection between premises, is called the **conclusion.** The following syllogism takes the earlier example about mental hospitals one step further:

MAJOR PREMISE   The state hospitals' treatment of chronic patients relies exclusively on drugs.
MINOR PREMISE   Drugs do not cure chronic patients.
CONCLUSION   Therefore, the state hospitals' treatment of chronic patients will not cure them.

Unlike an inductive conclusion, which requires a leap, the deductive conclusion derives necessarily from the premises: as long as the reasoning process is valid and the premises are accepted as true, then the conclusion must also be true. To be valid, the reasoning must conform to the process outlined above. The following syllogism is *not* valid, even though the premises are true:

All radicals want to change the system.
Georgia Allport wants to change the system.
Therefore, Georgia Allport is a radical.

The flaw in this syllogism is that not *only* radicals want to change the system, so Allport does not *necessarily* fall within the class of radicals just because she wants to change the system. The conclusion, then, is invalid.

A syllogism can be valid without being true if either of the premises is untrue. For example:

All people who want political change are radicals.
Georgia Allport wants political change.
Therefore, Georgia Allport is a radical.

The conclusion here is valid because Allport falls within the class of people who want political change. But the conclusion is untrue because the major premise is untrue. As commonly defined, a radical seeks extreme change, often by revolutionary means. But other forms and means of change are also possible; Allport, for instance, may be interested in improving the delivery of services to the poor and in achieving passage of tougher environmental-protection laws—both political changes, to be sure, but neither radical.

In arguments, syllogisms are rarely spelled out as neatly as in these examples. Sometimes the order of the statements is reversed, as in this sentence paraphrasing a Supreme Court decision:

> The state may not imprison a man just because he is too poor to pay a fine; the only justification for imprisonment is a certain danger to society, and poverty does not constitute certain danger.

The buried syllogism can be stated thus:

> MAJOR PREMISE   The state may imprison only those who are a certain danger to society.
>
> MINOR PREMISE   A man who is too poor to pay a fine is not a certain danger to society.
>
> CONCLUSION   Therefore, the state cannot imprison a man just because he is too poor to pay a fine.

Often, one of a syllogism's premises or even its conclusion is implied but not expressed. Each of the following sentences omits one part of the same syllogism:

> All five students cheated, so they should be expelled. [Implied major premise: cheaters should be expelled.]
>
> Cheaters should be punished by expulsion, so all five students should be expelled. [Implied minor premise: all five students cheated.]
>
> Cheaters should be punished by expulsion, and all five students cheated. [Implied conclusion: all five students should be expelled.]

Fallacies

Inappropriate emotional appeals and flaws in reasoning—called **fallacies**—can trap you as you construct an argument. Watch out for the following, which your readers will find if you don't:

- **Hasty generalization:** an inductive conclusion that leaps to include *all* instances when at best only *some* instances provide any evidence. Hasty generalizations form some of our worst stereotypes:

> Physically challenged people are mentally challenged, too.
> African Americans are good athletes.
> Italian Americans are volatile.

- **Oversimplification:** an inductive conclusion that ignores complexities in the evidence that, if heeded, would weaken the conclusion or suggest an entirely different one. For example:

> The newspaper failed because it couldn't compete with television.

Although television may have taken some business from the paper, hundreds of other papers continue to thrive; thus television could not be the only cause of the paper's failure.

- **Begging the question:** assuming a conclusion in the statement of a premise, and thus begging readers to accept the conclusion — the question — before it is proved. For example:

> We can trust the president not to neglect the needy, because he is a compassionate man.

This sentence asserts in a circular fashion that the president is not uncompassionate because he is compassionate. He may indeed be compassionate, but this is the question that needs addressing.

- **Ignoring the question:** introducing an issue or consideration that shifts the argument away from the real issue. Offering an emotional appeal as a premise in a logical argument is a form of ignoring the question. The following sentence, for instance, appeals to pity, not to logic:

> The mayor was badly used by people he loved and trusted, so we should not blame him for the corruption in his administration.

- **Ad hominem** (Latin for "to the man"): a form of ignoring the question by attacking the opponents instead of the opponents' arguments. For example:

> O'Brien is married to a convict, so her proposals for prison reform should not be taken seriously.

- **Either-or:** requiring that readers choose between two interpretations or actions when in fact the choices are more numerous.

> Either we imprison all drug users, or we will become their prisoners.

The factors contributing to drug addiction, and the choices for dealing with it, are obviously more complex than this statement suggests. Not all either-or arguments are invalid, for sometimes the alternatives encompass all the possibilities. But when they do not, the argument is false.

- **Non sequitur** (Latin for "it does not follow"): a conclusion derived illogically or erroneously from stated or implied premises. For instance:

  > Young children are too immature to engage in sex, so they should not be taught about it.

  This sentence implies one of two meanings, both of them questionable: only the sexually active can learn anything about sex, or teaching young children about sex will cause them to engage in it.

- **Post hoc** (from the Latin *post hoc, ergo propter hoc*, "after this, therefore because of this"): assuming that because one thing preceded another, it must have caused the other. For example:

  > After the town banned smoking in closed public places, the incidence of vandalism went up.

  Many things may have caused the rise in vandalism, including improved weather and a climbing unemployment rate. It does not follow that the ban on smoking, and that alone, caused the rise.

DEVELOPING AN ARGUMENTATIVE AND PERSUASIVE ESSAY

Getting Started

You will have many chances to write arguments, from defending or opposing a policy such as progressive taxation in an economics course to justifying a new procedure at work to persuading a company to refund your money for a bad product. To choose a subject for an argumentative essay, consider a behavior or policy that irks you, an opinion you want to defend, a change you would like to see implemented, a way to solve a problem. The subject you pick should meet certain criteria:

- It should be something you have some knowledge of from your own experience or observations, from class discussions, or from reading, although you may need to do further research as well.

- It should be limited to a topic you can treat thoroughly in the space and time available to you—for instance, the quality of computer instruction at your school rather than in the whole nation.
- It should be something that you feel strongly about so that you can make a convincing case. (However, it's best to avoid subjects that you cannot view with some objectivity, seeing the opposite side as well as your own; otherwise, you may not be open to flaws in your argument, and you may not be able to represent the opposition fairly.)

With your subject in hand, you should develop a tentative thesis. Because the thesis is essentially a conclusion from evidence, you may have to do some preliminary reading to be sure the evidence exists. This step is especially important with an issue like welfare cheating or tax advantages for the wealthy that we all tend to have opinions about whether we know the facts or not. But don't feel you have to prove your thesis at this early stage; fixing it too firmly may make you unwilling to reshape it if further evidence, your audience, or the structure of your argument so demands.

Stating your thesis in a preliminary thesis sentence can help you form your idea. Make this sentence as clear and specific as possible. Don't resort to a vague generality or a nondebatable statement of fact. Instead, state the precise opinion you want readers to accept or the precise action you want them to take or support. For instance:

VAGUE   Computer instruction is important.

NONDEBATABLE   The school's investment in computer instruction is less than the average investment of the nation's colleges and universities.

PRECISE   Money designated for new dormitories and athletic facilities should be diverted to constructing computer facilities and hiring first-rate computer faculty.

VAGUE   Cloning research is promising.

NONDEBATABLE   Scientists have been experimenting with cloning procedures for many years.

PRECISE   Those who oppose cloning research should consider the potentially valuable applications of the research for human health and development.

Once you have framed a tentative thesis sentence, the next step is to begin gathering evidence in earnest. You should consult as broad a range of sources as necessary to uncover the facts and opinions supporting not only your view but also any opposing views. Though it may be tempting to ignore your opposition in the hope that readers know nothing of it, it is dishonest and probably futile to do so. Acknowledging and, whenever possible, refuting significant opposing views will enhance your credibility with readers. If you find that some counterarguments damage your own argument too greatly, then you will have to revise your thesis.

Where to seek evidence depends on the nature of your thesis.

- For a thesis derived from your own experiences and observations, such as a recommendation that all students work part-time for the education if not for the money, gathering evidence will be primarily a matter of searching your own thoughts and also uncovering opposing views, perhaps by consulting others.
- Some arguments derived from personal experience can also be strengthened by the judicious use of facts and opinions from other sources. An essay arguing in favor of vegetarianism, for instance, could mix the benefits you have felt with those demonstrated by scientific data.
- Nonpersonal and controversial subjects require the evidence of other sources. Though you might strongly favor or oppose a massive federal investment in solar-energy research, your opinions would count little if they were not supported with facts and the opinions of experts.

As you generate or collect evidence, it should suggest the reasons that will support the claim of your thesis—essentially the minor arguments that bolster the main argument. In an essay favoring federal investment in solar-energy research, for instance, the minor arguments might include the need for solar power, the feasibility of its widespread use, and its cost and safety compared with the cost and safety of other energy sources. It is in developing these minor arguments that you are most likely to use induction and deduction consciously—generalizing from specifics or applying generalizations to new information. Thus the minor arguments provide the entry points for your evidence, and together they should encompass all the relevant evidence you find.

As we have already seen, knowledge of readers' needs and expectations is absolutely crucial in argument. In explanatory writing, detail and clarity alone may accomplish your purpose, but you cannot hope to move readers in a certain direction unless you have some idea of where they stand. You need a sense of their background in your subject, of course. But even more, you need a good idea of their values and beliefs, their attitudes toward your subject—in short, their willingness to be convinced by your argument. In a composition class, your readers will probably be your instructor and your classmates, a small but diverse group. A good target when you are addressing a diverse audience is the reader who is neutral or mildly biased one way or the other toward your thesis. You can hope to influence this person as long as your argument is reasonable, your evidence is thorough and convincing, your treatment of opposing views is fair, and your appeals to readers' emotions are appropriate to your purpose, your subject, and especially your readers' values and feelings.

Organizing

Once you have formulated your thesis, gathered reasons and the evidence to support them, and evaluated these against the needs and expectations of your audience, you should plan how you will arrange your argument. The introduction to your essay should draw readers into your framework, making them see how the subject affects them and predisposing them to consider your argument. Sometimes, a forthright approach works best, but an eye-opening anecdote or quotation can also be effective. Your thesis sentence may end your introduction. But if you think readers will not even entertain your thesis until they have seen some or all of your evidence, then withhold your thesis for later.

The main part of the essay consists of your minor arguments or reasons and your evidence for them. Unless the minor arguments form a chain, with each growing out of the one before, their order should be determined by their potential effects on readers. In general, it is most effective to arrange the reasons in order of increasing importance or strength so as to finish powerfully. But to engage readers in the argument from the start, try to begin with a reason that they will find compelling or that they already know and accept; that way, the weaker reasons will be sandwiched between a strong beginning and an even stronger ending.

The views opposing yours can be raised and dispensed with wherever it seems most appropriate to do so. If a counterargument pertains to just one of your minor arguments, then dispose of it at that point. But if the counterarguments are more basic, pertaining to your whole thesis, you should dispose of them either after the introduction or shortly before the conclusion. Use the former strategy if the opposition is particularly strong and you fear that readers will be disinclined to listen unless you address their concerns first. Use the latter strategy when the counterarguments are generally weak or easily dispensed with once you've presented your case.

In the conclusion to your essay, you may summarize the main point of your argument and state your thesis for the first time, if you have saved it for the end, or restate it from your introduction. An effective quotation, an appropriate emotional appeal, or a call for support or action can often provide a strong finish to an argument.

Drafting

While you are drafting the essay, work to make your reasoning clear by showing how each bit of evidence relates to the reason or minor argument being discussed, and how each minor argument relates to the main argument contained in the thesis. In working through the reasons and evidence, you may find it helpful to state each reason as the first sentence in a paragraph and then support it in the following sentences. If this scheme seems too rigid or creates overlong paragraphs, you can always make changes after you have got the draft down on paper. Draw on a range of methods to clarify your points. For instance, define specialized terms or those you use in a special sense, compare and contrast one policy or piece of evidence with another, or carefully analyze causes or effects.

Revising and Editing

When your draft is complete, use the following questions to guide your revision and editing.

- *Is your thesis debatable, precise, and clear?* Readers must know what you are trying to convince them of, at least by the end of the essay if not up front.
- *Is your argument unified?* Does each minor claim support the thesis? Do all opinions, facts, and examples provide evidence for a minor claim? In behalf of your readers, question every sentence you have written to be sure it contributes to the point you are making and to the argument as a whole.
- *Is the structure of your argument clear and compelling?* Readers should be able to follow easily, seeing when and why you move from one idea to the next.

- *Is the evidence specific, representative, and adequate?* Facts, examples, and expert opinions should be well detailed, should fairly represent the available information, and should be sufficient to support your claim.

- *Have you slipped into any logical fallacies?* Detecting fallacies in your own work can be difficult, but your readers will find them if you don't. Look for the following fallacies discussed earlier (pp. 311–13): hasty generalization, oversimplification, begging the question, ignoring the question, ad hominem, either-or, non sequitur, and post hoc. (All of these are also listed in the Glossary under *fallacies*.)

EDWARD I. KOCH

The feisty, opinionated mayor of New York City from 1978 to 1989, Edward Koch was born in the Bronx in 1924, the son of Polish immigrants. He attended the City College of New York for two years, left school to serve in the army during World War II, and returned to earn a law degree from New York University in 1948. He practiced law in New York City from 1949 to 1968, the last five years with a firm he cofounded. While still working as an attorney, Koch was elected a district leader for the Democratic party in 1963 and then a city councillor in 1966. In 1968 he was elected to the US House of Representatives, where he gained a reputation as a champion and supporter of social programs. He left Congress in 1977 to run for mayor of New York City on a platform stressing reduction in crime and in wasteful spending. He won that race and was reelected twice. Koch published two autobiographical books while in office: Mayor *(1984), a lively, candid view of New York politics; and* Politics *(1985), a memoir of his early years in politics. His latest books are* Murder on Broadway *(1997), a novel, and* I'm Not Done Yet! *(2000), a collection of autobiographical essays. "I'm the sort of person who will never get ulcers," Koch has said, "because I say exactly what I think. I am the sort of person who might give other people ulcers."*

Death and Justice

One issue over which Koch has been particularly outspoken—and particularly controversial—is capital punishment. In this essay, first published in the New Republic *in April 1985, he presents his argument in favor of the death penalty. The essay after this one, by David Bruck (page 327), responds directly to Koch in arguing against the death penalty.*

Last December a man named Robert Lee Willie, who had been convicted of raping and murdering an 18-year-old woman, was executed in the Louisiana state prison. In a statement issued several minutes before his death, Mr. Willie said: "Killing people is wrong. . . . It makes no difference whether it's citizens, countries, or governments.

319

Killing is wrong." Two weeks later in South Carolina, an admitted killer named Joseph Carl Shaw was put to death for murdering two teenagers. In an appeal to the governor for clemency, Mr. Shaw wrote: "Killing is wrong when I did it. Killing is wrong when you do it. I hope you have the courage and moral strength to stop the killing."

It is a curiosity of modern life that we find ourselves being lec-   2 tured on morality by cold-blooded killers. Mr. Willie previously had been convicted of aggravated rape, aggravated kidnapping, and the murders of a Louisiana deputy and a man from Missouri. Mr. Shaw committed another murder a week before the two for which he was executed, and admitted mutilating the body of the 14-year-old girl he killed. I can't help wondering what prompted these murderers to speak out against killing as they entered the death-house door. Did their newfound reverence for life stem from the realization that they were about to lose their own?

Life is indeed precious, and I believe the death penalty helps to   3 affirm this fact. Had the death penalty been a real possibility in the minds of these murderers, they might well have stayed their hand. They might have shown moral awareness before their victims died, and not after. Consider the tragic death of Rosa Velez, who happened to be home when a man named Luis Vera burglarized her apartment in Brooklyn. "Yeah, I shot her," Vera admitted. "She knew me, and I knew I wouldn't go to the chair."

During my 22 years in public service, I have heard the pros and   4 cons of capital punishment expressed with special intensity. As a district leader, councilman, congressman, and mayor, I have represented constituencies generally thought of as liberal. Because I support the death penalty for heinous crimes of murder, I have sometimes been the subject of emotional and outraged attacks by voters who find my position reprehensible or worse. I have listened to their ideas. I have weighed their objections carefully. I still support the death penalty. The reasons I maintained my position can be best understood by examining the arguments most frequently heard in opposition.

1. The death penalty is "barbaric." Sometimes opponents of capi-   5 tal punishment horrify with tales of lingering death on the gallows, of faulty electric chairs, or of agony in the gas chamber. Partly in response to such protests, several states such as North Carolina and Texas switched to execution by lethal injection. The condemned person is put to death painlessly, without ropes, voltage, bullets, or gas. Did this answer the objections of death penalty opponents? Of course not. On June 22, 1984, the *New York Times* published an editorial that sarcastically attacked the new "hygienic" method of death by injection, and stated that "execution can never be made humane through science." So it's not the method that really troubles opponents. It's the death itself they consider barbaric.

Admittedly, capital punishment is not a pleasant topic. However, one does not have to like the death penalty in order to support it any more than one must like radical surgery, radiation, or chemotherapy in order to find necessary these attempts at curing cancer. Ultimately we may learn how to cure cancer with a simple pill. Unfortunately, that day has not yet arrived. Today we are faced with the choice of letting the cancer spread or trying to cure it with the methods available, methods that one day will almost certainly be considered barbaric. But to give up and do nothing would be far more barbaric and would certainly delay the discovery of an eventual cure. The analogy between cancer and murder is imperfect, because murder is not the "disease" we are trying to cure. The disease is injustice. We may not like the death penalty, but it must be available to punish crimes of cold-blooded murder, cases in which any other form of punishment would be inadequate and, therefore, unjust. If we create a society in which injustice is not tolerated, incidents of murder—the most flagrant form of injustice—will diminish.   6

2. No other major democracy uses the death penalty. No other major democracy—in fact, few other countries of any description—are plagued by a murder rate such as that in the United States. Fewer and fewer Americans can remember the days when unlocked doors were the norm and murder was a rare and terrible offense. In America the murder rate climbed 122 percent between 1963 and 1980. During that same period, the murder rate in New York City increased by almost 400 percent, and the statistics are even worse in many other cities. A study at M.I.T. showed that based on 1970 homicide rates a person who lived in a large American city ran a greater risk of being murdered than an American soldier in World War II ran of being killed in combat. It is not surprising that the laws of each country differ according to differing conditions and traditions. If other countries had our murder problem, the cry for capital punishment would be just as loud as it is here. And I daresay that any other major democracy where 75 percent of the people supported the death penalty would soon enact it into law.   7

3. An innocent person might be executed by mistake. Consider the work of Adam Bedau, one of the most implacable foes of capital punishment in this country. According to Mr. Bedau, it is "false sentimentality to argue that the death penalty should be abolished because of the abstract possibility that an innocent person might be   8 executed." He cites a study of the 7,000 executions in this country from 1893 to 1971, and concludes that the record fails to show that such cases occur. The main point, however, is this. If government functioned only when the possibility of error didn't exist, government wouldn't function at all. Human life deserves special protection, and one of the best ways to guarantee that protection is to assure that convicted murderers do not kill again. Only the death penalty can accomplish this end. In a recent case in New Jersey, a man named Richard Biegenwald was freed from prison after serving 18 years for murder; since his release he has been convicted of committing four murders. A prisoner named Lemuel Smith, who, while serving four life sentences for murder (plus two life sentences for kidnapping and robbery) in New York's Green Haven Prison, lured a woman corrections officer into the chaplain's office and strangled her. He then mutilated and dismembered her body. An additional life sentence for Smith is meaningless. Because New York has no death penalty statute, Smith has effectively been given a license to kill.[1]

But the problem of multiple murder is not confined to the nation's   9
penitentiaries. In 1981, 91 police officers were killed in the line of duty in this country. Seven percent of those arrested in the cases that have been solved had a previous arrest for murder. In New York City in 1976 and 1977, 85 persons arrested for homicide had a previous arrest for murder. Six of these individuals had two previous arrests for murder, and one had four previous murder arrests. During those two years the New York police were arresting for murder persons with a previous arrest for murder on the average of one every 8.5 days. This is not surprising when we learn that in 1975, for example, the median time served in Massachusetts for homicide was less than two-and-a-half years. In 1976 a study sponsored by the Twentieth Century Fund found that the average time served in the United States for first-degree murder is ten years. The median time served may be considerably lower.

4. Capital punishment cheapens the value of human life. On the con-   10
trary, it can be easily demonstrated that the death penalty strengthens the value of human life. If the penalty for rape were lowered, clearly it would signal a lessened regard for the victims' suffering, humiliation, and personal integrity. It would cheapen their horrible experience, and expose them to an increased danger of recurrence. When we lower the penalty for murder, it signals a lessened regard for the

[1]When Koch was writing, in 1985, the US Supreme Court had in 1972 struck down capital punishment in all states as unconstitutional. New York State reinstated the death penalty in 1995. [Editor's note.]

value of the victim's life. Some critics of capital punishment, such as columnist Jimmy Breslin, have suggested that a life sentence is actually a harsher penalty for murder than death. This is sophistic nonsense. A few killers may decide not to appeal a death sentence, but the overwhelming majority make every effort to stay alive. It is by exacting the highest penalty for the taking of human life that we affirm the highest value of human life.

5. *The death penalty is applied in a discriminatory manner.* This fac- 11 tor no longer seems to be the problem it once was. The appeals process for a condemned prisoner is lengthy and painstaking. Every effort is made to see that the verdict and sentence were fairly arrived at. However, assertions of discrimination are not an argument for ending the death penalty but for extending it. It is not justice to exclude everyone from the penalty of the law if a few are found to be so favored. Justice requires that the law be applied equally to all.

6. *Thou shalt not kill.* The Bible is our greatest source of moral 12 inspiration. Opponents of the death penalty frequently cite the sixth of the Ten Commandments in an attempt to prove that capital punishment is divinely proscribed. In the original Hebrew, however, the Sixth Commandment reads, "Thou Shalt Not Commit Murder," and the Torah specifies capital punishment for a variety of offenses. The biblical viewpoint has been upheld by philosophers throughout history. The greatest thinkers of the 19th century—Kant, Locke, Hobbes, Rousseau, Montesquieu, and Mill—agreed that natural law properly authorizes the sovereign to take life in order to vindicate justice. Only Jeremy Bentham was ambivalent. Washington, Jefferson, and Franklin endorsed it. Abraham Lincoln authorized executions for deserters in wartime. Alexis de Tocqueville, who expressed profound respect for American institutions, believed that the death penalty was indispensable to the support of social order. The United States Constitution, widely admired as one of the seminal achievements in the history of humanity, condemns cruel and inhuman punishment, but does not condemn capital punishment.

7. *The death penalty is state-sanctioned murder.* This is the defense 13 with which Messrs. Willie and Shaw hoped to soften the resolve of those who sentenced them to death. By saying in effect, "You're no better than I am," the murderer seeks to bring his accusers down to his own level. It is also a popular argument among opponents of capital punishment, but a transparently false one. Simply put, the state has rights that the private individual does not. In a democracy, those rights are given to the state by the electorate. The execution of a lawfully condemned killer is no more an act of murder than is legal

imprisonment an act of kidnapping. If an individual forces a neighbor to pay him money under threat of punishment, it's called extortion. If the state does it, it's called taxation. Rights and responsibilities surrendered by the individual are what give the state its power to govern. This contract is the foundation of civilization itself.

Everyone wants his or her rights, and will defend them jealously. 14
Not everyone, however, wants responsibilities, especially the painful responsibilities that come with law enforcement. Twenty-one years ago a woman named Kitty Genovese was assaulted and murdered on a street in New York. Dozens of neighbors heard her cries for help but did nothing to assist her. They didn't even call the police. In such a climate the criminal understandably grows bolder. In the presence of moral cowardice, he lectures us on our supposed failings and tries to equate his crimes with our quest for justice.

The death of anyone — even a convicted killer — diminishes us all. 15
But we are diminished even more by a justice system that fails to function. It is an illusion to let ourselves believe that doing away with capital punishment removes the murderer's deed from our conscience. The rights of society are paramount. When we protect guilty lives, we give up innocent lives in exchange. When opponents of capital punishment say to the state: "I will not let you kill in my name," they are also saying to murderers: "You can kill in your *own* name as long as I have an excuse for not getting involved."

It is hard to imagine anything worse than being murdered while 16
neighbors do nothing. But something worse exists. When those same neighbors shrink back from justly punishing the murderer, the victim dies twice.

Meaning

1. What is the thesis of Koch's argument in favor of capital punishment? What main idea about the death penalty does he ask readers to agree with?
2. Koch focuses on two issues in the debate over capital punishment: the death penalty as a deterrent to murder and as a form of justice for murder done. Which of his arguments deal with the first issue, and which with the second? How is each issue related to his thesis?

Purpose and Audience

1. In the next essay, which rebuts Koch's argument, David Bruck implies that Koch's support of capital punishment served him well politically:

"The electric chair has been a centerpiece of each of Koch's recent political campaigns, and he knows better than anyone how little the facts have to do with the public's support for capital punishment" (paragraph 14, page 331). Does Koch's purpose in this essay seem political? Does he seem to be aiming for votes? Why, or why not?

2. Does Koch seem to expect his audience to agree or disagree with his position on capital punishment? In answering this question, consider the opening two paragraphs: what audience reaction does he seem to be seeking in his presentation of the examples and of himself?

3. In countering the final claim, that "the death penalty is state-sanctioned murder," Koch raises the issue of state versus individual responsibility (paragraphs 13–16). What responsibilities does he thus place on his readers?

Method and Structure

1. Locate examples of emotional, ethical, and rational appeals in Koch's argument. Which appeals do you consider most effective? Least effective? Why?

2. The pleas of convicted killers Willie and Shaw (paragraph 1) were based on a syllogism. Outline the syllogism and explain Koch's grounds for denying its validity (paragraph 13).

3. Analyze and explain Koch's strategy in countering the argument that "the death penalty is 'barbaric'" (paragraphs 5–6). Do you find his methods of argument in this section convincing? Why, or why not?

4. **Other Methods**   Among several other methods, Koch's argument depends in part in example. Search out all of his examples and determine what purpose each one serves.

Language

1. How would you characterize Koch's tone in this essay? What does his language contribute to this tone? To what extent does the tone influence your receptiveness to his argument? (If necessary, consult *tone* in the Glossary.)

2. Examine Koch's comments on his opponents' thinking in paragraphs 4, 5, 10, 13, and 15. What do the words he uses indicate about his attitudes toward opponents of capital punishment and their arguments?

Writing Topics

1. Proponents and opponents of the death penalty use statistics, expert opinions, and other evidence to support their arguments. But for

many people the issue is a matter only of morality: it is right to execute murderers, or it is not right. What are your moral views on this issue? Write a brief essay in which you defend or oppose capital punishment on moral grounds, explaining as best you can the sources of your views (family, religion, experience, and so on).

2. Use the library to investigate the status of the death penalty in your state, and report your findings in an essay. In your research, consider these questions: Is there a death-penalty law on the books? If so, who may be executed and under what conditions? What appeals are available to the defendant? How many people have been executed under the law, and how many more await execution? If there is no death-penalty law, has such legislation been proposed? What is its current status? Have views on capital punishment changed in recent years? In your essay, avoid taking sides on the issue. View your task as fact gathering for the purpose of providing yourself and others with objective background information.

3. Using the resources of the library as well as Koch's and Bruck's essays, write an essay supporting or refuting one of Koch's arguments. Make sure your own argument has a clear thesis and that it is supported to the extent possible by statistics, examples, and expert opinions. Remember to acknowledge arguments opposed to your own.

DAVID BRUCK

*Born in 1949, David Bruck is an attorney specializing in the repre-
sentation of persons facing death sentences. He received a BA from
Harvard College in 1971 and a law degree from the University of
South Carolina in 1975. After working four years as a public defender
in South Carolina, Bruck entered private practice in 1980 to defend
death-row inmates; he has since handled more than sixty appeals of
capital-punishment sentences and successfully argued six death-
penalty cases. Bruck also lectures and consults on capital punishment and the defense of capital cases, and he has appeared on*
Nightline, *the* Newshour with Jim Lehrer, *and other televised news
and affairs programs. His articles on the death penalty have appeared
in the* New York Times, *the* Washington Post, *and other newspapers
and magazines.*

The Death Penalty

This essay was published in the New Republic *in May 1985, one
month after Edward Koch's "Death and Justice" (page 319). In responding directly to Koch, Bruck lays out his own argument against capital
punishment.*

Mayor Ed Koch contends that the death penalty "affirms life." By 1
failing to execute murderers, he says, we "signal a lessened regard
for the value of the victim's life." Koch suggests that people who
oppose the death penalty are like Kitty Genovese's neighbors, who
heard her cries for help but did nothing while an attacker stabbed
her to death.

This is the standard "moral" defense of death as punishment: even 2
if executions don't deter violent crime any more effectively than
imprisonment, they are still required as the only means we have of
doing justice in response to the worst of crimes.

Until recently, this "moral" argument had to be considered in the 3
abstract, since no one was being executed in the United States. But
the death penalty is back now, at least in the southern states, where
every one of the more than 30 executions carried out over the last

two years has taken place.[1] Those of us who live in those states are getting to see the difference between the death penalty in theory, and what happens when you actually try to use it.

South Carolina resumed executing prisoners in January with the   4
electrocution of Joseph Carl Shaw. Shaw was condemned to death for helping to murder two teenagers while he was serving as a military policeman at Fort Jackson, South Carolina. His crime, propelled by mental illness and PCP, was one of terrible brutality. It is Shaw's last words ("Killing was wrong when I did it. It is wrong when you do it. . . .") that so outraged Mayor Koch: he finds it "a curiosity of modern life that we are being lectured on morality by cold-blooded killers." And so it is.

But it was not "modern life" that brought this curiosity into being.   5
It was capital punishment. The electric chair was J. C. Shaw's platform. (The mayor mistakenly writes that Shaw's statement came in the form of a plea to the governor for clemency: actually Shaw made it only seconds before his death, as he waited, shaved and strapped into the chair, for the switch to be thrown.) It was the chair that provided Shaw with celebrity and an opportunity to lecture us on right and wrong. What made this weird moral reversal even worse is that J. C. Shaw faced his own death with undeniable dignity and courage. And while Shaw died, the TV crews recorded another "curiosity" of the death penalty—the crowd gathered outside the death-house to cheer on the executioner. Whoops of elation greeted the announcement of Shaw's death. Waiting at the penitentiary gates for the appearance of the hearse bearing Shaw's remains, one demonstrator started yelling, "Where's the beef?"

For those who had to see the execution of J. C. Shaw, it wasn't   6
easy to keep in mind that the purpose of the whole spectacle was to affirm life. It will be harder still when Florida executes a cop-killer named Alvin Ford. Ford has lost his mind during his years of death-row confinement, and now spends his days trembling, rocking back and forth, and muttering unintelligible prayers. This has led to litigation over whether Ford meets a centuries-old legal standard for mental competency. Since the Middle Ages, the Anglo-American legal system has generally prohibited the execution of anyone who is

[1]Since the US Supreme Court struck down the death penalty in all states in 1972, thirty-eight states have reinstated or initiated capital punishment. The twelve that have not are Alaska, Hawaii, Iowa, Maine, Massachusetts, Michigan, Minnesota, North Dakota, Rhode Island, Vermont, West Virginia, and Wisconsin. [Editor's note.]

too mentally ill to understand what is about to be done to him and why. If Florida wins its case, it will have earned the right to electrocute Ford in his present condition. If it loses, he will not be executed until the state has first nursed him back to some semblance of mental health.

We can at least be thankful that this demoralizing spectacle   7
involves a prisoner who is actually guilty of murder. But this may not always be so. The ordeal of Lenell Jeter—the young black engineer who recently served more than a year of a life sentence for a Texas armed robbery that he didn't commit—should remind us that the system is quite capable of making the very worst sort of mistake. That Jeter was eventually cleared is a fluke. If the robbery had occurred at 7 PM rather than 3 PM, he'd have had no alibi, and would still be in prison today. And if someone had been killed in that robbery, Jeter probably would have been sentenced to death. We'd have seen the usual execution-day interviews with state officials and the victim's relatives, all complaining that Jeter's appeals took too long. And Jeter's last words from the gurney would have taken their place among the growing literature of death-house oration that so irritates the mayor.

Koch quotes Hugo Adam Bedau, a prominent abolitionist, to the   8
effect that the record fails to establish that innocent defendants have been executed in the past. But this doesn't mean, as Koch implies, that it hasn't happened. All Bedau was saying was that doubts concerning executed prisoners' guilt are almost never resolved. Bedau is at work now on an effort to determine how many wrongful death sentences may have been imposed: his list of murder convictions since 1900 in which the state eventually *admitted* error is some 400 cases long. Of course, very few of these cases involved actual executions: the mistakes that Bedau documents were uncovered precisely because the prisoner was alive and able to fight for his vindication. The cases where someone is executed are the very cases in which we're least likely to learn that we got the wrong man.

I don't claim that executions of entirely innocent people will occur   9
very often. But they will occur. And other sorts of mistakes already have. Roosevelt Green was executed in Georgia two days before J. C. Shaw. Green and an accomplice kidnapped a young woman. Green swore that his companion shot her to death after Green had left, and that he knew nothing about the murder. Green's claim was supported by a statement that his accomplice made to a witness after the crime. The jury never resolved whether Green was telling the truth, and when he tried to take a polygraph examination a few days

before his scheduled execution, the state of Georgia refused to allow the examiner into the prison. As the pressure for symbolic retribution mounts, the courts, like the public, are losing patience with such details. Green was electrocuted on January 9, while members of the Ku Klux Klan rallied outside the prison.

Then there is another sort of arbitrariness that happens all the 10 time. Last October, Louisiana executed a man named Ernest Knighton. Knighton had killed a gas station owner during a robbery. Like any murder, this was a terrible crime. But it was not premeditated, and is the sort of crime that very rarely results in a death sentence. Why was Knighton electrocuted when almost everyone else who committed the same offense was not? Was it because he was black? Was it because his victim and all 12 members of the jury that sentenced him were white? Was it because Knighton's court-appointed lawyer presented no evidence on his behalf at his sentencing hearing? Or maybe there's no reason except bad luck. One thing is clear: Ernest Knighton was picked out to die the way a fisherman takes a cricket out of a bait jar. No one cares which cricket gets impaled on the hook.

Not every prisoner executed recently was chosen that randomly. 11 But many were. And having selected these men so casually, so blindly, the death penalty system asks us to accept that the purpose of killing each of them is to affirm the sanctity of human life.

The death penalty states are also learning that the death penalty 12 is easier to advocate than it is to administer. In Florida, where executions have become almost routine, the governor reports that nearly a third of his time is spent reviewing the clemency requests of condemned prisoners. The Florida Supreme Court is hopelessly backlogged with death cases. Some have taken five years to decide, and the rest of the Court's work waits in line behind the death appeals. Florida's death row currently holds more than 230 prisoners. State officials are reportedly considering building a special "death prison" devoted entirely to the isolation and electrocution of the condemned. The state is also considering the creation of a special public defender unit that will do nothing else but handle death penalty appeals. The death penalty, in short, is spawning death agencies.

And what is Florida getting for all of this? The state went through 13 almost all of 1983 without executing anyone: its rate of intentional homicide declined by 17 percent. Last year [1984] Florida executed eight people—the most of any state, and the sixth highest total for any year since Florida started electrocuting people back in 1924.

Elsewhere in the US last year, the homicide rate continued to decline. But in Florida, it actually rose by 5.1 percent.

But these are just the tiresome facts. The electric chair has been a 14 centerpiece of each of Koch's recent political campaigns, and he knows better than anyone how little the facts have to do with the public's support for capital punishment. What really fuels the death penalty is the justifiable frustration and rage of people who see that the government is not coping with violent crime. So what if the death penalty doesn't work? At least it gives us the satisfaction of knowing that we got one or two of the sons of bitches.

Perhaps we want retribution on the flesh and bone of a handful of 15 convicted murderers so badly that we're willing to close our eyes to all of the demoralization and danger that come with it. A lot of politicians think so, and they may be right. But if they are, then let's at least look honestly at what we're doing. This lottery of death both comes from and encourages an attitude toward human life that is not reverent, but reckless.

And that is why the mayor is dead wrong when he confuses such 16 fury with justice. He suggests that we trivialize murder unless we kill murderers. By that logic, we also trivialize rape unless we sodomize rapists. The sin of Kitty Genovese's neighbors wasn't that they failed to stab her attacker to death. Justice does demand that murderers be punished. And common sense demands that society be protected from them. But neither justice nor self-preservation demands that we kill men whom we have already imprisoned.

The electric chair in which J. C. Shaw died earlier this year was 17 built in 1912 at the suggestion of South Carolina's governor at the time, Cole Blease. Governor Blease's other criminal justice initiative was an impassioned crusade in favor of lynch law. Any lesser response, the governor insisted, trivialized the loathsome crimes of interracial rape and murder. In 1912 a lot of people agreed with Governor Blease that a proper regard for justice required both lynching and the electric chair. Eventually we are going to learn that justice requires neither.

Meaning

1. What is the thesis of Bruck's argument? Where is this thesis stated most clearly? What is the relationship between Bruck's thesis and Koch's thesis in the previous essay (beginning on p. 319)?

2. To understand Bruck's strategy, make an outline of the main points in his argument. Which of these points directly counter points made by

Koch? Which of Koch's points does Bruck not address directly? In what ways is his emphasis different from Koch's?

3. What does Bruck mean by "symbolic retribution" (paragraph 9)? Why does he believe that the Green case represents an instance of symbolic retribution? Why is this notion particularly demoralizing and dangerous (15)?

Purpose and Audience

1. Given Bruck's obvious purpose of refuting Koch, how do you account for the striking difference in argument style between the two essays?

2. Whom does Bruck seem to be addressing in this essay: Mayor Koch? those who support capital punishment? those who oppose it? those who haven't made up their minds? some other group? What influence does he apparently hope to have on his readers' opinions? To what extent did he influence your opinions of capital punishment and of Koch's argument supporting it?

3. Compare Bruck's and Koch's accounts of the crime for which Joseph Carl Shaw was executed (paragraph 4 in Bruck; paragraph 1, pp. 319–20, in Koch). Which is more detailed? How does each author's use of detail — and the details themselves — reflect the way in which he hopes to influence readers' opinions?

Method and Structure

1. To what extent does Bruck use rational appeal in refuting Koch? ethical appeal? emotional appeal? Identify examples of each in your answer.

2. In paragraph 16 Bruck identifies and disputes a syllogism that he sees Koch and other proponents of capital punishment relying on. Tease out the faulty syllogism and explain what is wrong with it.

3. **Other Methods**   Much of Bruck's argument is developed by cause-and-effect analysis. Why is this method particularly effective for countering Koch's claims, given Bruck's main point?

Language

1. Bruck, more than Koch, relies on irony, saying one thing when he means another: for example, "it wasn't easy to keep in mind that the purpose of the whole spectacle [of Shaw's execution] was to affirm life" (paragraph 6). Locate other examples of irony. In your view, does irony strengthen or weaken Bruck's argument? Why? (If necessary, consult *irony* in the Glossary.)

2. Compare the tone of the first few paragraphs of Bruck's essay with that of the concluding paragraphs. Which is stronger? How does language create the difference? (See *tone* in the Glossary if you need a definition.)

Writing Topics

1. Taking off from the third question under "Purpose and Audience," use a periodical database or the Web to help locate accounts of the trial and execution of Joseph Carl Shaw. (He was electrocuted in January 1985.) Write a short essay evaluating the accuracy of Koch's and Bruck's descriptions of this case: Which facts did each include and omit? Did either distort the facts in any way? In your essay, account for their differing interpretations in light of their respective purposes.

2. Koch says the death penalty is not barbaric considering the purpose it serves; Bruck implies that it is barbaric. Think of some other practice of our society that could also be interpreted as barbaric by some and not by others—for instance, displaying the body at a funeral (Jessica Mitford's "Embalming Mr. Jones," page 192, could help with this topic), removing wrinkles by cosmetic surgery, or tattooing. In an essay, argue for or against the practice on specific grounds: Is it indeed barbaric? Why, or why not? Why do those who perform it do so? Does it serve society as a whole in any way? Is its performance currently restricted? Should it be less or more restricted? How?

3. Koch's and Bruck's essays provide a concise debate on many of the important questions concerning capital punishment. Using their essays as a guide to the issues, locate at least one more "pro" argument and one more "con" argument in a periodical database or on the Web. Draw on the arguments and the data in Koch's and Bruck's essays and the other sources to support your own argument for or against the death penalty. If you are still uncertain of your own opinion after reading the other sources, focus your argument on the strengths and weaknesses of each side in the debate, supporting your points with evidence.

WILLIAM F. BUCKLEY, JR.

William F. Buckley, Jr., is a prominent conservative commentator and founder of the National Review *magazine. Born in New York in 1925, he began publishing books and articles about conservative political values shortly after he graduated from Yale. His recent works include* Nuremburg: The Reckoning *(2003),* Miles Gone By: A Literary Autobiography *(2004), and* The Fall of the Berlin Wall *(2004), an account of the events leading to the end of the Cold War. From 1966 to 1999, he starred in the television debate program* Firing Line.

Why Don't We Complain?

An episode on an overheated commuter train triggers Buckley's argument against his and his fellow Americans' passive acceptance of circumstances. The essay first appeared in Esquire *in 1961.*

It was the very last coach and the only empty seat on the entire train, so there was no turning back. The problem was to breathe. Outside, the temperature was below freezing. Inside the railroad car the temperature must have been about 85 degrees. I took off my overcoat, and a few minutes later my jacket, and noticed that the car was flecked with the white shirts of the passengers. I soon found my hand moving to loosen my tie. From one end of the car to the other, as we rattled through Westchester County, we sweated; but we did not moan.

I watched the train conductor appear at the head of the car. "Tickets, all tickets, please!" In a more virile age, I thought, the passengers would seize the conductor and strap him down on a seat over the radiator to share the fate of his patrons. He shuffled down the aisle, picking up tickets, punching commutation cards. *No one addressed a word to him.* He approached my seat, and I drew a deep breath of resolution. "Conductor," I began with a considerable edge to my voice. Instantly the doleful eyes of my seatmate turned tiredly from his newspaper to fix me with a resentful stare: What question could be so important as to justify my sibilant intrusion into his stupor? I was shaken by those eyes. I am incapable of making a discreet

1

2

fuss, so I mumbled a question about what time we were due in Stamford (I didn't even ask whether it would be before or after dehydration could be expected to set in), got my reply, and went back to my newspaper and to wiping my brow.

The conductor had nonchalantly walked down the gauntlet of 3 eighty sweating American freemen, and not one of them had asked him to explain why the passengers in that car had been consigned to suffer. There is nothing to be done when the temperature *outdoors* is 85 degrees, and indoors the air conditioner has broken down; obviously when that happens there is nothing to do, except perhaps curse the day that one was born. But when the temperature outdoors is below freezing, it takes a positive act of will on somebody's part to set the temperature *indoors* at 85. Somewhere a valve was turned too far, a furnace overstocked, a thermostat maladjusted: something that could easily be remedied by turning off the heat and allowing the great outdoors to come indoors. All this is so obvious. What is not obvious is what has happened to the American people.

It isn't just the commuters, whom we have come to visualize as a 4 supine breed who have got on to the trick of suspending their sensory faculties twice a day while they submit to the creeping dissolution of the railroad industry. It isn't just they who have given up trying to rectify irrational vexations. It is the American people everywhere.

A few weeks ago at a large movie theater I turned to my wife and 5 said, "The picture is out of focus." "Be quiet," she answered. I obeyed. But a few minutes later I raised the point again, with mounting impatience. "It will be all right in a minute," she said apprehensively. (She would rather lose her eyesight than be around when I make one of my infrequent scenes.) I waited. It was *just* out of focus—not glaringly out, but out. My vision is 20-20, and I assume that is the vision, adjusted, for most people in the movie house. So, after hectoring my wife throughout the first reel, I finally prevailed upon her to admit that it *was* off, and very annoying. We then settled down, coming to rest on the presumption that: a) someone connected with the management of the theater must soon notice the blur and make the correction; or b) that someone seated near the rear of the house would make the complaint in behalf of those of us up front; or c) that—any minute now—the entire house would explode into catcalls and foot stamping, calling dramatic attention to the irksome distortion.

What happened was nothing. The movie ended, as it had begun, 6 *just* out of focus, and as we trooped out, we stretched our faces in a variety of contortions to accustom the eye to the shock of normal focus.

I think it is safe to say that everybody suffered on that occasion. 7
And I think it is safe to assume that everyone was expecting someone else to take the initiative in going back to speak to the manager.
And it is probably true even that if we had supposed the movie would
run right through the blurred image, someone surely would have
summoned up the purposive indignation to get up out of his seat and
file his complaint.

But notice that no one did. And the reason no one did is because we 8
are all increasingly anxious in America to be unobtrusive, we are
reluctant to make our voices heard, hesitant about claiming our rights;
we are afraid that our cause is unjust, or that if it is not unjust, that it
is ambiguous; or if not even that, that it is too trivial to justify the
horrors of a confrontation with Authority; we will sit in an oven or
endure a racking headache before undertaking a head-on, I'm-here-to-
tell-you complaint. That tendency to passive compliance, to a heedless
endurance, is something to keep one's eyes on—in sharp focus.

I myself can occasionally summon the courage to complain, but I 9
cannot, as I have intimated, complain softly. My own instinct is so
strong to let the thing ride, to forget about it—to expect that someone will take the matter up, when the grievance is collective, in my
behalf—that it is only when the provocation is at a very special key,
whose vibrations touch simultaneously a complexus of nerves, allergies, and passions, that I catch fire and find the reserves of courage and
assertiveness to speak up. When that happens, I get quite carried away.
My blood gets hot, my brow wet, I become unbearably and uncon-
scionably sarcastic and bellicose; I am girded for a total showdown.

Why should that be? Why could not I (or anyone else) on that rail- 10
road coach have said simply to the conductor, "Sir"—I take that
back: that sounds sarcastic—"Conductor, would you be good
enough to turn down the heat? I am extremely hot. In fact, I tend to
get hot every time the temperature reaches 85 degr—." Strike that
last sentence. Just end it with the simple statement that you are
extremely hot, and let the conductor infer the cause.

Every New Year's Eve I resolve to do something about the 11
Milquetoast in me and vow to speak up, calmly, for my rights, and
for the betterment of our society, on every appropriate occasion.
Entering last New Year's Eve I was fortified in my resolve because
that morning at breakfast I had had to ask the waitress three times
for a glass of milk. She finally brought it—after I had finished my
eggs, which is when I don't want it anymore. I did not have the man-
liness to order her to take the milk back, but settled instead for a
cowardly sulk, and ostentatiously refused to drink the milk—though

I later paid for it—rather than state plainly to the hostess, as I should have, why I had not drunk it, and would not pay for it.

So by the time the New Year ushered out the Old, riding in on my 12 morning's indignation and stimulated by the gastric juices of resolution that flow so faithfully on New Year's Eve, I rendered my vow. Henceforward I would conquer my shyness, my despicable disposition to supineness. I would speak out like a man against the unnecessary annoyances of our time.

Forty-eight hours later, I was standing in line at the ski repair store 13 in Pico Peak, Vermont. All I needed, to get on with my skiing, was the loan, for one minute, of a small screwdriver, to tighten a loose binding. Behind the counter in the workshop were two men. One was industriously engaged in servicing the complicated requirements of a young lady at the head of the line, and obviously he would be tied up for quite a while. The other—"Jiggs," his workmate called him—was a middle-aged man, who sat in a chair puffing a pipe, exchanging small talk with his working partner. My pulse began its telltale acceleration. The minutes ticked on. I stared at the idle shopkeeper, hoping to shame him into action, but he was impervious to my telepathic reproof and continued his small talk with his friend, brazenly insensitive to the nervous demands of six good men who were raring to ski.

Suddenly my New Year's Eve resolution struck me. It was now or 14 never. I broke from my place in line and marched to the counter. I was going to control myself. I dug my nails into my palms. My effort was only partially successful.

"If you are not too busy," I said icily, "would you mind handing me 15 a screwdriver?"

Work stopped and everyone turned his eyes on me, and I experi- 16 enced that mortification I always feel when I am the center of centripetal shafts of curiosity, resentment, perplexity.

But the worst was yet to come. "I am sorry, sir," said Jiggs defer- 17 entially, moving the pipe from his mouth. "I am not supposed to move. I have just had a heart attack." That was the signal for a great whirring noise that descended from heaven. We looked, stricken, out the window, and it appeared as though a cyclone had suddenly focused on the snowy courtyard between the shop and the ski lift. Suddenly a gigantic army helicopter materialized, and hovered down to a landing. Two men jumped out of the plane carrying a stretcher, tore into the ski shop, and lifted the shopkeeper onto the stretcher. Jiggs bade his companion good-bye and was whisked out the door, into the plane, up to the heavens, down—we learned—to a nearby army hospital. I looked up manfully—into a score of man-eating eyes. I put the experience down as a reversal.

As I write this, on an airplane, I have run out of paper and need to reach into my briefcase under my legs for more. I cannot do this until my empty lunch tray is removed from my lap. I arrested the stewardess as she passed empty-handed down the aisle on the way to the kitchen to fetch the lunch trays for the passengers up forward who haven't been served yet. "Would you please take my tray?" "Just a *moment*, sir!" she said, and marched on sternly. Shall I tell her that since she is headed for the kitchen *anyway*, it could not delay the feeding of the other passengers by more than two seconds necessary to stash away my empty tray? Or remind her that not fifteen minutes ago she spoke unctuously into the loudspeaker the words undoubtedly devised by the airline's highly paid public relations counselor: "If there is anything I or Miss French can do for you to make your trip more enjoyable, *please* let us—" I have run out of paper.

I think the observable reluctance of the majority of Americans to assert themselves in minor matters is related to our increased sense of helplessness in an age of technology and centralized political and economic power. For generations, Americans who were too hot, or too cold, got up and did something about it. Now we call the plumber, or the electrician, or the furnace man. The habit of looking after our own needs obviously had something to do with the assertiveness that characterized the American family familiar to readers of American literature. With the technification of life goes our direct responsibility for our material environment, and we are conditioned to adopt a position of helplessness not only as regards the broken air conditioner, but as regards the overheated train. It takes an expert to fix the former, but not the latter; yet these distinctions, as we withdraw into helplessness, tend to fade away.

Our notorious political apathy is a related phenomenon. Every year, whether the Republican or the Democratic Party is in office, more and more power drains away from the individual to feed vast reservoirs in far-off places; and we have less and less say about the shape of events which shape our future. From this alienation of personal power come the sense of resignation with which we accept the political dispensations of a powerful government whose hold upon us continues to increase.

An editor of a national weekly news magazine told me a few years ago that as few as a dozen letters of protest against an editorial stance of his magazine was enough to convene a plenipotentiary meeting of the board of editors to review policy. "So few people complain, or make their voices heard," he explained to me, "that we assume a dozen letters represent the inarticulated views of thousands of readers." In the past ten years, he said, the volume of mail has noticeably decreased, even though the circulation of his magazine has risen.

When our voices are finally mute, when we have finally suppressed   22
the natural instinct to complain, whether the vexation is trivial or grave, we shall have become automatons, incapable of feeling. When Premier Khrushchev[1] first came to this country late in 1959 he was primed, we are informed, to experience the bitter resentment of the American people against his tyranny, against his persecutions, against the movement which is responsible for the great number of American deaths in Korea, for billions in taxes every year, and for life everlasting on the brink of disaster; but Khrushchev was pleasantly surprised, and reported back to the Russian people that he had been met with overwhelming cordiality (read: apathy), except, to be sure, for "a few fascists who followed me around with their wretched posters, and should be horsewhipped."

I may be crazy, but I say there would have been lots more posters   23
in a society where train temperatures in the dead of winter are not allowed to climb to 85 degrees without complaint.

Meaning

1. How does Buckley account for his failure to complain to the train conductor? What reasons does he give for not taking action when he notices that the movie he is watching is out of focus?
2. Where does Buckley finally place the blame for the average American's reluctance to try to "rectify irrational vexations"?
3. By what means does the author bring his argument around to the subject of political apathy?

Purpose and Audience

1. What thesis does Buckley attempt to support? What is his purpose?
2. Judging from the vocabulary displayed in this essay, would you say that Buckley is writing for a highly specialized audience or an educated but nonspecialized general audience?

---

[1]Nikita Khrushchev (1894–1971) was premier of the former Soviet Union from 1958 to 1964. [Editor's note.]

Method and Structure

1. In taking to task not only his fellow Americans but also himself, does Buckley strengthen or weaken his charge that, as a people, Americans do not complain enough?

2. As a whole, is Buckley's essay an example of appeal to emotion or reasoned argument or both? Give evidence for your answer.

3. **Other Methods** Buckley includes as evidence four narratives of his personal experiences. What is the point of the narrative about Jiggs (paragraphs 13–17)?

Language

1. What does Buckley's use of the capital A in *Authority* (paragraph 8) contribute to the sentence in which he uses it?

2. What is Buckley talking about when he alludes to "the Milquetoast in me" (paragraph 11)? Notice how well Buckley's allusion fits into the paragraph, with its emphasis on breakfast and a glass of milk. (If necessary, see the definition of *allusion* in the Glossary.)

Writing Topics

1. Write an essay about one moment when you either spoke up against an annoyance or didn't complain when you should have. Narrate this incident to help explain why you did or did not act.

2. Think of some disturbing incident you have witnessed, or some annoying treatment you have received in a store or other public place, and write a letter of complaint to whomever you believe responsible. Be specific in your evidence, be temperate in your language, make clear what you would like to come of your complaint (your proposal), and be sure to put your letter in the mail.

3. Write a paper in which you analyze and evaluate any one of Buckley's ideas. For instance: Do we feel as helpless as Buckley says (paragraph 19)? Are we politically apathetic, and if so should the government be blamed (20)? For that matter, do we not complain? Support your view with evidence from your experience, observation, or reading.

MARTIN LUTHER KING, JR.

Born in 1929 in Atlanta, Georgia, the son of a Baptist minister, Martin Luther King, Jr., was a revered and powerful leader of the black civil rights movement during the 1950s and 1960s. He was ordained in his father's church before he was twenty and went on to earn degrees at Morehouse College (BA in 1948), Crozer Theological Seminary (BD in 1951), and Boston University (PhD in 1955). In 1955 and 1956, while he was pastor of a church in Montgomery, Alabama, King attracted national attention to the plight of Southern blacks by leading a boycott that succeeded in desegregating the city's buses. He was elected the first president of the Southern Christian Leadership Conference and continued to organize demonstrations for equal rights in other cities. By the early 1960s his efforts had helped raise the national consciousness so that the landmark Civil Rights Act of 1964 and Voting Rights Act of 1965 could be passed by Congress. In 1964 King was awarded the Nobel Peace Prize. When leading sit-ins, boycotts, and marches, King always insisted on nonviolent resistance "because our end is a community at peace with itself." But his nonviolence often met with violent opposition. Over the years he was jailed, beaten, stoned, and stabbed. His house in Montgomery was bombed. And on April 4, 1968, at a motel in Memphis, Tennessee, he was assassinated. He was not yet forty years old.

I Have a Dream

On August 28, 1963, one hundred years after Abraham Lincoln's Emancipation Proclamation had freed the slaves, 200,000 Americans marched on Washington, DC, to demand equal rights for blacks. It was the largest crowd ever to assemble in the capital in behalf of a cause, and the high point of the day was this speech delivered by King on the steps of the Lincoln Memorial. Always an eloquent and inspirational speaker, King succeeded in articulating the frustrations and aspirations of America's blacks in a way that gave hope to the oppressed and opened the eyes of many oppressors.

Five score years ago, a great American, in whose symbolic shadow we stand, signed the Emancipation Proclamation. This momentous decree came as a great beacon light of hope to millions of Negro slaves who had been seared in the flames of withering injustice. It came as a joyous daybreak to end the long night of captivity.

But one hundred years later, we must face the tragic fact that the 2 Negro is still not free. One hundred years later, the life of the Negro is still sadly crippled by the manacles of segregation and the chains of discrimination. One hundred years later, the Negro lives on a lonely island of poverty in the midst of a vast ocean of material prosperity. One hundred years later, the Negro is still languishing in the corners of American society and finds himself an exile in his own land. So we have come here today to dramatize an appalling condition.

In a sense we have come to our nation's capital to cash a check. 3 When the architects of our republic wrote the magnificent words of the Constitution and the Declaration of Independence, they were signing a promissory note to which every American was to fall heir. This note was a promise that all men—yes, black men as well as white men—would be guaranteed the unalienable rights of life, liberty, and the pursuit of happiness.

It is obvious today that America has defaulted on this promissory 4 note insofar as her citizens of color are concerned. Instead of honoring this sacred obligation, America has given the Negro people a bad check, a check which has come back marked "insufficient funds." But we refuse to believe that there are insufficient funds in the great vaults of opportunity of this nation. So we have come to cash this check—a check that will give us upon demand the riches of freedom and the security of justice. We have also come to this hallowed spot to remind America of the fierce urgency of *now*. This is no time to engage in the luxury of cooling off or to take the tranquilizing drugs of gradualism. *Now* is the time to make real the promises of Democracy. *Now* is the time to rise from the dark and desolate valley of segregation to the sunlit path of racial justice. *Now* is the time to open the doors of opportunity to all of God's children. *Now* is the time to lift our nation from the quicksands of racial injustice to the solid rock of brotherhood.

It would be fatal for the nation to overlook the urgency of the 5 moment and to underestimate the determination of the Negro. This sweltering summer of the Negro's legitimate discontent will not pass until there is an invigorating autumn of freedom and equality; 1963 is not an end, but a beginning. Those who hope that the Negro needed to blow off steam and will now be content will have a rude awakening if the nation returns to business as usual. There will be neither rest nor tranquility in America until the Negro is granted his citizenship rights.

The whirlwinds of revolt will continue to shake the foundations of our nation until the bright day of justice emerges.

But there is something that I must say to my people who stand on 6 the warm threshold which leads into the palace of justice. In the process of gaining our rightful place we must not be guilty of wrongful deeds. Let us not seek to satisfy our thirst for freedom by drinking from the cup of bitterness and hatred. We must forever conduct our struggle on the high plane of dignity and discipline. We must not allow our creative protest to degenerate into physical violence. Again and again we must rise to the majestic heights of meeting physical force with soul force. The marvelous new militancy which has engulfed the Negro community must not lead us to a distrust of all white people, for many of our white brothers, as evidenced by their presence here today, have come to realize that their destiny is tied up with our destiny and their freedom is inextricably bound to our freedom. We cannot walk alone.

And as we walk, we must make the pledge that we shall march 7 ahead. We cannot turn back. There are those who are asking the devotees of civil rights, "When will you be satisfied?" We can never be satisfied as long as the Negro is the victim of the unspeakable horrors of police brutality. We can never be satisfied as long as our bodies, heavy with the fatigue of travel, cannot gain lodging in the motels of the highways and the hotels of the cities. We cannot be satisfied as long as the Negro's basic mobility is from a smaller ghetto to a larger one. We can never be satisfied as long as a Negro in Mississippi cannot vote and a Negro in New York believes he has nothing for which to vote. No, no, we are not satisfied, and we will not be satisfied until justice rolls down like waters and righteousness like a mighty stream.

I am not unmindful that some of you have come here out of great 8 trials and tribulations. Some of you have come fresh from narrow jail cells. Some of you have come from areas where your quest for freedom left you battered by the storms of persecution and staggered by the winds of police brutality. You have been the veterans of creative suffering. Continue to work with the faith that unearned suffering is redemptive.

Go back to Mississippi, go back to Alabama, go back to South 9 Carolina, go back to Georgia, go back to Louisiana, go back to the slums and ghettos of our northern cities, knowing that somehow this situation can and will be changed. Let us not wallow in the valley of despair.

I say to you today, my friends, that in spite of the difficulties and 10 frustrations of the moment I still have a dream. It is a dream deeply rooted in the American dream.

I have a dream that one day this nation will rise up and live out 11
the true meaning of its creed: "We hold these truths to be self-
evident, that all men are created equal."

I have a dream that one day on the red hills of Georgia the sons 12
of former slaves and the sons of former slaveowners will be able to
sit down together at the table of brotherhood.

I have a dream that one day even the state of Mississippi, a desert 13
state sweltering with the heat of injustice and oppression, will be
transformed into an oasis of freedom and justice.

I have a dream that my four little children will one day live in a 14
nation where they will not be judged by the color of their skin but by
the content of their character.

I have a dream today. 15

I have a dream that one day the state of Alabama, whose gover- 16
nor's lips are presently dripping with the words of interposition and
nullification, will be transformed into a situation where little black
boys and black girls will be able to join hands with little white boys
and white girls and walk together as sisters and brothers.

I have a dream today. 17

I have a dream that one day every valley shall be exalted, every hill 18
and mountain shall be made low, the rough places will be made
plain, and the crooked places will be made straight, and the glory of
the Lord shall be revealed, and all flesh shall see it together.[1]

This is our hope. This is the faith with which I return to the 19
South. With this faith we will be able to hew out of the mountain of
despair a stone of hope. With this faith we will be able to transform
the jangling discords of our nation into a beautiful symphony of
brotherhood. With this faith we will be able to work together, to pray
together, to struggle together, to go to jail together, to stand up for
freedom together, knowing that we will be free one day.

This will be the day when all of God's children will be able to sing 20
with new meaning

> My country, 'tis of thee,
> Sweet land of liberty,
>   Of thee I sing:
> Land where my fathers died,
> Land of the pilgrims' pride,
> From every mountainside,
>   Let freedom ring.

[1]This paragraph quotes the Bible, Isaiah 40:4–5. [Editor's note.]

So let freedom ring from the prodigious hilltops of New Hampshire. 21
Let freedom ring from the mighty mountains of New York. Let freedom ring from the heightening Alleghenies of Pennsylvania. Let freedom ring from the snowcapped Rockies of Colorado. Let freedom ring from the curvaceous peaks of California.

But not only that. Let freedom ring from Stone Mountain of 22
Georgia. Let freedom ring from Lookout Mountain of Tennessee. Let freedom ring from every hill and molehill of Mississippi. From every mountainside, let freedom ring.

When we let freedom ring, when we let it ring from every village 23
and every hamlet, from every state and every city, we will be able to speed up that day when all of God's children, black men and white men, Jews and Gentiles, Protestants and Catholics, will be able to join hands and sing in the words of the old Negro spiritual, "Free at last! Free at last! Thank God almighty, we are free at last!"

Meaning

1. In a sentence, state the main point of King's speech.
2. How does King depict the general condition of the nation's African Americans? What specific injustices does he cite?
3. What reasons does King give for refusing to resort to violence? What comfort does he offer those who have been jailed or beaten?
4. Summarize the substance of King's dream. What does he mean when he says, "It is a dream deeply rooted in the American dream" (paragraph 10)?

Purpose and Audience

1. What do you think King wanted to achieve with this speech? How does each part of the speech relate to his purpose?
2. What group of people does King seem to be addressing primarily in this speech? Where does he seem to assume that they agree with his ideas? Where does he seem to assume that they have reservations or need reassurance?
3. What about King's purpose and audience leads him to rely primarily on emotional appeal? Where does he appeal specifically to his listeners' pride and dignity? to their religious beliefs? to their patriotism?
4. Where does King seem to suppose that doubters and opponents of the civil rights movement might also hear his speech? What messages about the goals and determination of the movement does he convey to these hearers?

Method and Structure

1. Analyze the organization of King's speech. What is the main subject of paragraphs 3–5? 6–9? 10–23? How does this structure suit King's purpose?

2. Why does King's first paragraph refer to the hope generated by Lincoln's Emancipation Proclamation? Is the contrast King develops in paragraphs 1 and 2 an effective introduction to the speech? Why, or why not?

3. **Other Methods**   Paragraph 3 and the first half of paragraph 4 are developed by comparison and contrast. What are the main points of comparison, and what purpose does it serve? Do you think it is effective? Why, or why not?

Language

1. In paragraph 6 King says, "Let us not seek to satisfy our thirst for freedom by drinking from the cup of bitterness and hatred." To what extent in this speech does King follow his own suggestion? How would you characterize his attitudes toward oppression and segregation? Choose words and phrases in the speech to support your answer.

2. King's speech abounds in metaphors, such as "manacles of segregation" and "chains of discrimination" (paragraph 2). Locate as many metaphors as you can (consulting the Glossary under *figures of speech* if necessary), and analyze what five or six of them contribute to King's meaning. Which metaphors are repeated or restated, and how does this repetition help link portions of the speech?

Writing Topics

1. King's speech had a tremendous impact when it was first delivered in 1963, and it remains influential to this day. Pick out the elements of the speech that seem most remarkable and powerful to you: ideas, emotional appeals, figures of speech, repetition and parallelism, or whatever you choose. Write an essay in which you cite these elements and analyze their effectiveness.

2. Reread paragraph 6, where King outlines a strategy for achieving racial justice. In an essay, briefly explain an unjust situation that affects you directly—in school, in your family, at work, in your community—and propose a strategy for correcting the injustice. Be specific about the steps in the strategy, and explain how each one relates to the final goal you want to achieve.

3. King says that his dream is "deeply rooted in the American dream" (paragraph 10). Write an essay in which you provide your own definition of the American dream. Draw on the elements of King's dream as you see fit. Make your definition specific with examples and details from your experiences, observations, and reading.

VIRGINIA WOOLF

Virginia Woolf was born in London in 1882. She is regarded as one of the most important writers of the twentieth century for her insightful, poetic essays, some of which are collected in The Common Reader *(1925) and* The Second Common Reader *(1933), as well as her acclaimed novels, including* Mrs. Dalloway *(1925),* To the Lighthouse *(1927),* Orlando *(1928), and* The Waves *(1931). Woolf was at the center of the Bloomsbury Group, a circle of artists and writers named after the neighborhood where she lived. In 1912, she married Leonard Woolf, and they soon founded Hogarth Press, which published her books as well as works by T. S. Eliot and Sigmund Freud. For much of her life, Woolf suffered from severe depression, and in 1941, she committed suicide.*

Professions for Women

Published in The Death of the Moth and Other Essays *(1942), this essay abridges a speech that Woolf gave to the Women's Service League in 1931. Woolf argues that despite the freedom gained to choose their own occupations, women still face barriers and challenges.*

When your secretary invited me to come here, she told me that your 1
Society is concerned with the employment of women and she suggested that I might tell you something about my own professional experiences. It is true I am a woman; it is true I am employed; but what professional experiences have I had? It is difficult to say. My profession is literature; and in that profession there are fewer experiences for women than in any other, with the exception of the stage — fewer, I mean, that are peculiar to women. For the road was cut many years ago — by Fanny Burney, by Aphra Behn, by Harriet Martineau, by Jane Austen, by George Eliot[1] — many famous women, and many more unknown and forgotten, have been before me, making the path smooth, and regulating my steps. Thus, when I came to write, there

---

[1]English women writers of the seventeenth through nineteenth centuries. (George Eliot was the pseudonym of Mary Ann or Marian Evans.) [Editor's note.]

were very few material obstacles in my way. Writing was a reputable and harmless occupation. The family peace was not broken by the scratching of a pen. No demand was made upon the family purse. For ten and sixpence one can buy paper enough to write all the plays of Shakespeare—if one has a mind that way. Pianos and models, Paris, Vienna and Berlin, masters and mistresses, are not needed by a writer. The cheapness of writing paper is, of course, the reason why women have succeeded as writers before they have succeeded in the other professions.

But to tell you my story—it is a simple one. You have only got to   2 figure to yourselves a girl in a bedroom with a pen in her hand. She had only to move that pen from left to right—from ten o'clock to one. Then it occurred to her to do what is simple and cheap enough after all—to slip a few of those pages into an envelope, fix a penny stamp in the corner, and drop the envelope into the red box at the corner. It was thus that I became a journalist; and my effort was rewarded on the first day of the following month—a very glorious day it was for me—by a letter from an editor containing a cheque for one pound ten shillings and sixpence. But to show you how little I deserve to be called a professional woman, how little I know of the struggles and difficulties of such lives, I have to admit that instead of spending that sum upon bread and butter, rent, shoes and stockings, or butcher's bills, I went out and bought a cat—a beautiful cat, a Persian cat, which very soon involved me in bitter disputes with my neighbours.

What could be easier than to write articles and to buy Persian cats   3 with the profits? But wait a moment. Articles have to be about something. Mine, I seem to remember, was about a novel by a famous man. And while I was writing this review, I discovered that if I were going to review books I should need to do battle with a certain phantom. And the phantom was a woman, and when I came to know her better I called her after the heroine of a famous poem, "The Angel in the House."[2] It was she who used to come between me and my paper when I was writing reviews. It was she who bothered me and wasted my time and so tormented me that at last I killed her. You who come of a younger and happier generation may not have heard of her— you may not know what I mean by the Angel in the House. I will describe her as shortly as I can. She was intensely sympathetic. She was immensely charming. She was utterly unselfish. She excelled in

[2]A poem by the English poet Coventry Patmore (1823–96). The poem's heroine symbolizes the ideal nineteenth-century woman. [Editor's note.]

the difficult arts of family life. She sacrificed herself daily. If there was chicken, she took the leg; if there was a draught she sat in it—in short she was so constituted that she never had a mind or a wish of her own, but preferred to sympathize always with the minds and wishes of others. Above all—I need not say it—she was pure. Her purity was supposed to be her chief beauty—her blushes, her great grace. In those days—the last of Queen Victoria[3]—every house had its Angel. And when I came to write I encountered her with the very first words. The shadow of her wings fell on my page; I heard the rustling of her skirts in the room. Directly, that is to say, I took my pen in my hand to review that novel by a famous man, she slipped behind me and whispered: 'My dear, you are a young woman. You are writing about a book that has been written by a man. Be sympathetic; be tender; flatter; deceive; use all the arts and wiles of our sex. Never let anybody guess that you have a mind of your own. Above all, be pure.' And she made as if to guide my pen. I now record the one act for which I take some credit to myself, though the credit rightly belongs to some excellent ancestors of mine who left me a certain sum of money—shall we say five hundred pounds a year?—so that it was not necessary for me to depend solely on charm for my living. I turned upon her and caught her by the throat. I did my best to kill her. My excuse, if I were to be had up in a court of law, would be that I acted in self-defence. Had I not killed her she would have killed me. She would have plucked the heart out of my writing. For, as I found, directly I put pen to paper, you cannot review even a novel without having a mind of your own, without expressing what you think to be the truth about human relations, morality, sex. And all these questions, according to the Angel of the House, cannot be dealt with freely and openly by women; they must charm, they must conciliate, they must—to put it bluntly—tell lies if they are to succeed. Thus, whenever I felt the shadow of her wing or the radiance of her halo upon my page, I took up the inkpot and flung it at her. She died hard. Her fictitious nature was of great assistance to her. It is far harder to kill a phantom than a reality. She was always creeping back when I thought I had despatched her. Though I flatter myself that I killed her in the end, the struggle was severe; it took much time that had better have been spent upon learning Greek grammar; or in roaming the world in search of adventures. But it was a real experience; it was an experience that was found to befall

---

[3]Queen of the United Kingdom from 1837 to 1901. The sentiments of the long Victorian era are often characterized as refined and moralistic. [Editor's note.]

all women writers at that time. Killing the Angel in the House was part of the occupation of a woman writer.

But to continue my story. The Angel was dead; what then 4 remained? You may say that what remained was a simple and common object — a young woman in a bedroom with an inkpot. In other words, now that she had rid herself of falsehood, that young woman had only to be herself. Ah, but what is 'herself'? I mean, what is a woman? I assure you, I do not know. I do not believe that you know. I do not believe that anybody can know until she has expressed herself in all the arts and professions open to human skill. That indeed is one of the reasons why I have come here — out of respect for you, who are in process of showing us by your experiments what a woman is, who are in process of providing us, by your failures and successes, with that extremely important piece of information.

But to continue the story of my professional experiences. I made 5 one pound ten and six by my first review; and I bought a Persian cat with the proceeds. Then I grew ambitious. A Persian cat is all very well, I said; but a Persian cat is not enough. I must have a motor car. And it was thus that I became a novelist — for it is a very strange thing that people will give you a motor car if you will them a story. It is a still stranger thing that there is nothing so delightful in the world as telling stories. It is far pleasanter than writing reviews of famous novels. And yet, if I am to obey your secretary and tell you my professional experiences as a novelist, I must tell you about a very strange experience that befell me as a novelist. And to understand it you must try first to imagine a novelist's state of mind. I hope I am not giving away professional secrets if I say that a novelist's chief desire is to be as unconscious as possible. He has to induce in himself a state of perpetual lethargy. He wants life to proceed with the utmost quiet and regularity. He wants to see the same faces, to read the same books, to do the same things day after day, month after month, while he is writing, so that nothing may break the illusion in which he is living — so that nothing may disturb or disquiet the mysterious nosings about, feelings round, darts, dashes and sudden discoveries of that very shy and illusive spirit, the imagination. I suspect that this state is the same both for men and women. Be that as it may, I want you to imagine me writing a novel in a state of trance. I want you to figure to yourselves a girl sitting with a pen in her hand, which for minutes, and indeed for hours, she never dips into the inkpot. The image that comes to my mind when I think of this girl is the image of a fisherman lying sunk in dreams on the verge of a deep lake with a rod held out over the water. She was letting her imagination sweep unchecked round every rock and cranny of the world that lies submerged in the depths of our unconscious being. Now came the experience, the experience that I believe to be far commoner with women writers than with men. The line raced through the girl's fingers. Her imagination had rushed away. It had sought the pools, the depths, the dark places where the largest fish slumber. And then there was a smash. There was an explosion. There was foam and confusion. The imagination had dashed itself against something hard. The girl was roused from her dream. She was indeed in a state of the most acute and difficult distress. To speak without figure she had thought of something, something about the body, about the passions which it was unfitting for her as a woman to say. Men, her reason told her, would be shocked. The consciousness of what men will say of a woman who speaks the truth about her passions had roused her from her artist's state of unconsciousness. She could write no more. The trance was over. Her imagination could work no longer. This I believe to be a very common experience with women writers—they are impeded by the extreme conventionality of the other sex. For though men sensibly allow themselves great freedom in these respects, I doubt that they realize or can control the extreme severity with which they condemn such freedom in women.

These then were two very genuine experiences of my own. These were two of the adventures of my professional life. The first—killing the Angel in the House—I think I solved. She died. But the second, telling the truth about my own experiences as a body, I do not think I solved. I doubt that any woman has solved it yet. The obstacles against her are still immensely powerful—and yet they are very difficult to define. Outwardly, what is simpler than to write books? Outwardly, what obstacles are there for a woman rather than for a man? Inwardly, I think, the case is very different; she has still many ghosts to fight, many prejudices to overcome. Indeed it will be a long time still, I think, before a woman can sit down to write a book without finding a phantom to be slain, a rock to be dashed against. And if this is so in literature, the freest of all professions for women, how is it in the new professions which you are now for the first time entering? 6

Those are the questions that I should like, had I time, to ask you. And indeed, if I have laid stress upon these professional experiences of mine, it is because I believe that they are, though in different forms, yours also. Even when the path is nominally open—when there is nothing to prevent a woman from being a doctor, a lawyer, 7 a civil servant—there are many phantoms and obstacles, as I believe, looming in her way. To discuss and define them is I think of great value and importance; for thus only can the labour be shared, the difficulties be solved. But besides this, it is necessary also to discuss the ends and the aims for which we are fighting, for which we are doing battle with these formidable obstacles. Those aims cannot be taken for granted; they must be perpetually questioned and examined. The whole position, as I see it—here in this hall surrounded by women practising for the first time in history I know not how many different professions—is one of extraordinary interest and importance. You have won rooms of your own in the house hitherto exclusively owned by men. You are able, though not without great labour and effort, to pay the rent. You are earning your five hundred pounds a year. But this freedom is only a beginning; the room is your own, but it is still bare. It has to be furnished; it has to be decorated; it has to be shared. How are you going to furnish it, how are you going to decorate it? With whom are you going to share it, and upon what terms? These, I think are questions of the utmost importance and interest. For the first time in history you are able to ask them; for the first time you are able to decide for yourselves what the answers should be. Willingly would I stay and discuss those questions and answers—but not tonight. My time is up; and I must cease.

Meaning

1. What does Woolf mean by the "Angel in the House" (paragraph 3)? Why is it necessary that she kill the Angel?
2. What struggle does Woolf describe in paragraph 5? Why does this represent a greater obstacle to her than does coping with the Angel in the House?
3. What point is Woolf making in her final two paragraphs, and why is it central to her theme? Is this point still relevant today?

Purpose and Audience

1. Woolf spends most of this essay relating her personal experience as a writer, but her purpose is clearly something larger. How would you characterize that purpose?
2. Keeping in mind that "Professions for Women" was originally written as a speech, point to some particular techniques that Woolf uses to connect with a listening audience.

3. What is the effect of Woolf's opening description of the ease with which she was able to become a writer? How does she present herself to her audience?

Method and Structure

1. Woolf does not state her thesis until her final paragraph. What is the thesis? Is its placement effective? Why, or why not?
2. What is the function of paragraph 6? How does it lead into Woolf's concluding paragraph?
3. **Other Methods**   In paragraph 5 Woolf compares and contrasts female and male novelists. What similarities and differences does she point out? How do these relate to the point she is making in the paragraph?

Language

1. What image does Woolf use to describe the work of the novelist (paragraph 5)? Do you find this image in any way surprising?
2. Discuss Woolf's use of the pronoun *he* in paragraph 5. How might a contemporary writer make the point here differently?

Writing Topics

1. Develop an essay in which you argue that women and men today face essentially the same obstacles in their personal and professional lives or that they face essentially different obstacles. In supporting your argument, draw on your own experiences and on your observations of contemporary culture.
2. Woolf makes the point that, in her day, well-bred women were constrained from being open about their "passions" (that is, their sexuality). Today's society, in contrast, is much more open about sexuality. Do you see this change as essentially positive or negative? In an essay, make a case for your views.
3. In her opening paragraph, Woolf lists some women writers of earlier centuries. In the nineteenth century most women writers were read primarily by women, while most male writers had a following among both men and women. Many commentators believe that the same holds true today: for example, men are unlikely to attend movies with a "female" sensibility ("chick flicks"), while movies with a more "male" sensibility (involving violence or vulgar humor, say) attract a mixed audience. If you agree that this is the case,

write an essay in which you explore the causes of a female/male divide in popular entertainment tastes and argue for or against its legitimacy. If you disagree, write an essay in which you argue that women and men have basically the same tastes in popular entertainment.

JONATHAN SWIFT

Jonathan Swift was an Anglican priest, a poet, and a political pamphleteer, but he is best known as a satirist with a sharp wit and a sense of outrage at human folly and cruelty. He was born in 1667 in Dublin, Ireland, to English parents. After receiving a diploma from Trinity College in Dublin, he went to England in 1689 and there became involved in the political and literary life of London. He was ordained in the Church of Ireland in 1694 and in 1713 became dean of St. Patrick's Cathedral in Dublin, where he served until his death in 1745. Several of Swift's works, including The Tale of a Tub *and* The Battle of the Books *(both 1704), ridicule the religious extremism and literary pretensions of his day.* Gulliver's Travels *(1726), his most famous book, is often abridged for children into a charming fantasy about tiny people and giants and a wise race of horses; but unabridged it takes a bitter swipe at humankind's lack of humanity and abuse of reason.*

A Modest Proposal

In Swift's time Ireland had already suffered almost two centuries of exploitation by the English. Mostly from abroad, the English controlled much of Ireland's farmland, exacted burdensome taxes from the Irish, and repressed the people in countless other ways. Swift, who had often lashed out at the injustices he saw, was moved in 1729 to his most vicious attack. Several years of crop failures had resulted in widespread starvation among the Irish poor, yet the government of England, the English landowners, and the well-to-do Irish had done nothing to help. In response, Swift wrote "A Modest Proposal," subtitled "For Preventing the Children of the Poor People in Ireland from Being a Burden to Their Parents or Country, and for Making Them Beneficial to Their Public." The essay is a model of satire, the combination of wit and criticism to mock or condemn human foolishness or evil. Like much satire, the essay is also heavily ironic, saying one thing but meaning another. (Satire and irony are both explained more fully in the Glossary.) Assuming the role of a thoughtful and sympathetic observer, Swift proposes a solution to the troubles of the Irish that, in the words of the critic Gilbert Highet, is "couched in terms of blandly persuasive logic, but so atrocious that no one could possibly take it as serious."

It is a melancholy object to those who walk through this great town[1]   1
or travel in the country, when they see the streets, the roads, and cabin doors, crowded with beggars of the female sex, followed by three, four, or six children, all in rags and importuning every passenger for an alms. These mothers, instead of being able to work for their honest livelihood, are forced to employ all their time in strolling to beg sustenance for their helpless infants, who, as they grow up, either turn thieves for want of work, or leave their dear native country to fight for the Pretender in Spain, or sell themselves to the Barbados.[2]

I think it is agreed by all parties that this prodigious number of chil-   2
dren in the arms, or on the backs, or at the heels of their mothers, and frequently of their fathers, is in the present deplorable state of the kingdom a very great additional grievance; and therefore whoever could find out a fair, cheap, or easy method of making these children sound, useful members of the commonwealth would deserve so well of the public as to have his statue set up for a preserver of the nation.

But my intention is very far from being confined to provide only   3
for the children of professed beggars; it is of a much greater extent, and shall take in the whole number of infants at a certain age who are born of parents in effect as little able to support them as those who demand our charity in the streets.

As to my own part, having turned my thoughts for many years   4
upon this important subject, and maturely weighed the several schemes of other projectors,[3] I have always found them grossly mistaken in their computation. It is true, a child just dropped from its dam may be supported by her milk for a solar year, with little other nourishment; at most not above the value of two shillings,[4] which the mother may certainly get, or the value in scraps, by her lawful occupation of begging; and it is exactly at one year that I propose to

---

[1]Dublin. [Editor's note.]

[2]The Pretender was James Stuart (1688–1766). He laid claim to the English throne from exile in Spain, and many Irishmen joined an army in support of his cause. Irishmen also shipped out for the British colony of Barbados, in the Caribbean, exchanging several years' labor there for their passage. [Editor's note.]

[3]People who develop projects or schemes. [Editor's note.]

[4]A shilling was then worth less than twenty-five cents. [Editor's note.]

provide for them in such a manner as instead of being a charge upon their parents or the parish, or wanting food and raiment for the rest of their lives, they shall on the contrary contribute to the feeding, and partly to the clothing, of many thousands.

There is likewise another great advantage in my scheme, that it will prevent those voluntary abortions, and that horrid practice of women murdering their bastard children, alas, too frequent among us, sacrificing the poor innocent babes, I doubt, more to avoid the expense than the shame, which would move tears and pity in the most savage and inhuman breast.

The number of souls in this kingdom being usually reckoned one million and a half, of these I calculate there may be about two hundred thousand couples whose wives are breeders; from which number I subtract thirty thousand couples who are able to maintain their own children, although I apprehend there cannot be so many under the present distress of the kingdom; but this being granted, there will remain an hundred and seventy thousand breeders. I again subtract fifty thousand of those women who miscarry, or whose children die by accident or disease within the year. There only remain an hundred and twenty thousand children of poor parents annually born. The question therefore is, how this number shall be reared and provided for, which, as I have already said, under the present situation of affairs, is utterly impossible by all the methods hitherto proposed. For we can neither employ them in handicraft or agriculture; we neither build houses (I mean in the country) nor cultivate land. They can very seldom pick up a livelihood by stealing till they arrive at six years old, except where they are of towardly parts;[5] although I confess they learn the rudiments much earlier, during which time they can however be looked upon only as probationers, as I have been informed by a principal gentleman in the country of Cavan, who protested to me that he never knew above one or two instances under the age of six, even in a part of the kingdom so renowned for the quickest proficiency in that art.

I am assured by our merchants that a boy or a girl before twelve years old is no salable commodity; and even when they come to this age they will not yield above three pounds; or three pounds and half a crown at most on the Exchange;[6] which cannot turn to account either to the parents or the kingdom, the charge of nutriment and rags having been at least four times that value.

---

[5]Natural abilities. [Editor's note.]

[6]A pound consisted of twenty shillings; a crown consisted of five shillings. [Editor's note.]

I shall now therefore humbly propose my own thoughts, which I   8
hope will not be liable to the least objection.

I have been assured by a very knowing American of my acquain-   9
tance in London, that a young healthy child well nursed is at a year
old a most delicious, nourishing, and wholesome food, whether
stewed, roasted, baked, or boiled; and I make no doubt that it will
equally serve in a fricassee or a ragout.

I do therefore humbly offer it to public consideration that of the   10
hundred and twenty thousand children, already computed, twenty
thousand may be reserved for breed, whereof only one fourth part to
be males, which is more than we allow to sheep, black cattle, or
swine; and my reason is that these children are seldom the fruits of
marriage, a circumstance not much regarded by our savages, therefore one male will be sufficient to serve four females. That the
remaining hundred thousand may at a year old be offered in sale to
the persons of quality and fortune through the kingdom, always
advising the mother to let them suck plentifully in the last month, so
as to render them plump and fat for a good table. The child will
make two dishes at an entertainment for friends; and when the family dines alone, the fore or hind quarter will make a reasonable dish,
and seasoned with a little pepper or salt will be very good boiled on
the fourth day, especially in winter.

I have reckoned upon a medium that a child just born will weigh   11
twelve pounds, and in a solar year if tolerably nursed increaseth to
twenty-eight pounds.

I grant this food will be somewhat dear, and therefore very proper   12
for landlords, who, as they have already devoured most of the
parents, seem to have the best title to the children.

Infant's flesh will be in season throughout the year, but more plen-   13
tiful in March, and a little before and after. For we are told by a grave
author, an eminent French physician,[7] that fish being a prolific diet,
there are more children born in Roman Catholic countries about
nine months after Lent than at any other season; therefore, reckoning a year after Lent, the market will be more glutted than usual,
because the number of popish infants is at least three to one in this
kingdom; and therefore it will have one other collateral advantage,
by lessening the number of Papists among us.

I have already computed the charge of nursing a beggar's child (in   14
which list I reckon all cottagers, laborers, and four-fifths of the farmers) to be about two shillings per annum, rags included; and I believe

[7]François Rabelais, a sixteenth-century French humorist. [Editor's note.]

no gentleman would repine to give ten shillings for the carcass of a good fat child, which, as I have said, will make four dishes of excellent nutritive meat, when he hath only some particular friend or his own family to dine with him. Thus the squire will learn to be a good landlord, and grow popular among the tenants; the mother will have eight shillings net profit, and be fit for work till she produces another child.

Those who are more thrifty (as I must confess the times require) 15 may flay the carcass; the skin of which artifically[8] dressed will make admirable gloves for ladies, and summer boots for fine gentlemen.

As to our city of Dublin, shambles[9] may be appointed for this pur- 16 pose in the most convenient parts of it, and butchers we may be assured will not be wanting; although I rather recommend buying the children live, and dressing them hot from the knife as we do roasting pigs.

A very worthy person, a true lover of his country, and whose 17 virtues I highly esteem, was lately pleased in discoursing on this matter to offer a refinement upon my scheme. He said that many gentlemen of his kingdom, having of late destroyed their deer, he conceived that the want of venison might be well supplied by the bodies of young lads and maidens, not exceeding fourteen years of age nor under twelve, so great a number of both sexes in every county being now ready to starve for want of work and service; and these to be disposed of by their parents, if alive, or otherwise by their nearest relations. But with due deference to so excellent a friend and so deserving a patriot, I cannot be altogether in his sentiments; for as to the males, my American acquaintance assured me from frequent experience that their flesh was generally tough and lean, like that of our schoolboys, by continual exercise, and their taste disagreeable; and to fatten them would not answer the charge. Then as to the females, it would, I think with humble submission, be a loss to the public, because they soon would become breeders themselves; and besides, it is not improbable that some scrupulous people might be apt to censure such a practice (although indeed very unjustly) as a little bordering upon cruelty; which, I confess, hath always been with me the strongest objection against any project, how well soever intended.

But in order to justify my friend, he confessed that this expedient 18 was put into his head by the famous Psalmanazar,[10] a native of the

---

[8]Artfully. [Editor's note.]

[9]Slaughterhouses. [Editor's note.]

[10]Georges Psalmanazar was a Frenchman who gulled London society into thinking he was an exotic Formosan. [Editor's note.]

island Formosa, who came from thence to London above twenty years ago, and in conversation told my friend that in his country when any young person happened to be put to death, the executioner sold the carcass to persons of quality as a prime dainty; and that in his time the body of a plump girl of fifteen, who was crucified for an attempt to poison the emperor, was sold to his Imperial Majesty's prime minister of state, and other great mandarins of the court, in joints from the gibbet, at four hundred crowns. Neither indeed can I deny that if the same use were made of several plump young girls in this town, who without one single groat to their fortunes cannot stir abroad without a chair,[11] and appear at the playhouse and assemblies in foreign fineries which they never will pay for, the kingdom would not be the worse.

Some persons of desponding spirit are in great concern about the 19 vast number of poor people who are aged, diseased, or maimed, and I have been desired to employ my thoughts what course may be taken to ease the nation of so grievous an encumbrance. But I am not in the least pain upon the matter, because it is very well known that they are every day dying and rotting by cold and famine, and filth and vermin, as fast can be reasonably expected. And as to the younger laborers, they are now in almost as hopeful a condition. They cannot get work, and consequently pine away for want of nourishment to a degree that if any time they are accidentally hired to common labor, they have not strength to perform it; and thus the country and themselves arc happily delivered from the evils to come.

I have too long digressed, and therefore shall return to my subject. 20 I think the advantages by the proposal which I have made are obvious and many, as well as of the highest importance.

For first, as I have already observed, it would greatly lessen the 21 number of Papists, with whom we are yearly overrun, being the principal breeders of the nation as well as our most dangerous enemies; and who stay at home on purpose to deliver the kingdom to the Pretender, hoping to take their advantage by the absence of so many good Protestants, who have chosen rather to leave their country than to stay at home and pay tithes against their conscience to an Episcopal curate.

Secondly, the poorer tenants will have something valuable of their 22 own, which by law may be made liable to distress,[12] and help to pay their landlord's rent, their corn and cattle being already seized and money a thing unknown.

[11]A groat was a coin worth a few pennies. In a sedan chair, one person is carried about by two others on foot. [Editor's note.]

[12]Seizure for payment of debts. [Editor's note.]

Thirdly, whereas the maintenance of an hundred thousand children, from two years old and upwards, cannot be computed at less than ten shillings a piece per annum, the nation's stock will be thereby increased fifty thousand pounds per annum, besides the profit of a new dish introduced to the tables of all gentlemen of fortune in the kingdom who have any refinement in taste. And the money will circulate among ourselves, the goods being entirely of our own growth and manufacture. 23

Fourthly, the constant breeders, besides the gain of eight shillings sterling per annum by the sale of their children, will be rid of the charge of maintaining them after the first year. 24

Fifthly, this food would likewise bring great custom to taverns, where the vintners will certainly be so prudent as to procure the best receipts[13] for dressing it to perfection, and consequently have their houses frequented by all the fine gentlemen, who justly value themselves upon their knowledge in good eating; and a skillful cook, who understands how to oblige his guests, will contrive to make it as expensive as they please. 25

Sixthly, this would be a great inducement to marriage, which all wise nations have either encouraged by rewards or enforced by laws and penalties. It would increase the care and tenderness of mothers toward their children, when they were sure of a settlement for life to the poor babes, provided in some sort by the public, to their annual profit instead of expense. We should see an honest emulation among the married women, which of them could bring the fattest child to the market. Men would become as fond of their wives during the time of their pregnancy as they are now of their mares in foal, their cows in calf, or sows when they are ready to farrow; nor offer to beat or kick them (as is too frequent a practice) for fear of a miscarriage. 26

Many other advantages might be enumerated. For instance, the addition of some thousand carcasses in our exportation of barreled beef, the propagation of swine's flesh, and improvements in the art of making good bacon, so much wanted among us by the great destruction of pigs, too frequent at our tables, which are no way comparable in taste or magnificence to a well-grown, fat, yearling child, which roasted whole will make a considerable figure at a lord mayor's feast or any other public entertainment. But this and many others I omit, being studious of brevity. 27

Supposing that one thousand families in this city would be constant customers for infants' flesh, besides others who might have it 28

[13]Recipes. [Editor's note.]

at merry meetings, particularly weddings and christenings, I compute that Dublin would take off annually about twenty thousand carcasses, and the rest of the kingdom (where probably they will be sold somewhat cheaper) the remaining eighty thousand.

I can think of no one objection that will possibly be raised against 29 this proposal, unless it should be urged that the number of people will be thereby much lessened in the kingdom. This I freely own, and it was indeed one principal design in offering it to the world. I desire the reader will observe, that I calculate my remedy for this one individual kingdom of Ireland and for no other that ever was, is, or I think ever can be upon earth. Therefore let no man talk to me of other expedients: of taxing our absentees at five shillings a pound: of using neither clothes nor household furniture except what is of our own growth and manufacture: of utterly rejecting the materials and instruments that promote foreign luxury: of curing the expensiveness of pride, vanity, idleness, and gaming in our women: of introducing a vein of parsimony, prudence, and temperance: of learning to love our country, in the want of which we differ even from Laplanders and the inhabitants of Topinamboo:[14] of quitting our animosities and factions, nor acting any longer like the Jews, who were murdering one another at the very moment their city was taken:[15] of being a little cautious not to sell our country and conscience for nothing: of teaching landlords to have at least one degree of mercy toward their tenants: lastly, of putting a spirit of honesty, industry, and skill into our shopkeepers; who, if a resolution could not be taken to buy only our native goods, would immediately unite to cheat and exact upon us in the price, the measure, and the goodness, nor could ever yet be brought to make one fair proposal of just dealing, though often and earnestly invited to it.

Therefore I repeat, let no man talk to me of these and the like 30 expedients, till he hath at least some glimpse of hope that there will be some hearty and sincere attempt to put them in practice.

But as to myself, having been wearied out for many years with 31 offering vain, idle, visionary thoughts, and at length utterly despairing of success, I fortunately fell upon this proposal, which, as it is wholly new, so it hath something solid and real, of no expense and little trouble, full in our own power, and whereby we can incur no

[14]Lapland is the northernmost part of Scandinavia, above the Arctic Circle. The primitive tribes of Topinamboo, in Brazil, were notorious in Swift's day for their savagery. [Editor's note.]

[15]Jerusalem was seized by the Romans in AD 70. [Editor's note.]

danger in disobliging England. For this kind of commodity will not bear exportation, the flesh being of too tender a consistence to admit a long continuance in salt, although perhaps I could name a country which would be glad to eat up our whole nation without it.

After all, I am not so violently bent upon my own opinion as to 32 reject any offer proposed by wise men, which shall be found equally innocent, cheap, easy, and effectual. But before something of that kind shall be advanced in contradiction to my scheme, and offering a better, I desire the author or authors will be pleased maturely to consider two points. First, as things now stand, how they will be able to find food and raiment for an hundred thousand useless mouths and backs. And secondly, there being a round million of creatures in human figure throughout this kingdom, whose sole subsistence put into a common stock would leave them in debt two millions of pounds sterling, adding those who are beggars by profession to the bulk of farmers, cottagers, and laborers, with their wives and children who are beggars in effect; I desire those politicians who dislike my overture, and may perhaps be so bold to attempt an answer, that they will first ask the parents of these mortals whether they would not at this day think it a great happiness to have been sold for food at a year old in this manner I prescribe, and thereby have avoided such a perpetual scene of misfortunes as they have since gone through by the oppression of landlords, the impossibility of paying rent without money or trade, the want of common sustenance, with neither house nor clothes to cover them from the inclemencies of the weather, and the most inevitable prospect of entailing the like or greater miseries upon their breed forever.

I profess, in the sincerity of my heart, that I have not the least per- 33 sonal interest in endeavoring to promote this necessary work, having no other motive than the public good of my country, by advancing our trade, providing for infants, relieving the poor, and giving some pleasure to the rich. I have no children by which I can propose to get a single penny; the youngest being nine years old, and my wife past childbearing.

Meaning

1. In your own words, explain Swift's "modest proposal," the chief problems it is designed to solve, and how it would solve those problems.
2. What reasonable solutions does Swift mention to Ireland's problems? Why does he reject these solutions in favor of his outrageous one?

Purpose and Audience

1. Like all satirists, Swift writes on two levels: as his narrator, the *I* of the essay, and as himself. What is the narrator's purpose? What is Swift's real purpose? Where do these two purposes overlap? Where do they diverge?

2. Ever since this essay was first published, many readers have failed to grasp its irony and have condemned Swift for his inhumanity. Yet Swift provides clues that make his true intentions clear, as in his statement that the landlords, "as they have already devoured most of the parents, seem to have the best title to the children" (paragraph 12). What other such clues do you find after that point? Why do you think Swift provides them?

3. What was your own reaction to Swift's essay? Did you appreciate the irony? To what extent—and in what ways—did the repulsiveness of the proposal affect your willingness to accept his argument? What do your own responses and those of your classmates suggest about the advantages and disadvantages of satire as a technique of argument?

Method and Structure

1. Swift casts his essay in a fairly standard argumentative structure. Outline the essay roughly to see its parts, and analyze what each part contributes to the whole.

2. What steps does Swift take to establish the ethical appeal of his narrator? Cite sentences or passages that seem designed to gain the reader's trust and confidence in the author.

3. **Other Methods** Swift furthers his argument through skillful use of several methods of development, including process analysis and cause-and-effect analysis. Locate one example of each of these methods, and explain what each contributes to the persuasiveness of the argument.

Language

1. Locate several passages where Swift's irony strikes you as particularly apt or intriguing, and explain the contrast between their ironic and literal meanings. At whom is the ironic barb directed? Is it bitter or humorous? (If necessary, consult the Glossary for a definition of *irony*.)

2. Swift refers to the poor people of Ireland in terms normally reserved for livestock—for example, "breeders" (paragraph 6) and "fore or hind quarter" (10). Locate other expressions or sentences in this vein. What do they lend to the satire?

3. How would you characterize Swift's writing style? Give examples to support your answer. To what extent does his style contribute to or detract from your appreciation of the essay, and why? (See *style* in the Glossary if you need a definition.)

Writing Topics

1. Just as Swift was outraged by conditions in Ireland, you may be similarly moved by some current condition—perhaps terrorism, increasing crime, a newly discovered health hazard, or a dangerous traffic intersection the authorities persist in ignoring. Imitate Swift's strategy and write a "modest proposal" to end the condition. Like Swift's, your proposal should be fairly simple and argued with the most careful and detailed logic you can muster.

2. Ireland's problems did not end with the publication of Swift's essay but in fact have endured. Consult an encyclopedia or Web site to find an overview of the history of Ireland and its relations with England from Swift's time until the present. Focus on one of the specific problems Swift mentions—prejudices against "Papists," for example, or food shortages or absentee landlords—and research it in at least several other sources. Write an essay explaining the origins of the problem, the extent of its persistence, the attempts to resolve it, and the results of those attempts.

3. In analyzing Swift's essay, you have observed many of the elements of good satire. Using what you now know about satire, write an essay examining the strategy and effectiveness of one of the other satiric essays in this book, such as Jessica Mitford's "Embalming Mr. Jones" (p. 192) or Judy Brady's "I Want a Wife" (p. 241).

Writing with the Method
Argument and Persuasion

Choose one of the following statements, or any other statement they suggest, and support *or* refute it in an argumentative essay. The statement you decide on should concern a topic you care about so that argument is a means of convincing readers to accept an idea, not an end in itself.

Media
1. Pornographic magazines and films should be banned.
2. Violence and sex should be prohibited from television.
3. Advertisements for consumer products (or political candidates) should be recognized as serving useful purposes.
4. Recordings of popular music should be specially labeled if their lyrics contain violent or sexual references.

Sports
5. Professional athletes should not be allowed to compete in the Olympics.
6. Professional athletes are overpaid for their work.
7. The school's costly athletic programs should be eliminated in favor of improving the academic curriculum.

Health and Technology
8. People should have the right to choose when to die without interference from the government or medical community.
9. Private automobiles should be restricted in cities.
10. Laboratory experiments on dogs, cats, and primates should be banned.
11. Smoking should be banned in all public places, including outdoors in congested places.

Education
12. Students caught in any form of academic cheating should be expelled.
13. Students should not be granted high school diplomas until they can demonstrate reasonable competence in writing and mathematics.
14. Like high school textbooks, college textbooks should be purchased by the school and loaned to students for the duration of a course.

Social and Political Issues

15. The elderly are entitled to unlimited free medical care.
16. Private institutions should have the right to make rules that would be unconstitutional outside those institutions.
17. Children should be able to sue their parents for negligence or abuse.
18. A citizen should be able to buy and keep a handgun for protection without having to register it.
19. When they turn eighteen, adopted children should have free access to information about their birth parents.

Glossary

Abstract and concrete words   An **abstract** word refers to an idea, quality, attitude, or state that we cannot perceive with our senses: *democracy, generosity, love, grief*. It conveys a general concept or impression. A **concrete** word, in contrast, refers to an object, person, place, or state that we can perceive with our senses: *lawnmower, teacher, Chicago, moaning*. Concrete words make writing specific and vivid. See also *general and specific words*.

Allusion   A brief reference to a real or fictitious person, place, object, or event. An allusion can convey considerable meaning with few words, as when a writer describes a movie as "potentially this decade's *Star Wars*" to imply both that the movie is a space adventure and that it may be a blockbuster. But to be effective, the allusion must refer to something readers know well.

Analysis (also called **division**)   The method of development in which a subject is separated into its elements or parts and then reassembled into a new whole. See Chapter 4 on division or analysis, p. 122.

Anecdote   A brief narrative that recounts an episode from a person's experience. See, for instance, Cole, paragraph 2, p. 288. See also Chapter 2 on narration, p. 60.

Argument   The form of writing that appeals to readers' reason and emotions in order to win agreement with a claim or to compel some action. This definition encompasses both argument in a narrower sense—the appeal to reason to win agreement—and persuasion—the appeal to emotion to compel action. See Chapter 10 on argument and persuasion, p. 305.

Assertion   A debatable claim about a subject; the central idea of an argument.

Audience   A writer's audience is the group of readers for whom a particular work is intended. To communicate effectively, the writer should estimate readers' knowledge of the subject, their interests in it, and their biases toward it and should then consider these needs and expectations in choosing what to say and how to say it. For further discussion of audience, see pp. 2, 10–11, 15.

Body   The part of an essay that develops the main idea. See also pp. 17–18.

Cause-and-effect analysis   The method of development in which occurrences are divided into their elements to find what made an event happen (its causes) and what the consequences were (its effects). See Chapter 9 on cause-and-effect analysis, p. 267.

Chronological order   A pattern of organization in which events are arranged as they occurred over time, earliest to latest. Narratives usually follow a chronological order; see Chapter 2, p. 60.

Classification   The method of development in which the members of a group are sorted into classes or subgroups according to shared characteristics. See Chapter 5 on classification, p. 146.

Cliché   An expression that has become tired from overuse and that therefore deadens rather than enlivens writing. Examples: *in over their heads, turn over a new leaf, march to a different drummer, as heavy as lead, as clear as a bell.*

Climactic order   A pattern of organization in which elements—words, sentences, examples, ideas—are arranged in order of increasing importance or drama.

Coherence   The quality of effective writing that comes from clear, logical connections among all the parts, so that the reader can follow the writer's thought process without difficulty.

Colloquial language   The language of conversation, including contractions *(don't, can't)* and informal words and expressions (*hot* for new or popular, *boss* for employer, *ad* for advertisement, *get away with it, flunk the exam*). Most dictionaries label such words and expressions *colloquial* or *informal.* Colloquial language is inappropriate when the writing situation demands precision and formality, as a college term paper or a business report usually does. But in other situations it can be used selectively to relax a piece of writing and reduce the distance between writer and reader. (See, for instance, Hughes, p. 66.) See also *diction.*

Comparison and contrast   The method of development in which the similarities and differences between subjects are examined. Comparison examines similarities and contrast examines differences, but the two are generally used together. See Chapter 7 on comparison and contrast, p. 202.

Conclusions   The endings of written works—the sentences that bring the writing to a close. A conclusion provides readers with a sense of completion, with a sense that the writer has finished. Sometimes the final point in the body of an essay may accomplish this purpose, especially if it is very important or dramatic (for instance, see Eighner, p. 182). But usually a separate conclusion is needed to achieve completion. It may be a single sentence or several paragraphs, depending on the length and complexity of the piece of writing. And it may include one of the following, or a combination, depending on your subject and purpose:

- A summary of the main points of the essay (see Visser, pp. 133–37)
- A statement of the main idea of the essay, if it has not been stated before (see Klass, p. 98), or a restatement of the main idea incorporating information from the body of the essay (see Naylor, p. 251)
- A comment on the significance or implications of the subject (see Dillard, p. 71; Gould, p. 294)
- A call for reflection, support, or action (see Quindlen, p. 104; Ericsson, p. 164)
- A prediction for the future (see King, pp. 341–47)
- An example, anecdote, question, or quotation that reinforces the point of the essay (see Brady, p. 241; Ehrenreich, p. 282)

Excluded from this list are several endings that should be avoided because they tend to weaken the overall effect of an essay: (1) an example, fact, or quotation that pertains to only part of the essay; (2) an apology for your ideas, for the quality of the writing, or for omissions; (3) an attempt to enhance the significance of the essay by overgeneralizing from its ideas and evidence; (4) a new idea that requires the support of an entirely different essay.

Concrete words   See *abstract and concrete words*.

Connotation and denotation   A word's **denotation** is its literal meaning: *famous* denotes the quality of being well known. A word's **connotations** are the associations or suggestions that go beyond its literal meaning: *notorious* denotes fame but also connotes sensational, even unfavorable, recognition.

Contrast   See *comparison and contrast*.

Critical reading   Reading that looks beneath the surface of a work, seeking to uncover both its substance and the writer's interpretation of the substance.

Deductive reasoning   The method of reasoning that moves from the general to the specific. See Chapter 10 on argument and persuasion, especially pp. 309–11.

Definition   An explanation of the meaning of a word. An extended definition may serve as the primary method of developing an essay. See Chapter 8 on definition, p. 234.

Denotation   See *connotation and denotation*.

Description   The form of writing that conveys the perceptions of the senses—sight, hearing, smell, taste, touch—to make a person, place, object, or state of mind vivid and concrete. See Chapter 1 on description, p. 21.

Diction   The choice of words you make to achieve a purpose and make meaning clear. Effective diction conveys your meaning exactly, emphatically, and concisely, and it is appropriate to your intentions and audience. **Standard English,** the written language of educated native speakers, is expected in all writing for college, business and the professions, and publication. The vocabulary of standard English is large and varied, encompassing, for instance, both *comestibles* and *food* for edible things, both *paroxysm* and *fit* for a sudden seizure. In some writing situations, standard English may also include words and expressions typical of conversation (see *colloquial language*). But it excludes other levels of diction that only certain groups understand or find acceptable. Most dictionaries label expressions at these levels as follows:

- **Nonstandard:** words spoken among particular social groups, such as *ain't*, *them guys*, *hisself*, and *nowheres*.
- **Slang:** words that are usually short-lived and that may not be understood by all readers, such as *smashed* for drunk, *bling* for jewelry or money, and *honcho* for one in charge.
- **Regional** or **dialect:** words spoken in a particular region but not in the country as a whole, such as *poke* for a sack or bag, *holler* for a hollow or small valley.
- **Obsolete:** words that have passed out of use, such as *cleam* for smear.

See also *connotation and denotation* and *style*.

Division or analysis   See *analysis*.

Dominant impression   The central ideal or feeling conveyed by a description of a person, place, object, or state of mind. See Chapter 1 on description, especially p. 22.

Effect   See *cause-and-effect analysis*.

Emotional appeal In argumentative and persuasive writing, the appeal to readers' values, beliefs, or feelings in order to win agreement or compel action. See pp. 307–8.

Essay A prose composition on a single nonfictional topic or idea. An essay usually reflects the personal experiences and opinions of the writer.

Ethical appeal In argumentative and persuasive writing, the sense of the writer's expertise and character projected by the reasonableness of the argument, the use and quality of evidence, and tone. See p. 307.

Evidence The details, examples, facts, statistics, or expert opinions that support any general statement or claim. See pp. 309 and 314–15 on the use of evidence in argumentative writing.

Example An instance or representative of a general group or an abstract concept or quality. One or more examples may serve as the primary method of developing an essay. See Chapter 3 on example, p. 93.

Exposition The form of writing that explains or informs. Most of the essays in this book are primarily expository, and some essays whose primary purpose is self-expression or persuasion employ exposition to clarify ideas.

Fallacies Flaws in reasoning that weaken or invalidate an argument. Some of the most common fallacies are listed below (the page numbers refer to further discussion in the text).

- **Oversimplification,** overlooking or ignoring inconsistencies or complexities in evidence: *If the United States banned immigration, our unemployment problems would be solved* (p. 312).
- **Hasty generalization,** leaping to a conclusion on the basis of inadequate or unrepresentative evidence: *Every one of the twelve students polled supports the change in the grading system, so the administration should implement it* (pp. 311–12).
- **Begging the question,** assuming the truth of a conclusion that has not been proved: *Acid rain does not do serious damage, so it is not a serious problem* (p. 312).
- **Ignoring the question,** shifting the argument away from the real issue: *A fine, churchgoing man like Charles Harold would make an excellent mayor* (p. 312).
- **Ad hominem** ("to the man") **argument,** attacking an opponent instead of the opponent's argument: *She is just a student, so we need not listen to her criticisms of foreign policy* (p. 312).

- **Either-or,** presenting only two alternatives when the choices are more numerous: *If you want to do well in college, you have to cheat a little* (pp. 312–13).

- **Non sequitur** ("It does not follow"), deriving a wrong or illogical conclusion from stated premises: *Because students are actually in school, they should be the ones to determine our educational policies* (p. 313).

- **Post hoc** (from *post hoc, ergo propter hoc,* "after this, therefore because of this"), assuming that one thing caused another simply because it preceded the other: *Two students left school in the week after the new policies were announced, proving that the policies will eventually cause a reduction in enrollments* (p. 313).

Figures of speech   Expressions that imply meanings beyond or different from their literal meanings in order to achieve vividness or force.

Some figures of speech involve comparisons of two unlike objects:

- A **simile** equates two unlike things using *like* or *as*: *The crowd was restless, like bees in a hive.*

- A **metaphor** compares two unlike things by saying that one is the other: *Bright circles of ebony, her eyes smiled back at me.*

- **Personification** gives human qualities to things or abstractions: *The bright day smirked at my bad mood.*

Other figures of speech consist of deliberate misrepresentations:

- **Hyperbole** is a conscious overstatement or exaggeration: *The desk provided an acre of work surface.* (The opposite of hyperbole is understatement, discussed under *irony*.)

- A **paradox** is a seemingly self-contradictory statement that, on reflection, makes sense: *Children are the poor person's wealth* (wealth can be monetary, or it can be spiritual). *Paradox* may also refer to a situation that is inexplicable or contradictory, such as the restriction of one group's rights to secure the rights of another group.

Formal style   See *style.*

Freewriting   A technique for discovering ideas for writing: writing for a fixed amount of time without stopping to reread or edit. See p. 16.

General and specific words   A **general** word refers to a group or class: *car, mood, book.* A **specific** word refers to a particular member of a group or class: *Toyota, irritation, dictionary.* Usually, the more specific a word is, the more interesting and informative it will be for readers. See also *abstract and concrete words.*

Generalization   A statement about a group or a class derived from knowledge of some or all of its members: for instance, *Dolphins can be trained to count* or *Television news rarely penetrates beneath the headlines.* The more instances the generalization is based on, the more accurate it is likely to be. A generalization is the result of inductive reasoning; see p. 309.

Hasty generalization   See *fallacies.*

Hyperbole   See *figures of speech.*

Image   A verbal representation of sensory experience—that is, of something seen, heard, felt, tasted, or smelled. Images may be literal: *Snow stuck to her eyelashes; The red car sped past us.* Or they may be figures of speech: *Her eyelashes were snowy feathers; The car rocketed past us like a red missile.* Through images, a writer touches the readers' experiences, thus sharpening meaning and adding immediacy. See also *abstract and concrete words.*

Inductive reasoning   The method of reasoning that moves from the particular to the general. See Chapter 10 on argument and persuasion, especially p. 309.

Informal style   See *style.*

Introductions   The openings of written works, the sentences that set the stage for what follows. An introduction to an essay identifies and restricts the subject while establishing your attitude toward it. Accomplishing these purposes may require anything from a single sentence to several paragraphs, depending on your purpose and how much readers need to know before they can begin to grasp the ideas in the essay. The introduction often includes a thesis sentence stating the main idea of the essay (see pp. 14–15). To set up the thesis sentence, or as a substitute for it, any of the following openings, or a combination, may be effective:

- Background on the subject that establishes a time or place or that provides essential information (see Momaday, p. 50; Swift, p. 356)
- An anecdote or other reference to the writer's experience that forecasts or illustrates the main idea or that explains what prompted the essay (see Dillard, p. 71; Brady, p. 241)
- An explanation of the significance of the subject (see Naylor, p. 251)
- An outline of the situation or problem that the essay will address, perhaps using interesting facts or statistics (see King, p. 341)
- A statement or quotation of an opinion that the writer will modify or disagree with (see Bruck, p. 327)
- An example, quotation, or question that reinforces the main idea (see Klass, p. 98)

A good introduction does not mislead readers by exaggerating the significance of the subject or the essay, and it does not bore readers by saying more than is necessary. In addition, a good introduction avoids three openings that are always clumsy: (1) beginning with *The purpose of this essay is...* or something similar; (2) referring to the title of the essay in the first sentence, as in *This is not as hard as it looks* or *This is a serious problem;* and (3) starting too broadly or vaguely, as in *Ever since humans walked upright...* or *In today's world....*

Irony   In writing, irony is the use of words to suggest a meaning different from their literal meaning. Swift's "A Modest Proposal" presents an ironic statement relying on reversal: he says the opposite of what he really means (pp. 356–66). But irony can also derive from understatement (saying less than is meant) or hyperbole (exaggeration). Irony can be witty, teasing, biting, or cruel. At its most humorless and heavily contemptuous, it becomes **sarcasm:** *Thanks a lot for telling Dad we stayed out all night; that was really bright of you.*

Metaphor   See *figures of speech*.

Narration   The form of writing that tells a story, relating a sequence of events. See Chapter 2 on narration, p. 60.

Nonstandard English   See *diction*.

Oversimplification   See *fallacies*.

Paragraph   A group of related sentences, set off by an initial indentation, that develops an idea. By breaking continuous text into units, paragraphing helps the writer manage ideas and helps the reader follow those ideas. Each paragraph makes a distinct contribution to the main idea governing the entire piece of writing. The idea of the paragraph itself is often stated in a topic sentence, and it is supported with sentences containing specific details, examples, and reasons. Like the larger piece of writing to which it contributes, the paragraph should be unified, coherent, and well developed. For examples of successful paragraphs, see the paragraph analyses in the introduction to each method of development (Chapters 1–10).

Parallelism   The use of similar grammatical form for ideas of equal importance. Parallelism occurs within sentences: *The doctor recommends swimming, bicycling, or walking.* It also occurs among sentences: *Strumming her guitar, she made listeners feel her anger. Singing lines, she made listeners believe her pain.*

Personification   See *figures of speech*.

Persuasion See *argument*.

Point of view The position of the writer in relation to the subject. In description, point of view depends on the writer's physical and psychological relation to the subject (see pp. 22–23). In narration, point of view depends on the writer's place in the story and on his or her relation to it in time (see p. 61). More broadly, point of view can also mean the writer's particular mental stance or attitude. For instance, an employee and employer might have different points of view toward the employee's absenteeism or the employer's sick-leave policies.

Premise The generalization or assumption on which an argument is based. See *syllogism*.

Process analysis The method of development in which a sequence of actions with a specified result is divided into its component steps. See Chapter 6 on process analysis, p. 176.

Pronoun A word that refers to a noun or other pronoun: *Six days after King picked up his Nobel Peace Prize in Norway, he was jailed in Alabama*. The personal pronouns (the most common) are *I, you, he, she, it, we,* and *they*.

Proposition A debatable claim about a subject; the central idea of an argument.

Purpose The reason for writing, the goal the writer wants to achieve. The purpose may be primarily to explain the subject so that readers understand it or see it in a new light; to convince readers to accept or reject an opinion or to take a certain action; to entertain readers with a humorous or exciting story; or to express the thoughts and emotions triggered by a revealing or instructive experience. The writer's purpose overlaps the main idea—the particular point being made about the subject. In effective writing, the two together direct and control every choice the writer makes. See also p. 14, and *thesis* and *unity*.

Rational appeal In argumentative and persuasive writing, the appeal to readers' rational faculties—to their ability to reason logically—in order to win agreement or compel action. See pp. 308–11.

Repetition and restatement The careful use of the same words or close parallels to clarify meaning and tie sentences together.

Revision The stage of the writing process devoted to "re-seeing" a draft, divided into fundamental changes in content and structure (revision) and more superficial changes in grammar, word choice, and the like (editing). See pp. 19–20.

Rhetoric   The art of using words effectively to communicate with an audience, or the study of that art. To the ancient Greeks, rhetoric was the art of the *rhetor*—orator, or public speaker—and included the art of persuasion. Later the word shifted to mean elegant language, and a version of that meaning persists in today's occasional use of *rhetoric* to mean pretentious or hollow language, as in *Their argument was mere rhetoric.*

Sarcasm   See *irony.*

Satire   The combination of wit and criticism to mock or condemn human foolishness or evil. The intent of satire is to arouse readers to contempt or action, and thus it differs from comedy, which seeks simply to amuse. Much satire relies on irony—saying one thing but meaning another (see *irony*).

Simile   See *figures of speech.*

Slang   See *diction.*

Spatial organization   A pattern of organization that views an object, scene, or person by paralleling the way we normally scan things—for instance, top to bottom or near to far. See also p. 24.

Specific words   See *general and specific words.*

Standard English   See *diction.*

Style   The *way* something is said, as opposed to *what* is said. Style results primarily from a writer's characteristic word choices and sentence structures. A person's writing style, like his or her voice or manner of speaking, is distinctive. Style can also be viewed more broadly as ranging from formal to informal. A very formal style adheres strictly to the conventions of Standard English (see *diction*); tends toward long sentences with sophisticated structures; and relies on learned words, such as *malodorous* and *psychopathic*. A very informal style, in contrast, is more conversational (see *colloquial language*); tends toward short, uncomplicated sentences; and relies on words typical of casual speech, such as *smelly* or *crazy*. Among the writers represented in this book, King (p. 341) writes quite formally, Hughes (p. 66) quite informally. The formality of style may often be modified to suit a particular audience or occasion: a college term paper, for instance, demands a more formal style than an essay narrating a personal experience. See also *tone.*

Syllogism   The basic form of deductive reasoning, in which a conclusion derives necessarily from proven or accepted premises. For example: *The roof always leaks when it rains* (the major premise). *It is raining* (the minor premise). *Therefore, the roof will leak* (the conclusion). See Chapter 10 on argument and persuasion, especially pp. 309–11.

Symbol   A person, place, or thing that represents an abstract quality or concept. A red heart symbolizes love; the Golden Gate Bridge symbolizes San Francisco's dramatic beauty; a cross symbolizes Christianity.

Thesis   The main idea of a piece of writing, to which all other ideas and details relate. The main idea is often stated in a **thesis sentence** (or sentences), which asserts something about the subject and conveys the writer's purpose. The thesis sentence is often included near the beginning of an essay. Even when the writer does not state the main idea and purpose, however, they govern all the ideas and details in the essay. See also pp. 14–15 and *unity*.

Tone   The attitude toward the subject, and sometimes toward the audience and the writer's own self, expressed in choice of words and sentence structures as well as in what is said. Tone in writing is similar to tone of voice in speaking, from warm to serious, amused to angry, joyful to sorrowful, sympathetic to contemptuous. For examples of strong tone in writing, see White (p. 26), Mitford (p. 192), Brady (p. 241), and King (p. 341).

Transitions   Links between sentences and paragraphs that relate ideas and thus contribute to clarity and smoothness. Transitions may be sentences beginning paragraphs or brief paragraphs that shift the focus or introduce new ideas. They may also be words and phrases that signal and specify relationships. Some of these words and phrases—by no means all—are listed below:

- **Space:** above, below, beyond, farther away, here, nearby, opposite, there, to the right
- **Time:** afterward, at last, earlier, later, meanwhile, simultaneously, soon, then
- **Illustration:** for example, for instance, specifically, that is
- **Comparison:** also, in the same way, likewise, similarly
- **Contrast:** but, even so, however, in contrast, on the contrary, still, yet
- **Addition or repetition:** again, also, finally, furthermore, in addition, moreover, next, that is
- **Cause or effect:** as a result, consequently, equally important, hence, then, therefore, thus
- **Summary or conclusion:** all in all, in brief, in conclusion, in short, in summary, therefore, thus
- **Intensification:** indeed, in fact, of course, truly

Understatement   See *irony*.

Unity   The quality of effective writing that occurs when all the parts relate to the main idea and contribute to the writer's purpose.

ACKNOWLEDGMENTS

Maya Angelou. "Champion of the World." From *I Know Why the Caged Bird Sings* by Maya Angelou. Copyright © 1968 and 1987 by Maya Angelou. Used by permission of Random House, Inc.

Barbara Lazear Ascher. "The Box Man." From *Playing After Dark* by Barbara Lazear Ascher. Copyright © 1982, 1983, 1984, 1985, 1986 by Barbara Lazear Ascher. Used by permission of Doubleday, a division of Random House, Inc.

Russell Baker. "The Plot Against People." From *The New York Times*, 1968. Copyright © 1968, Russell Baker. Reprinted by permission.

Judy Brady. "I Want a Wife." Originally published in *Ms*. Magazine, Vol. 1, No. 1, December 31, 1971. Reprinted by permission of the author.

Suzanne Britt. "Neat People vs. Sloppy People." From *Show & Tell* by Suzanne Britt. Reprinted by permission of the author.

David Bruck. "The Death Penalty." Published in *The New Republic*, May 1985. Copyright © 1985. Reprinted by permission of the author.

William F. Buckley, Jr. "Why Don't We Complain?" Copyright © 1961 by William Buckley, Jr. First printed in *Esquire Magazine*. Used by permission of the Wallace Literary Agency, Inc.

Bruce Catton. "Grant and Lee: A Study in Contrasts." From *The American Story*. Copyright © 1990. Reprinted by permission.

Judith Ortiz Cofer. "Silent Dancing." Copyright © 1990. Reprinted with permission from the publisher of *Silent Dancing: A Partial Remembrance of a Puerto Rican Childhood*. Arte Publico Press, University of Houston.

K. C. Cole. "Women in Science." From *The New York Times*, December 3, 1981. Copyright © 1981 by K. C. Cole. Reprinted by permission.

Joan Didion. "The Santa Ana." From *Slouching Towards Bethlehem* by Joan Didion. Copyright © 1966, 1968 and renewed 1996 by Joan Didion. Reprinted by permission of Farrar, Straus & Giroux, LLC.

Annie Dillard. "The Chase." From *An American Childhood* by Annie Dillard. Copyright © 1987 by Annie Dillard. Reprinted by permission of HarperCollins Publishers, Inc.

Barbara Ehrenreich. "Cultural Baggage." From *The Snarling Citizen* by Barbara Ehrenreich. Copyright © 1995 by Barbara Ehrenreich. Reprinted by permission of Farrar, Straus & Giroux, LLC.

Lars Eighner. "Dumpster Diving." From *Travels with Lizbeth* by Lars Eighner. Copyright © 1993 by Lars Eighner. Reprinted by permission of St. Martin's Press, LLC.

Stephanie Ericsson. "The Ways We Lie." Originally published by *The Utne Reader* in the November/December issue, 1992. Copyright © 1992 by Stephanie Ericsson. Reprinted by permission of Dunham Literary, Inc., as agents for the author.

Malcolm Gladwell. "The Tipping Point." From *The Tipping Point* by Malcolm Gladwell. Copyright © 2000, 2002 by Malcolm Gladwell. By permission of Little, Brown & Company.

Stephen Jay Gould. "Sex, Drugs, Disasters, and the Extinction of Dinosaurs." From *The Flamingo's Smile: Reflections in Natural History* by Stephen Jay Gould. Copyright 1984 by Stephen Jay Gould. Used by permission of W. W. Norton & Company, Inc.

Langston Hughes. "Salvation." From *The Big Sea* by Langston Hughes. Copyright © 1940 by Langston Hughes. Copyright renewed 1968 by Arna Bontemps and George Houston Bass. Reprinted by permission of Hill and Wang, a division of Farrar, Straus & Giroux, LLC.

Martin Luther King, Jr. "I Have a Dream." Copyright © 1963 Martin Luther King, Jr. Copyright renewed 1991 by Coretta Scott King. Reprinted with arrangement with the Estate of Martin Luther King, Jr. c/o Writer's House as agent for the proprietor, New York, NY.

Perri Klass. "She's Your Basic L.O.L. in N.A.D." From *A Not Entirely Benign Procedure* by Perri Klass. Copyright © 1987 by Perri Klass. Used by permission of G. P. Putnam's Sons, a division of Penguin Group (USA) Inc.

Edward I. Koch. "Death and Justice." Published in *The New Republic,* May 1985. Copyright 1985. Reprinted by permission of the author.

Anne Lamott. "The Crummy First Draft." From *Bird by Bird* by Anne Lamott. Copyright © 1994 by Anne Lamott. Used by permission of Pantheon Books, a division of Random House, Inc.

Nancy Mairs. "Disability." From *Carnal Acts* by Nancy Mairs. Copyright © 1990 by Nancy Mairs. Reprinted by permission of Beacon Press, Boston.

Jessica Mitford. "Embalming Mr. Jones." Copyright © 1998 by the Estate of Jessica Mitford. Reprinted by permission of The Estate of Jessica Mitford.

N. Scott Momaday. "The Way to Rainy Mountain." Introduction from *The Way to Rainy Mountain* by N. Scott Momaday. Reprinted by permission of the University of New Mexico Press.

Gloria Naylor. "The Meanings of a Word." Copyright © 1986 by Gloria Naylor. Reprinted by permission of SSL/Sterling Lord Literistic, Inc.

George Orwell. "Shooting an Elephant." From *Shooting an Elephant and Other Essays* by George Orwell. Copyright © 1946 by Sonia Brownell Orwell and renewed 1974 by Sonia Orwell. Reprinted by permission of Harcourt, Inc.

Noel Perrin. "The Androgynous Man." From *The New York Times,* February 5, 1984. Copyright © 1984 by The New York Times Company. Reprinted by permission.

Emily Prager. "Our Barbies, Ourselves." Originally published in *Interview* Magazine, December 1991. Courtesy Brant Publications, Inc.

Anna Quindlen. "Homeless." From *Living Out Loud* by Anna Quindlen. Copyright © 1987 by Anna Quindlen. Used by permission of Random House, Inc.

Richard Rodriguez. "Private Language, Public Language." From *Hunger of Memory* by Richard Rodriguez. Copyright © 1985 by Richard Rodriguez. Reprinted by permission of David R. Godine, Publisher, Inc.

Scott Russell Sanders. "The Men We Carry in Our Minds." From *The Paradise of the Bombs* by Scott Russell Sanders. Copyright © 1984 by Scott Russell Sanders. First appeared in *Milkweed Chronicle.* Reprinted by permission of the author and the author's agents, the Virginia Kidd Agency, Inc.

David Sedaris. "Remembering My Childhood on the Continent of Africa." From *Me Talk Pretty One Day* by David Sedaris. Copyright © 2000 by David Sedaris. Reprinted by permission of Little, Brown & Company (Inc.).

Brent Staples. "Black Men and Public Space." Reprinted by permission of the author.

Amy Tan. "Mother Tongue." Copyright © 1990 by Amy Tan. First appeared in *The Threepenny Review.* Reprinted by permission of the author and the Sandra Dijkstra Literary Agency.

Deborah Tannen. "But What Do You Mean?" From *Talking from 9 to 5* by Deborah Tannen. Copyright © 1994 by Deborah Tannen. Reprinted by permission of HarperCollins Publishers, Inc.

Margaret Visser. "The Ritual of Fast Food." From *The Rituals of Dinner* by Margaret Visser. Copyright © 1991 by Margaret Visser. Published by HarperCollins. Used by permission of the author.

E. B. White. "Once More to the Lake." From *One Man's Meat* by E. B. White. Text copyright © 1941 by E. B. White. Copyright renewed. Reprinted by permission of Tilbury House, Publishers, Gardiner, Maine.

Virginia Woolf. "Professions for Women." From *The Moth and Other Essays* by Virginia Woolf. Copyright © 1942 by Harcourt, Inc. and renewed 1970 by Marjorie T. Parsons, Executor. Reprinted by permission of the publisher.

Index of Authors and Titles

bedfordstmartins.com

Online Research and Reference Aids for Students

The Bedford Research Room

bedfordstmartins.com/researchroom

Mike Palmquist, *Colorado State University*

This site offers a rich array of resources to support the research process, including online manuals on using search engines and other digital research and writing tools, tutorials on evaluating and citing sources, and links to online style and citation guides. The site also provides more than 30 downloadable research activities and checklists that will help you develop a research topic, evaluate sources, plan a research project, and much more.

Research and Documentation Online

bedfordstmartins.com/resdoc

Diana Hacker, late of *Prince George's Community College*

This online version of Hacker's popular booklet provides clear guidelines on how to integrate outside material into your paper, how to cite sources correctly, and how to format your paper in MLA, APA, *Chicago*, or CBE style.

Exercise Central

bedfordstmartins.com/exercisecentral

The largest collection of editing and writing exercises available online, Exercise Central includes diagnostic tests and thousands of exercises that help you improve your grammar and usage skills.